I0475969

The State of the Constitution--2017

Cases, Events and People that Shaped the Constitution from 2000 to 2016

by C. Paul Smith

Library of Congress Cataloging in Publication Data

Smith, C. Paul, 1951 –
        The State of the Constitution—2017
                Political and legal commentary and index

International Standard Book Number: 13-978-1544077628
Frederick Printing, Frederick, Maryland 21701
© 2017 by C. Paul Smith. All rights reserved.
Printed in the United States of America
02/17

The meaning of the Constitution is shaped not only by the Judicial Branch of the federal government (the Supreme Court), but also by the Executive and the Legislative Branches (the President and Congress), as they carry out their respective responsibilities, as provided in the Constitution.

TABLE OF CONTENTS

Introduction

By its innate nature, the United States Constitution is constantly changing as new rights are recognized by the Supreme Court and as the parameters of conflicting rights are defined and as old laws collide with new technologies and changing values of society. Political parties debate whether and to what extent changes should be made by the Court in interpreting the meaning of the Constitution, but the changing nature of the Constitution is undeniable.

The sixteen years that mark the George W. Bush and the Barack Obama Administrations represent a period of time of some of the greatest changes that the Constitution has ever experienced. In 2017 the United States Constitution is not what it was in 2000, prior to 9-11 and prior to the razor-thin presidential election victory for George W. Bush. The election in 2008 of the nation's first black President, Barack Obama, and the tumultuous 2016 presidential campaign that resulted in the election of Donald J. Trump as President of the United States are both symbolic of the change and tumult that mark this time in the nation's history.

This sixteen-year span (2000-2016) brought major changes to the Constitution. This book chronicles and analyzes the conflicts and debates that gave rise to many of these changes. A review of these debates is certainly helpful to understand and interpret the history of this time period. And the debates are not over. Understanding the intellectual conflicts that shaped recent changes will help going forward as the eternal conflict between agency and security continues to play out in America.

This book is a compilation of seventeen editions of the newsletter, *Constitutional Law Updates* (from 2001-2017). Many of these writings continue to have great significance and relevance today for politicians, historians and informed citizens. These writings were written to supplement the text, *The State of the Constitution* (2002), but the value of many of these essays, commentaries and opinion pieces warrants the publication of this book as a stand-alone volume. Those who love the Constitution will cherish this book, and they will find it a valuable resource in addressing many of the important moral, legal and political issues that continue to shape the political debates today in America.

C. Paul Smith - March 2017

Who Will Want to Read this Book

The continued vitality, prosperity and greatness of America depend upon this nation's continuing to embrace the conservative principles of government. America was founded as a land of opportunity, not a land of entitlements. But if a majority of Americans reject this premise, then American will suffer greatly. Hard work, creativity, ingenuity and the incentive to achieve are the foundation of America's economic greatness. If these become replaced by an entitlement mentality, then the foundation and incentive for economic prosperity will be lost. As the right to entitlements to the government pie grows bigger, the number of people making that pie will dwindle; as the right to entitlements increases there will be a corresponding decrease in the benefits to be bestowed. Historically socialism always fails because it destroys the incentive to produce. The free enterprise system, on the other hand, produces enough so that those who have in abundance can help those who lack. Historically, this is what has happened in America. But the Democrat Party openly attacks the free enterprise system as being greedy, heartless and uncaring. These attacks were certainly rebuffed in the 2016 Presidential election, but because of the closeness of the election, we know those philosophical attacks on the free enterprise system will continue. The rich and successful will be vilified, and advocacy for socialism will increase. The liberals will not be satisfied until they have destroyed the free enterprise system and established an entitlement system so burdened with debt that it will undermine the economy of America.

This book is dedicated to preserving and strengthening the free enterprise system and the other basics of a limited federal government that will preserve and strengthen America.

It is of critical importance that America's elected leaders—at every level—understand and implement the views of conservative government in order to make and keep America great. This book will help. Here's how. Understanding and articulating the principles of conservatism empowers people to win the thousands of local and national debates that are needed to elect a majority of conservative leaders.

Although the reader is welcome to read through this book like a novel, its greatest value will be as a resource on multiple, important issues. The Table of Contents, Table of Cases and Index will be very helpful. Here are some examples of how this book will be helpful.

During the 2016 Presidential campaign, Hillary Clinton decried the Supreme Court decision in *Citizens United*. She was wrong. If you don't understand why that Supreme Court case was correctly decided, you should go to the Table of Cases and read about the *Citizens United* case (pp. 264-265).

The political platforms of President Obama in 2012 and of Hillary Clinton in 2016 were seriously flawed. President Obama's agenda was harmful to America, and Hillary Clinton's agenda would have been equally harmful. If you don't understand the problems with their platforms, then you should go to the Table of Contents or to the Index and find the sections in this book that describe and analyze their agendas and the better agendas of Mitt Romney (pp. 234, 266 & 282) and Donald Trump (285).

Perhaps the most controversial and important of all Supreme Court cases in the last 50 years is *Roe v. Wade*. There were multiple significant results from that decision—some good, such as recognizing a woman's right to control her own body—but some were bad, such as eliminating the right of states to protect fetal life. By using the Table of Cases, you will find some helpful commentary and analysis of this important case (pp. 111-115, 170-172 & 246-247).

Two Supreme Court cases that have established a personal liberty to engage in same-sex relations and same-sex marriage are *Lawrence v. Texas* (2003) and *Obergefell v. Hodges* (2015). Most people understand that these new rights have been established, but a reading of my commentary and analysis of these rulings shows how in these cases the Supreme Court abandoned and discarded its traditional standards of neutrality and judicial self-restraint to establish new rights. These cases are examples of extreme judicial activism that threaten the foundations of separation of powers under the Constitution. You can use either the Table of Contents or the Table of Cases to find an informative discussion and analysis of these cases (pp. 111-116 for *Lawrence*, and pp. 308-310 for *Obergefell*).

A brief look at the Table of Contents will show where these and other important issues are discussed.

There is a great political divide in America. The five Presidential elections from 2000 to 2016 make this perfectly clear. There are several primary issues that distinguish the liberal views of the Democrats from the more conservative views of the Republicans. The liberals promise virtually unlimited government benefits for all, to be paid for by increasing taxes on the rich. The conservatives want a limited federal government that stops undermining the economic vitality of its people. While there are other important points of division between the two parties, it is the above issues that are the fundamental philosophical difference between the Democrat and Republican parties. These differences include conflicting views about the following: the role of the federal government, entitlements, re-distributing wealth, taxation, economic health and personal liberties. The Democrat Party has become the party of socialism, while the Republican Party is the party of the free enterprise system.

The answer to which direction America will go in the future depends upon who wins the local and national elections in America at every level—city, county, state and national levels. Saving America from the socialists will require that elected officials learn and articulate the fundamentals of freedom and limited government that are discussed and analyzed in this book. Those who do this will have greater strength and influence to get elected and to govern wisely.

Measuring the Health of the Constitution

A measure of the state or condition (or health, if you will) of the Constitution first requires the identification of those standards which would represent the ideal state of the Constitution. The Constitution itself is silent about any such standards except for the broad statement in Article III that "the judicial Power of the United States shall be vested in one supreme Court." In *Marbury v. Madison* (1803), the Supreme Court (in an opinion authored by Chief Justice John Marshall) asserted that it is the role and power of the Supreme Court to determine what laws are and are not constitutional. Ever since, the principle that the Supreme Court has the ultimate say on what the Constitution means has been a major part of our nation's constitutional foundation.

Nevertheless and notwithstanding this bedrock principle of power, it must also be acknowledged that the actions and non-actions of both Presidents and Congress continue to play a major role in what the Constitution means and in what the Constitution allows and does not allow. For example, despite the existence of laws restricting immigrants from entering America, the Executive Branch also affects the meaning of those laws by its actions in enforcing and/or not enforcing those laws. The Legislative Branch also exerts influence on the meaning of immigration laws by its role in passing laws, investigating matters and in vetting judicial and administrative appointees.

Each of these may have its own philosophy and belief on what the ideal state of the Constitution should be. Pressures from the public also affect what the Constitution means and how it is applied.

I submit that there are two primary principles that are ingredients of a healthy condition for our Constitutional government: The predominant existence of law and order, and a Supreme Court that adjudicates controversies with neutrality and impartiality.

1. Rule of law exists in the nation, where the nation accepts and complies with the
rulings of the Supreme Court, whether or not people work to change such rulings.

2. Judicial restraint is exercised by the judiciary such that it applies neutral, established legal principles in interpreting the Constitution and laws so as not to convert the judiciary into a super legislature. The Supreme Court is the primary guardian and protector of the Constitution. This protection is achieved when judges do not use their own political views in determining the cases and controversies that come before them, except to the extent that the proper role of the judiciary becomes a political issue.

Applying these standards to the state of the Constitution in 2017, it must be observed that the nation is primarily in order, but there is significant division in the nation, as witnessed by the many demonstrations about current political happenings (i.e., protests about the Election of Donald Trump and his policies and statements). Nevertheless, the rule of law is mostly in place. But as to the judicial restraint standard, during the last sixteen years, a narrow majority of the Supreme Court has abandoned the neutrality standard in determining many cases, and this narrow majority have applied their personal political views to establish some new rights and liberties, and at the same time to diminish or destroy other rights, liberties and values. Therefore, to this extent the Constitution has been impaired; this narrow majority of Justices have turned the Court into a kind of super Legislature who are converting the Supreme Court from a neutral adjudicator to a political super agent—enacting the agenda of political activists, and in the process changing and dispensing with the neutral legal principles that should govern the Court in determining cases and controversies.

Whether such recent changes will continue or stop or be reversed remains to be seen.

Cases that make it to the Supreme Court are often determined by principles and philosophies that transcend the normal parameters of routine cases where questions of fact are determined by a judge or jury. In fact, virtually every case discussed in this book is significant because of how the Supreme Court invoked, established and decreed standards and rules that will have broad and far-reaching application and effect in America. These rulings come from cases where controversial issues of national interest are involved. And in this process, the legal arguments invariably involve political, religious and moral philosophies that are controversial, polarizing and emotionally charged. Such is the case with much of the subject matter treated in this book.

Analyzing these controversial matters is often both political and legal. And the analysis often focuses on the philosophies and politics of the individual Justices. To ignore the existence and influence of these underlying views would be to deny the ultimate sources of influence and power that are shaping the Constitution and America.

The politicizing of the Supreme Court is a concern because the Court has become a super legislature more than a neutral, impartial adjudicator. The judiciary has become infected with partisanship, which is demonstrated through their writings. This is a major crisis for the Constitution. There is no virtue in not acknowledging this problem and in ignoring (or denying) this major difference in the platforms of the political parties. This problems need to be exposed and corrected if the Supreme Court is to be restored to its proper role as a neutral adjudicator of cases and controversies, and stop functioning as a super legislature. This can be corrected through political processes, in the election of officials who will endorse and appoint judicial appointees who embrace the philosophies of judicial restraint, political neutrality, and a limited federal government.

CONSTITUTIONAL LAW UPDATES

1:i	April 2001	No. 1

Creating Special Rights for Gays
Threatens America .... Insert 8.4.5 (8 pages)

America has been duped to embrace the erroneous, but popular, belief that gays are born that way and that they cannot change their homosexual orientation. Scientific studies have not substantiated this hypothesis. Militant gay researchers report that studies "suggest" that there may be a genetic link. But the studies do not bear this out. Rather, the scientific studies prove the opposite—they prove that environment and experience are causative factors. This article exposes the myth that gays are born that way and cannot change. This article takes a look at the brief of the American Psychological Association in the Supreme Court case of the *Boy Scouts of America v. Dale* (2000). In this brief the APA advanced its best argument for the proposition that gays are born that way. A close look at that article reveals how feeble that argument is. Neither the APA nor the militant gays want people to learn the scientific truth about these issues, and thus far they have been pretty successful. This article exposes the reveals the truth that could pull the rug out from under the gay rights movement.

One Crisis with China is Resolved; Other Tough Issues Remain and
Souring Relations with China Can Impinge on Constitutional Liberties ...Insert 7.6 (2 pages)

During the 2000 Presidential Campaign, both candidates avoided the brewing conflict between Taiwan and China. Now, after the election, a half dozen issues are coming to a boil, including the question of whether the U.S. should sell Aegis destroyers to Taiwan to defend against any attack from China. The dynamics of this issue have been adjusted following the emergency landing of 24 U.S. soldiers on the Chinese Island of Hainan after a Chinese jet collided with a U.S. plane in international air space. After extracting an apology of sorts from the U.S., the Chinese eventually released the Americans. A major crisis was averted for the time being, but the effect of this incident is still reverberating throughout the nation.

Inaugural Issue of CONSTITUTIONAL LAW UPDATES--The *CLU* newsletter will provide quarterly updates on important developments in the U.S. Constitution. The *CLU* updates are prepared to be inserted into various sections of the text, **The State of the Constitution.** For an explanation of this education and retrieval system............ See pages A2 and A3

Coming Attractions in the next issue of *CLU*:
* Constitutional Problems with Campaign Finance Reform Legislation
* Adverse Effects of Hate Crime Laws
* The Aftermath of the 2000 Presidential Election

CONSTITUTIONAL LAW UPDATES is a quarterly newsletter edited and published by C. Paul Smith, J.D. Subscription cost is $25.00 per year. To subscribe, send a check or money order to CONSTITUTIONAL LAW UPDATES, P.O. Box 1204, Frederick MD 21702-0204. For further information, visit C. Paul Smith's web site at www.geocities.com/cpaulsmithlaw

Welcome to CLU!

This is the inaugural issue of **CONSTITUTIONAL LAW UPDATES** (**CLU** for short). Responsible citizens, young and old, want to better understand the Constitution—from the basics of its initial organization to the complex issues involved in the recent Supreme Court cases of *Bush v. Gore*, and *Boy Scouts of America v. Dale*. But where do you turn for this understanding? Neither the newspapers nor the television news shows nor talk radio adequately provides this. These industries are so driven by market and entertainment forces that they do not meet this need. **CLU** meets this need. **CLU** will treat the major constitutional issues of the day on a quarterly basis—updating concerned citizens on significant developments in important national issues.

CLU is published to be used in tandem with the text, **The State of the Constitution**. Here's how they work together. **The State of the Constitution** is a book that analyzes how current events, laws, trends and developments impact the United States Constitution. The organization of the book is shown on the adjacent page (A3). This book is addressed to educated people who want a quick-reference source to assist them in identifying and analyzing constitutional issues that concern them. **The State of the Constitution** is printed on letter-size paper and is compiled in an attractive burgundy, 3-ring notebook. Inside each **CLU** edition are pre-punched inserts that are intended to go into certain sections of **The State of the Constitution**. At the top, right-hand corner of each **CLU** insert page there is a number that corresponds to the section where it should be inserted in **The State of the Constitution**. For example, in the first issue of **CLU**, the article "Crisis with China Is Averted" should be inserted at section 7.6—Chapter 7 (International Relations), section 6 (Relations with Specific Countries). And for another example, the first edition's article on gay rights should be inserted at section 8.4.5 – Chapter 8 (the Fourteenth Amendment), section 4 (Civil Rights Laws), and subsection 5 (Protected Classes). Each insert will also have a date written at the bottom to indicate when the insert was written.

The greatest experts on the Constitution use indexes and update services to stay abreast with the most current developments in the law. *U. S. Law Week* publishes such a service with dozens of updates each year. The cost for this is several hundred dollars per year. But as excellent as this service is, it is too broad in scope to be helpful to non-lawyers, who have neither the time nor the money to study hundreds of complex issues in which they have no interest. **CLU** is directed to non-lawyer, responsible citizens, who are interested only in the major constitutional/political issues of the day. **CLU** is just the right service for them—giving them access to insightful and easy-to-understand analysis of the most important political, judicial, and legislative issues of our time.

The combination package of **CLU** and **The State of the Constitution** is an affordable, insightful, and interesting constitutional law information and retrieval service that will empower its readers to be influential leaders in their communities and among their associates. This combination one-two punch will inform, entertain, educate and empower its readers.

****

About the Editor--

C. Paul Smith has a general litigation law practice in Montgomery County, Maryland. He practices primarily in the areas of Family Law, Probate, Wills and Estates, Adoption, Bankruptcy, Juvenile Law and some Criminal Law. He opened the practice in 1978, after receiving a J.D. degree from the J. Reuben Clark Law School at Brigham Young University in 1978. He is admitted to practice in all state and federal courts in Maryland and before the Fourth Circuit U.S. Court of Appeals and the U. S. Supreme Court. He is active in the Bar Association of Montgomery County, Maryland, one of the most prestigious bar associations in the country (having nearly 3,000 members). He chaired the Bar's Speakers Bureau from 1996 to 2000. In connection with this, he founded the Bar's annual Constitutional Law Seminars in 1998; and he organized, hosted, and lectured at the Bar's 8-part seminar series on Constitutional Law. He appeared on two of the Bar Association's televised programs on the Constitution in 1998. From 1987 – 1989 he edited *The East Coast Addendum*, a quarterly constitutional law and religion newsletter. While still in law school, he wrote and published *The Fetal Right to Life Argument* (1977).

The State of the Constitution
Table of Contents

CLU 04/01

Professors Can Be Ordered
To Change Grades

The Third Circuit U.S. Court of Appeals has ruled that professors at public universities can be ordered by their schools to change grades or be fired if they refuse, even if the university's order is bad or stupid. Why? Because the Court said that "grading is padagogic" and because the university and not the professor has the "freedom to determine how a course is to be taught." The courts will not second-guess the university on the wisdom of its pedagogic policies, even if the court might agree that they are ill-advised.

So what's a professor to do? He must take it or leave it.

Now to give you a little sympathy for Professor Bob Brown (62), who was fired at the California University of Pennsylvania in 1996 because he would not pass a student that he wanted to fail, listen to his sad plight. Professor Brown gave a failing grade to a student who missed 12 of 15 class meetings and who did not do most of the assign-ments. When ordered by university President Angelo Armenti, Jr. to change the failing grade, Professor Brown refused. The university did change the grade, and then it fired Professor Brown. Professor Brown sued to retain his job, claiming that the university had the right to change the grade, but not to fire him for his refusing to change the grade. The Third Circuit agreed with the university, so Professor Brown loses his suit to be reinstated.

One has to wonder why the college was not supportive of Professor Brown, who is reported to be an excellent teacher. But that issue is apparently irrelevant for purposes of this case.

Professor Brown plans to appeal, but the Supreme Court is not likely to take the case, let alone reverse it.

Montgomery County, Maryland Passes Law Recognizing and Protecting Individuals from Genetic-Based Discrimination

Effective March 21, 2001, Montgomery County, Maryland now has a law protecting individuals from discrimination based on his/her genetics. (See Montgomery County Code, Chapter 27 (Human Relations and Civil Liberties.) The County believes it is the first local government in the country to enact such a law. What the law means, however, is not clear.

On the one hand, I would agree that governments may properly identify as "protected classes" those individuals who are powerless to change a condition about themselves, such as color and race. By the same reasoning, I would argue that "sexual orientation" therefore should not be a protected class. Of course, Montgomery County has already made "sexual orientation" a protected class. Exactly who the county is trying to protect with this new law is not exactly clear.

One potential problem with this law is whether the law will require the genetic factor to be a "controlling, determinative" factor, or whether the law will be enforced to protect individuals for whom a genetic factor merely contributes to the individual's condition or being. For example, would an employer be prevented from firing an employee who is often drunk because the employee can show that he has a genetic intolerance to alcohol that causes him to get drunk when others would not be impaired. We'll see.

****

Coming Attractions--

"The Aftermath of the 2000 Election"
The legal chess match to determine whether Al Gore or George Bush won the Florida electoral votes is as fascinating as the election was close. The Supreme Court has been greatly criticized by some for its decision in *Bush v. Gore.* But such criticism is not warranted; the Supreme Court got it right.

"Constitutional Problems with Campaign Finance Reform Legislation"
A majority seem to agree that political campaigns are driven by money and that there is too much of it and too much improper manipulation of voters. But how to correct our system is a more difficult issue. Limiting contributions does not begin to address the campaign problems that stem from our two-party system of government. Even if the McCain-Feingold bill (or some variation of it) ever becomes law, there is serious doubt as to whether it will survive constitutional scrutiny.

"The Adverse Effects of Hate Crime Laws"
These laws add an unnecessary cost to government, and they are of minimal value when they do work as intended. But they have a chilling effect on speech and they create a hierarchy of wrongful intents that lacks soundness.

CREATING SPECIAL RIGHTS FOR GAYS THREATENS AMERICA

In April of 2001, the Maryland Legislature just passed a law making "sexual orientation" a protected class in Maryland. This will protect gays from all public and from much private discrimination. Maryland Governor Parris Glendening had championed this legislation in part because of his sympathy towards his brother, now deceased, who had been a closet gay for much of his life. This development is extremely significant, not only for Maryland, but for the entire nation. It represents a trend that is dangerous for our children and that bodes for dire consequences for future families and for our nation if the trend is not stopped and reversed.

I. Two Avenues for Advancing Gay Rights—
The "Fundamental Rights" Approach and the "Protected Class" Approach

Militant gays seek to obtain recognition and protection for their lifestyle through two primary legal avenues. First, they seek to obtain legal recognition that there is a "fundamental" individual right to engage in whatever private sexual activity they may choose. Second, they seek to enact local, state and federal laws making "sexual orientation" a "protected class" against which neither public nor private individuals may discriminate.

In constitutional law, the term "fundamental right" has a significant, technical meaning, it identifies rights that may not be specifically enumerated in the law, but which nevertheless are so "fundamental" that they are protected by the Constitution. In 1972, the Supreme Court said that one such right was the right of an "individual . . . to be free from unwarranted governmental intrusion into matters so fundamentally affecting a person as the decision whether to bear or beget a child." *Eisenstadt v. Baird*, 405 U.S. 438, 92 S.Ct. 1029, 1038 (1972). "Fundamental" rights are sometimes a part of or synonymous with the right to privacy. A year later, the Supreme Court held that a woman's right to control her own body was also a "fundamental" personal right that was included in the right to privacy protected under the Constitution. *Roe v. Wade*, 410 U.S. 113, 152, 96 S.Ct. 705, 726 (1973). Thus far, the Supreme Court has specifically declined to extend the fundamental right of privacy in sexual relations to include consensual homosexual conduct. *Bowers v. Hardwick*, 478 U.S. 186, 106 S.Ct. 2841 (1986).

However, while the advancement of gay rights has been stalled on the "fundamental rights" avenue, those rights have been advancing under the "protected class" approach. Over twenty years ago Montgomery County, Maryland passed a law including "sexual orientation" in its list of "protected classes." Since then many other local governments around the country passed similar laws. The District of Columbia passed such a law in 1987. New Jersey passed such a law, of course, and this led to the recent case that resulted in the Supreme Court's June 2000 ruling in *Boy Scouts of America v. Dale*, ___ U.S. ___, 120 S.Ct. 2446 (2000). Despite the fact the Supreme Court ruled in *BSA v. Dale* that a private organization's expressive association right trumped a state law that made sexual orientation a "protected class," the current national trend seems to be towards the protection of gays and towards accommodating the homosexual lifestyle. This is a situation that presents serious concerns for America and for the world. (See also the discussion of *Romer v. Evans*, in *The State of the Constitution* (2001 ed.).)

The dissenting justices in *BSA v. Dale* contended that gays have been "harmed" by society's refusal to protect gays from discrimination. They make this conclusion without empirical evidence of any harm and without scientific proof that gays can't help being that way. The dissenters, and much of American society, have been duped into accepting the fiction that gays are born that way, and that they can't change. Despite the absence of scientific proof of this hypothesis, and in spite of scientific studies that refute this hypothesis, the dissenting justices and the gay propagandists hold tenaciously to the fiction that homosexual orientation is genetically determined. The main purpose

1

8.4.5

of this article is to expose this falsehood. Correcting this widely-held but false belief about homosexual orientation is the key to stemming the trend to protect and encourage homosexual orientation and homosexual conduct. Correcting this can help us protect our nation's youth from being ensnared in sexual experimentation that can harm them.

If the 2000 presidential debates are any gauge of the national attitude regarding the gay rights issues, there appears to be a great reluctance to even address the issue. No candidate wanted to openly encourage homosexual conduct, but neither did any candidate wish to attack the gay lifestyle, all candidates sought to avoid the issue. To his credit, George W. Bush did express his disapproval of establishing "special rights" for gays; he said that they should be protected in their constitutional rights just like everybody else. Neither candidate wanted to be labeled a "homophobe"—that would have been political suicide. Never mind that the definition of "homophobe" has quickly evolved from meaning "one who harbors an unreasonable and unjustified fear of homosexuals" to "one who opposes homosexuality." The predominant national attitude towards homosexuality today seems to be one of a cowering tolerance, much like the emperor's subjects who dared not state the obvious - that the emperor's new clothes were merely no clothes at all. The emperor's subjects are apparently alive and well in America today, as our public schools, elected officials, judges, and now more and more laws are being made to encourage homosexual experimentation. It seems as if no one dares state that homosexual conduct is wrong. With our educational and political leaders waffling on this issue, our children need someone to speak up for the truth. The virtual absence of a spokesman on this issue compels me to speak up. I feel compelled to speak out because I am concerned that our current national dialogue and attitude is one that allows false and pernicious ideas about homosexuality to flourish and to attack and infect my children. So I am going to address and expose the myth that protecting homosexuality has any virtue. I don't want my children to experiment with homosexual conduct. I don't want my children to begin to wonder whether they might be gay, and then to experiment with homosexual gay relationships in an attempt to answer this question.

II. Improper Expression of Sexual Drives Can Lead to Perverted Habits and Desires.

No one dares use the word "perversion" any more when identifying homosexual conduct. But that is really the most appropriate word to describe it because such conduct is a perversion of powerful desires and conduct that are appropriate only between a man and woman in marriage and which are inappropriate outside of marriage. So strong and powerful are the sexual drives within humans that they incite, entice, drive or motivate men and women to do things. They can certainly help keep a married couple together; they can help a couple to resolve differences, to be united in purpose, and to work together for the good of their marriage and their children. But exercised outside of marriage, in same-sex relations, these desires can be come perverted. And the power of the drives can lead to enslaving, bad habits. Sexual conduct is habit forming, for better or for worse. And some of the worst habits are literally perverted sexual expression.

III. Social Ills Attend Homosexual Conduct

It is remarkable how rarely one hears any discussion of the many social ills that attend homosexual conduct. But from the very earliest days of this nation, we have acknowledged these adverse by-products of extra-marital sexual relations of all kinds. Outside the bonds and covenants of marriage, giving expression to sexual drives can lead to irresponsibility, to children born out of wedlock, to single-parent homes, to serious economic pressures on a family, to welfare problems for individuals and state, to increased juvenile delinquency and crime, and to unhappy and dysfunctional families. These ills are promoted by extramarital heterosexual relations and from

CLU 04/01

homosexual relations because both are destructive of the traditional two-parent family – which has been the foundation of American society.

As will be discussed in more detail below, many experts deny that there is such a thing as a "homosexual" individual because the use of such a term implies the existence of a condition that one is helpless to change. Thus, what happens is that some people may experiment with homosexual activity, but few end up becoming committed to "homosexual-only" lifestyles. And even those people need not remain that way. Society's tolerance of homosexual activity promotes promiscuity, and consequently it promotes all of the above-listed attendant societal ills. And of course, some mention should be made of the high incidence of acquiring AIDS from individuals who have previously had homosexual contacts. While this cause-effect relationship is known and acknowledged by all moderately intelligent humans, for some reason the prevailing societal attitude today is that one dare not mention the risk of acquiring AIDS from homosexual contacts. This has been replaced with the politically acceptable warning to have safe sex (i.e., use a condom), as if that will take care of everything. Well, since we're exposing lies, let's stop for a second to expose this one. First, use of a condom does not avoid all risks of acquiring AIDS, neither does it avoid all risks of pregnancy. And second, the very act of engaging in extra-marital sex brings consequences that are both adverse to society and harmful to the individuals. Extra-marital sexual activity promotes increased single-parent homes, increased economic problems, increased welfare demands, increased juvenile delinquency and crime, and increased children who perpetuate these lifestyles by parenting a new generation of socially handicapped children.

If our nation would become committed to live by the principle that sexual relations should be limited to those who are married, in one generation this simple commitment would result in a gigantic reduction in our national social ills; crime would be reduced; welfare needs would be reduced; and a greater percentage of our society would be living happy, productive lives. Local governments have passed laws to protect "homosexual orientation" because they have ignored these bad effects. These laws have found widespread support because of one argument that has been persuasive, although not completely logical--that is, that we should not be allowed to hurt others just because we disagree with their lifestyle. It is this tolerance that has undoubtedly led to the support for making homosexual orientation a protected class. I believe, however, that the tolerance is excessive—it crosses the line over to an undesirable indulgence.

IV. A Misleading Distinction Between Homosexual Conduct and Homosexual Orientation

Let us return to the more narrow issue of our nation's current excessive tolerance of homosexual conduct and homosexual orientation. There is a distinction between the two of these, but the distinction is often more illusory than helpful. Our laws should certainly distinguish between "conduct" and "thoughts," and therefore, we should not pass laws punishing mere thought. But here is where, militant gay logic goes astray; it does not follow that we should make "homosexual orientation" a protected class. And here is why.

First, I prescribe to the view that whatever "homosexual orientation" exists, does so only to the extent that the individual allows himself/herself to develop it; once developed it may bedifficult to change, but it can be changed. More fundamentally, I take issue with the belief that an individual is or becomes a "homosexual"; such a conclusion presumes that such a mind-set is a legitimate mental condition that one is powerless to resist and which cannot be changed or corrected; such a conclusion rejects the traditional notion that homosexual conduct is a perversion of normal sexual drives and desires. So, by seeking to find acceptance for the term "homosexual orientation," the militant gays seek to legitimize the implicit opinion that a condition exists that one cannot help and which one cannot change. But these opinions have not been scientifically proven, and they have been scientifically refuted. And here is the root of the problem or the key to the problem of exposing the homosexual orientation myth. Once this fact is made known and acknowledged, all the other militant gay arguments that are built upon this lie dissipate.

Second, there is no legitimate or desirable reason for protecting "homosexual orientation" because it is a principle cause of multiple behaviors and conditions that are inimical to society. Our laws should not seek to promote, encourage and foster a state of mind that is preventable and which leads to conduct and conditions that are unhealthy and otherwise harmful to individuals and society.

Third, gay individuals do not need special rights; they are protected by the same constitutional rights that protect every other citizen. They have the same rights under the Fourth, Fifth, Sixth and Eighth Amendments that protect all others accused of crimes.

Fourth, the recognition of "protected classes" should be made only for classes the identification of which are dependent solely upon conditions about which the individuals in that class have no control, such as race, color, national origin and handicap.

V. People Aren't Born That Way—Homosexual Orientation Results from the Exercise of Choices, and Homosexual Orientation Can Be Changed.

If homosexual orientation is a choice or is the result of choices, and if homosexual conduct is harmful to society, then it is counterproductive for society to protect the mind-set that produces the societal ills. The key element of this reasoning is whether or not homosexual orientation is a choice. It all boils down to whether one **is born that way** and whether one **can change**. But if one is not born that way, and if one can change, and if one is responsible for being homosexually-oriented, **then** our laws should not give special protection to this inimical mind set any more than it should give special protection to alcoholics, drug addicts and pedophiles—all of whom become addicted to bad behavior.

VI. Homosexual Orientation Is Caused by Multiple Factors, Including Environment, Habits and Experiences.

Scientific studies have proven that homosexual orientation is the result of multiple factors, including environment, habits, and experiences. (See the studies cited in comments on page 8.) No study has proven that a person is born that way. Many people will take issue at these two prior sentences because they conflict with the current thinking of a large segment of our society. The militant gays have been successful in creating and fostering the false notion that people are born that way and that they can't change. The widespread acceptance of this erroneous notion is primarily responsible for the current societal attitude of catering to the gays. But the attitude is based on falsehood. If and when society becomes educated and enlightened on this issue, then the unhealthy promoting of the gay lifestyle can be stopped.

Why do so many people believe that people are born that way and that they can't change? It is because of a combination of things: (1) We are a tolerant and forgiving people; (2) we cherish our freedom and our privacy so much and to such an extent that we want to protect the privacy of other as well as our own; and (3) the militant gays have conducted a successful campaign to brainwash people to think that homosexual orientation is genetically determined and that people who have such orientation are born that way and can't change.

VII. The Brief of the APA in the *BSA v. Dale* Case Demonstrates That the Militant Gays Know that There Is No Scientific Proof that Homosexual Orientation Is Genetically Determined.

One of the best ways to refute the militant gay campaign to brainwash society to accept that people "are born that way" is to address head-on their best argument in support of this opinion.

Refuting this argument should expose the factual flaws that are the foundation of their propaganda. I believe that the best argument that the militant gays can make was contained in the amicus curiae brief of the American Psychological Association (APA) that was filed in support of Mr. Dale in the Supreme Court case of *Boy Scouts of America v. Dale*. Immediately following this article (at page 7) is a copy of pages 4-7 of the APA brief, together with seven reference notes in the margin, referring the reader to comments on the following page that expose the patent biases and misleading statements in the APA brief. Those comments address the contention that people are born that way and that they can't change. However, a close review of what the APA stated shows that the APA does not actually state that it has been proven that people are born that way, nor that they cannot change.

The APA, who is openly supportive of the militant gay movement, only grudgingly acknowledges that studies exist that refute the "suggestion" that people are born that way; and they only grudgingly acknowledge "one" expert who works with homosexuals to help change or convert them to be heterosexual. But this acknowledgement is so begrudging that it borders on being dishonest; there are many psychological therapists that work with individuals who seek to rid themselves of erotic same-sex attractions that they had allowed themselves to develop. (See comments at page 8.) The APA's acknowledgement of only one such psychologist evidences their refusal to face the truth on this issue. Hundreds of men who have developed same-sex attractions have sought psychological help to rid themselves of these mental thought patterns so that they can have healthy and happy marriages and family lives. And a significant percentage of such men have been successful in such therapy. Percentages of success have varied between 50 and 70 percent, depending upon the therapist; and, of course, the success of the therapy also depends upon the individual; and successful treatment can take a couple of years to achieve. The length of treat-ment required is an indication of the immense power of the human sexual drives and the power of perverse habits that people develop. But to conclude (erroneously) that the possession of a powerful habit means that one cannot change is not scientifically warranted; and it defies the common experience of human nature that many people are dragged down and hurt by bad habits that they develop; and it blocks the people who are afflicted with such desires from learning the truth and obtaining the assistance that can relieve the affliction. *People can change; and studies prove that people with erotic same-sex attraction can, with therapy and time, have these attractions replaced.*

VIII. Gay Parents Cannot Model Healthy Heterosexual Relations Between a Husband and a Wife.

The APA is so much in bed with the militant gays, that they devoted a large portion of their Supreme Court brief to reciting numerous studies that demonstrate that gay people can do as good a job as heterosexual parents in rearing children in some areas. Well this may be true in some areas, but one important area in which they cannot perform as well as heterosexual parents is in modeling an ideal relationship between a mother and a father (a husband and a wife). The militant gays and APA trivialize the importance of a strong and appropriate relationship between a father and a mother in a marriage. The militant gays discount and deny the emotional and mental differences between a man and a woman and the need for children to have the input of both in order to give them the best chance to live happy and productive lives. Having two women raise a child does not equal having a father and a mother raise a child; neither is two men the equivalent of a father and a mother.

In my opinion, the ideal association for raising children is a family with a father and a mother. All children would be best served if they could be raised in a home with both a father and a mother, and if possible with some other children. For over 200 years America has embraced this core belief in passing laws making sexual relations illegal outside of marriage. Marriage licensing laws were enacted to ensure that parents would be for their children. Our laws should continue to do this. Our laws should prohibit same-sex marriages, and our laws should discourage rather than encourage people from falling prey to the popular fiction that they could be "homosexually-oriented."

IX. Opposing the Legislation to Make "Homosexual Orientation" a Protected Class Does Not Make One a Gay-Hater.

Lest anyone interpret my strong opinion on this matter with hatred for gays, let me point out that I have vigorously represented and defended at least one gay individual. The issue of my client's homosexuality was obvious in this matter because my client was inheriting from his partner who died of AIDS. The decedent's sister fought the inheritance that her brother had left for my client. But my disapproval of the gay life style was irrelevant legally in this case, and it did not affect me in the least from fighting for my client's rights. I know that my representation of him was aggressive and vigilant. I consider the man my friend, and I believe his regard for me was mutual. I harbor no animosity towards gays that makes me want to hurt them in any way. I only wish to help them, to the extent that I can and that it is appropriate. My opposition to making "sexual orientation" a "protected class" is not part of any desire to hurt gays; my opposition is primarily geared at protecting my children and our society, and it is secondly geared at helping gays and everyone else to understand that the most enlightened policy is to not encourage people to adopt a homosexual orientation, but is to teach people that they are responsible for developing and maintaining an appropriate heterosexual orientation.

Until recently, the gay rights movement did not present any significant constitutional issues. But now the gay rights issues are one of the most important constitutional issues now facing our nation. As more and more jurisdictions make "homosexual orientation" a "protected class," this gives more and more encouragement to a life style that is inimical to our society. This life style causes a multitude of societal ills. And those who seek to recognize same-sex marriages and gay-parent families make a mockery of the word "family." Both are perversions that attack our society at its roots. Good and honorable people need to understand this. The word "perversion" needs to be rediscovered—not in order to attack the individuals who cling desperately to their gay identity—but to discourage and prevent my children and yours and other children from falling prey to the invitations of the militant propagandists who would entice our children to experiment with conduct that can enslave and entrap them and lead them to unhealthy life styles.

* *

The following two pages (**Pages 4-7 of the APA Brief, from *BSA v. Dale*)** are extremely significant because they contain the best argument that the APA can make that gays are born that way and that they cannot change. But as you will see by reading these four pages and by reading the seven reference notes on the following page commenting on the APA brief, it is clear (1) that scientific studies do not support the "born that way" contention; (2) that the APA brief is blatantly biased in favor of the militant gays; (3) that there is a considerable amount of scientific evidence that supports the conclusion that people become "that way" from environmental and experiential factors; and (4) that there is considerable scientific evidence that people can change their erotic, same-sex attractions. In summary, there is neither scientific evidence nor any good argument that supports the opinion that gay people are born that way; scientific evidence proves the opposite—that environment and experience cause it.

religion, or gender. Further, the research provides considerable support for anti-discrimination legislation, such as N.J.S.A. 10:5-1 to 5-49, as a means to reduce prejudice in addition to reducing overt discrimination, by increasing interpersonal contact between members of the majority and minority groups.

Conferring broad-based organizations with a readily available means to insulate themselves from anti-discrimination legislation thwarts state policy aimed at alleviating the potentially significant negative psychological, as well as physical and economic, effects of discrimination and prejudice.

ARGUMENT

I. THE NATURE OF SEXUAL ORIENTATION

A. What Causes a Particular Sexual Orientation?

Scientific research and clinical experience indicate that sexual orientation is not "voluntary" for most people. Most people - especially men - do not experience their sexual orientation as the result of conscious choice.[9] The available studies of gay men indicate that the core feelings and attractions that form the basis for adult sexual orientation

typically emerge by early adolescence.[10] For some people, adult sexual orientation is predicable by early childhood.[11] "By the time boys and girls reach adolescence, their sexual preference is likely to be already determined, even though they may not yet have become sexually very active."[12]

Scientific investigation into developmental precursors of adult sexual orientation has not yet consistently identified those factors for the population as a whole.[13] It is not yet clear to what extent and in what way genetic, other biological traits, or early childhood experience may contribute to its development. Studies of identical twins have found that "heritabilities were substantial under a wide range of assumptions."[14] However,

---

9/ For example, 80% of the 60 gay men in one community sample said they had "no choice at all" about their sexual orientation. See Gregory M. Herek, J.C. Cogan, J.R. Gillis & E.K. Glunt, Correlates of internalized homophobia in a community sample of lesbians and gay men, 2 J. Gay and Lesbian Med. Ass'n 17-25 (1998). In a larger, not-yet-published study, the same researchers found 72% of the 898 gay men studied reported having "no choice," and another 13% reported "very little choice" (on file with the APA). Summarizing the prevalent view, one researcher explained: "The concept of voluntary choice is as much in error here as in its application to handedness or native language." John Money, Sin, Sickness or Status? Homosexual Gender Identity and Psychoneuroendocrinology, 42 Am. Psychologist 384 (1987).

10/ See Alan P. Bell, Martin S. Weinberg & Sue Kiefer Hammersmith, Sexual Preference: Its Development in Men and Women 186-87 (1981); Richard R. Troiden, The Formation of Homosexual Identities, 17 J. Homosexuality 43, 43-73 (1989) (reviewing research literature).

11/ See J. Michael Bailey & Kenneth J. Zucker, Childhood Sex-Typed Behavior and Sexual Orientation: A Conceptual Analysis and Quantitative Review, 31 Dev. Psychol. 43 (Jan. 1995); Richard Green, The Immutability of (Homo)sexual Orientation: Behavioral Science Implications for a Constitutional (Legal) Analysis, 16 J. Psychiatry & L. 537 (1988); Richard Green, The "Sissy Boy Syndrome" and the Development of Homosexuality 370 (1987).

12/ Bell et al., supra note 10, at 186.

13/ See Bell et al., supra note 10 at 193-211.

14/ J. Michael Bailey & Richard C. Pillard, A Genetic Study of Male Sexual Orientation, 48 Archives Gen. Psychiatry 1089 (1991). Bailey and Pillard's study, which has since been replicated, found: where one identical twin was gay, the other was gay in 52% of the cases; where one fraternal twin was gay, the other was also gay in 22% of the cases; and where one brother by adoption was gay, his adoptive brother was gay in just 11% of the cases. Id. at 1089. See also J. Michael Bailey and Khytam Dawood, Behavioral Genetics, Sexual Orientation, and the Family, in Lesbian, Gay, and Bisexual Identities in Families 3 (Charlotte J. Patterson and Anthony R. D'Augelli eds. 1998) (reviewing research); J.

---

molecular studies of one aspect of DNA have reached inconsistent conclusions with respect to a linkage with sexual orientation.[15] Another study, as yet unreplicated, reported differences between heterosexual and gay men in the volume of a cell group in the anterior hypothalamus, a brain structure involved in sexual behavior.[16] Results of a study of women suggests that women who were exposed to certain prenatal estrogens are more likely to be lesbian or bisexual.[17] Other researchers, critical of this research, have proposed an "interactionist" model, in which genetic factors are

conceptualized as indirect influences on the development of sexual orientation.[18]

B. Can Sexual Orientation Be Changed?

Once established, sexual orientation is highly resistant to attempts to change it.[19] Although some therapists report that their clients changed their sexual orientation in treatment, no scientific comparison with a control group has been reported. Closer scrutiny has shown that such changes were more likely among bisexuals who were highly motivated to reject a homosexual behavior pattern. Many interventions aimed at changing sexual orientation have succeeded only in reducing or eliminating homosexual behavior rather than in creating heterosexual attractions. One scholar concluded upon review of reports on "conversion therapy" that there is no reliable evidence that "sexual orientation is amenable to redirection or significant influence from psychological intervention."[20]

Michael Bailey, Richard C. Pillard, Michael C. Neale & Yvonne Agyei, Heritable Factors Influence Sexual Orientation In Women, 50 Archives Gen. Psychiatry 217 (1993); J. Michael Bailey & Deana S. Benishay, Familial Aggregation of Female Sexual Orientation, 150 Am. J. Psychiatry 272 (1993); Frederick L. Whitam, Milton Diamond & James Martin, Homosexual Orientation in Twins: A Report of 61 Pairs and Three Triplet Sets, 22 Archives Sexual Behav. 187 (1993).

15/ See Dean H. Hamer, Stella Hu, Victoria L. Magnuson, Nan Hu & Angela M.L. Pattatucci, A Linkage Between DNA Markers on the X Chromosome and Male Sexual Orientation, 261 Science 321 (1993) (study of 76 gay males and 40 gay brother pairs), Stella Hu et al., 11 Nature Genet. 248 (1995) (follow-up study of 33 additional gay brother pairs); William J. Turner, Homosexuality: Type I: An Xq28 Phenomenon, 24 Archives Sexual Behav. 109 (1995); but see George Rice, Carol Anderson, Neil Risch & George Ebers, Male homosexuality: Absence of linkage to microsatellite markers at Xq28, 284 Science 665-667 (1999) (attempting, but failing, to replicate the Hamer et al. results with a sample of 52 gay sibling pairs).

16/ Simon LeVay, A Difference in Hypothalamic Structure Between Heterosexual and Homosexual Men, 253 Science 1034 (1991); see also Simon LeVay, The Sexual Brain (1993).

17/ See Heino F.L. Meyer-Bahlburg, Anke A. Ehrhardt, Laura R. Rosen & Rhoda S. Green, Prenatal Estrogens and the Development of Homosexual Orientation, 31 Developmental Psychology 12 (1995).

18/ William Byne & Bruce Parsons, Human Sexual Orientation: The Biologic Theories Reappraised, 50 Archives Gen. Psychiatry 228 (1993).

19/ See Douglas C. Haldeman, The Practice and Ethics of Sexual Orientation Conversion Therapy, 62 J. Consulting & Clinical Psych. 221 (1994) [hereinafter Haldeman, Practice]; Douglas C. Haldeman, Sexual Orientation Conversion Therapy for Gay Men and Lesbians: A Scientific Examination, in Homosexuality: Research Implications for Public Policy 149-60 (John C. Gonsiorek & James D. Weinrich eds. 1991) [hereinafter Homosexuality]; A. Damien Martin, The Emperor's New Clothes: Modern Attempts to Change Sexual Orientation, in Innovations in Psychotherapy with Homosexuals 23-58 (E.S. Hetrick & T.S. Stein eds. 1984).

20/ Haldeman, Practice, supra note 19, at 224. Moreover, attempts to change someone's sexual orientation runs a risk of causing depression, anxiety, and self-destructive behavior. See American Psychiatric Ass'n, No. 98-56, Position Statement on Psychiatric Treatment and Sexual Orientation (Dec. 11, 1998) [opposing psychiatric treatment based on the assumption that a patient should change sexual orientation] <http://

845

Comments on APA Brief, pages 4-7

[1] That most people do not make a conscious choice of their sexual orientation is just stating the obvious; most people are instinctively attracted to the opposite sex. The fact that sexual attraction does not typically emerge in an individual until early adolescence does not support a finding that homosexual orientation is innate, rather it highlights the fact that there are years of opportunities for influences on impressionable children that can shape or distort their orientation at adolescence.

[2] This statement is significant because it is an admission that even the militant gays cannot say that homosexual orientation is genetically determined. The clever thing about this APA brief is that while on the one hand they acknowledge there is no proof that a gay person is born that way, the APA nevertheless argues that one is. They make every argument they can to support what they wish were true. But the plain language they use admits that there is no scientific evidence to prove what they desperately hoped to prove. Their language, however, acknowledges that their best argument is that only "suggestions" exist where they need "proof."

[3] The studies of identical twins do not support any genetic causation or "linkage" with homo-sexual orientation. The study by Rice, Anderson, Risch and Ebers (discussed in note 6, below), specifically refutes Hamer's conclusions that studies of identical twins show any genetic "linkage" with sexual orientation. The APA brief does not account for the environmental and interactional factors that could easily account for the findings of Bailey and Pillard.

[4] This is an incredible sentence; it shows how desperate the APA is to drum up support for its hypothesis that gays are born that way. The APA states that scientific studies "of DNA have reached *inconsistent conclusions* with respect to a linkage with sexual orientation." In other words, there is no proof of the linkage they were hoping to find. And the study by Dean H. Hamer that they cite has been criticized in the scientific community for improper methods.

[5] Again, in the APA's desperation to cite anything to support its hypothesis that gays are born that way, they cite the study by Simon LeVay, which they acknowledge has not been "replicated." In other words, it is not yet reliable. In fact, the study by Byne and Parsons (which is discussed below, and which is referenced in an APA footnote) specifically refuted LeVay's findings. Byne and Parsons pointed out that a man's experiences and behavior could account for the differing volume in that part of the brain.

[6] A comment must be made about the APA's reference to "other researchers" who have "proposed" an "inter-actionist" theory as to what factors may cause a person to be homosexually oriented. The APA brief cites only one study—the study by Byne and Parsons; however, there are several studies that support the Byne and Parsons conclusions, and the critical aspects of the Byne and Parsons conclusions **have been replicated.** (See e.g., Ruth Hubbard and Elijah Wald, *Exploding the Gene Myth* (1993), Richard C. Friedman and Jennifer Downey, "Neurobiology and Sexual Orientation: Current Relationships, *Journal of Neuropsychiatry*, Vol. 5, No. 2 (Spring 1993), and George Rice, Carol Anderson, Neil Risch, and George Ebers, "Male Homosexuality: Absence of Linkage to Microsatellite Markers at XQ28," *Science*, Vol. 284 (April 1999). Satinover (1996) and Consiglio, Ferre have also published studies that support the findings of Byne and Parsons. Further, the APA puts its own slant on the Byne and Parsons study that makes it sound like even their study concludes that "genetic factors are . . . indirect influences." This statement is misleading because it mentions only the genetic factor; in fact the Byne and Parsons study specifically refuted the LeVay study that had "suggested" a genetic causation of homosexual orientation. Byne and Parsons concluded that homosexuality results from an interaction between the environment and personality characteristics, that biologic factors may affect a person's personality does not mean they cause homosexuality. Byne and Parsons found that an individual's interaction with others appears responsible for one's developing a homosexual orientation.

[7] This particular statement is such a grave distortion that it approaches outright dishonesty. The APA cites "one" scholar who criticizes what they call "conversion therapy" as being ineffective and as having the potential to cause "depression" and "self-destructive behavior." What the APA does not tell you is that the conclusions of this "one" scholar are vehemently disputed by many psychologists who have successfully worked with hundreds of men with same-sex attractions to help these men change. Dr. A. Dean Byrd has treated approximately 300 such men and has achieved a 70% success rate in helping these men to manage, repress and lose the desires they want to change. Other therapists have success ratios in excess of 50% around the nation. (See study by Satinover, 1996.) The APA has a well documented bias against those who attempt "conversion therapy"; according to Dr. Byrd, at one time the APA condemned and prohibited such therapy; however, they later rescinded this condemnation, in part because of the large number of individuals who were plagued with same-sex attractions and who sought psychological help. This put the APA in the position of turning its back on these individuals, until they rescinded their condemnation stance.

One Crisis with China Is Resolved; Other Tough Issues Remain

Heightened tensions between the U. S. and China were defused, at least for the time being, when China chose to accept President Bush's letter of regret as an apology. Tension between the nations rapidly grew following the in-air collision between a U.S. plane and a Chinese jet that resulted in the death of the Chinese pilot and the emergency landing of the U. S. plane and 24 Americans on the Chinese Island of Hainan. Dire consequences were averted when the Chinese chose to interpret President Bush's statement as an apology. But many other issues remain between the U.S. and China, such that uncertainty continues to pervade our relations.

Problems with China have been brewing for some time. The massacre of hundreds of student protesters by the Chinese government at Tiananmen Square in 1989, followed by that government's executing large numbers of people suspected of being protesters has led to loud and indignant criticism of China from the U.S. And although civil rights violations have continued in China, President Clinton recently bestowed on China the "most favored nation" trade status. Many Americans wanted to see China make progress in recognizing fundamental civil rights before blessing them with this. And this development nearly coincided with the theft of national security secrets (believed to be by the Chinese) from the Los Alamos labs. Add to this mix the illegal campaign contributions to President Clinton from Chinese-related donors during his administration and the pending Chinese bid to host the Olympics. All of this makes for strange and strained relations between the U.S. and China.

But that's not all. Now add the heightened tensions between China and Taiwan as Taiwan threatens to declare its independence from China, and as China threatens to take military action to prevent this. And to this, add the question of whether the U.S. should sell the Aegis destroyers to Taiwan, so they can have guided missiles to defend against any attack from China. Sum it all up and you've got an extremely sensitive and volatile issue. All of this was percolating during our recent Presidential election campaign; at the time, both candidates were able to avoid becoming embroiled in any particular answer to this problem. But now President Bush is having to respond.

All of these issues have been hovering in the air for many months, threatening to precipitate into a serious problem at any time. Then, just before the air craft

collision, the Chinese arrested Gao Zhan, a sociology professor from American University, who was travelling in China with her five-year-old son. The Chinese accused Ms. Zhan of spying, put her in prison, and took her son from her.

With this backdrop, the Chinese pilot collided with the U.S. plane, torquing U.S.-China tensions to crisis level. Despite its responsibility for the whole affair, China announced its determination to extract an apology from the U.S., and in so doing they complicated things. Should the U. S. apologize if we did nothing wrong? No, we felt that an expression of regret was as far as we could go. Petty issues like this frequently arise in human relations, but on the international stage the consequences of such pettiness can lead to war. In light of all of this, the apparent peaceful resolution, including the safe return of the 24 soldiers, is quite remarkable. Nevertheless, continuing conflicts with China must be anticipated, given the other issues that continue to fester.

At the height of the uncertainty about whether the 24 soldiers would be returned, one flippant radio personality even suggested putting American Chinese into isolation camps, as the nation did to many Japanese Americans during World War II. We would like to believe that the U.S. would never repeat that, but the prospect is really haunting. And the mere discussion of this is troubling.

President Bush declares he will not stop the reconnaissance missions near China; and American arm sales to Taiwan are going forward; albeit without the Aegis destroyers. The Chinese have yet to return our downed plane, nor have they yet released the captive American University professor.

Because of the aggressive and offensive actions of China, many Americans were gearing up to boycott Chinese goods. If those 24 Americans had not been quickly returned, there is no doubt that millions of Americans would have spontaneously begun a boycott of Chinese goods. China is currently on probation; and they certainly must sense this.

A major crisis has been averted, for now.

Souring Relations with China Can Impinge on Constitutional Liberties

The most important international issues facing the nation today involve our relations with China and Taiwan. For the last 6 to 8 months, tensions between the U. S. and China have become increasingly tense. The recent episode with the U.S. reconnaissance plane that was forced to land on the Chinese Island of Hainan is only the tip of the iceberg. And the apparent peaceful resolution of that crisis has not solved the many other issues that remain.

U. S. relations with China is extremely important to us for several reasons, not the least of which is the fact that China, with over 1.2 billion people and twenty percent of the world's population, is now the biggest nation in the world, with five times as many people as the United States. They also have the atomic bomb, and they export a lot of products to the U.S. So, for the last eight months, while Taiwan and China have wrestled with the issue of whether Taiwan will declare independence from China, and whether China will employ military force to attempt to prevent it, the U. S. has been confronted with the issue of whether we will defend our long-time friend, Taiwan, or whether we will waffle and take the course of deliberate ambiguity.

For quite some time, ambiguity has been the theme of our response to the Taiwan-China issue, even though the Taiwan Relations Act of 1979 committed the U.S. to help assure a peaceful determination of Taiwan's future.

The U.S. had engaged in friendly relations with Taiwan for years before we recognized mainland China as a legitimate nation (during the Nixon administration). The United States has the duty of a loyal friend to continue to stand up for our democratic friend, Taiwan.

President George Bush recently stated that the U.S. would do "whatever it takes" to help Taiwan. But official actions both before and after this statement continue to leave us in the posture of considerable ambiguity. For example, President Bush declined to sell any Aegis destroyers to Taiwan, and he announced that he is dispensing with the procedure of conducting set annual evaluations of the China-Taiwan situation to determine what adjustments should be made in our relations with both nations.

How the China-Taiwan issue will ultimately be resolved is not known. But because it has the potential to erupt into a gigantic conflict, including military action, it must be dealt with properly.

Following the return of the 24 American soldiers from China, the U.S. proceeded to sell a large package of military equipment to Taiwan. Noticeably missing from this package were any Aegis destroyers (battleships with sophisticated defense equipment). Even without the Aegis destroyers, China protested this. Then, most recently, the U.S. Army announced that its troops would not wear any of the 600,000 berets that the Army had previously ordered from China. If China continues its oppressive acts towards the U.S. and Taiwan, then China can expect to face a widespread and spontaneous boycott of its goods in America.

The effects of our relations with China are connected to the preservation of our constitutional rights and liberties. Four reasons for this connection are given below.

First, if another nation were to conquer the United States, then all of our constitutional rights would be lost or jeopardized. This is not currently a likely probability, but at least it illustrates the point that the most fundamental responsibility of the federal government is to protect the states from foreign invasion. Defending against China is clearly a current national priority.

Second, and something that is clearly quite probable, when the U. S. becomes engaged in military action around the globe we put at risk the lives of many Americans. Even if the risk of being conquered by an enemy remains remote, any military engagement risks some American lives. The right to life is the most fundamental of all rights protected by the Constitution, and when we engage in military actions we put at risk the lives of many of us.

Third, military engagements and other strained foreign relations often result in limits to our right to control and enjoy our personal property. The Constitution protects this right and liberty, but foreign actions often impinge on the extent to which we can control and enjoy our property. Almost all Americans experience the economic consequences of military actions, as taxes are increased to support the actions, as the manufacture of military equipment and products increase, as the manufacture and availability of other products is reduced, as boycotts occur, and as embargo sanctions are enacted. These economic consequences are interconnected with the fundamental right to own and enjoy property. To the extent that something deprives a person economically it also diminishes that person's liberty to control his/her property. In other words, if someone confiscates either all of my property or only 10 percent of my property, both actions would deprive me of liberty—the former deprives me of a lot of liberty by taking all of my property, but the latter also deprives me of a portion of my liberty.

Fourth, there are valuable long-term benefits from maintaining good relations with foreign nations. When we treat other nations honorably and honestly, the same treatment is often reciprocated. If and when the day comes that we need allies to support us in a conflict, we can expect to reap more support if we have dealt honorably with others. We certainly enjoyed such support in the war against Iraq in 1990. And such benefit translates into fuller enjoyment of our rights and liberties.

In conclusion, our relations with other nations affect the enjoyment of our constitutional rights and liberties. And specifically, the current conflicts with China jeopardize these liberties. We cannot avoid these conflicts; and sometimes the United States must take a stand to defend one country from another, such as defending Taiwan from China. But these issues are not isolated from the enjoyment of constitutional rights and liberties—they are interconnected.

15

CONSTITUTIONAL LAW UPDATES

| I:ii | July - August 2001 | No. 2 |

The Aftermath of the 2000 Presidential Election...Insert 3.1

Eight months after the momentous ruling of the U. S. Supreme Court that ended the Florida recounts and sealed the presidency for George W. Bush, this case continues to be a divisive topic. Discussion and analysis of this ruling will remain an intriguing subject for years to come. The Equal Protection and Due Process Clauses required Florida to apply uniform standards in counting votes. The failure to do so invalidated the recounts, and time deadlines precluded further recounts. The Supreme Court got it right.

Senator Jeffords Switches Parties....................................Insert 2.2

In a surprise move in May 2001, Senator Jeffords bolted from the GOP and announced that he was becoming an "Independent" who would "caucus" with the Democrats. This unprecedented switch threw control of the Senate from the Republicans to the Democrats. Is Senator Jeffords really an Independent? Was this move motivated by principle or was it a power play?

Supreme Court Review..............................Inserts 8.4.4, 9.1, 9.2 & 10.4

Recent Supreme Court decisions worthy of note include:
--Illegally taped private conversations can be legally broadcast and published;
--Seat belt violators can be arrested;
--Public school cannot exclude religious group from meeting on the premises;
--City ordered not to keep the Ten Commandments (a plaque thereof, that is);
--Police must obtain warrant before searching home with thermal imaging device;
--States cannot make ballots that identify candidates for House and Senate
   who will not pledge support for term limits.

CONSTITUTIONAL LAW UPDATES is a quarterly newsletter edited and published by C. Paul Smith, J.D. Subscription cost is $25.00 per year. To subscribe, send a check or money order to CONSTITUTIONAL LAW UPDATES, P. O. Box 1204, Frederick MD 21702-0204. For further information, visit C. Paul Smith's web site at www.cpaulsmith.com

Supreme Court Review

Each year during the months of May and June the U. S. Supreme Court issues a string of rulings, as it prepares to leave town for a summer break. The Court then shuts down until October 1st, except for emergency matters. October 1, 2001 will mark the beginning of a new "term" for the Court—this fall it will be the 2001 Term; that term will end on June 30th of the next year. This routine has been followed for many years, and it results in a number of important cases being decided each year in May and June. The insert pages of this issue, describe several of the significant cases that were recently decided by the Supreme Court.

How to Research a Supreme Court Case

When references are made to cases in **CLU**, there will usually be a reference citation immediately following the name of the case. This is to assist those who may wish to independently review the case. This section will explain how to research cases. Many large libraries have the U. S. Supreme Court cases—either the hard bound volumes or computer-accessed texts.

The name of each court ruling is underlined, like the title of a book. This is followed by a citation, indicating where the case can be found. For those of you who have not received legal training, the following explanation may be helpful: The official reports of U. S. Supreme Court cases is called, *United States Reports,* and it is referred to by a citation that indicates the volume and page number of the first page of the case. For example, the citation for the *Roe v. Wade* case is 410 U.S. 113. The citation is usually followed by the year that the case was decided (in parenthesis). Thus, the official citation for *Roe v. Wade* is: *Roe v. Wade,* 410 U.S. 113 (1973).

Supreme Court cases are also reported in unofficial publications. The two most widely used unofficial publications are the *Supreme Court Reporter* (published by West Publishing Co.) and the *United States Supreme Court Reports—Lawyers Edition* (published by The Lawyers Co-Operative Publishing Co.). Both of these unofficial reports are valuable in doing legal research because they are annotated, whereas the official reports are not. The citations for both of these unofficial sources and are frequently listed following the official citation. In addition, with the advent of computerized research, additional citations are sometimes given. For example, I subscribe to the LEXIS research service. So, to illustrate, the reference citation for the *Roe v. Wade* case, which gives all four of the above-discussed references is as follows:

Roe v. Wade, 410 U.S. 113; 93 S.Ct. 706; 35 L.Ed.2d 147; 1973 U.S. LEXIS 159 (1973)

As you read some of the recent Supreme Court cases that are discussed in this issue of **CLU**, you will find blanks for the volume and page numbers of the official citation for these cases. This is because the official publication is not yet available, so we don't know the volume and page numbers yet.

How to Use the Inserts

At the top right-hand corner of each **CLU** insert is a number that tells where this page should be inserted in **The State of the Constitution**, the text that will be available later this year.

2A

Subscribe to CLU

CONSTITUTIONAL LAW UPDATES (CLU for short), is a unique newsletter for conscientious individuals to help them keep abreast of important developments in constitutional law that affect all of us, as citizens. The quarterly CLU summaries discuss and analyze the most significant recent developments in constitutional law. The CLU reference system, which is used in conjunction with the text 𝕿𝖍𝖊 𝕾𝖙𝖆𝖙𝖊 𝖔𝖋 𝖙𝖍𝖊 𝕮𝖔𝖓𝖘𝖙𝖎𝖙𝖚𝖙𝖎𝖔𝖓, makes it possible for non-lawyers to quickly access up-to-date information on current issues. Lawyers can benefit from these materials, too, since there is no other publication that attempts to monitor and report these issues as does the CLU.

All news programs and publications make judgments as to what are the most important matters to cover. This means that the news items you see and hear are filtered through someone's judgment of what is important for you. This is true for CLU also, and it is the CLU editorial judgment that makes CLU so valuable.

Regardless of your political point of view, the CLU articles will be informative and probing. The arguments and analysis in CLU can help the reader to be a more effective and influential leader. Knowledge is the foundation of power in leadership, and CLU can help empower the reader. If you have not yet subscribed, please fill out the accompanying form and mail it in. If you have relatives and friends who may be interested, please let them know. A gift subscription to CLU is a great idea.

Do You Have Access to Daily Editions of *The Washington Post* and *The Washington Times*?

It is my experience that most people do not regularly read or even scan the daily editions of *The Washington Post* and *The Washington Times*. It is my observation that these two newspapers give the most thorough treatment of the daily issues relating to our federal government and affecting our constitutional rights. As a subscriber to both of these newspapers, I observe the daily constitutional debates that are occurring. And make no mistake about it, the constitutional debates are being waged in these two newspapers and a few other major newspapers around the country.

Without such a regular review of these two Washington, D. C. newspapers, it is extremely difficult for citizens to keep abreast of the Congressional, Judicial and Executive happenings in our federal government that affect our constitutional rights. The CLU can help make up for this deficiency from which most citizens in the United States are suffering. It takes time to follow all the happenings in government that impact upon the lives of the citizens. I know because I take a lot of time to do this. But those who will read the CLU newsletter can quickly get a reliable, in-depth discussion of important civic, constitutional issues of our day. Subscribe today. You'll be glad you did.

If you don't have a clue, you don't have CLU.

3A

Oregon Democratic Party Seeks to Impeach the Five U. S. Supreme Court Justices Who Voted to Stop the Florida Election Recount

On July 23, 2001, *The Washington Post* reported that the Oregon Democratic Party voted to begin a campaign to impeach the five Supreme Court Justices who voted on December 12, 2000 to stop the recount of presidential election votes in Florida.

Former representative Charles Porter (D-Ore.) accused the five justices of "egregiously bad behavior, high crimes and misdemeanors." Apparently Mr. Porter was not paying attention during the Clinton impeachment proceedings. There isn't any rational, constitutional scholar who could endorse such a fanatical reading of "high crimes and misdemeanors."

Too Frequent Use of the Phrase "BILL OF RIGHTS"—A Persuasive Devise for Attempting to Get Votes

This nation is pretty much united in its dissatisfaction with many current practices in health care services. When that is coupled with a bill in Congress known as the "Patients' Bill of Rights," you would think that passage of the bill would be a sure thing, regardless of the substance of the bill. But that is a very scary, a very dangerous situation. When Congress passes laws based upon superficial reasons or mere appearances, then we run the danger of suffering from bad laws that were passed because of excellent marketing, rather than because the proposed law was the best and proper solution to a problem.

The too frequent use of the solemn title, "Bill of Rights" should be avoided. But Senator Charles Schumer (D-NY) has recently proposed yet another bill that invokes the title, "Bill of Rights."

We must be wary of tactics that attempt to marshal support for a bill based upon its title, without regard to the actual substance of the bill. When appearances and not substance govern our politics, we are in serious trouble.

The National Gay Rights Battle Has Moved to Maryland

On July 19th, Maryland Election officials announced that in the year 2002 there would be a state-wide referendum vote to determine whether "sexual orientation" would be added to the list of protected classes in Maryland. The vote in November of 2002 will determine whether to repeal the recently passed law that would have extended special protections for gays and lesbians.

The referendum vote is now required because of a state-wide petition drive to invalidate the law that had been championed by Governor Parris N. Glendening (D). 47,539 citizens throughout the state signed petitions calling for the referendum vote. This was 1,400 more than the required minimum.

Tres Kerns, from Severna Park, MD, played an instrumental role in this achievement. Mr. Kerns, a father of five children, was instrumental in setting up an organization known as "TakeBackMaryland.org," which helped gather the signatures.

On July 30, 2001, a suit was filed in Annapolis, MD challenging the validity and sufficiency of the petition votes. If successful, the suit would terminate the referendum.

Recently gay rights initiatives lost referendum votes in California and Maine, even though preliminary polls had indicated a contrary public opinion.

The 5-4 holding of the Supreme Court in *BSA v. Dale* (2000) has not settled that case for some people. On June 21, 2001, the D.C. Commission on Human Rights ruled that the Boy Scouts of America violated the city's anti-discrimination law by expelling two gay, adult leaders. The D. C. Commission has seemingly defied the Supreme Court ruling of last year in a virtually identical situation. The ruling is being appealed. *CLU* will follow this case.

On a related matter, on June 29, 2001, the Surgeon General of the United States, David Satcher (a Clinton appointee) issued a report criticizing those who do not embrace homosexual behavior as acceptable and healthy.

Coming Attractions--

In late July, a court upheld the constitutionality of Virginia's "moment of silence" that is administered each morning at the beginning of public school. Some contend that this practice violates the Establishment Clause of the First Amendment. We will address this in the next issue.

Campaign Finance Reform legislation has been temporarily derailed in Congress, despite the recent Supreme Court decision in *FEC v. Colorado RFCC* that upheld the right of Congress to regulate certain political party campaign expenditures. More will be said about this in the next issue. We will also address Hate Crime Legislation in the future.

Bush v. Gore (2000):
A Momentous Supreme Court Decision—and the Court Got It Right!

Make no mistake about it, the 2000 presidential election was one of the most exciting elections in American history. It will be the subject of discourse and debate for years to come. This is the first presidential election to be decided by court litigation resulting in a Supreme Court ruling.

For 36 days following the November 8th Election, our nation lived through a political drama that had never before been seen. Each day brought new happenings and new legal maneuvers that might affect the final outcome of the vote. The nation's eyes were riveted to the television, as we monitored the several recounts and court battles. It wasn't until the announcement of the Supreme Court at 10:00 p.m. on December 12th, that anyone knew who would prevail, Bush or Gore. And even then it took some time to figure out what the Court had ruled, since the ruling came with six separate written opinions.

For the seven-and-a-half months since the Supreme Court handed down its ruling, many critics have chastised the five conservative justices who voted to stop the vote recount, accusing them of political bias and otherwise condemning them. As recent as July 22, 2001, the Oregon Democratic Party voted to begin a drive to impeach those five justices.

While I have read much criticism of the Court ruling, I have read little in support of it. This article is intended to remedy that. The ruling was right. In fact, it was a no-brainer; the Supreme Court corrected blatant violations of the Equal Protection and Due Process Clauses of the Fifth and Fourteenth Amendments. Not one of the nine Justices denied that such violations existed. The two Justices who refused to rule that the Florida recount was fatally defective (Stevens and Ginsberg) preferred to ignore the recount flaws, deferring to the sovereignty of the State in this matter—never mind the fact that these two Justices had consistently voted against

states' rights vis-à-vis federal rights, in resolving previous conflicts between the two.*

Let us first review some presidential election history, and then analyze the Florida case that worked its way up to the Supreme Court.

I. HISTORICAL BACKGROUND

The 2000 Presidential election was one of the three closest presidential elections ever. The elections of 1824 and 1876 were also close—so close that no candidate received a majority of the electoral votes, requiring Congress to choose the president in both cases.

In 1824, no candidate received a majority of electoral votes, so the matter was settled pursuant to the Twelfth Amendment that was ratified in 1804. This Amendment provides that upon counting the electoral votes, "if no person have such majority, then from the persons having the highest numbers not exceeding three on the list of those voted for as President, the House of Representatives shall choose immediately, by ballot, the President." Pursuant to this authority, in 1824, the House chose John Quincy Adams to be President, even though he had received fewer electoral votes than his opponent, Andrew Jackson. I suppose Andrew Jackson could complain that there was a conspiracy to keep him from the presidency. In a sense there was. Henry Clay, the candidate with the third most popular votes in 1824, threw his support behind Adams, giving him the presidency. (Jackson did win the presidency in the next election, 1828.)

In the 1876 election, Democrat Samuel J. Tilden ended up with a slight lead in the popular

*See, e.g., *United States v. Morrison*, 529 U.S. 598; 120 S.Ct. 1740; 2000 U.S. LEXIS 3422 (2000), where the Violence Against Women Act , 42 U.S.C. sec. 13981, was struck down as an unconstitutional exercise of congressional power vis-à-vis the states; it was not valid under either the Commerce Clause of Article I or under section 5 of the Fourteenth Amendment); *Alden v. Maine*, 527 U.S. 706; 119 S.Ct. 2240; 1999 U.S. LEXIS 4374 (1999), where the Court held that Article I does not give Congress power to make a State subject to private suits; and *College Savings Bank v. Florida Prepaid Postsecondary Education Board*, 527 U.S. 666; 119 S.Ct. 2219; 1999 U.S. LEXIS 4375 (1999), where the Court held that Congress lacks the power to abrogate the States' sovereign immunity from private suits in federal court. Justices Stevens and Ginsberg dissented and opposed recognizing states rights in all of these cases.

vote, but he needed to win the electoral votes from either South Carolina, Louisiana or Florida in order to win the presidency. Each of these states and Oregon had sent two conflicting sets of electoral returns to Congress It became the lot of Congress to determine which state electors were the authentic ones. The Twelfth Amendment empowers the President of the Senate to count the electoral votes in the presence of a joint session of the House and Senate. But the Constitution does not spell out how Congress should resolve a dispute between two competing electoral slates. This dilemma was politically volatile in 1876 because the Democrats controlled the House and the Republicans controlled the Senate. Congress set up a special commission to resolve the disputes. The commission was comprised of seven Democrats and eight Republicans, and was chaired by Supreme Court Justice Joseph P. Bradley, a Republican who was highly regarded as brilliant and moral. The commission ruled in favor of the Republican electoral slates, giving the election to Republican candidate Rutherford Hayes by one electoral vote (the closest electoral margin of victory ever). The basis for the commission's decision is no longer readily available; the history books merely point out that the result came on a party-line vote

In 1960 the popular vote between John F. Kennedy and Richard M. Nixon was very close; but Kennedy's victory in the electoral vote was not close.

II. The Night That Would Not End

As Election Night came to a close on November 8, 2000, the vote appeared to be a dead heat. Several weeks later, when all the votes, including absentee ballots were counted, Al Gore prevailed by a slight margin in the popular vote. But prevailing in the popular vote count can be a hollow victory, as Al Gore can testify. By the evening's end on November 8th, it became apparent to all that whoever would win Florida's 25 electoral votes would win the presidency.

Early Tuesday night all of the networks had projected Florida for Vice President Al Gore. Later in the evening all the networks backed off this projection. When I retired at 2:00 a.m. there was no projected winner. When I awoke the

next morning nothing had changed. The election was truly too close to call. George Bush carried a lead of slightly more than a thousand votes (out of 6 million votes) in Florida. But with absentee ballots to be counted and the possibility of recounts, no one could project a winner. And that, of course, introduces us to the key issue in *Bush v. Gore*--**recounts**.

No doubt entire books will be written to relate the drama of the 2000 Presidential Election litigation in Florida. Both candidates used the courts to attempt to secure victory. And the closeness of the vote made normally small election problems to become gigantic. This article, however, will focus on the narrow issues addressed by the Supreme Court. Because of the accusations that the Court's decision was politically biased and was a departure from the Court's precedents, an analysis of the two key issues in that case is very important.

The two issues at the heart of the Court's *Bush v. Gore* ruling were: (1) Was the Florida recount being conducted in a way that violated the Equal Protection and Due Process guarantees of the Fourteenth and Fifth Amendments? And assuming there was such a violation, (2) Should the U. S. Supreme Court nevertheless defer to the Supreme Court of Florida and abstain from correcting these problems, in deference to Florida's sovereignty?

III. Setting, Factor I—The Rehnquist Court Has Championed States Rights.

One of the hallmarks of the Rehnquist Court is its unprecedented recognition of the sovereignty of the states in connection with many matters in which there were competing state and federal interests. (The footnote above cites three specific, recent cases that demonstrate this.) Because of this championing of states' rights, when George Bush asked the U., S. Supreme Court to review and reverse the decision of the Florida Supreme Court, many Constitutional experts expressed doubt as to whether the Rehnquist Court would even agree to review the case.

There are six Republican appointees and three Democratic appointees among the nine Supreme Court Justices, so the Court appears to have a political slant in favor of the Republican Party. Obviously, the Court's opinions do not address the political motivations and biases that they may have. But the nation is very much aware of these factors, and in deciding a case that would in turn decide a presidential election, the nation expects the High Court's ruling to be void of political motives. And that is again the reason it is important to analyze what the Court did rule, and why.

IV. Setting, Factor II—The Democratic Themes: "Discern the Voter's Intent" and "Count Every Vote."

And the problem that eventually made its way to the Supreme Court was the insistence of the Florida courts that the admonition to "discern the voters' intent" was an adequate standard for counting ballots notwithstanding the fact that similarly marked ballots would be counted differently in different counties. This refusal to insist on uniform standards was the fatal flaw in the Gore battle campaign to "count every vote."

Surely the Gore campaign must have contemplated the risk it was taking by not insisting upon a uniform standard. But to my knowledge they have not openly acknowledged this. I suspect the reason is that there was no such standard that could be expected to yield sufficient votes. Perhaps they have a different explanation, but their silence on this issue warrants speculation.

What we do know is that the Gore camp boldly argued that the "discern the voter intent" directive was sufficient, pretending that no Equal Protection problem existed. Then, as long as the Florida Supreme Court would rule in their favor, maybe the U. S. Supreme Court would decline to become involved.

The "count every vote" theme played well with the Gore supporters, but it was seen by others as a cover for biased counting that could arbitrarily change standards to reach a desired result. These were the Equal Protection and Due Process flaws in the Florida recount.

V. The First Law Suit Is Filed

The first law suit filed in connection with the Florida recount, was the one filed by George Bush in U. S. District Court, alleging that the absence of applying uniform standards in the different counties was a violation of the Equal Protection and Due Process Clauses of the Fourteenth Amendment. This case did not receive the greatest coverage during the 36-day ordeal. The case quickly worked its way up the the Fifth Circuit Court of Appeals in Atlanta, Georgia, which indicated its agreement that such violations appeared to be occurring, but the Appeals Court refrained from acting until the matter were to become ripe; the Appeals Court was giving Florida every conceivable opportunity to correct the problems.

VI. The Case That Would Make Its Way to the U. S. Supreme Court

While the federal court case reached an impasse, one of the state court cases did get to the Supreme Court. That case started when the Gore campaign sued to force Secretary of State Katherine Harris to extend the November 14th deadline for submitting vote counts. Leon County Judge Terry Lewis ruled that the Secretary of State had discretion to extend the deadline. Thereafter, when late-submitted votes were presented to Katherine Harris, she declined to accept them stating that no good grounds were given for missing the deadline. Al Gore then again filed suit to reverse Ms. Harris' ruling, but Judge Lewis quickly ruled that the Secretary of State did not abuse her discretion in failing to include recount results that were submitted after the deadline. Vice President Gore immediately appealed this ruling to the intermediate State appeals court, but just as quickly the Florida Supreme Court took the case in order to expedite a final resolution to this urgent matter.

When the case was argued before the Florida Supreme Court, the disparate standards used in counting punch ballots was only one of several issues. David Boies argued for Al Gore that rather than applying a strict standard in counting punch card ballots (i.e., requiring the chad to be completely dislodged in order to count as a vote), he advocated a more lenient standard. He argued that the legislative charge to "discern the voter's intent" required the use of a flexible standard. Mr. Boies convinced the Florida Supreme Court to side with him, but at the same time he boxed himself into the position that would ultimately bring defeat: The failure to apply uniform standards in determining what constituted a legal vote, i.e.--whether the punch-card ballot was completely punched out, whether it was hanging by one chad, or two chads, or whether it had just been indented with the stylus—this violated the principles of equal protection and due process. Staring at a close election loss, Al Gore's only hope was that perhaps a flexible standard—"discern the voter's intent"—would increase the votes for him.

After the oral argument before the Florida Supreme Court, commentators evaluated the performances of the attorneys, and most gave David Boies the highest marks, since most of the justices seemed to agree with him. Bush attorney, Michael A. Carvin, took the biggest beating in the press. Bush attorney Barry Richard, and Katherine Harris' attorney, Joe Klock were also impressive, but David Boies was touted by the press as having been the best attorney. After the Court announced its ruling in favor of Al Gore, the accolades for Mr. Boies became even more glowing. But the final results on December 12th made it clear that Gore's success before the Florida Supreme Court had much more to do with the make-up of that Court rather than the quality of performance of the attorneys arguing before it.

On November 21st, a unanimous Florida Supreme Court ruled in favor of Al Gore and in favor of proceeding with the recounts. The Bush camp had to anticipate the adverse ruling by the Florida Court that was comprised of six Democrats and one Independent. The next day (November 22nd) George Bush announced that he would appeal to the U. S. Supreme Court. The day after that (November 23rd—Thanksgiving Day) the Bush attorneys filed a petition for certiorari, and both sides filed briefs.

But there was no assurance for George Bush that the U. S. Supreme Court [hereafter "Supreme Court"] would take the case. And, of course, the Bush campaign had no right to an automatic appeal to the Supreme Court; the Court would accept the Bush appeal only if it deemed the case significant and sufficiently meritorious. The Bush attorneys filed a petition for certiorari, and then waited and hoped the high Court would "grant certiorari" and do so on an expedited basis. Again, the issue that gave the Bush attorneys the greatest concern was the fact

that the Rehnquist Court had historically given so much deference to state rights that they worried that the Justices might let an admittedly bad Florida decision stand just because of their deference to state sovereignty. The Bush attorneys argued that the federal questions incident to a national election (3 U.S.C. sec. 5), federal election laws, and due to the constitutional issues involved under Article II and under the Twelfth Amendment—all served to make this a case where the Supreme Court should intervene.

On Friday, November 24th, the Court announced that it would take the case. This was a very positive sign for George Bush. He knew there had to be at least four justices who voted to take the case, and the brief Per Curium opinion that accompanied the order indicated that there was probably a majority in favor of taking the case. And if the Court would even agree to review the Florida decision, this seemed to signal that the Court might also be willing to address the Equal Protection problem that the Florida Supreme Court [hereafter "Florida Court"] had tried to ignore.* If the Court was not willing to overturn the Florida Court, then it could have so indicated by deciding not to hear Bush's appeal. From this point on, the burden seemed to have shifted to Gore, even though technically Bush had the normal burden of an appellant.

While the law suit was quickly working its way up to the Supreme Court, recounts had been taking place in Broward, Miami-Dade and Palm Beach Counties, and certain disturbing voting irregularities were widely reported. On November 20th, *The Washington Times* reported that "Broward County alters 'chad' rules midcount." The same day another report included charges that someone had eaten chads. And the nation watched on television as Judge Charles E.

---

*One interesting item to note here is that when the Supreme Court accepted the case, they accepted it for the limited purpose of reviewing the Equal Protection issue, but not the Due Process issue. This is interesting because when the Court issued its final ruling, it held that the Florida recount violated both the Equal Protection and Due Process clauses. Thus, the Supreme Court eventually did consider the due process arguments when the case made its way back to the High Court later.

Burton, chairman of the Palm Beach County canvassing board urged a state court to establish uniform standards for determining whether or not a marked ballot constituted a vote. The nation also saw that this approach was rejected in favor of the flexible, "discern the voter's intent" instruction. Thus, as this case made its way to the U. S. Supreme Court, the Equal Protection argument had acquired considerable attention and support throughout the nation.

At oral argument, the Gore team chose the well-respected lawyer-scholar Lawrence Tribe to represent them. The Bush team selected Ted Olson to speak for them. Within hours after the completion of oral arguments, a united Supreme Court sent the case back to the Florida Supreme Court, directing it to address the issue of the non-uniformity of standards in counting ballots in the different counties. If the Florida justices ever needed a hint as to what the Supreme Court would do if push came to shove—this was it. By remanding the case back to Florida, the U. S. Supreme Court sought to stay out of the fray. The remand was a gentle threat that if the case came back without having resolved the Equal Protection problems, then the Supreme Court would address those problems; and that, of course, would mean that any recounts would either begin again from scratch or that they would be stopped altogether.

While a united Supreme Court remanded the case back to Florida, it was apparent from the Justices comments at oral argument, that the Supreme Court would not be united if it should have to address the Equal Protection issue. But at least the Court was able to unite in remanding the case.

Despite the clear warning signals from the Supreme Court, the Florida Court refused to correct the Equal Protection problem, i.e., the disparate standards problem. Whether the Florida justices were blind or defiant or whatever, I do not know; I presume they wanted to force the U. S. Supreme Court to get involved and to expose the political fractures that would certainly be manifest in the Court if it were to take on the Equal Protection problem. But for whatever reasons, the Florida Court again refused to correct the lack of uniformity of

standards in counting votes; they continued to insist that "discerning the voter intent" was an appropriate standard and a cure-all for any discrepancy in standards. But this time, the Florida Court was not united; Chief Justice Charles T. Wells dissented; he followed the Supreme Court's lead; he decried the unequal standards and argued that the recounts were fatally defective.

Whether or not the Florida Supreme Court's second ruling would have been unanimous, that would not have affected the result in the U. S. Supreme Court. But the Chief Justice's dissent sure made it easier for the U. S. Supreme Court to rule as it did. This helped shield them from some of the inevitable accusations of political bias; for if the Chief Justice of Florida (a Democrat) spoke out against the arbitrary and unfair standards, then this would bolster the credibility of the Republican Supreme Court Justices who likewise condemned the recount for lacking uniform standards.

Anyway, back to the chronology— immediately after the second ruling by the Florida Supreme Court—ruling in favor of Gore and calling for an immediate resumption of the recount, the Bush team again immediately appealed to the Supreme Court. Predictably, the High Court again promptly agreed to take the case and scheduled oral arguments for 36 hours later. But in addition, the Supreme Court ordered a halt to the recount that the Florida Supreme Court had ordered. This was clearly not a good sign for Al Gore.*

The issues before the Court this time were

*Some critics have also criticized the Supreme Court for staying the recount that was in process when the Court agreed to take the case on December 9th. But this is a ridiculous criticism. The recount was a waste of time because it was flawed. Allowing the flawed recount to have continued would not have accomplished anything except perhaps raise some false hopes dependent upon what the flawed results may have been.

The Supreme Court had to invalidate the Florida recount procedures because they were not applying uniform standards to similar ballots in the different counties. This is an obvious defect. Yet the Democratic Justices on the Florida Supreme Court refused to see this flaw. If you want to see political bias in the judiciary, you need not look further than the Florida Supreme Court.

essentially identical to those that were argued the first time. Ted Olson again argued the case for George Bush, but this time Al Gore selected David Boies to argue for him. Within 36 hours after the conclusion of oral arguments, the Supreme Court announced its ruling—and this time they addressed the Equal Protection and Due Process issues head on; seven of the nine Justices agreed that the Florida recount had been conducted in violation of the Equal Protection and Due Process Clauses; the lack of uniform standards in recounting votes in the different Florida counties made the recount results invalid. And as I pointed out at the outset, even the two dissenting justices did not deny the unfairness of the recount methods—they merely voted to defer to the Florida Supreme Court—to look the other way at the unfairness.

VII. Stopping the Recount

The remaining issue was whether to stop the recount or to allow it to continue. And this is the part of the ruling on which the complaining Democrats choose to focus, attempting to paint the Court as being obstructionists (preventing a recount), without ever acknowledging either the unfairness of the recount that had been stopped, the requirement under Florida law that the electors be determined by December 12th, or the impossibility of completing a new one by December 18th (even assuming there should be an additional six days given to do it).* Five justices voted to stop the recount—this, of course, is only the slimmest of a majority.

The Chief Justice stated that the recent order of the Florida Supreme Court to extend recounting beyond December 12th was a departure from Florida law. When the Florida

Court extended deadlines, it "significantly departed from the statutory framework in place on November 7, and authorized open-ended further proceedings which could not be completed by December 12." *

VIII. Was It a 5-4 Vote or a 7-2 Vote?

Democratic critics have characterized the court's vote as having been a narrow 5-4 vote. Stated this way, this would be a misrepresentation, yet those who criticize this ruling insist on labeling the ruling in this manner. But for the record, seven of the nine justices agreed that the Florida recount violated the Equal Protection and Due Process Clauses of the Constitution. And even the other two did not deny that violations had occurred. Two of the seven Justices would have allowed Florida to continue the recount, even though insufficient time remained to complete a proper recount and to allow for the inevitable court contests and appeals—all of which had to be concluded by December 12th, according to the Florida Legislature's stated intent to complete the process six days prior to the date for casting or electoral votes. The Legislature set this deadline in order to take advantage of the federal "safe harbor" provision pursuant to 3 U.S.C. sec. 5, to insure that it would be Florida and not Congress who selected their electors.**

IX. In Retrospect—A Tactical Mistake

When the Gore camp initially prevailed upon the Florida Supreme Court to postpone the date by which the Secretary of State must certify the

---

*To appreciate the correctness of this part of the ruling, one need only project how much time it would take to (a) conduct a proper recount; (b) allow sufficient time for the inevitable protests; and (c) allow sufficient time for judicial review, including the inevitable appeals. The majority pointed out that all of this could not have been completed by December 18th (within six days). But in any event, because Florida law required the recount, protest and judicial review processes to be completed by December 12th, five of the justices concluded that in the absence of fraud or some other serious irregularity, Florida law precluded any other recounts.

---

*To make things even more confusing, Justices O'Connor and Kennedy voted with the Chief Justice and Justices Scalia and Thomas to stop all recounts, but they neither joined in the Chief Justice's concurring opinion, nor did they write separate opinions as to why they voted to stop the counts.

**Justice Souter, in his dissent argued that the state deadline should be extended to December 18th—the date when the electors were to officially cast their votes. However the Florida Legislature specifically provided for the selection to be completed six days prior to that— December 12th. But even if a majority of the Court had agreed, this would not have been a sufficient time to complete the task; it would have been an exercise in futility.

6

election results, they at the same time decreased the time they would later have to protest the results through judicial review. In retrospect, this appears to have been a tactical mistake that ultimately gave them less time for protests, judicial review and further recounts. As it turned out, Al Gore later needed the time that he had initially sacrificed, but it was too late.

X. Contingency Electors

If the Supreme Court had not ended the recount, another mechanism would have gone forward, further complicating matters; the State Legislature was geared up and prepared to name its own set of electors. The Republican party controlled both houses, and it was ready to independently authorize the Bush electors to vote in the electoral college in the event the electors might not be timely certified by the Secretary of State or if the selection of the electors violated Florida law.* Thus, if the selection of Florida electors were not completed by December 12th, either because of a pending recount or otherwise, then the Legislature was prepared to appoint a slate of electors to cast their votes on December 18th.

The Democrats spoke out against this contingency plan, but it was a plausible solution to the dilemma. You will recall that in the 1876 election, Florida sent two slates of electors to vote in the electoral college, and that the U. S. Congress ended up deciding which slate of electors was the right one. Shortly thereafter, Florida passed a law to prevent this result from happening again; and their law provided that protests and judicial reviews must be completed by December 12th to insure that the problem of 1876 (two sets of electors) does not recur.

This statement of priorities and principles by the Florida Legislature was a key factor in the Supreme Court's ruling to stop the recount.

---

* A state constitutional crisis was brewing with this latter possible scenario. The Florida Legislature (controlled by Republicans) asserted that the Florida Supreme Court (dominated by Democrats) improperly acted to change the Florida voting laws after the election. Thus, if the Supreme Court had not settled the matter on December 12th, the Legislature was expected to promptly makes its own selection of electors. Undoubtedly, someone would have challenged this in court.

Those who wanted the recount did not even pretend that they could complete the recount, the protests and the judicial review by December 18th. Therefore, under Florida law completing the recount procedures would have become an impossibility. Those wanting to continue the recounting refused to recognize the Legislature's safe harbor policy, and they refused to accept the Legislature's policy that the recount procedures must be concluded by December 12th

XI. Conclusion

The Democratic themes, "Count Every Vote" and "Discern the Voter's Intent" were nice-sounding, compelling slogans, but they were also smoke-screens, that served to divert attention away from their efforts to harvest as many Gore votes as they could by discarding any uniform standards evenly applied in all Florida counties. The United States Supreme Court exposed and corrected this unfairness.

If the Supreme Court had not corrected this problem, it would be tantamount to telling all the states that in a presidential election there are no enforceable standards of fairness and equal protection. Does anyone really wish the Supreme Court had ruled that way?

3.1

Exerpts from the Majority Opinion
in *Bush v. Gore—*

SUPREME COURT OF THE UNITED STATES

No. 00–949

GEORGE W. BUSH, ET AL., PETITIONERS *v.*
ALBERT GORE, JR., ET AL.

ON WRIT OF CERTIORARI TO THE FLORIDA SUPREME COURT

[December 12, 2000]

PER CURIAM.

The petition presents the following questions: whether the Florida Supreme Court established new standards for resolving Presidential election contests, thereby violating Art. II, §1, cl. 2, of the United States Constitution and failing to comply with 3 U. S. C. §5, and whether the use of standardless manual recounts violates the Equal Protection and Due Process Clauses. With respect to the equal protection question, we find a violation of the Equal Protection Clause.

The individual citizen has no federal constitutional right to vote for electors for the President of the United States unless and until the state legislature chooses a statewide election as the means to implement its power to appoint members of the Electoral College. U. S. Const., Art. II, §1. This is the source for the statement in *McPherson* v. *Blacker*, 146 U. S. 1, 35 (1892), that the State legislature's power to select the manner for appointing electors is plenary; it may, if it so chooses, select the electors itself, which indeed was the manner used by State legislatures in several States for many years after the Framing of our Constitution. *Id.*, at 28–33.

The State, of course, after granting the franchise in the special context of Article II, can take back the power to appoint electors. See *id.*, at 35 ("[T]here is no doubt of the right of the legislature to resume the power at any time, for it can neither be taken away nor abdicated") (quoting S. Rep. No. 395, 43d Cong., 1st Sess.).

The right to vote is protected in more than the initial allocation of the franchise. Equal protection applies as well to the manner of its exercise. Having once granted the right to vote on equal terms, the State may not, by later arbitrary and disparate treatment, value one person's vote over that of another. See, *e.g.*, *Harper* v. *Virginia Bd. of Elections*, 383 U. S. 663, 665 (1966) ("[O]nce the franchise is granted to the electorate, lines may not be drawn which are inconsistent with the Equal Protection Clause of the Fourteenth Amendment").

The recount mechanisms implemented in response to the decisions of the Florida Supreme Court do not satisfy the minimum requirement for non-arbitrary treatment of voters necessary to secure the fundamental right.

The want of those rules here has led to unequal evaluation of ballots in various respects.

The Supreme Court of Florida has said that the legislature intended the State's electors to "participat[e] fully in the federal electoral process," as provided in 3 U. S. C. §5. ___ So. 2d, at ___ (slip op. at 27); see also *Palm Beach Canvassing Bd.* v. *Harris*, 2000 WL 1725434, *13 (Fla. 2000). That statute, in turn, requires that any controversy or contest that is designed to lead to a conclusive selection of electors be completed by December 12. That date is upon us, and there is no recount procedure in place under the State Supreme Court's order that comports with minimal constitutional standards. Because it is evident that any recount seeking to meet the December 12 date will be unconstitutional for the reasons we have discussed, we reverse the judgment of the Supreme Court of Florida ordering a recount to proceed.

When contending parties invoke the process of the courts, however, it becomes our unsought responsibility to resolve the federal and constitutional issues the judicial system has been forced to confront.

CLU 07/01

Senator Jeffords Switches Parties and Shifts Control of Senate From GOP to Dems

On May 24, 2001, Senator James Jeffords (R., Vt.) announced that he was leaving the Republican Party to become an Independent, and that henceforth he would caucus with the Democratic Party. This announcement has sent shock waves throughout the nation, as it has reversed the effect of the Republican victory in the 2000 Senatorial Elections.

For weeks after the announcement, additional aftershocks and repercussions continued to manifest as all the pundits weighed in on the matter. The June 2nd headline in *The Washington Post* stated that "McCain Is Considering Leaving GOP," as Republican Senator John McCain (AZ) is hosting the new Senate Majority Leader, Tom Daschle (D., S.D.) for a visit over the weekend. *The Washington Times* reported on the same day that unhappy Vermonters who donated to Jeffords' campaign as a Republican candidate now want their money back. There will certainly be additional aftereffects as well.

While elected Senators and Congressmen have occasionally switched parties from time to time during the nation's history, this is the first time that such a switch has caused the control of one of the houses to shift from one party to the other. Thus, this party-switch is the most significant one ever.

From a constitutional law perspective, this switch is interesting because it highlights the inner workings of the two-party system by which our Congress, and especially the Senate, operates.

I. The Two-Party Legislative System

Nowhere in the Constitution is it set forth that we shall have two main political parties in Congress and that the workings of the House and Senate shall be made to accommodate two parties, with each party having a leader to marshal and direct that party's agenda. However, the Constitution does not prohibit this, and it does authorize each house to make its own rules. Article I, Section 5, clause 2 states: "Each House may determine the Rules of its Proceedings ...." Based upon this, both houses have enacted rules that empower the two most prominent parties, and that leave little power and influence to any third or fourth parties that may succeed in electing a candidate to one of the houses. In fact, it is this two-party system that discourages any third party candidate from seeking election to Congress; obviously neither of the two main parties are interested in backing such a candidate, and even if such a candidate were to be elected, he or she could

not be expected to have the backing (votes) to enact legislation. Consensus-building is essential for a senator or representative to be effective in Congress, and the two-party system is conducive to this.

Existing rules in the Senate and the House give the majority party considerable control, through setting the agenda and through control of committees. Committees control whether a proposed law (or bill) is voted upon by both the House and the Senate. Thus, while any member of Congress may submit a bill for consideration, it must first make it out of the committee to which it is assigned before a vote can be taken on it. And the party in control of that house can table a bill or otherwise keep it from coming to a vote. This is how the party in control can block a bill from even coming to vote. Similarly, in the Senate, the majority party can prevent the confirmation of judges and high officials in the President's administration by stalling, even without voting to reject one of the President's nominations.

II. A Plug for a Three-Party System

Let me digress for a moment. I am convinced that there would be some advantages to having a three-party system; it would promote creativity and cooperation; and I believe it would discourage bitter partisan attacks. By giving voice to a third opinion on many issues, I believe it could act as a shield against some of the frequent propaganda techniques that are frequently employed in political debate-- specifically, the either/or fallacy and *ad hominem* attacks. The participation of a viable third party in our politics would make it more difficult for one party to get away with sleazy and deceptive propaganda devices; it would promote a more honest treatment of the facts and issues in political debate. All of this is wishful thinking, however. At this point it would take a constitutional amendment to force Congress to set up a system that accommodates at least three parties, and I cannot foresee ever getting a majority of votes to weaken the majority party.

III. Senator Jeffords' Switch Was Motivated by the Desire for Power, Not by Other Principles

Pardon my digression. Now, back to the Jeffords matter. As we all know, Jeffords announced that he was leaving the Republican Party to become an Independent, not a Democrat. What does this mean? Surely Senator Jeffords understands all that was discussed above about the two-party system. As the facts unfolded, it is clear that Jeffords made this switch to increase his power. No sooner had Senator Jeffords finished listing the topics that he called "principles" that impelled him to switch parties, then it was announced that the Democrats had promised him the leadership of one of the Senate Committees once he left the Republican Party. So much for Senator Jeffords' principles; his influence was bought by the Democrats, who would gladly give the liberal Republican a committee chair if he could give the Democrats control of the Senate. This was not about matters of principle, as Senator Jeffords attempted to characterize it; this was about his seizing a unique opportunity to expand his own power and influence in a Senate that was evenly split. It was this even split that created the power opportunity for Senator Jeffords, and he has gambled that the Senate's even split will continue for a considerable length of time because once a clear majority party emerges, further leadership opportunities for an Independent will clearly be in jeopardy.

Perhaps Vermonters can call Senator Jeffords a traitor, especially the Republican voters who voted for him and gave him money for his campaign. And whether this will cost Senator Jeffords in a subsequent election 5 ½ years from now, we don't know. Vermont has taken pride in being independent, so maybe Senator Jeffords will fare just fine. And there is talk that he might run for governor in Vermont. Vermonters will have to judge Senator Jeffords for his bait-and-switch tactic. But no one else has standing to accuse Jeffords of betrayal, certainly not the GOP.

But, interestingly, the GOP is not accusing Senator Jeffords of betrayal; they are treating it rather matter-of-factly – this was not something within their control.

IV. Was Senator Jeffords' Switch Based upon Principle or Was It the Result of a GOP Blunder?

Also interestingly, liberal pundits have been anxious to characterize Jeffords defection as both "principled" and "the result of GOP blunders." Such characterizations are both inconsistent and erroneous. In fact, this double-breasted criticism is illogical, and manifests the lack of principles of those who advance it. Clearly, if Jeffords' actions were based upon principle, it would not have been possible to persuade Jeffords not to switch through pampering him and catering to his special desires, unless either he or the GOP compromised principles. So if Jeffords' actions were truly principle-based, there is nothing that President Bush and the GOP could have done to prevent it. Conversely, if Jeffords' actions were not based upon principles, then perhaps the GOP could have kept Jeffords by abandoning some of their principles.

I previously pointed out that the switch was motivated by power, not principle. But to further demonstrate the disingenuouness of the "principle" argument, consider the following.

Last fall Jeffords ran for re-election as a Republican, accepting campaign funds from the Republican Party and implicitly endorsing the election of George Bush as president. Now, however, Senator Jeffords states that it is because of the election of President Bush that his principles require that he leave the Republican Party. This reasoning would make sense only if President Bush had begun to govern differently than he promised in his campaign. But he has not, and neither did Jeffords allege that he had. This statement by Senator Jeffords shows that it is his own lack of principles that motivated his switch. Additionally, Senator Jeffords listed several topics, which he called "principles" that required him to sever ties with the Republican Party. These topics included budget, choice, judiciary, tax and spending, missile defense, energy, environment and education. But even a cursory analysis of this basis for his switch leads to the inescapable conclusion that principles had nothing to do with his actions. Senator Jeffords had differed with most of the Republican Party on these topics for many years, going as far back as 1981 when he (then a Congressman) voted against President Reagan's tax cut legislation. Jeffords had a long record of voting with Democrats on many matters, including voting against the conviction of President Clinton on the impeachment charges.

The drooling of the Democrats over Senator Jeffords' "principled" act of repudiating the GOP is just simply nonsense—it is so divorced from being a principled act. And everyone knows it. This was purely about power, and only about power.

If Senator Jeffords were to have waited until 98-year-old Republican Senator Strom Thurmond should die – which is expected to bring a temporary Democratic replacement until another election could be held (see Seventeenth Amendment), then control of the Senate would switch to Democrats without the aid of Senator Jeffords. But under this scenario, Jeffords would have had no clout to demand the chairmanship of a committee. Only by acting now could he exact such a concession from the Democratic leadership.

V. Why Would Any Senator Want to Be an Independent?

Some comment is due on the question of why anyone would want to call himself a member of the "Independent Party" in the first place. We have already pointed out some of the disadvantages, since he cannot normally expect to be given any party leadership posts.

The incentive to be an "Independent" rests with the notion that somehow an Independent thinks for himself and is not dictated to by others, especially by one of the parties. This, of course, sounds great, and implicit in it is the thought that Democrats and Republicans are not independent thinkers and that they are merely pawns of their parties, marching to party orders. But this latter view is an insult to the hundreds of independent thinkers that choose to align themselves with the two main parties. Such thinking is merely pseudo-intellectual; such thinking may convince some that a representative is more independent than those from the two main parties, but it has no basis in fact; it is a self-deception that frankly operates to prevent their representatives from having increased power in Congress. And if the representative should believe that he or she is more independent than others just by belonging to the Independent Party, then that representative is either ignorant or dishonest.

If the truth be known, Jeffords is really not an Independent; he is a Democrat who likes to call himself an Independent. Not only does Senator Jeffords vote with most Democrats, but he will now chair a Senate Committee and caucus with the majority party in the Senate, the Democratic Party. As the saying goes, if it looks like a duck, walks like a duck, and quacks like a duck, it is a duck. So is Senator Jeffords a Democrat.

VI. What Is the Expected Effect of the Jeffords' Defection?

In many respects the Jeffords' defection will have virtually no effect on Congress; his leaving the GOP does not signal any change in the overall expected voting in the Senate. And, the House of Representatives continues to be controlled by the GOP, even though control of the Senate has shifted to the Democrats. The only area of impact will be in the work of the Senate committees, where the Democrats will now have more power to block Republican bills and actions.

The potential effect of Jeffords' switch to the Democrats is that it gives the Democrats the opportunity to block President Bush from making needed appointments to his administration and making judicial appointments. Four months into the Bush administration, only 11% of the executive appointments had been made. This delay is largely due to the backlog of Senatorial confirmation of the nominees proposed by President Bush. As the majority power shifts to the Democrats, this confirmation process can be dragged to a halt or otherwise blocked. In a recent editorial, *The*

Washington Post urged the Democrats to take this opportunity and revamp the Senate's existing rules to expedite a process that has become archaic and counterproductive. The party that has complained of gridlock for several years now, has the opportunity to break up one species of gridlock that no longer serves a useful purpose.

VII. Campaign Finance Reform Implications

The occurrence of the Jeffords switch amidst the campaign finance reform debate, highlights a big inadequacy in both the existing campaign finance law and in the proposed new legislation, including the McCain-Feingold bill. These laws and proposed laws only deal superficially with a symptom, and they fail to address the root of the problem that brings corruption to politics. One of those roots is our national, two-party political system that encourages national parties to influence local elections in order to control the national agenda. It is the national, two-party system that is the foundation behind the corruption; the money is only a symptom.

Ironically, Senator Jeffords accepted Republican Party campaign funds to help secure his reelection in November; and shortly after his victory he left the party that had helped pay for his campaign. Obviously Senator Jeffords was not bought by the Republican Party through his acceptance of their money. But again, it was the very rare power opportunity that was presented to Jeffords that bought him away from the party that had succored him for over twenty years.

VIII. Conclusion

Senator Jeffords' switching parties from Republican to "Independent" is interesting to analyze because it is the first time a Congressman making such a switch actually shifted the control of one of the chambers of Congress from one party to another. The move highlights the inner workings of the Senate and the rules that give the majority party the power to block legislation and certain executive actions. Finally, the disingenuousness of Senator Jeffords (claiming to act out of principle, and claiming to be and Independent rather than a Democrat) give this event an intriguing component. It is the very absence of principle as a basis for this switch that makes it a fascinating story.

Congress Can Limit A Political Party's Campaign Expenditures

FEC v. Colorado Republican Federal Campaign Committee, ___ U.S. ___; 121 S.Ct. 2351; 2001 U.S. LEXIS 4668 (2001)

On June 25th, 2001, the Supreme Court ruled (5-4) that a political party's expenditures for a federal candidate can be limited. *FEC v. Colorado Republican Federal Campaign Committee*. Justice Souter, writing for the majority, ruled that Congress can regulate a party's coordinated campaign expenditures in order to prevent parties from having a corrupting influence on elected officials. The four dissenting justices (Thomas, Rehnquist, Scalia and Kennedy) argued that this was an improper regulation of speech protected by the First Amendment.

In 1976, in *Buckley v. Valeo*, 424 U.S. 1, the Supreme Court held that limits could be set on the amount of contributions to campaigns, but not on expenditures. *FEC v. Colorado RFCC* modifies that to permit regulation of "coordinated" party expenditures. This ruling will certainly be encouraging for the proponents of the current campaign finance reform legislation because it answers some of the arguments that it would be unconstitutional.

But campaign finance reform legislation will never cure our political system of the possibility of corruption from those who seek to buy influence with contributions. There will always be ways to circumvent laws intended to prevent the buying of influence. It is the two-party system that gives the impetus to coordinate and combine efforts to elect candidates around the country who will promote a party's interests. And if the two-party system is not modified, campaign finance reform won't work. What would work would be a political system that gives ample broadcast time and press coverage to at least three or four candidates in elections. This would provide a self-policing feature that could check major corrupt influences by giving a forum to four individuals who could advocate for their positions and who could expose and denounce corruption that they saw. By doubling the number of candidates given public forums, it would double the difficulty of corrupting a campaign.

See also 9.1.4

States Cannot Impose Term Limits on Candidates for the House and Senate Except By Not Voting for Them

Cook v. Gralike, ___ U.S. ___, 121 S.Ct. 1029 (2001)

On February 28, 2001, a unanimous Supreme Court struck down a Missouri law that sought to print on election ballots the statement, "DECLINED TO PLEDGE TO SUPPORT TERM LIMITS" next to the name of every candidate for the United States Senate and House who would not take such a pledge. The Supreme Court struck down this state law, ruling that it violated Article I, Section 4, clause 1 of the U. S. Constitution, and was an improper attempt by Missouri to regulate the times, places and manner of holding federal elections.

The Supreme Court said that the 1995 case of *U. S. Term Limits, Inc. v. Thornton*, 514 U.S. 749, was controlling in deciding the Missouri case. In *Thornton*, the Supreme Court struck down an Arkansas law that would have prohibited a three-term Representative or a two-term Senator from running for reelection again.

Government Cannot Force Company to Subsidize Message Against Its Will

USDA v. United Foods, ___ U.S. ___; 121 S.Ct. 2334; 2001 U.S. LEXIS 4904 (2001)

On June 25, 2001, the Supreme Court ruled that a federal regulation that required a mushroom producer to pay an assessment that funded a message with which the producer disagreed was a violation of the mushroom producer's First Amendment freedom of speech rights.

Commercial speech is entitled to some protection under the First Amendment, albeit lesser protection. *Virginia Board of Pharmacy v. Virginia Citizens Consumer Council, Inc.* (1976).

The United States Department of Agriculture (USDA) had required United Foods to pay an assessment based upon the Mushroom Promotion, Research, and Consumer Information Act of 1990, *7 U.S.C.S. sec. 6101 et seq.* United Foods objected and refused to pay the assessment, claiming that it was used to promote something with which United Foods disagreed. The Government sued United Foods in the U. S. District Court for the Western District of Tennessee. The government prevailed at the District Court level. United Foods appealed to the Sixth Circuit Court of Appeals who reversed. The U. S. Supreme Court affirmed the Sixth Circuit decision.

The Supreme Court had recently ruled that mandatory fees can be required where they are necessitated by a comprehensive regulatory scheme. *Glickman* (1997). However, this was not the case with United Foods and the mushroom assessment, where the assessment was to be used to promote a message with which United Foods disagreed and which was not a part of a "valid scheme of economic regulation."

Illegally-Taped, Private Phone Call That Is a "Public Concern" May Be Legally Broadcast

Bartniki v. Vopper, ___ U.S. ___; 121 S.Ct. 1753; 2001 U.S. LEXIS 3815 (2001)

On May 21, 2001 the Supreme Court ruled (6-3) that an intentional publication of a private phone conversation that was known to have been illegally taped was protected under the First Amendment because the content of the conversation was a public issue. Consequently, the state and federal laws that prohibited the publication of these private communications over the radio and in the newspapers was unconstitutional.

Justice Stevens writing for the majority, justified the publication of the private conversation because of our nation's "profound national commitment to the principle that debate on public issues should be uninhibited, robust and wide-open," 121 S.Ct. 1753, at 1765, citing *New York Times v. Sullivan*, 376 U.S. 254, *at* 270 (1964). Justice Stevens stated that [o]ne of the costs associated with participation in public affairs is an attendant loss of privacy." *Id.* Finally, Justice Stevens concluded that "a stranger's illegal conduct does not suffice to remove the First Amendment shield from speech about a matter of public concern." *Id.*

Justices Breyer and O'Connor filed a concurring opinion, to explain that they concurred with Justice Stevens only because of the very "narrow" holding of this particular case. They warned against using this case broadly to immunize the media in other situations.

Chief Justice Rehnquist, joined by Justices Scalia and Thomas, dissented, arguing that the Court's ruling was a violation of privacy, and that the First Amendment did not override the important privacy concerns that the state and federal laws had sought to protect.

Congress Can Limit A Political Party's Campaign Expenditures

FEC v. Colorado Republican Federal Campaign Committee, ___ U.S. ___: 121 S.Ct. 2351; 2001 U.S. LEXIS 4668 (2001)

On June 25th, 2001, the Supreme Court ruled (5-4) that a political party's expenditures for a federal candidate can be limited. *FEC v. Colorado Republican Federal Campaign Committee.* Justice Souter, writing for the majority, ruled that Congress can regulate a party's coordinated campaign expenditures in order to prevent parties from having a corrupting influence on elected officials. The four dissenting justices (Thomas, Rehnquist, Scalia and Kennedy) argued that this was an improper regulation of speech protected by the First Amendment.

In 1976, in *Buckley v. Valeo,* 424 U.S. 1, the Supreme Court held that limits could be set on the amount of contributions to campaigns, but not on expenditures. *FEC v. Colorado RFCC* modifies that to permit regulation of "coordinated" party expenditures. This ruling will certainly be encouraging for the proponents of the current campaign finance reform legislation because it answers some of the arguments that it would be unconstitutional.

But campaign finance reform legislation will never cure our political system of the possibility of corruption from those who seek to buy influence with contributions. There will always be ways to circumvent laws intended to prevent the buying of influence. It is the two-party system that gives the impetus to coordinate and combine efforts to elect candidates around the country who will promote a party's interests. And if the two-party system is not modified, campaign finance reform won't work. What would work would be a political system that gives ample broadcast time and press coverage to at least three or four candidates in elections. This would provide a self-policing feature that could check major corrupt influences by giving a forum to four individuals who could advocate for their positions and who could expose and denounce corruption that they saw. By doubling the number of candidates given public forums, it would double the difficulty of corrupting a campaign.

8.4.4

Compassionate Judicial Action Allows Martin to Stay in the PGA

PGA Tour, Inc. v. Martin, ___ U.S. ___; 121 S.Ct. 1879 (2001)

On May 29, 2001, the Supreme Court in a 7-2 vote ruled that Casey Martin, who has a physical handicap that prevents him from walking the course when he plays golf, can nevertheless participate in the PGA Tour because the Americans With Disabilities Act (ADA) requires the PGA to make accommodations for such a disability. The Court ruled that making such an accommodation would not disrupt the fundamental nature of the game of golf.

The PGA has no special place in my heart, but it concerns me that the Court is taking control in a private matter that is none of its business. I'm happy for Casey Martin, but I hope this case does not become precedent for other intrusions into private affairs that should not be the concern of the Court.

In Justice Scalia's dissent (joined by Justice Thomas), he said: "In my view today's opinion exercises a benevolent compassion that the law does not place it within our power to impose. The judgment distorts the text of Title III, and the structure of the ADA, and common sense."

Court Orders City Not to Keep the Ten Commandments

Elkhart v. Books, ___ U.S. ___; 121 S.Ct. 2209; 2001 U.S. LEXIS 4120 (2001)

On May 29, 2001, the Supreme Court decided not to review the case from the Seventh Circuit Court of Appeals in which the city of Elkhart, Indiana had been ordered by the Seventh Circuit to remove the monument bearing the Ten Commandments from the grounds in front of the Elkhart Municipal Building. The Seventh Circuit reversed the federal district court and held the monument's existence violated the Establishment Clause of the First Amendment.

The Supreme Court will not get an opportunity to rule on this case because only three justices voted to take the case. (At least four justices must vote to hear a case on certiorari.)

Normally, no written opinions accompany a ruling that denies certiorari to a case. But in this case, Chief Justice Rehnquist prepared a dissent because of his great disagreement with the ruling of the divided Seventh Circuit. This, in turn, prompted Justice Stevens to write a brief majority opinion, pointing out that opinions that accompany the denial of certiorari have no precedential significance at all.

Notwithstanding this disclaimer, Justice Rehnquist argued that the continued maintenance of the Ten Commandment monument did not violate the Establishment Clause; its erection in 1958 was a project that was jointly backed by Jews, Catholics and Protestant faiths, and it did not advance or inhibit any one religious faith.

What this case clearly holds is that the Seventh Circuit Court of Appeals commands the City of Elkhart, Indiana to not keep the Ten Commandments.

Public School Cannot Exclude Religious Group from Meeting in School Where the Facilities Are Made Available to the Public

Good News Club v. Milford Central School, ___ U.S. ___; 121 S.Ct. 2093; 2001 U.S. LEXIS 4312 (2001)

On June 11, 2001, the Supreme Court ruled (6-3) that Milford Central School violated the free speech rights of the Good News Club when it excluded the Club (a private Christian organization) from meeting at the school after hours. The Court ruled that no Establishment Clause concern justified Milford's violation.

This case resolved a conflict among the circuits on the question of whether speech can be excluded from a limited public forum on the basis of the religious nature of the speech.

The Milford Central School invited the public to use its facilities for educational, recreational and character-building purposes, but not for religious purposes. The School sought to prohibit proselytizing speech but not speech from a religious point of view. The majority found such a distinction to be an impossible one to make; the majority said that it is unnecessary to do so because in either event the limitation was a violation of free speech rights.

The result of this ruling is initially, to allow the Good News Club to meet on school property after school hours, where they will be allowed to begin and close their meetings with prayer and to attempt to lead children to Christ.

If the school should close its doors to all non-school groups, then it could perhaps exclude the Good News Club.

35

Seat Belt Violators Can Be Arrested

Atwater v. City of Lago Vista, ___ U.S. ___; 121 S.Ct. 1536; 2001 U.S. LEXIS 3366 (2001)

On April 24, 2001 the Supreme Court ruled in a 5-4 decision that the Fourth Amendment does not forbid a warrantless arrest of an individual for a minor criminal offense, such as a seatbelt violation punishable only by a fine.

This ruling is troubling to me for two reasons. It strikes me as unreasonable and unfair to allow the police to arrest someone for an offense that is not an incarcerable offense. Second, once an arrest is made on a seatbelt violation, the police would then have the right to search the vehicle incident to a lawful arrest. This back door approach will allow the police to circumvent the protections that would otherwise exist to protect an individual's privacy through the Fourth Amendment.

The dissent in this case, authored by Justice O'Connor, called this a "new rule," that is "unsupported by our precedent, but runs contrary to the principles that lie at the core of the Fourth Amendment." 121 S.Ct. 1536, 1561. But the majority did not see it this way; they found no specific violation of the Fourth Amendment by the Texas law that authorized the police to arrest someone for a seatbelt violation.

Warrant Required to Search Home with Thermal Imaging Device

Kyllo v. United States, ___ U.S. ___; 121 S.Ct. 2038; 2001 U. S. LEXIS 4487 (2001)

On June 11, 2001, the Supreme Court ruled (5-4) that the use of a thermal-imaging device aimed at a private home from the public street to detect relative amounts of heat within the home constitutes a "search" within the meaning of the Fourth Amendment, and that consequently a search warrant must be obtained before such a device is used by the State in obtaining evidence. Absent such a warrant, the resulting evidence obtained is inadmissible, since it was from an unlawful search.

The breakdown of the Justices voting on this case is interesting. Justice Scalia delivered the opinion of the majority; he was joined by Justices Souter, Thomas, Ginsburg and Breyer. Justice Stevens wrote a dissent, joined by the Chief Justice and by Justices O'Connor and Kennedy.

Warrant Required by State Hospitals to Perform Nonconsensual Diagnostic Tests

Ferguson v. City of Charleston, ___ U.S. ___; 121 S.Ct. 1281; 2001 U.S. LEXIS 2460 (2001)

On March 21, 2001, the Supreme Court ruled (6-3) that a Charleston, South Carolina law requiring state hospitals to perform diagnostic tests on patients in order to obtain evidence of criminal conduct (drug abuse) is a nonconsensual, unconstitutional search in violation of the Fourth Amendment. The Court ruled that the threat of criminal sanctions to deter pregnant women from using cocaine does not justify an exception from the Fourth Amendment right to be protected from warrantless searches. The majority ruled that this was not the type of "special needs" situation that would justify an exception to the requirement of obtaining a warrant.

STEM CELL RESEARCH—Don't Fund It

President Bush has given much deliberation to the question of whether he will agree to governmental funding of stem cell research. On July 23, 2001, President Bush met with the Pope, who urged the President not to give governmental support to stem cell research. As of this writing, President Bush has not decided what position his administration will take on the issue; the President acknowledged the issue to be a difficult one because there seems to be so many potential benefits from the stem cells.

Notwithstanding the potential benefits, if the scientific research is dependent upon harvesting stem cells from human embryos, whose continued living is sacrificed for the production of the stem cells, then such a harvesting industry is wrong. Such a practice is the sacrificing of one independent human life in order to try to help another life. Such a sacrifice would be clearly illegal and immoral if the human life were a born human being.

Some would argue that the Supreme Court ruling in *Roe v. Wade* (1973) has resolved the moral issue, and makes it okay to have abortions and to harvest stem cells any time before birth. But since the U. S. Supreme Court is not God, the Court's rulings do not necessarily resolve the moral issues.

Regardless of the fact that the Supreme Court held that a fetus is not a "person" under the Constitution, it may nevertheless be a "person" in the eyes of God, and it is for this reason that many people continue to seek to overturn *Roe v. Wade*. At the very least, a human embryo or fetus is an independent biological human life that is sacred and entitled to protection and reverence.

Some will attempt to distinguish embryos that are created for harvesting and those that are the result of a legal abortion. But is an embryo in a petri dish entitled to any less protection than an embryo that is in a woman's womb? From the point of view of the embryo, this should make no difference. Some may argue that a week-old embryo does not have a point of view because its consciousness has not yet developed—only the potential for consciousness is there.

Nevertheless, the preciousness of life and the sanctity of potential human life cause me to resolve this dilemma in favor of protecting both week-old embryos and nine-month-old fetuses.

Perhaps science will yet discover other ways to address illnesses such as Parkinsons Disease and Alzheimer's Disease. A recent column by Nat Hentolf in *The Washington Times* suggested that adults may produce a type of stem cell in their bone marrow, and that such stem cells may be able to provide the type of benefits that we expect from embryonic stem cells.

37

CONSTITUTIONAL LAW UPDATES

I:iii   November 2001   No. 3

The Effects of Terrorism on Constitutional Rights

In the wake of the terrorist attacks of September 11, 2001, with the United States at war against enemies known and unknown, life will be forever changed in America. There will be a multitude of changes in our rights and liberties. Constitutional rights and duties have been impacted by the terrorism on the American mainland.............................Inserts 2.8, 3.5.1, 3.10 & 7.7

Prayer in School—Has the Supreme Court Become Hostile towards God and Prayer?

As the United States unites in praying for God's blessings in combating terrorism, the Supreme Court's "hostility" towards prayer in public school becomes visible and out of harmony with the great majority of citizens. Does the Virginia, Moment of Silence case stand as a change in the Supreme Court's position on school prayer? Or will the *Santa Fe v. Doe* case (no prayer at school football games) continue to govern in Establishment Clause jurisprudence?.........Insert 9.2

Significant Issues Pending Before the Supreme Court

A preview of issues that the Court will decide this term.......................Pages 3A & 4A

Second Amendment Cases

The Fifth Circuit U. S. Court of Appeals ruled that the right to bear arms is an individual right, independent of whether one belongs to a militia.............................Page 2A (Insert 12.1)

CONSTITUTIONAL LAW UPDATES is a quarterly newsletter edited and published by C. Paul Smith, J.D. Subscription cost is $25.00 per year. To subscribe, send a check or money order to CONSTITUTIONAL LAW UPDATES, P. O. Box 1204, Frederick MD 21702-0204. For further information, visit C. Paul Smith's web site at www.cpaulsmith.com.

1 2 .1

Federal Court Rules the Right to Bear Arms Belongs Directly to the Individual, Not to an Individual Through the Militia

On October 16, 2001, the United States Court of Appeals for the Fifth Circuit, based in New Orleans, ruled that the Second Amendment "right to bear arms" protects the rights of individuals, whether or not those individuals may be a member of any militia. *United States v. Emerson* (5th Cir. 2001).

This decision is significant because it is one of the rare times a federal appeals court has weighed in on this issue since the Supreme Court case of *United States v. Miller*, 307 U.S. 174 (1939). In *Miller,* the Supreme Court sustained a statute requiring that sawed-off shotguns be registered under the National Firearms Act. *Miller* establishes that the Second Amendment right to bear arms is not absolute. But the Court's language in *Miller* has not resolved the national debate as to whether the Second Amendment right to bear arms belongs directly to the individual, or whether this right belongs only to individuals who belong to a militia.

The Fifth Circuit took this issue head-on and resolved it in favor of the individuals who claim a right to own guns independent of belonging to any militia. The Fifth Circuit reasoned that the reference to militia was not intended to limit those individuals who would have a right to bear arms. The Fifth Circuit said that their interpretation was in total harmony with the Supreme Court's holding in *Miller*.

Attorney General Ashcroft has recently expressed the same opinion about the Second Amendment as that of the Fifth Circuit.

Supreme Court Refuses to Take Case of Product-Liability Suit Against Gun Manufacturer—This Protects Gun Makers and Owners

Earlier this fall (2001), the Supreme Court announced that it would not review the Louisiana case, in which New Orleans Mayor Marc Morial had sued the gun-maker Smith & Wesson, alleging that the guns were an "unreasonably dangerous" product because they did not have mechanisms to prevent the guns from being fired by unauthorized users. *Morial v. Smith & Wesson,* (Louisiana, 2001). The case made its way to the Supreme Court of Louisiana, which upheld the lower court's dismissal of the law suit. The U. S. Supreme Court refused to take the case, thereby upholding the Louisiana Court ruling.

This ruling is indirectly supportive of an individual's Second Amendment right. It is also an example of courts striking down extremist governmental regulations that would interfere with a legitimate business.

CLU 11/01

Significant Issues Pending Before the Supreme Court

The Child Online Protection Act (COPA) as enacted in 1998, makes it unlawful to make any communication for commercial purposes by means of the World Wide Web that is available to minors and is harmful to them, unless good faith efforts are made to prevent children from obtaining access to such material. 47 U.S.C. 231. In enforcing this law, the government has applied community standards to determine if material is "harmful to minors." The question before the Supreme Court is whether the application of community standards to determine if material is "harmful to minors" violates the First Amendment.

Ashcroft v. ACLU

Does the Fourteenth Amendment's Due Process Clause require a State to prove that a sexually violent predator "cannot control" his criminal sexual behavior before the State can civilly commit him for residential care and treatment?

Kansas v. Crane

In 1976, in *Young v. American Mini Theatres,* the Supreme Court upheld the use of zoning ordinances to limit the concentration of adult establishments in the city of Detroit. Los Angeles recently enacted a law which would prohibit the operation of more than one adult entertainment business at a single location. This law was challenged by a business which contends that this law is invalid because the city did not study the negative effects of such combinations of adult businesses, but rather relied on judicially approved statutory precedent from other jurisdictions.

Los Angeles v. Alameda Brooks, Inc.

Defendant Lee Remon requested a 19-hour continuance during a trial to enable him to contact his three subpoenaed alibi witnesses, when these witnesses did not return after a lunch break. The U. S. District Judge denied Mr. Remon's request, and the Eighth Circuit Court of Appeals affirmed. Mr. Remon contends that his rights under the Fifth and Fourteenth Amendments were denied.

Remon v. Kemna

In 1935 Congress stated that regulation of the transmission of energy to retail customers within a state "was subject to regulation by the states" (Section 201 of the Federal Power Act (FPA)). May the Federal Energy Regulatory Commission (FERC) now preempt state jurisdiction over such intrastate retail transmission of electric energy?

New York v. Ferc

The Family Education Right and Privacy Act, 20 U.S.C. 1232g, requires educational institutions to preserve the confidentiality of "education records" pertaining to students. Does this law prohibit school teachers from utilizing their students to grade each other's homework papers, quizzes and tests by having the students exchange papers and mark the correct and incorrect answers thereon as the teacher goes over the answers aloud in class?

Owasso Indep. Sch. Dist. v. Falvo

The Child Pornography Prevention Act of 1996 prohibits the distribution, reproduction, sale or possession of any visual depiction that "appears to be of a minor engaging in sexually explicit conduct" 18 U.S.C. 2252A et seq. (1998). Do these prohibitions violate the First Amendment to the Constitution?

Reno v. Free Speech Coalition

CLU 11/01

Does the ex post facto application of a judicial ruling abrogating the substantive rule of criminal law known as the "year-and-a-day rule" to a homicide committed five years prior to the change in the substantive rule of law violate the Fifth and Fourteenth Amendments of the Constitution?

Rogers v. Tennessee

May the U.S. Army Corps of Engineers, consistent with the Clean Waters Act and the Commerce Clause of the U. S. Constitution, assert jurisdiction over isolated intrastate waters solely because those waters do or potentially could serve as habitat of migratory birds?

*Solid Waste Agency v. U.S.
Army Corps of Engineers*

Does a temporary moratorium on land development constitutes a taking of property requiring compensation under the Taking Clause of the U. S. Constitution?

*Tahoe-Sierra Preservation v.
Tahoe Regional Planning*

A government program in Chicago is designed to rescue economically disadvantaged children from a failing public school system by providing scholarships that may be used in private, religious or suburban public schools. In the early stages of this program, most of the schools that have taken on scholarship students are religiously affiliated. Does this violate the Establishment Clause of the First Amendment?

Taylor v. Simmons-Harris

Does the Establishment Clause prohibit the State of Ohio from authorizing parents to use state scholarship funds at any private school, whether religious or not?

*Zelman, Supt. of Public Instr.
v. Simmons-Harris*

A municipal ordinance in Stratton, Ohio requires one to obtain a permit prior to engaging in the door-to-door advocacy of a political cause and to display upon demand the permit (which contains one's name). Does enforcing that ordinance against an individual who is proselytizing or distributing religious pamphlets violate the First Amendment?

Watchtower Bible v. Stratton, Ohio

A Case the Supreme Court Chose Not to Take

Antonio Contreras, a forklift operator, was injured in an accident in 1995. One of results of Mr. Contreras' accident was that he could thereafter have sex only once a month—down from five times a week before the injury. Subsequently, Mr. Contreras had a dispute with his employer that led to a law suit where Mr. Contreras insisted that his employer must make special accommodations to people such as him with sex problem disabilities such as his. His employer disagreed. A judge agreed with the employer; impaired virility is not a disability under the Americans with Disabilities Act. Mr. Contreras asked the Supreme Court to set things straight, but the Court declined to get involved.

Prayer in School--Has the Supreme Court Become Hostile towards God and Prayer?

Following the terrorist attacks on September 11th, there has been an outpouring of spontaneous invocations for God's help from federal, state and local governments around the nation. President Bush called for a national day of prayer on Friday, September 14th. Congress convened on the Capitol steps and unitedly sang "God Bless America." A public school in California placed a banner on its exterior wall, bearing the words, "God Bless America." Despite complaints from the ACLU that displaying the banner violated the Establishment Clause, the school defiantly kept the banner posted. With uncanny timing, a school board in Madison, Wisconsin picked this time to enact a policy that its schools could not allow the Pledge of Allegiance to be recited because they asserted that the phrase in the Pledge of "one nation under God" violated the Establishment Clause. This policy met quick and massive protests and led the school board to reconsider and reinstate the Pledge as a part of its daily routine.

In the near future the Supreme Court can be expected to address the question of whether the phrases, "in God we trust" and "God bless America," on our money and in our public schools violate the Establishment Clause. It appears at present that a majority of the Supreme Court would rule that these actions, as well as the public schools' endorsement of the phrase "one nation under God" in the Pledge of Allegiance, are unconstitutional.

For the first 150 years of its existence, the Establishment Clause of the First Amendment was interpreted to accommodate governmental endorsement of belief in God and prayer. However, during the last 55 years, the Supreme Court's interpretation of the Establishment Clause has changed to prohibit the public schools from invoking God's blessings. Between 1947 and 1992, the Supreme Court went astray (1) by establishing a "neutrality" doctrine, and (2) by establishing a preference for non-religion over religion. Last year (2000) in a Texas case about prayer at football games (*Santa Fe School Board v. Doe* 530 U.S. 290 [2000]), the Supreme Court showed that its "neutrality" towards religion has been translated into "hostility" towards God and prayer. However, the Court's recent ruling on Virginia's moment of silence, (*Brown v. Gilmore*, ___ U.S. ___ (2001)) raises the prospect that the Court may be willing in the future to retreat from its hostility towards God and prayer in government.

Following the September 11th terrorist attacks, the nation has manifest a heightened desire to acknowledge God and to invoke His blessings upon the nation. The Supreme Court was aware of all of this prior to announcing that it would not accept the Virginia moment of silence case. Perhaps this national reawakening will lead the Supreme Court to reconsider and to correct its interpretation of the Establishment Clause that is hostile to God and prayer.

I. Virginia's Moment of Silence.

On Monday, October 29, 2001, the Supreme Court announced that it would not review the Virginia Moment of Silence Case.[1] This ruling (without an opinion) allows the mandatory moment of silence to continue in Virginia public schools. The Virginia law specifically permits, but does not require, students to have a silent prayer

---

[1] The Court announced this ruling from the Prettyman United States Courthouse, where the U. S. Court of Appeals for the District of Columbia Circuit is seated. The Supreme Court building was temporarily closed after traces of Anthrax were found in the Court's mail room.

each morning during the minute of silence.

This is a victory for those who favor the government's endorsing prayer in school. This ruling will probably have only a small effect on current Establishment Clause law. But in light of the nation's spontaneous turning to God following the terrorist attacks, it is appropriate to take a close look at this case and where the Supreme Court currently stands on the Establishment Clause.

The Virginia Moment of Silence case rapidly made its way to the Supreme Court beginning in early 2000, after Virginia enacted a law requiring its public schools to observe a minute of silence at the beginning of each school day "to the end that each pupil may, in the exercise of his or her individual choice, meditate, pray, or engage in any other silent activity which does not interfere with, distract or impede other pupils in the like exercise of individual choice." Virginia Code, Sec. 22.1-203. The law was to go into effect July 1, 2000. Shortly before this date, Ed Brown and two dozen other Petitioners filed suit against Virginia Governor James Gilmore and others in the United States District Court for the Eastern District of Virginia, seeking to stop the implementation of this law on the grounds that it violated the Establishment Clause of the First Amendment. On October 26, 2000, the U. S. District Court ruled against the Petitioners, who then appealed to the U.S. Court of Appeals for the Fourth Circuit. On July 24, 2001, the Fourth Circuit also ruled against Petitioners. Immediately thereafter Petitioners filed a Petition for a Writ of Certiorari, asking the Supreme Court to review the case. *Brown v. Gilmore* (No. 01-384).

The State of Virginia did not want the Supreme Court to take the case because Virginia had prevailed in the litigation up to this point. But the Petitioners, represented by the ACLU, contended that the Fourth Circuit's ruling conflicted with the Supreme

Court's ruling in *Wallace v. Jaffree,*472 U.S. 38 (1985), where an Alabama moment of silence law was struck down. The central issue in *Brown v. Gilmore* was whether there was a secular purpose for the Virginia law. Virginia implicitly conceded that there existed a religious purpose for its law, but they argued that a secular purpose also existed, and that this was sufficient. The Supreme Court stated in *Wallace* that "a statute must be invalidated if it is *entirely* motivated by a purpose to advance religion." 472 U.S. at 56 [emphasis added]. Virginia offered evidence to show that the purpose of the law included promoting meditation, promoting discipline, and restoring a sense of calm and civility in public schools. (Respondents' Brief in Opposition to Writ [hereafter "Opposition"] p. 10.)

Petitioners contended that the law was wholly motivated to advance religion. They pointed out that only a year earlier the Supreme Court had addressed a similar contention in *Santa Fe Independent School District v. Doe*, 530 U.S. 290 (2000), where the Court said it should "refuse to turn a blind eye to the context in which [a law] arose, and that context quells any doubt that [the law] was implemented with the purpose of endorsing school prayer." 530 U.S. at 315. In the *Santa Fe* case, the Court invalidated a Texas law calling for prayer before high school football games. Petitioners also argued that the 1985 case of *Wallace v. Jaffree*, 472 U.S. 38, was controlling because in that case the Court had invalidated an Alabama moment of silence law. Virginia argued that its law was different because there were secular purposes for it, unlike the laws in Texas and Alabama.

To be sure, the Virginia law does specifically mention "prayer" as one of the silent activities that could be undertaken during the minute of silence. So the question for the court was whether this specific accommodation of prayer fatally infected the moment of silence policy. Virginia pointed out that all nine of the Justices in *Wallace* acknowledged that a moment of silence statute can be valid if a secular purpose exists for it. Opposition Brief, at 2, citing *Wallace*, 472 U.S. at 56, 59, 66, 76, 84, 90 and 91.

Warren E. Barry, the sponsor of the Virginia law, stated in a floor speech that prayer was specifically mentioned in the law in order for the people to know that "prayer would not be discriminated against." Opposition at 7.

The Supreme Court stated in *Santa Fe* that the First Amendment protects the right of students to pray before, during and after school. 530 U.S. 290, 301; *Wallace v. Jaffree*, 427 U.S. 59, 81-84 (O'Connor, J. concurring). This being the case, then what harm can there be for a school to provide an optional opportunity each day for students to exercise this right? In *Wallace*, the Court ruled that such a policy in Alabama crossed over the line of permissibility, even though Alabama did nothing to mandate prayer nor to dictate the content of any prayers that might be offered.

It was the Supreme Court, and not Alabama that crossed the line of impropriety in *Wallace*. It is one thing for a state to dictate the words that it requires students to utter in prayer. And the Court properly so ruled in *Engel v. Vitale*, 370 U.S. 421 (1962) and *Murray v. Curlett* 374 U.S. 203 (1963). But the Court failed to distinguish these cases from the Alabama case. For Alabama to adopt a policy that favors a belief in God and provides an opportunity for daily, silent prayer does not establish any religion in violation of the Establishment Clause—at least it was not a violation prior to 1985.

Notwithstanding any hostility that the Court may have developed towards religion, the Court in *Wallace v. Jaffree* nevertheless did describe a way for a state

moment of silence policy to pass First Amendment muster. In invalidating the Alabama "moment of silence" practice in *Wallace*, the Court found that *this* moment of silence practice was intended to promote prayer, and that it was this " purpose" that violated the Establishment Clause. Thus, if precedent is followed, Virginia's moment of silence could be upheld if Virginia could convince the Court that there is a "secular" purpose for it.

Virginia successfully defended its moment of silence policy based on its argument that there is a secular purpose for it. Under *Wallace*, the existence of a coexisting religious purpose is not necessarily fatal if there is a secular purpose as well. Sixteen years earlier, Alabama, had argued that it had a secular purpose for its moment of silence. But the Court found that argument to be merely an afterthought; the Court found that the Alabama purpose was specifically to promote prayer.

After reviewing briefs from both parties, on October 29, 2001, the Supreme Court decided not to accept the Virginia moment of silence case.

Although those who would like to see prayer in school will be happy with the Virginia Moment of Silence victory, that victory is really quite limited. Virginia argued that it was the existence of a "secular purpose" that made the moment permissible. Virginia did not argue that the Supreme Court should reverse some of its hostility towards God and prayer. Thus, the Virginia case side-stepped the more important issue—Can the government promote prayer and belief in God without violating the Establishment Clause of the First Amendment? This issue will have to wait for another day.

Why did the Court decline to take the Virginia Moment of Silence case? I submit it was because the Court wanted to avoid battling a divisive issue that was gaining popular momentum. The more important issue could be avoided by letting stand the ruling of the lower courts that Virginia had proved that a secular purpose existed for the moment of silence. If the Court had accepted the case and overturned the Virginia law, this would have shown an increased hostility of the Court towards religion at a time when the nation is reaching out towards God, and when some are reassessing what the proper relationship should be between government and God.

Had the Court taken the case, there is no question that the Chief Justice and Justices Scalia and Thomas would have once again argued that the Establishment Clause is perfectly compatible with school prayer, because it does not rise to the level of "establishing" any one particular religion by the state. But the six other Justices are undoubtedly tired of defending their majority view on this. In June of 2001, Chief Justice Rehnquist issued a written dissenting opinion with the Court's refusal to take the case from Elkhart, Indiana, where that city sought to be allowed to keep the Ten Commandment monument on its courthouse grounds. *Elkhart v. Books*, ___ U.S. ___, 121 S.Ct. 2209 (2001). The City of Elkhart was ordered to remove the Ten Commandments. It is extremely rare for any opinion to accompany a ruling by the Supreme Court denying a petition for certiorari. The Chief Justice's dissent was certainly intended to point out how the Court has gone astray in the Establishment Clause area. He succinctly pointed out that maintaining a monument of the Ten Commandments does not contribute to the establishment of any one, particular religion. Therefore the monument's continued presence should not be a ruled a violation of the Establishment Clause. Perhaps the Chief Justice is attempting to build increased awareness of the Court's apostasy with the hope of building public awareness of the

problem and ultimately changing the votes of enough Justices to correct the problem.

Although the Supreme Court did not take this case, it is important because it addresses the issue of whether it is unconstitutional for the federal and state governments to pray or to have policies that allow prayers in public school and other public meetings and events There now exist Supreme Court precedents that would deny this, but there also exist some long-established federal practices that accommodate governmental prayers. Before looking at these, first consider the recent Supreme Court ruling against prayer at public high school football games.

II. Prayer at School Football Games Case—*Santa Fe School District v. Doe* (2000)

Only last year the Supreme Court (in a 6-3 vote) stated in *Santa Fe School District v. Doe*, 530 U.S. 290 (2000) that **"the Constitution is abridged when the State affirmatively sponsors the particular religious practice of prayer."** (Emphasis added) 530 U.S. 313. The Court went on to invalidate the Santa Fe School policy of having student prayers prior to high school football games.

The Chief Justice (joined by Justices Scalia and Thomas) dissented in *Santa Fe*, and stated that majority opinion **"bristles with hostility to all things religious in public life."** (Emphasis added.) The Chief Justice accused the 6-Justice majority in *Santa Fe* of "distort[ing] existing precedent" in order to invalidate the school district's program for prayer at football games. He further stated that "[n]either the holding nor the tone of the opinion is faithful to the meaning of the Establishment Clause, when it is recalled that George Washington himself, at the very request of the very Congress which passed the Bill of Rights, proclaimed a day of 'public thanksgiving and prayer, to be observed by acknowledging with grateful hearts the many and signal favors of Almighty God." 530 U.S. 318 (Rehnquist dissenting).

The majority of Justices would prefer to characterize their position as being "neutral" rather than "hostile" towards religion. This is certainly true in some contexts. For example, just this June, in *Good News Club v. Milford Central School*, ___ U.S. ___, 121 S.Ct. 2093 (2001), the Court struck down a state school policy that specifically excluded religious groups from being allowed to use school premises after school hours. But as will be shown below, in the context of prayer in public schools, the Chief Justice is right. Regardless of how one characterizes the Court's decision in *Santa Fe*, it is indisputably a departure from the original meaning of the Establishment Clause of the First Amendment; and it is hostile to governmental endorsement of prayer and belief in God.

III. Establishment Clause Background.

Originally, the founders viewed the Establishment Clause to be merely a prohibition against religious persecution and to prevent the establishment of a national religion.[2] The Congressional Research Service of the Library of Congress confirms this and points out that the Court has altered the meaning of the Establishment Clause: "This interpretation has long since been abandoned by the Court, beginning, at least, with *Everson v. Board of Education*, [330 U.S. 1 (1947)] in which the Court, without dissent on this point, declared that the Establishment Clause forbids not only practices that 'aid one religion' or 'prefer

[2]The Congressional Research Service of the Library of Congress publishes an annotated book on the Constitution that includes an excellent discussion of this point. *The Constitution of the United States of America, Analysis and Interpretation (1992), 969-71.*

one religion over another,' but as well those that 'aid all religions.'" *Id.*, at 971. With the above language from *Everson*, the Court sowed the seeds of apostasy from the original intent of the Establishment Clause. Although the *Everson* ruling upheld the government's giving some financial aid to private, religious schools in New Jersey, the Court replaced the 155-year-old accommodation approach with a new rationale that has come to be characterized as the "neutrality" approach.

The infection that was introduced in *Everson* became worse in 1962, when the Court in *Engel v. Vitale*, 370 U.S. 421, invalidated a New York policy that required public school students to recite each morning a "nondenominational" prayer that the school board had prescribed. The invalidation of this practice was certainly correct, but the Court's rationale was hostile towards God and religion, and led to increased hostility in subsequent cases.[3]

The next year, in *Abington v. Schempp*, 374 U.S. 203, 223 (1963), the Court invalidated the daily reading in public schools of selections from the Bible. In this opinion, the Court responded to the argument that by eliminating the recitation of the Lord's prayer and reading from the Bible that it was establishing a religion of secularism:

> We agree of course that the State may not establish a "religion of secularism" in the sense of affirmatively opposing or showing hostility to religion, thus "preferring those who believe in no religion over those who do believe." *Zorach v. Clauson*, supra at 314. We do not agree, however, that this decision in any sense has that effect.

374 U.S. 203, 225. However, contrary to

[3]A year later, the Court also overturned the Maryland public school practice of reciting the Lord's prayer at the start of each day. *Murray v. Curlett*, 374 U.S. 203 (1963).

the Court's prediction, *Schempp* and the later cases to follow it did indeed establish a preference for secularism and nonreligion.

In 1970, the Court characterized its neutrality as a "benevolent" neutrality. *Walz v. Tax Comm'n*, 397 U.S. 664, 694-97 (1970). The next year, in *Lemon v. Kurtzman*, 403 U.S. 602 (1971), the Court adopted a three-part test to determine whether governmental laws and practices violate the Establishment Clause. To be valid, the law must (1) have a secular [nonreligious] purpose; (2) the law's primary effect must neither enhance nor inhibit religion; and (3) the law must not cause excessive entanglement between the government and the religious body that benefits from the law. This test confirms the neutrality principle. However, these tests are prone to subjective judgment, making this area of law one that is uncertain and marked with seemingly inconsistent rulings. These tests continue to govern Establishment Clause cases today (2001).

As late as 1984, there was a basis for saying that some "benevolent neutrality" continued to exist in Establishment Clause jurisprudence. In *Lynch v. Donnelly*, 465 U.S. 668, 673 (in a 5-4 ruling), a majority of the Court stated that the Constitution does not "require complete separation of church and state [but] affirmatively mandates accommodation, not merely tolerance, of all religions, and forbids hostility towards any." *Id.* But only the next year, in *Wallace v. Jaffree*, 472 U.S. 38 (1985), by a 5-4 vote, the Court clearly abandoned all "benevolence" in its "neutrality" when it struck down the Alabama moment of silence law. Later, in 1992, the Court struck down school-sponsored prayer at a high school graduation—transforming the "neutrality" into antagonism or hostility towards God and prayer. *Lee v. Weisman*, 505 U.S. 577 (1992). Thus, by 2000, when the Court delivered its ruling

prohibiting prayer at football games *(Santa Fe)*, the Court was firmly entrenched in its hostility towards God and prayer.

With this background, you can understand why the ACLU argued that Virginia's moment of silence law violated the Court's "neutrality" principle. In June 2001, when the Supreme Court, by a 6-3 vote, declined to hear the Elkhart, Indiana Ten Commandment case, the Court reaffirmed its hostility to religion and its continued apostasy from the original intent of the Establishment Clauses—that belief in God and prayer should be accommodated. Thus, had the Supreme Court taken the Virginia case, it would have pitted a majority of hostile Justices against a society that was experiencing a reemergence of support for governmental expressions of gratitude to God and invocations of God's blessings as we go to war against terrorism.

IV. Where the Court's Current Rationale Will Take Us, If Not Corrected.

If the First Amendment prohibits the government from mentioning God or from acknowledging God's existence or from invoking God's blessings, then the following results may also ensue:

"In God We Trust" must be removed from all our money,[4] and from the third verse of our national anthem;

The inscription, "In God We Trust," which is chiseled in stone and prominently displayed on the wall in the House of Representatives, must be obliterated;

The phrase "under God" must be removed from the Pledge of Allegiance;[5]

---

[4] This phrase was first put on national currency in 1864. In 1955 Congress passed a law requiring that all U.S. coins and paper money carry this motto. "Money." *The World Book Encyclopedia*, 1969.

[5] In 1954 Congress added this phrase to the Pledge of Allegiance. "Pledge of Allegiance." *The World Book Encyclopedia*, 1969.

Congress must be reprimanded from singing "God Bless America" in unison on the steps of the Capitol Building;

Prayers must be henceforth prohibited at the beginning of sessions of Congress, and the paid chaplains who delivered them must be fired forthwith;[6]

The President must be reprimanded for calling for a national day of prayer;

We must remove from all public school texts the words of Lincoln in his second Inaugural address, where he said that America "must acknowledge God";

We must reprimand George Washington for daring to pray at Valley Forge and from proclaiming a national "day of thanksgiving and prayer" to "Almighty God";

We must repudiate the cherished words in the Declaration of Independence that "All men are endowed by their Creator with certain inalienable rights";

And of course, once elected, our Presidents must be barred from ever again saying the words, "God bless America." And why must all of these practices stop?— Because they violate the Court's current view of the Establishment Clause of the First Amendment. The ACLU is certainly lying in wait for the right opportunity to try to remove all of these remaining vestiges of God from our government; they will not rest until atheism and secularism are established as our national religion.

The mere statement of these results points up the absurdity of this interpretation. The Establishment Clause was not intended to preclude these things. The Establishment Clause was intended to prevent the government from establishing any one religion or from attacking any one religion. But the Establishment Clause was not intended to excise God and belief in God from government. But they have been excised; governmental accommodation of God and religion

---

[6] The Supreme Court upheld this practice in *Marsh v. Chambers*, 463 U.S. 783 (1983).

in public schools is now forbidden. In its place the Supreme Court has adopted what it calls a "neutrality" towards religion. But this "neutrality" is a repudiation of the founders' belief that God favored and blessed this nation and that we should acknowledge His hand in our blessings. This "neutrality" is really a "hostility," as the Chief Justice pointed out. 530 U.S. 318.

Where did the Supreme Court go astray? It did so in two distinct ways: (1) In establishing a "neutrality" doctrine; and (2) In prohibiting government from favoring belief in a Supreme Being. All of these were an abandonment of the view that the Establishment Clause only prohibited government from favoring with any particular religious organization.

In his dissent in *Elkhart*, the Chief Justice advocated a return to the pre-*Everson* interpretation of the Establishment Clause, when the word "religion" precluded the government from advancing or inhibiting any one particular faith, but did not preclude the government from praying to God. Establishment Clause jurisprudence has changed with the redefining of this word.

This flaw was partly introduced when they began treating the word "religion" as if there were an "s" at the end. In other words, rather than construing the Establishment Clause to prohibit the establishment of *any particular religion*, by adding an "s" to make the word plural, they transformed the Establishment Clause into a phrase that prohibits the establishment *of any and all religions*. With this change, the Establishment Clause becomes a broader prohibition against any religion and all religions—changing the meaning from prohibiting one religion from getting special treatment, to prohibiting the government from accommodating many or all religions. This a clear, albeit implicit preference for non-religion (including atheism and secularism) over belief in God. Thus, through redefining the word "religion," the Court introduced a "neutrality" toward religions that has effectively become a "hostility" towards religion. This is not what Congress and the States intended when they passed and ratified the First Amendment.

V. The Supreme Court Should Reverse Its Decisions in *Wallace, Lee* and *Santa Fe.*

The Supreme Court should endorse the position that the government can acknowledge God and express thanks to Him and invoke His blessings without violating the Establishment Clause. This result would require overturning the *Santa Fe, Lee* and *Wallace* cases. This would have a positive effect on students and would not result in the establishment of any one religion as the church of state. It would restore the meaning that our First Congress and the People intended when they passed and ratified the First Amendment; and that intent was that it is good and proper for the government to acknowledge God, to express gratitude for his providential blessings, and to continue to invoke his choicest blessings on our nation, which we the people proclaim was established "under God."

Many Americans believe that God has protected and preserved this nation, and that He will continue to do so as long as we the people worship God and serve our fellow man in truth and love. This belief in God does not include any attempt to establish ties between any specific religion and the state; it merely establishes a national preference to acknowledge a Supreme Being, without defining his attributes nor expressing a preference for any specific "religion." It does express a preference for religion over atheism and secularism. And that is the preference that our founders intended when they proposed and ratified the First Amendment.

President Bush Proclaims September 14th as National Prayer Day

President George W. Bush unabashedly issued a President's Proclamation making Friday, September 14th to be a national day of prayer, following the September 11th terrorist attacks. Accompanying President Bush at the Friday prayer service in the National Cathedral were members of both political parties and people from diverse religious faiths— Muslims, Jews, Christians, Sikhs, Buddhists, and Hindus—shoulder to shoulder, unitedly praying to God. Those participating in the service included Catholic Archbishop Cardinal Theodore McCarrick; Protestant Evangelist, the Reverend Billy Graham; Rabbi Joshua Haberman; Episcopal Bishop Jane Holmes Dixon, and Muslim Imam Muzammi H. Siddiqi.

"Grieving atheists 'excluded' as nation unites under God"

This is the headline of a short report from Nicole Ziegler Dizon of the Associated Press that ran in *The Washington Times* on October 13, 2001.

Ms. Dizon reported that the atheists feel left out as most of the nation is finding unity under God in their grieving. Ron Barrier, spokesman for American Atheists, Inc. complains that atheists are being formally "left out" of "the grieving process."

The Effects of Terrorism on Constitutional Rights

Life in the United States will be forever different following the terrorist attacks of September 11, 2001 on the World Trade Center in New York City and on the Pentagon. For the first time since Britain invaded the U.S. during the War of 1812 has an enemy attacked the mainland U.S.A. So extensive are and will be the effects from this attack that volumes will be written about them for years to come. It would be impossible to thoroughly discuss the many effects in a short article. Nevertheless, at the very least, it must be observed that a world-altering event has occurred. The rights and liberties of Americans will be altered because of this.

On the back of this page is an outline of some of the effects from the terrorist attacks and from the war the nation is waging against terrorism. The outline indicates a couple of dozen effects. In addition, the following paragraphs will discuss some of the following areas of impact on the Constitution:

I. Declaring War;
II. Exercising Power as Commander in Chief-- Prosecuting War against Hidden Enemies;
III. Economic Effects; and
IV. Curtailed Liberties.

The Terrorist Attacks of September 11, 2001--What Will Be Their Effects on Rights and Liberties under the Constitution?

I. Declaration of War
    A. Congress Has Power to Declare War (Article 1, Section 8)
    B. President Is Commander in Chief (Article II, Section 2)
    C. What Warrants Such a Declaration?
        1. What Burden of Proof Must Be Met? (a) Beyond a Reasonable Doubt; (b) Clear and Convincing Evidence; (c) Preponderance of Evidence; (d) Probable Cause.
    D. Do We Ever Have a Moral Obligation to Go to War?
    E. Can the President Wage War without Congressional Authorization?
    F. What Military Operations Can the President Conduct without Congressional Authorization?   (The War Powers Act)
    G. Must a Declaration of War Specifically Use the Word, "War"?
    H. Must a Declaration of War Specify a Nation or Entity Against Whom the War Is Waged?
    I. Why Should Congress Declare War Without Using the Word, "War"?

II. Prosecuting War
    A. What Principles and Laws Should Guide Our Actions in War?
    B. What International Alliances Should We Make and Maintain?
        1. NATO invokes Article 5 for first time (attack on USA is attack on all)
        2. United Nations serves role as consensus-builder
        3. Pakistan Demands $1 Billion in Aid for Assisting the U.S.
    C. What Sovereignty Should We Relinquish in Exchange for Cooperation and Assistance from Other Nations?
    D. What Responsibility Do We Have to the World to Present a Case that Justifies Our Acts of War?
    E. Nuclear Testing (ABM Treaty—revoking ratification or joint withdrawal)
    F. Missile Defense System

III. The War Against Terrorism
    A. What Particular Challenges Do We Face in the War Against an Enemy That No Nation Will Claim as Hers?
    B. What Principles Would Justify Killing Innocent People in Attempting to Eliminate Terrorists?
    C. How Do You Know When the War is Won? When Do You Stop Fighting?
    D. Biological Threats (Anthrax, Smallpox)

IV. Direct Effects on Rights and Liberties
    A. Limitations on Freedom of Speech
        1. Speech That Incites or Promotes Terrorist Acts Can Be Censored—Should It Be Punished?
    B. Limitations on Right to Privacy
    C. Limitations on Right to Travel
    D. Discriminatory, Unwarranted Reprisals
    E. Establishment Clause Issues
    F. National ID Cards
    G. Relaxed regulations on wiretapping
    H. Monitoring Attorney-Client conversations
    I. Martial Law, Curfews, Suspending Habeas Corpus, Intern Camps for Suspects
    J. Anti-Terrorism Bill

V. Economic Consequences of War. Terrorism, Poverty, Recession, Death. Injury & Illness
    A. Fear Undermines the Economy—Domino Effect (worst week on Wall Street in 68 years)
        1. Fear of Flying and Fear of Being Part of a Large Gathering
        2. Effects on Transportation, Travel, Hotel, Restaurant & Entertainment
    B. Tightened Security Measures Will Affect the Economy
    C. Predicting Changes in the American Way of Life

2.8

3.5.1

I. DECLARING WAR

A. Seeking Justice. One of the first and strongest effects following the mass destruction is the widespread and powerful desire to bring to justice those responsible for it. Some seek vengeance, but almost all Americans feel the need to bring justice to the evil perpetrators remaining alive in the world. As long as our national response to the terrorism is based upon just principles, this is a worthy motivation. Responsible citizens seek to establish justice for society so that we can maintain our liberties and peace. Some times it is necessary to declare war to accomplish this. It is up to Congress to decide whether and when to engage the nation in war.

B. Are We at War or Aren't We? There comes a point where a crime becomes so extensive or so aggressive an attack that it becomes an act of war. This threshold was crossed by the concerted effort to hi-jack four planes at one time and to crash them into buildings, killing more than five thousand people. A unanimous Senate and 434 out of 435 Representatives regarded the terrorist acts on September 11, 2001 to be acts of war. That they are also crimes doesn't matter.

The Constitution gives Congress the power to declare war (Article I, Section 8). Without such congressional authorization, the President has limited authority to direct the military in defensive matters. Following the Viet Nam (war/conflict), Congress passed the War Powers Act to delineate with more specificity what the president can and cannot do in using military force in conditions of war and in situations that do not rise to the level of war.

Following the terrorist attacks, both Houses of Congress passed a Joint Resolution [see the back of this page for text] authorizing the President to use such force as necessary to attack the terrorists and those who aide them and harbor them. The word "war" was not used in the Joint Resolution itself. But the authorization for the President to conduct such a war was clear and unmistakable. There is no requirement that the word, "war," itself must be used in order to validate a declaration of war. In fact, omission of the word "war" may serve to tone down the rhetoric and could serve to make the authorization more palatable for countries whose aid and support we may need in prosecuting the war. This seems to be what is transpiring as America is building international consensus in the war against terrorism.

The Joint Resolution of war that was just passed does not identify a particular nation, organization or people as our opponents in war. The Constitution does not require this.

Joint Resolution of Congress
September 14, 2001

To authorize the use of United States armed forces against those responsible for the recent attacks launched against the United States.

Whereas, on Sept. 11, 2001, acts of despicable violence were committed against the United States and its citizens; and

Whereas, such acts render it both necessary and appropriate that the United States exercise its rights to self-defense and to protect United States citizens both at home and abroad, and

Whereas, in light of the threat to the national security and foreign policy of the United States posed by the grave acts of violence, and

Whereas, such acts continue to pose an unusual and extraordinary threat to the national security and foreign policy of the United States,

Whereas the president has authority under the Constitution to take actin to deter and prevent acts of international terrorism against the United States.

Resolved by the Senate and the House of Representatives of the United States of America assembled.

Section 1. Short Title

This joint resolution may be cited as the "Authorization for Use of Military Force"

Section 2. Authorization for Use of United States Armed Forces

(a) That the president is authorized to use all necessary and appropriate force against those nations, organizations, or persons he determines planned, authorized, committed, or aided the terrorist attacks that occurred on Sept. 11, 2001, or harbored such organizations or persons, in order to prevent any future acts of international terrorism against the United States by such nations, organizations or persons.

(b) War Powers Resolution Requirements

(1) Specific Statutory Authorization—Consistent with section 8(a)(1) of the War Powers Resolution, the Congress declares that this section is intended to constitute specific statutory authorization within the meaning of section 5 (b) of the War Powers Resolution.

(2) Applicability of Other Requirements —Nothing in this resolution supersedes any requirement of the War Powers Resolution.

II. EXERCISING POWER AS COMMANDER IN CHIEF—PROSECUTING WAR AGAINST HIDDEN ENEMIES

A. Commander in Chief. Article II, Section 2 of the Constitution states: "The President shall be Commander in Chief of the Army and Navy of the United States, and of the Militia of the several States, when called into the actual Service of the United States."

The Constitution does not spell out the limits and extent of the President's power as Commander in Chief. Thus, much is left to be determined in the exigencies of the moment, subject to the checks and balances of Congress and the Courts.

It is certainly clear in today's world that if the U.S. is to have the backing of other nations, we must wage a moral war. The President is obviously responsible to attend to this.

B. Be Sure That There Is Proof of Wrongdoing Before Administering Justice. We cannot allow our anger to lead us to be guilty of heinous acts like those committed against us. America, of all nations, understands that there must be evidence of guilt against an individual before the state punishes him. We will certainly succeed at this.

C. Present Our Case to the World. At some point we will have to present to the world the evidence we have that proves that we are or were justified in destroying people and things. We want the good people of the world to support us now and in the future.

D. Burden of Proof. Before the U.S. attacks someone, we must have proof that the attacks are warranted. One important question is What burden of proof should we meet before acting? (a) Proof beyond a reasonable doubt? (b) Clear and convincing evidence? (c) Preponderance of evidence? (d) Probable cause? or (e) Some other standard?

If Osama bin Laden were a citizen of the U.S. charged with a crime in connection with the destruction of the World Trade Center, then he would be protected by requiring the U.S. to meet the strictest burden of proof before convicting and punishing him. But he is not a citizen, he lives abroad, and his actions amount to war—therefore our Constitution neither bestows the protection of presumption of innocence nor the strictest burden of proof; neither does our Constitution limit how we may address our enemies who engage in war against us. This does not mean that we should not have standards and principles to guide us in how we wage war, but we have the flexibility to carve out the principles that serve us best. The preponderance of evidence standard may be appropriate one for us to use. But when faced with threats of devastating terrorism, the lesser, probable cause standard may be sufficient.

E. Evaluating the Success of the Terrorist Acts. Unfortunately, as the terrorist leaders look at the success of the acts wrought by their kamikaze pawns, they must marvel at their victory. But perhaps they were too successful. Among the 5,000+ people killed in the twin towers were victims from an estimated 80 nations—all innocent civilians. Attacking American civilians would have been bad enough, but by attacking the "world trade center," the terrorists in essence declared war on the world. This is a tactical blunder that will help the U.S. marshal sufficient international support to wage a sustained and effective war on the terrorists. Woody Deem, my professor in criminal law, taught us that criminals are stupid—sooner or later they would made a dumb mistake or mistakes that would help to apprehend and convict them. In that light, the first dumb mistake of the terrorist plot was to wage war on the world. Tactically, they may have been more effective in their dastardly plans to have targeted only U.S. citizens.

F. Attacks on Evil or on Good. We must assume that the terrorists had been blinded into the belief that striking the World Trade Center would strike a blow at Satan. Yet it is the terrorists who were doing Satan's bidding. The prophet Isaiah foretold that in the latter days wicked people would call evil good and good evil. This certainly has found fulfillment in the recent terrorist attacks. Any religion that is not founded in principles of justice, freedom, and concern for others is confused and in error. It is part of Satan's plan to dispense with virtuous principles because someone concludes that another person is evil.

III. ECONOMIC EFFECTS OF TERRORISM

A. Attacks on American Capitalism.
Terrorist Target—The Twin Towers of the World Trade Center. These monuments of America's free enterprise system were certainly viewed by the terrorists as being symbols of our capitalistic wealth and prosperity. Certainly, to the evil terrorists, the twin towers were also regarded as symbols of U.S. aggression, oppression and evil. But the attacks must be regarded as attacks on the free enterprise capitalism system that is the engine of the American economy. The ignorant terrorists attacked the hand that feeds them and much of the world.

B. Striking Fear Into the Hearts of Men. The success of the terrorist plot that leveled the Twin Towers and severely damaged the Pentagon has wrought fear into the lives of many Americans. It has shot down the commercial airlines industry and has crippled the hundreds of industries that feed off of it. Thus, in one week following the attacks, stocks lost 13% of their value in the largest one-week decline in 68 years. This great loss was not due to the destruction of the Twin Towers or to the declaration of war—the loss is due to the fear of people to fly and to resume our former lifestyles. And this paralyzing fear may yet prove to be the biggest victim of the September 11th attacks.

IV. TERRORISM WILL BRING CURTAILED LIBERTIES

A. Tightened Security Measures.
Who expected that terrorists would fly fully fueled commercial jets into the two World Trade Center towers and into the Pentagon? Apparently no one. Real life has produced a horrific story that eclipses anything Tom Clancy could have imagined.

The horror of the tragedy is heightened by the fact that we all see now that the U.S. was powerless to stop the terrorism once the hi-jackings were discovered. Jet fighters were dispatched from Massachusetts and Langley Air Force Base (130 miles from Washington, D. C.) to track down and intercept the hi-jacked planes. But they were too late.

Our vulnerability is obvious, and it is not acceptable. We fully expect the government to remedy this vulnerability, and the nation is prepared to give up additional conveniences in order to obtain the necessary level of security that we desire. The nation will, for the most part, willingly sacrifice some liberty to obtain the desired security in air travel. No constitutional amendment will be required to take these rights from us—we will freely give them up for some protection. Nevertheless, the terrorist attacks will be the cause of this loss of liberty.

B. Prohibit Speech that Condones, Promotes, Encourages, Incites, and Rewards Terrorism. During the last few years our society has not tolerated joking about bringing a weapon or a bomb onto a plane. As a society, this threat has been of such a serious nature, and we have gone to such great expense and effort to prevent such terrorism that we have not tolerated joking about this. We must now ratchet this prohibition even tighter. Because of the serious threats that such acts pose to our safety and to the strength of our economy (both in America and around the world), we can no longer tolerate an atmosphere that in any way supports or encourages terrorism. It must not be tolerated in America, and it cannot be tolerated throughout the world. And inasmuch as our enemies have infiltrated all nations throughout the world, many of whom have the capacity to hurt us abroad and at home, we must eliminate these spawning grounds for terrorism wherever they are. It is now a matter of self-defense for us. Heretofore, in America people could discuss revolutions and the overthrow of our own country as long as such talk did not "incite to imminent action" or as long as it did not create a "clear and present danger." But it seems to me that the "clear and present danger" that now exists warrants the prohibition of a much broader range of speech than we have previously tolerated. Current conditions require the elimination and disallowance of some speech that may contribute to death and disaster.

55

CONSTITUTIONAL LAW UPDATES

| II·i | March 2002 | No. 4 |

Table of Contents

CONSTITUTIONAL LAW UPDATES is a quarterly newsletter edited and published by C. Paul Smith J.D. Subscription cost is $25.00 per year (plus $1.25 tax in MD). To subscribe, send a check or money order to CONSTITUTIONAL LAW UPDATES, P. O. Box 1204, Frederick, MD 21702. For further information, visit Paul Smith's web site www.cpaulsmith.com.

Grading of Student Papers by Peers Is Okay!

On February 19, 2002, the Supreme Court ruled unanimously that the grading of students' papers by peers is permissible and does not violate the federal education privacy law. *Owasso Independent School District v. Falvo*, 122 S.Ct. 934 (2002). Thus, whatever privacy rights a student does have does not extend to the keeping of his work secret from other students in peer grading exercises.

Oops! CNN Slips Up, Discloses that Good Looks Sell Network News

The public got a chuckle out of CNN's blunder in early January, when CNN ran a TV advertisement for its morning news program featuring Paula Zahn, whom the advertisement described as "provocative" and "sexy." Oops! The networks aren't supposed to acknowledge that a newscaster's looks help attract viewers to a program; they are supposed to pretend that content alone is what matters; they have a silent pack to keep the industry "secret" that looks are essential to a successful news program. And, of course, Ms. Zahn reacted as if it were an insult to be promoted for her good looks. (Everybody has to play along.) Maybe Congress should pass a law making it illegal to discriminate against someone based upon his or her looks.

Right to Compel Witnesses to Testify

The Sixth Amendment gives an accused the right to compel witnesses to appear in court and testify in his favor. The Supreme Court recently confirmed this principle by its 6-3 ruling in *Lee v. Kemna*, 122 S.Ct. 877 (2002).

Mr. Lee was charged with and convicted of a murder in Missouri in 1992. At his trial, Mr. Lee had subpoenaed three relatives, who were going to testify that Lee was in California at the time of the murder and therefore could not have committed it. All three were in court on the appointed day, but all three claimed that they left when a court official told them that their testimony would not be needed. Lee requested a delay when his witnesses did not show up in court. Lee requested a delay, so that the three witnesses could be located. But the trial judge denied the request, and subsequently Lee was convicted. (One must wonder if the witnesses' disappearance

was the result of their having second thoughts about the risks of committing perjury. But, this is just speculation.) The Supreme Court overturned the conviction on the grounds that Lee was not afforded his Sixth Amendment right to compel witnesses to appear and testify in his behalf. (Chief Justice Rehnquist authored the Court's opinion.)

Court Prohibits Dinner Prayers at VMI

On January 24, 2002, U. S. District Court Judge Norman K. Moon invalidated the traditional dinner prayer practice at the state-run college, Virginia Military Institute. *Mellen v. Bunting*, 181 F.Supp.2d 619. Despite recent Supreme Court cases that seemed quite clear on the issue, VMI continued its practice of directing the students in prayer each weekday prior to the evening meal. The VMI faculty drafted the prayers and led the students in reciting the prayers.

There is nothing surprising about this decision. While three of the U. S. Supreme Court Justices would argue that a state should be allowed to accommodate a time for prayer, the Court would be unanimous in finding state-directed prayers to violate the Establishment Clause.

VMI has a knack for getting in the news. Several years ago, VMI lost a court battle in which it sought to continue its tradition of excluding females from the school. And beginning this year, VMI is enforcing a rule that bans students who are married and who are parents. I presume there will soon be another court case to settle these disputes.

A New Cover-Up

Attorney General John Ashcroft recently had curtains installed to cover the Spirit of Justice statue that stands behind and above the speaker's dais in the Department of Justice. The purpose of the curtains is to cover-up the bare breast of the statue that has provided comic relief to observant news photographers for many years. You see, if the cameraman gets his camera right down on the floor in front and to the right of the speaker dais, he can get a nice photo of the Attorney General speaking at the podium with the bare-breasted statue in the background. For example, in 1986, when then Attorney General Ed Meese released the findings of a pornography commission, he was photographed with the exposed statue as he held up the report.

7.0

International News

China Man Sentenced to Death For Distributing Bibles

On January 6, 2002, *The Washington Post* reported that a Chinese businessman Li Guangqiang (38) had been indicted in Bejing, China on charges of assisting an "evil cult" because he tried to deliver thousands of Bibles to people in China.

This is no small matter to the Chinese government. On January 10, 2002, *The Washington Post* reported that Mr. Guangqiang was sentenced to death for his missionary efforts.

Farrakhan Says Bush Should Be Tried for War Crimes

On February 19, 2002, *The Washington Times* reported that the Rev. Louis Farrakhan, leader of the Nation of Islam, suggested in a speech in California that President Bush should be tried for war crimes for prosecuting the war in Afghanistan.

Mr. Farrakhan seems to have the unique ability to routinely come up with new and outrageous ideas. The news article reported that the condemnation of President Bush was part of a 2 ½ -hour speech by Mr. Farrakhan. Perhaps that is some of the problem. Anyone who speaks for two-and-a-half hours is likely to say something dumb sooner or later.

Muslim World Condemns U.S. for War in Afghanistan and Denies that Arabs Were Responsible for 9-11 Terrorist Attacks

A Gallup Poll released in late February reported that a majority of the Muslin world condemns the U.S. for the war in Afghanistan and denies that Arabs were responsible for the attacks on the World Trade Center and the Pentagon. The poll was conducted in nine Arab countries in the mid-east, and 9,924 people were questioned.

Assuming the results to be accurate, it is disconcerting to think that so much hatred exists for the United States. That the hatred is based upon ignorance is not reassuring. Getting out the message of truth is an important and daunting task. The war against international terrorism will not be won until the light of truth illuminates the minds of people around the world.

French General Convicted for Apologizing

Strange, but true. On January 25, 2002, a French criminal court convicted 83-year-old General Paul Aussaresses for apologizing for war crimes committed by the French against Algerians in the 1950's, during the Algerian war of independence from France. French law makes such an apology illegal. General Aussaresses is appealing the conviction.

CLU 02/02

Redistricting

Article I, Section 2 of the Constitution directs Congress to make an "actual Enumeration" of "free persons" living in the United States. Originally, non-taxed Indians were not counted, and slaves were counted at three-fifths per person. Section 2 of the Fourteenth Amendment deleted the "three-fifths" inequity and dropped the "free" modifier, such that the enumeration included all "persons" except the non-taxed Indians.

The purpose of the enumeration (or census) is to determine the apportionment of representatives in the House of Representatives among the states.

The census is directed to be made every ten years. (Article I, Section 2)

As the population shifts between the states, political conflicts are spawned both between the states and within states.

Interstate Conflict. One interstate conflict is exemplified in the current dispute between Utah and North Carolina. According to the Census Bureau, North Carolina narrowly edged out Utah in earning an extra seat in the House. But Utah sought relief in the courts to get this new seat from North Carolina. Utah alleged two different problems in two separate suits. First, Utah complained that the Census Bureau erred in not counting the Mormon missionaries **from** Utah, but serving in other states and nations. Had the Bureau counted these missionaries, Utah would have edged out North Carolina and secured the new seat. The Supreme Court unanimously ruled against Utah on this issue on November 26, 2001. *Utah v. Evans,* 122 S.Ct. 612. Second, Utah challenged the Bureau's practice of using estimates, rather than actual counts, in certain circumstances. After repeated and unsuccessful attempts to determine whether a particular house is occupied, census-takers will "impute" a certain number of residents to the house based upon statistical sampling of other houses in that area. Utah contends that this practice violates the Constitution's requirement that an "actual Enumeration" be made.

In 1999, in *Department of Commerce v. U. S. House of Representatives,* 525 U.S. 316, the Supreme Court ruled (5-4) that statistical sampling violated federal law. The Court did not address the Constitutional issue.

The Bush Administration has joined North Carolina in opposing Utah in the current contest. The case, also titled *Utah v. Evans,* is scheduled to be argued before the Supreme Court on March 27, 2002.

Intrastate Conflict. State legislatures have authority to change district boundaries whenever they want. And states attend to this with some frequency whether or not they gain or lose a seat in the House. The Supreme Court has struck down boundaries that are racially drawn. *Hunt v. Cromartie,* 526 U.S. 541 (1999). But there is nothing improper or illegal with redrawing boundaries to attempt to gain political advantage—such as redrawing boundaries to attempt to elect a Democrat over a Republican, or visa versa. *Id.* The party that controls a state's legislature therefore has considerable power where geographic areas are identified that are dominated by one party or the other. A prime example of such a situation is the Maryland legislature's redistricting that is geared to defeat incumbent Congresswoman Connie Morella, an eight-term Republican from Maryland's Eighth District.

Connie Morella's continued success at the polls in Democratic-controlled Montgomery County, Maryland, has long baffled political tacticians in Maryland. Democrats hope that the new redistricting plan can bring her defeat this fall. The new boundaries eliminated a heavily Republican part of northern Montgomery County (a rural area) and added an urban part of southeastern Montgomery County that has been a strong Democratic area.

If the Democrats are successful in their redistricting plan, this is expected to change the Maryland Democrat:Republican mix in the House of Representatives from 5:3 to 6:2. And the national implications of this are significant as well because the Republicans currently hold only a narrow majority in the House—222:211 (plus 2 Independents).

4

World-wide Assault on the Family

by C. Paul Smith

There is a worldwide assault being made on the family. Not an overt attack, but an insidious attack that gives lip service to the word "family," at the same time it attacks and seeks to undermine the virtues that make "family" so wonderful and important.

This battle is being waged in the United States Congress, in the United Nations, in state legislatures around the country, in public schools, in colleges and universities, and in the national media.

This article will address five specific battles that are currently being waged and are receiving considerable public attention. Most people are superficially aware of these battles without realizing the significance of the struggle. This article is intended to help remedy this. Good and honorable citizens should throw their influence and support behind the following five causes:

1. *Congress should reject the CRC treaty;*

2. *Congress should reject the CEDAW treaty;*

3. *Congress should not release funds to the UNFPA;*

4. *States should defeat legislation that would make sexual orientation a protected class; and*

5. *School systems should endorse and promote marriage*

It is my sense that most people in America have no idea what the CRC and CEDAW treaties are. Neither do they know what the UNFPA is nor why we should closely monitor its funding. This article can help bridge the ignorance gap. These five battles will be discussed in the order identified above.

1

I.   Congress Should Reject the CRC Treaty.

The CRC Treaty originated in the United Nations. Its purpose is to recognize and establish certain children's rights on an international basis. The formal name of the treaty is the *U. N. Convention on the Rights of the Child* (CRC). It was adopted by the U. N. General Assembly in 1989. [1] In 1995, the CRC was signed by Madeleine Albright, then U.S. Ambassador to the U. N. [2] Thereafter, President Clinton submitted the CRC to the U. S. Senate for ratification. [3] The CRC is in the Senate Foreign Relations Committee. If the CRC makes it out of that committee, then it will go before the full Senate, where it must receive a two-thirds vote to be ratified. (U.S. Const., Art. II, Sec. 2.) [4]

The protection of children and of their rights is a good objective, but it is not good to attempt to expand children's rights in a way that endangers them, in a way that robs them of the protection of their parents, or in a way that promotes self-destructive behavior. The CRC has all of these defects, and therefore should not be ratified. Those who are concerned about the welfare of children and families should oppose the ratification of the treaty and exert their influence to defeat the treaty around the globe.

The CRC has laudable general purposes, and some positive specific terms. For example, it expresses concerns about the effects of divorce on children; it urges protecting children from exposure to violence and pornography in the media; and it calls for action against child prostitution, child pornography and the sale of children. [5] However, these positive purposes

can be and are already being addressed in the United States, and the negative parts of the CRC are significant. Catherina Hurlburt summarized the flaws in the CRC:

> The *Convention on the Rights of the Child* goes beyond simply safeguarding society for children. It delves into the personal affairs of the family, pitting children against parents, thus endangering their innocence and well being. It would make the government the national guardian of children, charged with determining "the best interests of the child" (Article 3), subject to U. N. interpretation. Yet the Committee's definition of a child's best interests is often very different from a parent's definition. [6]

Perhaps the key problem with the CRC is its provision that each nation must submit to the authority of the U. N. Committee on the Rights of the Child. [7] As will be seen from the discussion below, this has proven to present a serious problem; witness the following specific, serious flaws: (1) Elimination of important parental rights; (2) Elimination of all corporal punishment; (3) Prohibition of all gender discrimination; (4) Promotion of homosexuality; (5) Promotion of abortion without parental knowledge or consent; and (6) Elimination of parental right to rear children in the parents' religion.

1. Elimination of Parental Rights. The Preamble of the CRC contains language supportive of the family as the fundamental group of society, but the CRC proceeds to undermine parental rights and family foundations. It does this by establishing children's rights that are superior to that of their parents. [8] And it does this through the on-going, expansive rule-making of the CRC Committee, which gives children autonomous decision-making power, unfettered by parental involvement. The CRC undermines the traditional concept in America that children need

---

[1] United Nations. "The Convention on the Rights of the Child." See http://www.unicef.org/crc/fulltext.htm.

[2] Hurlburt, Catherina. "U.N. Convention on the Rights of the Child: A Treaty to Undermine the Family." p. 1 This paper is published by Concerned Women for America, 1015 Fifteenth Street, N.W., Suite 1100, Washington, D.C. 20005—(202) 488-7000—www.cwfa.org.

[3] *Id.*

[4] Ratification of the CRC by the Senate would make this law fully binding on all of the State. The treaty would then become a part of our federal laws that are the "supreme Law of the Land." (U. S. Const. , Art. VI.)

[5] Hurlburt, 2.

---

[6] *Id.*

[7] Articles 2, 43 & 45 of the CRC.

[8] Articles 12, 13, 14 & 16 of the CRC.

parental protection and direction. The CRC seeks to drastically increase the role of government and decrease the authority of parents in rearing children.

2. Elimination of Corporal Punishment. The CRC rightly calls for the protection of children from physical and mental violence. The CRC does not ban corporal punishment or spanking, [9] but the CRC Committee does. The CRC Committee has called to ban spanking in Bolivia, Luxembourg, Austria, Congo, the United Kingdom, Tanzania, Bhutan, Monaco and Turkey. [10]

3. Prohibition of All Gender Discrimination. The CRC Committee urges the end of gender discrimination. [11] In the U.S., we have wrestled with this issue for many years. After years of debate, the States declined to ratify the Equal Rights Amendment. We celebrate many differences between the sexes, and we have laws against specific kinds of gender discrimination. It would be counter-productive for the United States to impose on ourselves a new law that does not take into account important differences in the sexes.

4. Promotion of Homosexuality. The CRC Committee recommends legislating to "prevent discrimination based on the grounds of sexual orientation." [12] This position takes the politically correct, if not erroneous and ill-informed, position that homosexual conduct is acceptable and that participants therein cannot change, have no responsibility for the existence of such desires, and should not be urged to refrain from such conduct.

5. Promotion of Abortion. Article 24 of the CRC gives the children the right to family planning services. The CRC Committee takes this a step further and "demands reproductive services for children *without parental knowledge or consent.*" [12] One of the principal components of these "reproductive services" is abortion. Some supporters of the CRC deny that the CRC would give children an international right to an abortion. [13] But the CRC Committee has criticized nations with restrictive abortion laws, and the U. N. Human Rights Commission has demanded that Guatemala legalize abortion. [14]

6. Elimination of Parental Right to Rear Children in the Parents' Religion. Articles 14 and 30 of the CRC give children the right to "profess and practise [sic] his or her own religion." [15] This could make it more difficult (if not impossible in some instances) for parents to rear their children. In addition, the American Bar Association has offered the opinion that Article 29 of the CRC could make religious schools in the United States illegal. [16]

The above-discussed flaws are ample reasons to reject the CRC. It is a flawed treaty that would do more harm than good to both families and children. Despite its ostensibly good purposes, it has already proven around the world to be a tool to weaken traditional families as it has become an arm for leftist groups and individuals who seek to replace parents with government. And, just as importantly, the ratification of the CRC would be an abdication of our republican form of government—selling our right to self-governance for the opinions of the U. N. CRC Committee.

The CRC has been ratified by virtually every nation in the United Nations except the U.S. and Somalia. The United States should continue to refuse to ratify it.

---

[9] Article 19 of the CRC.

[10] *Concluding Observations of the Committee on the Rights of the Child: Turkey,* CRC/C/15/Add.152 (Geneva, Switzerland: Office of the United Nations High Commissioner for Human Rights, 8 June 2001, para. 48; reported by Hurlburt, 3.

[11] Hurlburt, 4. Implicit in this is the CRC's endorsement of another U. N. treaty, CEDAW. This will be discussed in the following section of this article.

[12] Concluding Observations of the Committee on the Rights of the Child: United Kingdom of Great Britain and Northern Ireland (Isle of Man), CRC/C/15/Add.134 (Geneva, Switzerland: Office of the United Nations High Commissioner for Human Rights, 16 October 2000), para. 22-23; reported by Hurlburt, 4.

[13] Hurlburt, 5.

[14] Woodward, Joe. "The U.N. Quietly Wages War on Religion," *The Calgary Herald,* 11 Aug. 2001, reported by Hurlburt, 5.

[15] CRC Article 30. See also CRC Article 14.

[16] Sabom, Diane. "Symposium: Should the Senate ratify the Convention on the rights of the Child?", *Insight on the News,* 16 April 2001, 41; reported in Hurlburt, 5.

II.   Congress Should Reject the CEDAW Treaty

The CEDAW is also a treaty that originated in the United Nations. Its name describes its purpose: *"Convention on the Elimination of All Forms of Discrimination Against Women"* (hereafter CEDAW. It was adopted by the U. N. General Assembly in 1979 [17] and was signed by President Jimmy Carter in 1980. [18] The Senate Foreign Relations Committee passed it in 1994, but the full Senate has yet to ratify it. A two-thirds vote is required by Article II, Section 2 of the Constitution.

165 countries have already signed the treaty. [19] As with the CRC, the United States stands almost alone in not ratifying it. But also, like the CRC, while the CEDAW has some good purposes, it is also infected with problems that are destructive of families, several of which problems also infect the CRC. CEDAW would replace the sovereignty of the States in matters of family law with a federal law (the CEDAW treaty). Further, like the CRC, CEDAW is administered by a U. N. CEDAW Committee that would be empowered to interpret and implement the CEDAW around the world. [20] The Committee is comprised of 23 individuals from 23 different nations which have ratified the treaty. [21] The United States would have only one, or perhaps no representative on this committee. I, for one, would prefer to hang on to

the right of United States citizens to determine their own laws. I don't see any reason to depart from the position the thirteen colonies took in 1776, when we declared our independence from Great Britain in part because we wanted a say in the making of the laws that would affect us. The CEDAW would give too much legislative and interpretive power to an United Nations Committee that has already demonstrated it would use this power in ways that are destructive of important family values.

Specific problems with CEDAW include the following: (1) It attacks the role of mothers in the family; (2) It would replace parental rights with governmental control; (3) It would eliminate all gender discrimination; (4) It would undermine important fundamentals of our free enterprise economic system; (5) It promotes abortion; (6) It promotes homosexual conduct; and (7) It promotes legalized prostitution.

1. CEDAW Attacks the Role of Mothers in the Family. Article 1 of the CEDAW defines "discrimination against women" as follows:

> Any distinction, exclusion or restriction made on the basis of sex which has the effect or purpose of impairing or nullifying the recognition, enjoyment or exercise by women, irrespective of their marital status, on a basis of equality of men and women, of human rights and fundamental freedoms in the political, economic, social, cultural, civil or any other field.

The overbreadth of this definition creates some problems. According to MacLeod and Hurlburt, "CEDAW is actually a global Equal Rights Amendment, a tool for radical feminists, who deny any distinctions between men and women." [22] After debating issues respecting the equality of men and women, American law currently holds to the view that some distinctions between men and women continue to be justified and desirable. For example, most if not all states continue to promote heterosexual marriage and to prohibit same-sex marriages. The CEDAW would change this.

But additionally, the CEDAW attacks the traditional role of mothers in bearing and

---

[17] United Nations. "The Convention on the Elimination of All Forms of Discrimination Against Women." See http://www.un.org/womenwatch/daw/cedaw/cedaw.htm.

[18] MacLeod, Laurel and Hurlburt, Catherina. "Exposing CEDAW: The United Nations Convention on the Elimination of All Forms of Discrimination Against Women." P. 1. This paper is published by Concerned Women for America, 1015 Fifteenth Street, N.W., Suite 1100, Washington, D.C. 20005—(202) 488-7000— www.cwfa.org.

[19] *Id.*

[20] Articles 2 & 17-22 of CEDAW.

[21] Article 17 of CEDAW.

---

[22] MacLeod & Hurlburt, 2.

nurturing and rearing children. The CEDAW combats this traditional role, characterizing it as an undesirable "stereotype." The CEDAW Committee criticized the nation of Belarus, complaining that "Mothers Day" and "Mothers' Award" promoted traditional roles for women. [23] The CEDAW Committee disapproved of "the traditional stereotype of women in the noble role of mother." [24] And the Committee criticized "stereotypical attitudes that tend to portray men as heads of households and breadwinners, and women primarily as mothers and homemakers." [25]

2. CEDAW Would Replace Parental Rights with Governmental Control. Like the CRC, the CEDAW establishes the principal that the government, not the parents, know what is best for children. This differs from the fundamental right of parents to rear children, as recently confirmed by the U. S. Supreme Court in the case of *Troxel v. Granville,* 530 U.S. 57 (2000). Current constitutional law recognizes this parental right and establishes a presumption that the parents know what's best for their children, and that the burden is on others (including the government) to refute this presumption. The CEDAW is at odds with this.

One application of this by the CEDAW Committee is its promotion of day care as being preferable to direct parental care of children. The Committee criticized Slovenia because 70 percent of its children were missing out on the educational and social opportunities available in

day care facilities. [26] And the Committee promoted day-care services in Germany to encourage mothers to join the labor force. [27]

3. CEDAW Would Eliminate All Gender Discrimination. The CEDAW is a back-door attempt to accomplish what the Equal Rights Amendment sought to accomplish. Article 10c of CEDAW requires: "The elimination of any stereotyped concept of the roles of men and women at all levels and in all forms of education." Not only does this create problems in families, but it ignores the studies that recognize the different emotional and attitudinal needs of boys and girls in education. [28]

4. CEDAW Would Undermine Important Fundamentals of Our Free Enterprise System. The CEDAW mandate to enforce equal pay for men and women is an excessive and ill-conceived policy. Once again, the overbreadth of CEDAW would create some new problems at the same time it would attempt to solve others. The CEDAW seeks to enforce equal pay for women without regard to the quality and quantity of work performed. Such a mandatory scheme, broadly applied, would seriously disrupt and jeopardize national and global economies.

---

[23] *Concluding Observations of the Committee on the Elimination of Discrimination Against Women: Belarus,* CEDAW/C/2000/I/CRP.3/Add.5/Rev.1 (Geneva, Switzerland: Office of the United Nations High Commissioner for Human Rights, 31 January 2000), para. 27; reported by MacLeod & Hurlburt, 3.

[24] Jones, Susan, "In Defense of Mother's Day, Senator Blasts 'Anti-Family' Treaty," *CNS News*, 12 May 2000, quoted in MacLeod & Hurlburt, 3.

[25] *Concluding Observations of the Committee on the Elimination of Discrimination Against Women: Luxembourg,* CEDAW/C/2000/I/CRP.3/Rev.1 (Geneva, Switzerland: Office of the United Nations High Commissioner for Human Rights, 21 January 2000), para. 29; reported by MacLeod & Hurlburt, 3.

[26] *Concluding Observations of the Committee on the Elimination of Discrimination Against Women: Slovenia,* A/52/38/Rev.1, paras. 81-122 (Geneva, Switzerland: Office of the United Nations High Commissioner for Human Rights, 23 January 1997), para. 104; reported by MacLeod & Hurlburt, 3.

[27] *Concluding Observations of the Committee on the Elimination of Discrimination Against Women: Germany,* CEDAW/C/2000/I/CRP.3/Add.7/Rev.1 (Geneva, Switzerland: Office of the United Nations High Commissioner for Human Rights, 2 February 2000), para. 28; reported by MacLeod & Hurlburt, 3.

[28] See e.g., Christina Hoff Sommers, *The War Against Boys: How Misguided Feminism is Harming Our Young Men* (New York: Simon & Schuster, 2000), and Richard Lowry, "The Male Eunuch," *National Review,* 3 July 2000; both are reported and cited in MacLeod & Hurlburt, 4.

5. CEDAW Promotes Abortion.
Articles 12 and 14 of CEDAW ensures the access of men and women to "family planning" services. In the thirty plus years since its inception, the CEDAW has demonstrated that abortion services is the principal component of the family services it advocates. [29] Feminists, including those who shape the CEDAW Committee, view abortion as something that must be made available to all women in order for them to compete equally with men. [30] Globally, CEDAW has become a tool to help accomplish this. [31] The CEDAW Committee has encouraged the facilitation of abortion laws in Romania and Ireland. [32]

6. CEDAW Promotes Homosexual Conduct. The CEDAW makes no specific mention of homosexual rights; however, its sweeping mandate for total gender neutrality implicitly promotes homosexual conduct and prohibits discrimination against homosexuals. The CEDAW Committee has specifically advocated for recognizing the right to engage in homosexual conduct in Kyrgyzstan. [33]

7. CEDAW Promotes Legalized Prostitution. Article 6 of the CEDAW prohibits the exploitation of prostitution in women. However, Article 11 upholds the right of women to choose their profession and employment. Consequently, the right of women to pursue the

world's oldest profession has prevailed. And the CEDAW Committee has advocated for legalized prostitution in China, Germany and Greece. [34]

The CEDAW should not be ratified. As Senator Jesse Helms (R-NC—past chair of the Senate Foreign Relations Committee) said, it "demeans motherhood and undermines the traditional family." [35] While there is a great need to fight for the rights of abused and disadvantaged women around the world, CEDAW does much harm in addition to any good that it does. Opportunistic radical feminists cite international abuses of women as justification for adopting CEDAW. But as MacLeod and Hurlburt point out:

> Radical feminists in Western nations are using these women's disadvantages to push an agenda of sexual and reproductive rights for females as young as age 10. Hiding under the guise of "human rights," and veiling their intentions with appeals for needy women in developing nations, they insist CEDAW is necessary. . . . At its best, CEDAW is unnecessary. At its worst, CEDAW unravels America's families and forces women to model themselves after global feminists' ideal image. [p.36]

---

[29] MacLeod & Hurlburt, 5.

[30] MacLeod & Hurlburt, 5.

[31] *Id.*

[32] *Id.*, at 6. *Concluding Observations of the Committee on the Elimination of Discrimination Against Women: Kyrgyzstan,* A/54/38, paras. 95-142 (Geneva, Switzerland: Office of the United Nations High Commissioner for Human Rights, 27 January 1999), paras. 127-128

[33] *Concluding Observations of the Committee on the Elimination of Discrimination Against Women: Kyrgyzstan,* A/54/38, paras. 95-142 (Geneva, Switzerland: Office of the United Nations High Commissioner for Human Rights, 27 January 1999), paras. 127-128; reported by MacLeod & Hurlburt, 6.

[34] *Concluding Observations of the Committee on the Elimination of Discrimination Against Women: China,* A/54/38, paras. 251-336 (Geneva, Switzerland: Office of the United Nations High Commissioner for Human Rights, 3 February 1999), para. 289; *Concluding Observations: Germany,* para. 36; and *Concluding Observations of the Committee on the Elimination of Discrimination Against Women: Greece,* A/54/38, paras. 172-212 (Geneva, Switzerland: Office of the United Nations High Commissioner for Human Rights, 1 February 1999), para. 197; reported by MacLeod & Hurlburt, 7.

[35] MacLeod & Hurlburt, 7.

[36] *Id.,* 8.

III. Congress Should Not Give Funds to the UNFPA.

Because of on-going human rights violations in China, the United States should not give funds to the United Nations Population Fund (UNFPA) because UNFPA has been promoting an extremist family planning policy that oppresses women and families and denies women of fundamental human rights.

According to Nafis Sadik, director of the United Nations Population Fund (UNFPA), "China has every reason to feel proud of and pleased with its remarkable achievements made in its family planning policy." Sadik went on to recommend that China "could offer its experiences and special expert[ise] to help other countries." Then Ms. Sadik offered this: "The UNFPA firmly believes, and so does the government of the People" Republic of China, that their program is a totally voluntary program.""[37]

All of this sounds good enough, except that it appears to be a lie, and the United Nations appears to be providing the cover for countless atrocities and human rights violations in China. Congressman Chris Smith accused the UNFPA of being a contributor to the cover-up, and he opposes the use of American tax dollars to support China's human rights abuses as well as the UN's condoning of such abuses. In early 2001, the Population Research Institute (PRI) sent an undercover fact-finding team to Sihui County, China, to investigate the following claims about China's population control programs:

Mandatory abortions;
Birth permits;
Fines and imprisonment for non-compliance with mandatory population control programs;
Mandatory use of IUDs; and
Forced sterilization.

The PRI found evidence of all of this. [38] But no sooner than the results of the PRI report were made known, the UNFPA sent its own team to China, spending most of its short visit meeting with Chinese Population Control officials. [39] Not surprisingly, the UNFPA team reported that "[n]o one expressed any grievances or complaints of any kind, or knew of any abuses in recent years." [40]

Whether the UNFPA team was duped or is in full complicity with the Chinese government, is not known. But the American people need not turn a blind eye to the blatant flaw in the UNFPA methods for checking out the allegations that the Chinese government is guilty of human rights violations and atrocities in its population control policies. UNFPA must be brain dead to think that the Chinese government itself would disclose any human rights abuses; that would be an act of suicide in China. And UNFPA was equally ignorant to think that the witnesses that the Chinese Population Control officials arranged for UNFPA to interview would dare to say even a word of complaint about any program of the Chinese government. Predictably, the UNFPA team found only satisfied and happy citizens. The UNFPA interviews were not done with individuals whose identity and safety could be kept confidential. This flaw made the UNFPA findings absolutely unreliable.

Representative Smith urged Congress not to give money to UNFPA, a program that is so intent on limiting child birth that it will look the other way at human rights violations that are promoted to achieve forced abortions and forced sterilizations. Representative Smith condemns UNFPA for "aggressively defend[ing] ... barbaric polici[es] that makes brothers and sisters illegal, and makes women the pawns of population-control cadres." [41] The last thing Congress should do is give several million dollars in grants to UNFPA.

[37] Chris Smith (Rep., NJ), Letter published in *The Washington Post*, December 19, 2001.

[38] *Id.*

[39] *Id.*

[40] *Id.*

[41] *Id.*

IV. States Should Defeat Legislation That Would Make Sexual Orientation A Protected Class.

Making sexual orientation a legally-protected class attacks and endangers the family. The importance and urgency of this has been made obvious by two announcements during the first two weeks of February. First, the American Academy of Pediatrics (AAP) announced its endorsement of the adoption of children by homosexual couples. [42] This was followed by the release of a social science report on Valentine's Day that confirmed that marriage promotes in men and women--better physical health, better mental health, longer life, more happiness and more affluence. [43] The social science report highlights the problems in the AAP recommendation; without supporting evidence for its position, the AAP has endorsed a practice that is geared to provide less benefits and more health dangers to children. The juxtaposition of these two simultaneous announcements demonstrates the dilemma that society is currently grappling with in determining how to deal with homosexuals and with asserted special rights for homosexuals.

Scientific studies show that gays have a high incidence of HIV and AIDS that threatens their health and their very lives. [44]

Homosexual conduct has been proven to be unhealthy and dangerous. [45] In addition, practicing homosexuals have a higher incidence of suicide and other emotional problems than the heterosexual population. [46] Studies have demonstrated consistently, that the great majority of practicing homosexuals do not practice fidelity (in terms of limiting their sexual relations to one partner), but rather have multiple partners. [47] Conversely, studies continue to

---

PhD; Michael Lyons, PhD; Seth Eisen, MD; Ming T. Tsuang, MD, DSc, PhD; "Sexual Orientation and Sucidality," *Archives of General Psychiatry*, October, 1999.

One expert has estimated that by age thirty, 30% of gay men will be HIV-positive or dead of AIDS. Eric Goldman, "Psychological Factors Generate HIV Resurgence in Young Gay Men," *Clinical Psychiatry News*, October 1994, p.5., reported in "All the Facts about Youth and Homosexuality," published by The National Association for Research and Therapy of Homosexuality (NARTH) (see www.narth.com).

Gay men acquire sexually transmitted diseases at a rate 2.5 times higher than heterosexual men. The National Lesbian and Gay Health Association (NGLHA), *Health Implications Associated with Homosexuality* (1999, published by The Medical Institute for Sexual Health, P. O. Box 162306, Austin, TX 78716), cited in NARTH, "All the Facts." This same NGLHA report found that homosexual conduct was associated with high rates of health problems in the following areas: STDs; HIV/AIDS; traumatic rectal/ intestinal injury; hepatitis; human papillomavirus/genital warts; herpes; other viral and nonviral STDs; and gonorrhea.

Another study has shown that people with same-sex behavior are at a greater risk for psychiatric disorders. Theo G. M. Sandfort, PhD; Ron de Graaf, PhD; Rob V. Bijl, PhD; Paul Schnabel, PhD; "Same-Sex Sexual Behavior and Psychiatric Disorders," *Archives of General Psychiatry*, January, 2001.

[45] *Id.*

[46] *Id.*

[47] M. Sagir and E. Robbins, *Male & Female Homosexuality* (Baltimore: Williams & Wilkins, 1973) p.225, cited in Family Research Council [FRC], "Talking Points: How Homosexual 'Civil Unions' Harm Marriage," *INFOCUS*, No. 226, May 17, 2000, p.2. Sagir and Robbins found that the average homosexual relationship lasts between 2 and 3 years. A study by McWhirter and Mattison found no homosexual relationship lasting more than 5 years that was monogamous. David P. McWhirter and Andrew M. Mattison, *The Male couple: How*

---

[42] Committee on Psychosocial Aspects of Child and Family Health, a report published in *Pediatrics*, February 2002. *Pediatrics* is the official publication of The American Academy of Pediatrics (AAP). See commentary on AAP's endorsement of gay parenting in James C. Dobson, PhD, "Pediatricians vs. Children," *The Washington Times*, February 12, 2002.

[43] Institute for American Values and Center of the American Experiment, "Why Marriage Matters: 21 Conclusions from the Social Sciences," as reported in *The Washington Times*, February 14, 2002. *See also* Linda J. Waite and Maggie Gallagher, *The Case for Marriage* (Broadway Books, 2000), as reported in Joseph Perkins, "Ample Benefits of Marriage," *The Washington Times*, February 23, 2002.

[44] Several studies have found a higher incidence of suicide attempts in homosexual males than in heterosexual males. *See e.g.*, Richard Herrell, MS; Jack Goldberg, PhD; William R. True, PhD, MPH; Visvanathan Ramakrishnan,

8.4.5 / 6.1

demonstrate that married couples are happier, live longer, [48] make more money, and are more successful than either single individuals or gay couples. [49] Finally, scientific studies show that homosexual behavior is caused by multiple factors, including environment, habits and experiences. [50] A recent study reported that

29% of the adult children of homosexual parents had been sexually molested by at least one of the parents—which translates into an incest risk factor that is 50 times greater than for children of heterosexual parents. [51]

The studies cited above demonstrate why states should be able to discriminate against gays and in favor of heterosexual couples in adoption. And these studies show why states should also advocate for and favor married couples in adoption. Notwithstanding the scientific evidence, there are powerful forces at work to encourage states to protect and promote homosexual conduct. But today, an excessive vigilance to promote the gay lifestyle often prevails over common sense and sound health practices. But this "politically correct" trend should be checked. Let me put it to you this way: Why should our state enact a policy to encourage more of our youth to adopt a gay life style? Why should our state enact a policy to increase health problems; to increase health care expenses; to increase premature deaths, including suicides; to increase emotional problems; and to decrease happy marriages?

There is a correlation between the reduction in traditional marriages and an increase in the social ills that plague society—crime, poverty, drunkenness, drug use, broken homes, abuse. Happy marriages are the key to happy, educated and well-balance children. [52]

But both current and past studies show a strong correlation between traditional, two-parent homes and effective education. [53]

Relationships Develop (Englewood Cliffs, N.J.: Prentice-Hall, 1984), pp. 252-253, cited in FRC, p. 2.

Studies show that the average male homosexual has hundreds of sex partners during his life. *See, e.g., Timothy J. Dailey*, "The Negative Health Effects of Homosexuality," *Insight* (published by Family Research Council—see www.frc.org) Number 232, March 6, 2001, in which Dr. Dailey cites several studies, including the following: A. P. Bell and M. S. Weinberg, *Homosexualities: A Study of Diversity Among Men and Women* (New York: Simon and Schuster, 1978) pp.308; and Paul Van de Ven et al., "A Comparative Demographic and Sexual Profile of Older Homosexually Active Men," *Journal of Sex Research* 34 (1997): 354

In a study of homosexual households by Dr. Bradley Hayton, he concluded that such households "model a poor view of marriage to children. They are taught by example and belief that marital relationships are transitory and mostly sexual in nature. . . . And they are taught that monogamy in a marriage is not the norm [and] should be discouraged if one wants a good 'marital' relationship." Bradley P. Hayton, "To Marry or Not: The Legalization of Marriage and Adoption of Homosexual Couples," (Newport Beach: The Pacific Policy Institute, 1993), p. 9, cited in Timothy J. Dailey, "Homosexual Parenting: Placing Children at Risk," published by Family Research Council—see www.frc.org.

[48] Robert S. Hogg, et al., "Modeling the Impact of HIV Disease on Mortality in Gay and Bisexual Men," *International Journal of Epidemiology* 26 (1997): 657, cited in FRC, p.2.

[49] Institute for American Values and Center of the American Experiment, "Why Marriage Matters: 21 Conclusions from the Social Sciences," as reported in *The Washington Times*, February 14, 2002.

[50] *See, e.g.*, Jeffrey Satinover, MD, "The Gay Gene?" *The Journal of Human Sexuality* (1996); William Byne, MD, PhD; Bruce Parsons, MD, PhD, "Human Sexual Orientation: The Biologic Theories Reappraised," *Archives of General Psychiatry*, Vol. 50, March, 1993; and Joseph Nicolosi; A. Dean Byrd; Richard W. Potts; "Retrospective Self-Reports of Changes in Homosexual Orientation: A Consumer Survey of Conversion Therapy Clients," *Psychological Reports*, June 2000, vol. 86, pp. 1071-1088.

[51] P. Cameron and K. Cameron, "Homosexual Parents," *Adolescence* 31 (1996): 772, cited in FRC, *INFOCUS*, p.2.

[52] Paul Barton , "America's Smallest School: The Family," reported in George F. Will, "Broken Families and School Performance," *The Washington Post*, January 6, 2002.

[53] *Id.* Mr. Barton, (then of the Educational Testing Service) concluded that there were five factors that determined 90 percent of the differences in proficiency of the various state schools in student performance on SAT tests: (1) number of days absent from school; (2) number of hours watching television; (3) number of pages read for homework; (4) quantity and quality of reading material in the home; and (5) the presence of two parents in the home.

8.4.5 / 6.1

This should not be surprising. State laws have sought to protect and encourage strong and happy marriages since before the Revolutionary War. Studies confirm that the philosophies and understanding of our ancestors in this regard were exactly right. But despite this—notwithstanding the scientific studies that prove the negative effects that result when there is a large decline in the number of traditional families—many in our society seek and promote lifestyles that have been proven to bring increases in crime, poverty, illness and suffering. [54]

Speaking out against "alternate" but undesirable lifestyles is not an act of a fear or hatred; it is the enlightened, healthy and wise thing to do.

Psuedo-intellectuals attempt to characterize those who oppose the gay lifestyle as ignorant, uneducated, fearful and hateful. But this is a false and inaccurate generalization. There are certainly evil people who have harmed and killed gays. Such actions are and should be punished as the crimes they are. But to encourage proper heterosexual relations and to discourage homosexual conduct is right and proper; and it is in the best interests of both society and individuals to do so.

You would think that the medical doctors that comprise the AAP would have the intelligence and judgment to insist upon scientific support for its positions. But both were lacking when it made its recent announcement promoting adoption by gays. The AAP cited some studies by gay militants that concluded that they could find no difference in the effects of gay parenting verses heterosexual parenting in certain situations. But the AAP did not address the many past and recent studies that show multiple advantages of traditional heterosexual parents for children. This omission is blatant! The only explanation seems to be that the AAP is so

caught up in the forces of political correctness that they have become blinded to the exigencies of facts and reasoning.

The serious flaws of same-sex marriage and homosexual parenting is illustrated most strikingly by examining how children are influenced when reared by homosexual couples. Such an examination illustrates why special gay rights should not be extended to gays in the context of adoption laws. It is one thing for a state to allow a gay couple to adopt, but it is a totally different thing to make a law that prohibits the state and private agencies and individuals from discriminating against gays in the placement of children in adoption.

This distinction is not recognized in the State of Maryland, where Governor Parris Glendenning promulgated a regulation (effective since January 8, 2001) making it illegal to discriminate in adoption based upon sexual orientation. Code of Maryland Regulations (COMAR) 07.05.03.09. This regulation was enacted prior to the effective date of Maryland's new law (S.B. 205), which makes it illegal to discriminate in employment, housing and public accommodations based upon one's "sexual orientation." Now, in Maryland, these two, independent legal bases exist to make it illegal to discriminate against gays in adoption. (Nevertheless, religious-based adoption agencies have First Amendment protection in their discriminating in favor of married couples in adoption.) But, except for this limited First Amendment exception, in Maryland, the State cannot take a position favoring married couples over gay couples in placing children for adoption. Such a policy is ludicrous. It ignores the consistent and numerous social studies that prove that a child's best interests would be served by placing him or her with a heterosexual, married couple if at all possible. Maryland's commitment to celebrate and recognize all differences has moved to the extreme, where it tolerates and promotes actions and practices that endangers the most vulnerable of its citizens— the children.

---

[54] Interestingly, there is also evidence that indicates that those youth who do not engage in premarital sex do so because of their commitment to religious principles. Deborah Simmons. "The ABC's of teen parenthood— What are the facts about abstinence vs. birth control?" *The Washington Times*, February 15, 2002. This is one good reason why governments should encourage and promote its citizens to believe in God.

10

69

V. School Systems Should Endorse and Promote Marriage.

Public school systems should endorse and promote marriage as the best and proper relationship for sexual relations. It seems so obvious that one hardly knows how to begin in arguing that our government, including our schools, should promote marriage. Yet, incredibly, that is where we have come to in America. I will tell you about a recent battle regarding this in Frederick, Maryland. I would think that similar battles may have occurred elsewhere around the country.

On November 15, 2001, the headlines in *The Frederick Post* announced, "Board takes marriage out of sex ed." The News-Post reporter, Julia Robb, reported a handful of reasons that were given by the County Board of Education members for taking this surprise action. The reasoning of the Board caused many citizens of Frederick County, Maryland, to have grave concerns about the wisdom of the individuals on the board. Subsequently, because of the intense public reaction that ensued, the Board later reversed this action, but not with an expression of remorse or regret with what they did. Because the opposition to state-endorsement of marriage continues to be strong, it is important to shed some light on the specious reasoning that was used against marriage here.

The following arguments were advanced for removing the county's endorsement of marriage in its sex ed curriculum: [55]

(1) Curriculum specialist, W. Lynn Carr argued that the following statement in the county's sex ed curriculum was offensive and improper: "Sexual abstinence is 'appropriate behavior before marriage.'" Mr. Carr argued that this offending statement should be eliminated to reflect state guidelines. The state guidelines had recently been changed to protect gays (through making sexual orientation a protected class). Mr. Carr failed to address the fact that the State of Maryland continues to endorse marriage, as it has for over 200 years.

(2) Board member, Anne Hooper, argued that

[55] Based upon author's observations at Dec., 2001 Board meeting and Julia Robb, "Board takes marriage out of sex ed," *The Frederick Post,* November 15, 2001.

the schools should not be teaching religious values that are not universally shared. This is a ridiculous argument; it would shackle any government; it repudiates democratic principles.

(3) Board member, Steve Crawford, argued that it would be improper for the public schools to link sex with marriage because this would be a religious position. This argument is total nonsense. The coincidence of a state standard with that of a particular religion is not fatal to the state standard if the state standard is established by the democratic and republican principles of our Constitution. The mere coincidence of the two does not violate the First Amendment. See, e.g., *Bowen v. Kendrick,* 487 U.S. 589 (1988). Virtually every law will express someone's moral or religious opinions; such a coincidence cannot be avoided; neither does the Constitution forbid it.

(4) Another argument that is implicit in the above three arguments is the notion that it is possible to teach about sexual relations without stating a moral or religious point of view. This is a false notion that is held by many. But by eliminating all moral and religious judgments when teaching about a moral matter, the amoral, secular view is adopted—one that is hostile towards morality and religion.

(5) Another argument that is implicit in the above three arguments is the concept that toleration is an absolute virtue—i.e., that we should tolerate and embrace all lifestyles and conduct without judging. But this brand of tolerance is an abandonment of principle, virtue and morality. The Constitution does not prohibit us from being a people of principle and virtue. If we, as a community, do not stand for something, then we have become duped by the philosophy that seeks to make tolerance an absolute principle, rather than a quality that must be exercised with wisdom and discrimination.

In December, 2001, the Frederick County Board of Education re-established its endorsement of marriage in the public school sex education curriculum. But, I can tell you, by the comments that I heard and the debate that I witnessed at that December board meeting, that several members on the current board do not share my values and concerns for the education of our children. This battle will be resumed again, both in Maryland and in other states.

CLU 02/02

VI. The Worldwide Battle to Prostitute the Family—Wake Up! We're in It!

No one opposes the family. Everyone agrees that families are good and important. However, by changing the meaning of the word "family" from its traditional meaning, and expanding it or in some cases giving it a specialized meaning, today being pro-family does not necessarily denote that which is positive and good.

Today there are some powerful groups who promote and advocate elective abortions, mandatory sterilizations, prostitution, and mandatory third-party child care for children—all of which are presented as being **pro-family**. In fact, such programs are the antithesis of that which supports and strengthens the family; they are **anti-family**. Yet they masquerade as if they were pro-family. When the pro-family bus goes by, these enemies of the family, want to hop on the bus, waving their pro-family banners. They are fully intent on taking over the bus and transforming the substance of the pro-family message into their brand of life-style that is inimical to the good and virtuous traditional family.

Thus, the meaning of being pro-family has been prostituted; in a sense, today it means nothing because virtually every lifestyle and philosophy today claims to be a legitimate member of the "family." The most obvious example of this prostitution is the gay couples who seek to obtain for themselves every right and privilege and every legal advantage that is possessed by traditional married couples. "We are also a family," they say, as they seek for society to bless their unions under state marriage laws and to obtain for themselves all the rights and benefits and legal privileges of married couples.

The traditional family—consisting of a father and a mother and children—is under attack around the world. The battle is being waged all around us, and its effects are affecting and infecting us. If the forces opposing the family are not confronted and fought, then in America and around the world there will be further weakening of families.

Perhaps individual families, such as yours, will survive the onslaught. But it will soon catch up with your children and your grandchildren as their relationships with others are affected by the insidious false notions and debilitating practices that will promote poor health, shorten lives, increase depression and sadness, and undermine marriages.

There are ample scientific evidences that support society's tradition of encouraging marriage and discouraging sexual relations outside of marriage.

CONSTITUTIONAL LAW UPDATES

II:ii   July 2002   No. 5

Table of Contents

CONSTITUTIONAL LAW UPDATES is a quarterly newsletter edited and published by C. Paul Smith, J.D.
Subscription cost is $25.00 per year (plus $1.25 tax in MD). To subscribe, send a check or money order to
CONSTITUTIONAL LAW UPDATES, P. O. Box 1204, Frederick, MD 21702. For further information, visit Paul
Smith's web site: www.cpaulsmith.com.

1.1.3.1
13.4

STOCK MARKET PLUNGE—
Due to the Dishonesty of Businesses—
Threat to a Strong Economy and to
Personal Liberties

On Friday, July 19, 2002, the Dow Jones Industrial closed at its lowest point in four years, dropping 390 points—the seventh biggest one-day drop ever.

Analysts debate the cause and when the market will bounce back. Just a day earlier, Fed Chairman Alan Greenspan testified before Congress that the economy was recovering—that the future for stocks looked good. But the very next day the market plunged anyway.

To the untrained eye of this stock watcher, there appears to be a correlation between the several major integrity gaffs and the public's lack of trust of many businesses. Not only did Enron and Global Crossings collapse, but just recently WorldCom filed for bankruptcy protection. Qwest, Imclone and Merrill Lynch also had book-cooking problems. And on July 24th, five former executives of Adelphia Communications Corp. were arrested and charged with defrauding investors out of billions of dollars. Even the one-time model of integrity and competence, CPA firm of Arthur Andersen, admitted falsifying records, and consequently lost most of its partners. According to *The Washington Post* (July 19, 2002) two-thirds of its 1700 U.S. partners left this spring, and hundreds of other employees have left as well.

Democrats have attempted to put the blame on Bush and Cheney for the business integrity crisis. (President Bush had involvement with Harken Energy twelve years ago, and Dick Cheney had involvement at Halliburton.) But thus far, polls show that President Bush does not seem to be hurt much by this blame game. Minority House Leader, Richard Gephardt, is confident his party will win over some House seats in the coming fall election due to the business scandals. But Republicans are countering, blaming the losses on the greed and dishonesty of the 90's (when Clinton-Gore) were in office. What the ultimate political effect will be, is yet to be determined. On July 24th, the market made a 489 point gain on the Dow (second largest one-day gain ever). Will the re-election of incumbents be reflected by whether or not the market recovers? We'll see.

But for now, some analysts, such as William Rusher, submit that this integrity crisis is responsible for the precipitous, recent drop in the stock market.

If indeed it is dishonesty that has caused the recent decline, then one would expect that good, honest businesses will survive this current crisis.

Many lives and families have been wrecked because of the dishonesty and greed of business leaders. Not only is honesty the best moral policy, but it is the best foundation for economic success and security. Business dishonesty has hurt hundreds—even thousands of people economically during the past year. Put another way, the business dishonesty has cost thousands of people personal liberty, as they have been denied or deprived of economic benefits they thought they had earned.

Honesty must be the foundation of every politician, of every business and of every citizen. This is the best foundation to build both a strong economy and to preserve and protect personal liberties.

CENSUS AND REDISTRICTING CASES

The State of Utah recently lost two Supreme Court cases in seeking to gain a fourth congressional seat.

On June 20, 2002, in a 5-4 ruling, the Supreme Court held that the Census Bureau's "hot deck imputation" was valid and did not violate the Constitutional requirement to make an "actual enumeration" in the decennial census. *Utah v. Evans,* ___ U.S. ___, 122 S.Ct. 2191 (2002). Only three years earlier, the Supreme Court, by a 5-4 vote in *Department of Commerce v. United States House of Representatives,* 525 U.S. 316 (1999), had struck down a proposal of the Census Bureau to conduct the census by statistical sampling. But the Supreme Court found that the imputation method employed by the Census Bureau in 2000 was only employed sparingly with respect to segments of the population not responding to census inquiries. Chief Justice Rehnquist was the only Justice that differentiated this limited "imputation" case from the broad statistical sampling. The other eight justices saw the two statistical imputation/sampling cases similarly. Thus, the Chief Justice was the swing vote in the two cases.

Utah previously lost another 2000 Census case that made its way to the Supreme Court. On November 26, 2001, the Supreme Court affirmed the ruling of the United States District Court for the District of Utah that the Census Bureau properly did not count as a part of Utah, the Mormon missionaries around the world whose home state is Utah. *Utah v. Evans,* ___ U.S. ___; 122 S.Ct. 612 (2001).

The result of these two cases is that Utah will not gain a fourth congressional seat. Instead, North Carolina will acquire an additional seat in the House of Representatives beginning next year. (Mississippi lost a congressional seat following the Census.)

Redistricting cases often result in states that lose or gain legislative seats following a Census. Some litigation originates in state courts, based upon the setting of new geographic boundaries by state legislatures, in accordance with state laws. Recently, on June 11, 2002, Maryland's highest court, the Court of Appeals, invalidated the State Legislature's new districting. The Court then redrew some of the boundaries to comport with Maryland law requiring the boundaries to be geographically appropriate.

PERKS OF THE PRESIDENCY

In case you were concerned about how his disbarrment might have jeopardized former President Clinton's ability to make a living, you will be interested to learn that in 2001, in his first year after leaving office, Bill Clinton made $9.2 million. Most of this came from speeches, including a payment of $350,000 for speaking at a Chinese real estate seminar in Shanghai; $450,000 from a three-day stint in Tokyo; and $400,000 for three speeches to a Jewish philanthropy in Scotland. And Mr. Clinton's future looks even better. According to Wesley Pruden, Mr. Clinton has a contract guaranteeing him $10 million in advance for the publishing of his memoirs. All of this is in addition to his plush lifetime pension with extensive fringe benefits. Mr. Clinton should be well provided for even if he does not land the TV talk show job he is seeking.

Despite these substantial fringe benefits, on July 26th, Mr. Clinton asked to have taxpayers reimburse him for legal bills he ran up in connection with the Whitewater investigations. *The Washington Times* reported that Mr. Clinton's attorney's fees totaled from $1.75 million to $6.5 million. That is a wide disparity. The report did not say whether these included any impeachment-related bills.

2.2.2
9.1.4

CAMPAIGN FINANCE REFORM ACT—A Monument to the Ignorance of the American People and to the Phoniness of Congress

On March 27, 2002, President George Bush signed into law the Campaign Finance Reform Act of 2002. Even before it was signed, efforts were underway to challenge the constitutionality of this law in the courts. Indeed important portions of this law will certainly be struck down. But the real story behind the passage of this law is how it highlights the stupidity of the American people and how it demonstrates the superficiality and shallowness of Congress. This law will have little impact on Congressional politics, and those who say otherwise are either stupid or less than candid.

Here's why. The supporters of this law acknowledge that it will have little effect on separating the corrupting influence of money from federal elections, but they say it is a step in the right direction. No one expects this law to prevent those with money from influencing elections. At best, the supporters of this law **hope** that perhaps further laws can be enacted that will eliminate the possibility of buying elections. Is there any sane person who would bet on this happening? Of course not! It will never happen. A democratic government is based upon **popularity**; and popularity is inextricably connected to money. If the influence of money on elections could ever be eliminated, it would at the same time destroy the democratic nature of our government.

I suppose our astute senators and representatives would acknowledge this if they were forced to logically respond. But they nevertheless insist that we have to reduce or eliminate the influence of special interests on elections. But this is another incredibly stupid argument. To the extent that we could eliminate the influence of some special interests, to that extent we would be promoting other interests.

Well, perhaps our Congress would argue that we only want to eliminate or curtail **certain** special interests. Is that a reassuring thought to anyone? Do you think for one minute that Congress could agree on a specific list of special interests that must be silenced? No way! All interests are special. It is the multiple special interests of the American people that shape our civic debates and which is the foundation of our democratic republican government.

The only way the Campaign Finance Reform Act got enough votes was because it attempted to curtail financial influence by the application of regulations that applied to dollar amounts, without consideration of the point of view of the contributor. But does anyone seriously believe that these rules—even if they are upheld by the Supreme Court—will stop the flow of money into election campaigns? Of course it won't! Does anyone really think that the political parties won't figure out how to raise money in conformity with the new rules? Of course they will!

The whole campaign finance reform movement is just a massive parade of charades. It's a big joke. And if John McCain et al really do seriously think this will reform government, then this would only prove that they are lacking in *gravitas*. They lose much credibility in my eyes when they emphatically and forcefully argue that this is an important law that must be passed for the good of the nation, and then they make sure the law does not take effect until after the next election. Some analysts have aptly named the law—the Incumbent Protection Act.

And what about President Bush? He promised in his campaign to oppose such a law; but now he signed it. I suppose politically he did the best thing, because the issue basically died once he signed the act. Now, he can just wait for the Supreme Court to overturn some or all of it.

And even if the Act should survive intact, it won't affect Bush's campaign—he is the all-time best fund raiser this nation has ever seen; no one has ever received contributions from more individuals than he. If he were to lose the support of some special interest groups, he would make it up in more individual support—he knows it! The front page headline in *The Washington Post* said it best on March 28th: "Bush Signs Campaign Bill, Hits Road to Raise Money."

And about the signing of the bill—President Bush signed the bill into law unannounced, early in the morning, in the privacy of his office without any bill sponsors present to celebrate. Senators McCain and Feingold were nowhere to be seen. Why?--because President Bush was signing reluctantly, without any desire to celebrate. Senator McCain would have celebrated with an exuberance that would have only embarrassed President Bush. The President signed it with misgivings. He had campaigned against it. His signing it was an act of political expediency—his conservative backers would forgive him for it, and it would likely build his support from moderates.

Indeed there is much to be embarrassed about in the new law. Congress worked very hard to make itself look foolish and manipulative when it delayed the so-called important changes so they would not take effect until after the next election. Boy! Doesn't that provision send a powerful message? And for those who might ask to what message am I referring, it is this: The law is a joke and a sham; its only purpose is to allow them to convince their gullible constituents that they are acting to clean up politics and to eliminate those nasty special interests from buying elections. Unfortunately, in a democratic republic where the ignorant, the naïve, and those dependent on government for their support **can all vote**, this hollow, superficial and false message **will** win them some votes. Of course, this paragraph brings up a topic that we will not be able to fully discuss here—that is how the masters of deceit can manipulate the ignorant, the duped, the naïve and the evil among our voters.

The principal constitutional flaw with the Campaign Finance Reform Act is that it interferes with free speech—the right to an open and robust dialogue of the issues. The placing of the media and the press at a preferred station vis a vis the candidates also cannot stand under the First Amendment. With respect to the new prohibitions against "soft money," the Supreme Court may uphold them. In the 2001 case of *FEC v. Colorado Republican Federal Campaign Committee*, 533 U.S. 431 (2001), the Court showed its support of laws that regulated the spending of soft money (which they called "coordinated expenditures"). And even if the Supreme Court may have erred in its judgment in this matter, it ultimately won't matter much because the popular candidates will easily get around it.

Look! The best approach to campaign contributions is to require full disclosure and to provide some free air time and press space for candidates; this would do more to level the playing field and would do more to help the poor but qualified candidate compete with the rich candidate. But the complex and flawed campaign finance regulations fix nothing; they only create the opportunity for more loopholes, all the while its supporters go on the trail patting themselves on the back for passing a law that is as phony as fools gold.

NINTH CIRCUIT HOLDS THAT PLEDGE OF ALLEGIANCE IS UNCONSTITUTIONAL

On June 26, 2002, the United States Court of Appeals for the Ninth Circuit ruled that the words "under God" in the Pledge of Allegiance made it unconstitutional for a state school to practice daily recitation of the Pledge of Allegiance with those words in it. *Newdow v. United States Congress*, 292 F.3d 597 (9th Cir. 2002); 2002 U.S. App. LEXIS 12576.

This ruling was met with disapproval from President Bush, who called the ruling "ridiculous" and from most of Congress. Hopefully, this ruling will demonstrate the folly that will result if jurists continue to follow the anti-religion rationales that have come to be popular among many judges.

In an accompanying article, I have addressed the ACLU campaign to remove monuments of the Ten Commandments in many cities around the nation. It is virtually the same legal issue that governs both the monument cases and the Pledge of Allegiance case. I won't repeat those arguments here. However, I will reproduce below some of the language from the majority opinion and from the dissent opinion.

from the Majority Opinion (pp. 24-26)—

In the context of the Pledge, the statement that the United States is a nation "under God" is an endorsement of religion. It is a profession of a religious belief, namely, a belief in monotheism. The recitation that ours is a nation "under God" is not a mere acknowledgment that many Americans believe in a deity. Nor is it merely descriptive of the undeniable historical significance of religion in the founding of the Republic. Rather the phrase "one nation under God" in the context of the Pledge is normative. To recite the Pledge is not to describe the United States; instead, it is to swear allegiance to the values for which the flag stands: unity, indivisibility, liberty, justice, and – since 1954 – monotheism. The text of the official Pledge,

codified in federal law, impermissibly takes a position with respect to the purely religious question of the existence and identify of God. A profession that we are a nation "under God" is identical, for Establishment Clause purposes, to a profession that we are a nation "under Jesus," a nation "under Vishnu," a nation "under Zeus," or a nation "under no god," because none of these professions can be neutral with respect to religion. "The government must pursue a course of complete neutrality toward religion." *Wallace*, 472 U.S. at 60. **[1]** Furthermore, the school district's practice of teacher-led recitation of the Pledge aims to inculcate in students a respect for the ideals set forth in the Pledge, and thus amounts to state endorsement of these ideals. Although students cannot be forced to participate in recitation of the Pledge, **[2]** the

---

[1] The majority accurately cite the Supreme Court's statement in *Wallace v. Jaffre*, 472 U.S. 38, the 1984 case that struck down an Alabama law calling for a moment of silence each morning in public schools, providing a time for the children to pray. As discussed in another issue of *CLU*, this writer disagrees with the holding and the reasoning of the Supreme Court in that case. Of particular concern is the "complete neutrality" doctrine that is a departure from the original meaning of the First Amendment. However, even the Supreme Court does not regard its "neutrality" doctrine as an absolute, for the Supreme Court has also stated that the Constitution "affirmatively mandates accommodation, not merely tolerance" of religion. *Lynch v. Donnelly*, 465 U.S. 668, 473 (1984). And in 1952 the Supreme Court stated that "[w]e are a religious people whose institutions presuppose a Supreme Being." *Zorach v. Clauson*, 343 U.S. 306, 313.

At this point in First Amendment jurisprudence, the Supreme Court has rendered so many opinions, that it is not possible to reconcile every holding—at least not if every principle stated is made into an absolute, unmodifiable rule. Jurists must recognize and give deference to the most important underlying principles, when principles conflict.

[2] In 1943 the Supreme Court held in *West Virginia State Board of Education v. Barnette*, 319 U.S. 624, that a state could not compel students to recite the Pledge of Allegiance. This would be a violation of the Free Exercise Clause of the First Amendment. Implicit in that ruling, the Court upheld the state practice of leading the students each day in reciting the Pledge. This distinction should continue to govern where individuals complain about reciting the pledge. Individuals have the right to remain silent, and not to be punished therefor.

9.2

school district is nonetheless conveying a message of state endorsement of a religious belief when it requires public school teachers to recite, and lead the recitation of, the current form of the Pledge.

from the Dissenting Opinion (pp. 40, 42 & 46)—

We are asked to hold that inclusion of the phrase "under God" in this nation's Pledge of Allegiance violates the religion clauses of the Constitution of the United States. We should do no such thing. We should, instead, recognize that those clauses were not designed to drive religious expression out of public thought; they were written to avoid discrimination.

In *County of Allegheny*, 492 U.S. at 602-03, 109 S.Ct. at 3106, the Supreme Court had this to say: "Our previous opinions have considered in dicta the motto and the pledge, characterizing them as consistent with the proposition that government may not communicate an endorsement of religious belief.

My reading of the stelliscript suggests that upon Newdow's theory of our Constitution, accepted by my colleagues today, we will soon find ourselves prohibited from using our album of patriotic songs in many public settings. "God Bless America" and "America the Beautiful" will be gone for sure, and while use of the first and second stanzas of the Star Spangled Banner will still be permissible, we will be precluded from straying into the third. And currency beware! Judges can accept those results if they limit themselves to elements and tests, while failing to look at the good sense and principles that animated those tests in the first place.

The Ninth Circuit's Pledge of Allegiance case has certainly captured the nation's attention. Hopefully, this will help the nation to pay enough attention to this debate to learn how in the last fifty years the courts have gone astray from the traditional interpretation of the

Establishment Clause that was almost universally accepted for 150 years. The majority judges in the Pledge of Allegiance case have adopted the philosophy of those who seek to establish a freedom from religion. This they are already free to do for themselves. But the "neutrality" that they seek is nothing more than "hostility" towards God and religion. Retaining the words "under God" in the Pledge of Allegiance is right and proper; it imposes no burden on people, and it poses no coercion to making anyone practice one particular religion. It certainly does not establish a religion in violation of the First Amendment. The Ninth Circuit ruling should be reversed as soon as possible, and it should be rejected by other Circuit Courts who later address the same issue.

NATIONAL CAMPAIGN TO REMOVE TEN COMMANDMENTS MONUMENTS FROM CITY PROPERTIES

There is a national, constitutional battle being waged to prevent the government from expressing thanks to God, from invoking the blessings of God and from accommodating religion. A significant segment of Americans support this narrow interpretation of the First Amendment's Establishment Clause. This new and narrow view seeks a total separation of government from any and all references to a Supreme Being. This narrow viewpoint is held by a number of judges around the country, and it is reflected in the 2-to-1 majority votes of two three-judge panels on the Seventh Circuit Court of Appeals, which has recently ruled that two different monuments in Indiana displaying the Ten Commandments were unconstitutional. *Books v. City of Elkhart, Indiana*, 235 F.3d 292 (7th Cir. 2000) (monument in front of city municipal building); and *Indiana Civil Liberties Union v. O'Bannon*, 259 F.3d 766 (7th Cir. 2001) (monument on Statehouse grounds). The U. S. Supreme Court declined the request to review the Elkhart, Indiana case in May, 2001.

The battle to establish this recently created view of the Establishment Clause has now come to Frederick, Maryland. Frederick cannot avoid taking sides on this issue. Frederick will either acquiesce to the movement that is hostile to religion, or Frederick will side with the view that the government can accommodate religion and the belief in God.

The restrictive view of the Establishment Clause described above is a departure from the original intent and meaning of the First Amendment. But this new, restrictive view is not shared by all judges, governmental leaders or citizens. The initial view of the Establishment Clause of the First Amendment continues to be held by a large segment of society. This

traditional view disputes the correctness of the ruling and the rationale of the Seventh Circuit. The traditional interpretation of the Establishment Clause that was almost universally held in our nation for the first 150 years following the ratification of the First Amendment is that the Establishment Clause prohibits the government from establishing one religion over others, but it provides for the government to accommodate religion, and it upholds governmental action that acknowledges the blessings of God in our nation. This point of view is held by many judges in other federal courts and by some of the Justices of the U. S. Supreme Court. What the exact count is we cannot be sure. Until another circuit court of appeals issues a ruling that contradicts the Seventh Circuit's ruling in *Books v. Elkhart*, the U. S. Supreme Court cannot be expected to weigh in on this issue.

Some Frederick citizens have been quick to express their opinions that the Ten Commandments monument in their city/county memorial part is unconstitutional. Such opinions are hasty and ill-founded. Four reasons support the opposite conclusion.

First, even if the *Books v. Elkhart* ruling by the Seventh Circuit were binding on Frederick, Maryland (which it is not because we are in a different federal circuit—the Fourth), our monument is in full compliance with the requirements that the two Indiana monuments were found to violate. (a) The Frederick monument is in a memorial park, it is not in front of a city municipal building nor on the grounds of the chief building of a state or city government. (b) The Frederick monument is only one of six or seven monuments in this park, and it is only a minor monument in relation to the four large monument displays in the park. Taken in the totality of its circumstances, the Frederick monument display does not convey the message that one particular religion has been established by Frederick City.

Second, there is good reason to believe that the Fourth Circuit would embrace an Establishment Clause interpretation more in keeping with that of the Tenth Circuit and with the minority opinions in the two Seventh Circuit monument cases. The Tenth Circuit reached the opposite conclusion, holding that a Ten Commandments monument was proper in *Anderson v. Salt Lake City*, 475 F.2d 29, (1973). The Tenth Circuit reaffirmed this holding in *Summum v. Callaghan*, 130 F.3d 906 (1997). The Fourth Circuit reviewed a North Carolina Ten Commandments monument case in 1997, but the court decided the case before it reached the question of whether that monument violated the Establishment Clause. *Suhre v. Haywood County*, 131 F.3d 1083 (4th Cir. 1997). The next year, however, the Fourth circuit did decide a case with a similar Establishment Clause issue. *Peck v. Upshur County Board of Education*, 155 F.3d 274 (4th Cir. 1998). In *Peck*, the Fourth Circuit upheld a school policy that designated a single day each year on which private religious groups could make Bibles and other religious materials available on tables for students. The court said this practice did not violate the Establishment Clause because the policy was not adopted to advance religion, but for the secular purpose of opening a forum for public speech. The Fourth Circuit's reasoning conflicts with that of the Seventh Circuit in interpreting the Establishment Clause.

Third, there were three significant flaws in the reasoning of the majority opinions in the two Seventh Circuit Ten Commandments cases. (a) Those judges erroneously interpreted the first prong of the three-part test in *Lemon v. Kurtzman*, 403 U.S. 602 (1971) to require that the government purpose for keeping the monument must be exclusively secular; but *Lemon* only requires that the government have *a* secular purpose—this is a minimal requirement. (b) Those judges also went astray in their application of the second prong of the *Lemon v.*

Kurtzman test, where they concluded that "the primary effect" of the government in keeping the monument was to advance religion. This particular test is acknowledged to be susceptible to subjective analysis and manipulation to reach whatever result one desires. The dissenting judges in both *Books v. Elkhart* and *ICLU v. O'Bannon* concluded that the primary effect of keeping the monuments did not advance religion. (c) In addition, the third *Lemon* test should be either thrown out or modified because it introduced a drastic change in the meaning of the Establishment Clause: It made it unconstitutional to advance religion in general, rather than to advance one particular religion. When the Supreme Court made this change it drastically changed the meaning of the Establishment Clause. The Supreme Court and other courts should drop this third test and return to the original meaning.

Fourth, other Supreme Court Establishment Clause cases that use an entirely different line of reasoning (different from the *Lemon v. Kurtzman* analysis) support a government's retaining a monument of the Ten Commandments. The Supreme Court has upheld the constitutionality of government displays of purely religious symbols—a creche and a menorah—when they were a part of a larger display. *Lynch v. Donnelly*, 465 U.S. 668 (1984); and *Allegheny v. ACLU*, 492 U.S. 573 (1989). The Court has upheld the hiring of chaplains by Congress and the opening of Congressional sessions with prayer. *Marsh v. Chambers*, 463 U.S. 783 (1983). The Court upheld mandatory Sunday closing laws in *McGowan v. Maryland*, 366 U.S. 420 (1960). Numerous governmental practices which pay homage to our religious heritage are regarded as being in harmony with the First Amendment— Christmas and Thanksgiving holidays, military chaplains, the national motto ("In God We Trust," which is on our currency), and the Pledge of Allegiance. See *Lynch v. Donnelly*, in which the Supreme Court pointed out that the

Constitution does not require a complete separation of church and state, but rather "affirmatively mandates accommodation, not merely tolerance." *Lynch*, 465 U.S. at 473. And the Supreme Court stated in *Zorach v. Clauson*, 343 U.S. 306, 313 (1952) that "[w]e are a religious people whose institutions presuppose a Supreme Being."

Frederick City officials have voiced the concern that it would be costly to fight a legal battle to keep its monument. Costly is a relative term, and I would say that there would be some cost, but not a great cost. Organizations and individuals have already offered to do the legal work to help the city litigate this battle. So the cost would be minimal. The ACLU has threatened Frederick by stating that the City would have to pay for the ACLU legal fees if the ACLU wins. There are a lot of ifs in this threat, including "if the ACLU wins," which is no sure bet. But even if the ACLU were to win, this is a battle that is well worth the cost.

Some have objected to Frederick's using taxpayer monies to fight to keep a monument that some citizens don't want to pay to keep. Of course, the government regularly spends money to promote one cause and to oppose another, and invariably a minority will oppose how the government spends money. This cannot be avoided. But the Establishment Clause issue with the Ten Commandments monument is much larger than the six-food granite monument. And the battle is more than just a city battle. The battle is part of a national war about whether America will continue to openly thank God for His blessings, or whether America will cower and acquiesce to those who seek to purge God from American government.* This is an

important issue. It is worth the cost to fight against those who seek to turn a God-fearing nation into an atheist-fearing nation.

Regardless of the cost, this is a battle that Frederick should fight. Those who want the Ten Commandments monument removed will not be satisfied until they have also removed "under God" from the Pledge of Allegiance; until they have removed "In God We Trust" from our currency and off the wall in the House of Representatives; until the Supreme Court and Congress are prohibited from making any utterance that acknowledges a belief in God; and until all other favorable references to God by the President and all other government officials are made illegal. I believe it would be bad for our nation to go down that road. Now is the time to take a stand for permitting the government to express belief in and gratitude to God without compelling citizens to do anything except to perhaps have their hearing offended by listening to this humble expression.

Frederick City must decide whether it will fight the efforts of a vocal minority to remove the Ten Commandments monument from the memorial park. The Constitution does not require it. Frederick cannot avoid taking sides on this issue. Frederick should do the right thing and fight to keep the Ten Commandments monument.

Governmental acknowledgement of God did not use to be a violation of the Establishment Clause. It should not become so now. Governmental acknowledgement of God does not establish any one religion. If Frederick City chooses to subscribe to the narrow view that all references to God must be eliminated from government, then Frederick will contribute to the establishment of anti-religion and atheism as the official church-of-state. The First Amendment was never intended to bring this result. The First Amendment has historically accommodated governmental endorsement of the belief in God so long as it does not go so far as to establish one governmental religion.

---

* One organization that has sought to remove Ten Commandments monuments is The Freedom From Religion Foundation. The name, of course, reflects the goal of this organization—which is to convert the Establishment Clause into an anti-religion clause. This organization recently lost a court battle to remove a Ten Commandments monument in Colorado. *State v. Freedom From Religion Foundation*, 898 P.2d 1013 (Colo. 1995).

The government cannot take a position here that will avoid offending everyone. Our democratic republic allows for legislators, executives and judges to acknowledge God and express belief in a Supreme Being, so long as no one religion is established by the government. A state or city is free to adopt an atheistic policy under democratic principles. But states and cities are also free to express gratitude to God and to invoke God's blessings in song, ceremony and rhetoric.

Frederick must not cave in to the whining of those who fight against God. There is no constitutional requirement to do so. The Constitution does not require the government to be hostile towards God and religion. If Frederick shuns the fight, then Frederick will be supporting the movement that seeks to excise God from government.

30 YEARS OF TITLE IX—
Lack of Common Sense Lifts Women's Sports Programs as It Kills Men's Sports Programs

In the 1970's the Equal Rights Amendment failed to become ratified because it failed to acknowledge that our law should accommodate some differences between men and women. The ERA would have required absolute equality between the sexes.

But while the ERA failed, Title IX of the Civil Rights Act of 1972 has succeeded in establishing this absolute equality standard in college athletics. It is almost universally acknowledged that this is not good, but Title IX has become "a genie out of the bottle gone bad," and no one can put the genie back in.

An estimated 400 men's athletic programs have been eliminated from American colleges because of the strict equality standards imposed by Title IX,[1] and more eliminations are expected. It is mostly the minor sports that take the hit—wrestling teams, golf teams, tennis teams, swimming teams—but also some baseball teams. Football and basketball teams have survived—because they generate revenues for colleges, but Title IX forces colleges to eliminate other men's teams to bring the number of female and male athletes into balance. This rigid equality has not been good.

If Title IX could have been administered with more soundness, the women's programs could have been lifted without killing the non-income producing men's sports. There are no women's counterparts for either football or wrestling. And football requires so many male athletes that wrestling programs must often be eliminated to bring the men:women ratio in line. Title IX should either have been modified or interpreted so as to prevent the harsh result. Frankly, just exempting football programs from the numbers ratios would have prevented or solved most of this problem.

This is not merely an issue of elective athletics. Corresponding with the cuts in men's programs is a drop in men graduating from college. Only 43% of college graduates today are men. (Report in *The Washington Post*, June 25, 2002.) This raises a serious societal issue about the changing roles of men and women in our society. With women now graduating in greater numbers than men, this means that fewer women are leaving school to have families. This represents a growing rejection by women of the value to society of a woman's contribution as a mother and homemaker. This also means that more women are competing with men in the work force—therefore making it tougher for some men to find employment. It also means an increase in the trend to value women according to traditional standards for valuing men; this in turn rejects the different and important role of women as mothers and homemakers.

Christina Hoff Sommers, a scholar at the American Enterprise Institute, said this about the new trend:

> What does it mean in the long run that we have females who are significantly more literate, significantly more educated than their male counterparts? It is likely to create a lot of social problems. This does not bode well for anyone.

(Quoted in *The Washington Post*, June 25, 2002.)

Title IX is in large part responsible for the decreasing number of male college graduates. Ultimately men and women will suffer from the effects of laws that seek to establish absolute equality between the sexes. Sound discretion in celebrating the differences in men and women is the best approach. We are reaping the ill effects of Title IX, which rejects this approach.

---

[1] On May 30, 2002, the United States Court of Appeals for the Eighth Circuit ruled that Title IX "does not require proportionality," but it "does not forbid it either." *Chalenor v. Univ. of North Dakota*, ____ F.3d ____ ; 2002 U.S. App. LEXIS 14404 (8th Cir. 2002). By this ruling, the eight circuits that have now addressed this issue are all of one accord. The effect of this decision is to further strengthen the stranglehold that Title IX has on college athletics.

SUPREME COURT RULES DEATH PENALTY IS UNCONSTITUTIONAL FOR MENTALLY RETARDED

On June 20, 2002, the Supreme Court ruled (6-3) that the Eighth Amendment prohibition against cruel and unusual punishment now prohibits the execution of defendants having an IQ below 70. *Atkins v. Virginia*, ___ U.S. ___; 122 S.Ct. 2242 (2002). This result is not remarkable, but the Court's rationale is a little disconcerting.

Writing for the majority, Justice Stevens cited public opinion and the views of professional and religious organizations as its basis for creating a new standard on cruel and unusual punishment. This polling rationale is troubling because it amounts to nothing more than a subjective standard. Certainly some subjectivity will always make its way into the sentencing process, but the ruling in *Atkins* is more bold and audacious. Hopefully this new subjectivity test will be limited in application.

SUPREME COURT LIMITS THE RIGHT TO REMAIN SILENT

On June 10, 2002, the Supreme Court upheld a Kansas law requiring sex-offender inmates to admit their crimes and give details of their sexual history (including acts for which they were never charged) as prerequisites to getting out of maximum security cells and into treatment programs. *McKune v. Lile*, ___ U.S. ___, 122 S.Ct. ___ (2002).

Four justices (Stevens, Souter, Ginsberg & Breyer) viewed the Kansas law as violative of the Fifth Amendment privilege against self-incrimination. Four of the justices disagreed, stating that that these conditional requirements were "minimal incentives" for offenders who were "a serious threat." The deciding vote was cast by Justice O'Connor, who stated that the "liberty interests" involved in determining whether an inmate was in maximum security or a treatment program are not protected by the Constitution.

SUPREME COURT UPHOLDS MANDATORY DRUG TESTING FOR PARTICIPANTS IN PUBLIC SCHOOL EXTRA-CURRICULAR SPORTS

On June 27, 2002, the Supreme Court in a 5-4 ruling, held that public schools can test children for drugs as a prerequisite to participating in extracurricular activities. *Pottawatomie County v. Earls*, ___ U.S. ___, 122 S.Ct. 2559 (2002). Four justices said that the drug-testing program under scrutiny was "capricious, even perverse." But five justices disagreed.

SUPREME COURT STRIKES DOWN OHIO LAW REQUIRING PERMIT FOR DOOR TO DOOR PROSELYTIZING

On June 17, 2002, the Supreme Court (in an 8 –1 vote) struck down the town ordinance of Stratton, Ohio that required anyone going door to door in that community to register with the town and to carry a permit. *Watchtower Bible and Tract Society v. Stratton,* ___ U.S. ___, 122 S.Ct. 2080 (2002). The Jehovah's Witnesses' Watchtower Bible and Tract Society sued in federal district court to have the ordinance invalidated, contending that it violated their freedom of religious expression protected under the First Amendment. The district court ruled against the Jehovah's Witnesses as did the Sixth Circuit Court of Appeals. However, the Supreme Court agreed with the Jehovah's Witnesses and overturned the lower court decision. Only Chief Justice Rehnquist dissented.

This case is especially significant for Jehovah's Witnesses and Mormons and other religions that go home to home in sharing their religious messages. Justice Stevens, who wrote the opinion, said that the ruling would save the Jehovah's Witnesses from "petty prosecutions."

Stratton, Ohio had passed the ordinance in order to protect its citizens from unwanted peddlers and con artists. Chief Justice Rehnquist observed that the law did not give the own the right to deny a permit to Jehovah's Witnesses, but eight justices felt that even the registration requirement was too much. Justice Stevens wrote: "It is offensive—not only to the values protected by the First Amendment, but to the very notion of a free society—that in the context of everyday public discourse a citizen must first inform the government of her desire to speak to her neighbors and then obtain a permit to do so."

THIRD CIRCUIT HOLDS PUBLIC LIBRARIES CAN'T BAR ALL COMPUTER PORNOGRAPHY

On May 31, 2002, the United States District Court for the Eastern District of Pennsylvania held the Children's Internet Protection Act (CIPA) to be unconstitutional. *American Library Assoc., Inc. v. United States.* CIPA would have required public libraries to use filters on all their computers to block access to pornographic sites. The Court said that CIPA went too far, by blocking access to protected speech.

Attorneys for the United States argued that internet smut is so pervasive that filter protections are necessary to protect youth. Even though CIPA had a provision where adults could have the filters removed for their use, it was successfully argued that this procedure might embarrass the adult or cause him to lose his right to remain anonymous.

9.2

SUPREME COURT UPHOLDS
USE OF SCHOOL VOUCHERS

On June 27, 2002, the Supreme Court (by a 5-4 vote) upheld the Ohio School voucher law that allowed a state to give vouchers of up to $2,250 per pupil to families who put their students in private schools. *Zelman v. Simmons-Harris,* _____ U.S. _____; 122 S.Ct. 2460 (2002).

This ruling is significant because it holds that the Establishment Clause of the First Amendment is not violated by the use of state funds to help finance the education for children in private schools, including private religious schools.

This case may have some bearing on litigation aimed at removing Ten Commandments monuments from government property around the nation. The case demonstrates that the "wall of separation" analogy is inaccurate and misleading—there is no wall of separation between church and state. The nebulous "excessive entanglement" test is a more accurate analogy.

Opponents to school vouchers worry that the payment of such vouchers improperly mingles the operation of governments with religion. But the Supreme Court reaffirms that the Establishment Clause permits a certain involvement between government and religion. As the Supreme Court stated in *Lynch v. Donnelly,* 465 U.S. at 473, the Constitution "affirmatively mandates accommodation" of religion.

Fight for Freedom—
Struggle against Stupidity

Editorials and opinion pieces from just one day in one of my local papers, the April 11th issue of *The Frederick Gazette*, prompt me to pen my own opinion piece on one of the chief challenges to our liberties under the Constitution. I am speaking of the continuing battle against stupidity. To illustrate, consider key statements from three opinion pieces appearing in this community newspaper:

1. Helen G. Alexander writes:
"scientists who worked … at Ft. Detrick know the facts....Vaccines contaminated with the AIDS virus spread AIDS. **Vaccines put out by Merck Bionetics and Litton Bionetics started AIDS**....Actually, gays were inoculated with Hepatitis B vaccine in several large cities—New York, San Francisco and others—which contained the AIDS virus, in other words, contaminated vaccines, which was intentional."

2. In her piece titled, "Slavery reparations are right thing to do," Dawn S. Onley writes:
"Johnny Cochran [and others] filed three class-action lawsuits on behalf of 35 million American descendants of slavery. They named FleetBoston Financial Corp, ...Aetna, Inc.,...and CSX Corp as defendants that all profited from slavery's evil grasp....

The suit goes back to 1619, when the first Dutch ship arrived at Jamestown packed with slaves.

Let me explain why reparations are needed. They are needed to right America's wrongs. They are needed so that African-Americans can finally heal. They are needed to bring about a truce in race relations....

Affirmative action wasn't about slavery. It was about doing what was right. It was about discrimination. The best person should get the job regardless of his or her color....

[H]undreds of years of unpaid labor in America must be made right.

It was for the Jews. Holocaust victims won a $1.25 billion settlement from three Swiss banks to compensate for their slave labor....

Should women get reparations as well for not being allowed to vote prior to Aug. 26, 1920?"

3. Denise Branch, president of the Frederick County NAACP writes:
"[W]e need ...to address the criminalization of poor people and people of color....

In almost every state in this country, African American and Hispanic American children are being locked up at a disproportionate rate and given harsher sentences than their Caucasian peers, though they commit crimes at roughly the same rate and proportion....

[W]e know from experience that we are treated differently because of the color of our skin....

For certain racial and ethnic groups, being arrested and locked up is a given."

It is alarming to consider the extent to which people's beliefs and motives are based upon falsehood and irrational thought. Examine a little more closely the above, irrational arguments about:

1. The Cause of AIDS;
2. Slavery Reparations; and
3. False Bias Accusations.

I. The Cause of AIDS
Helen Alexander's assertion that the spread of AIDS was an "intentional" effort, accomplished by intentionally vaccinating gays with contaminated Hepatitis B vaccines is an astounding allegation. Ms. Alexander cites no specific support for this. Intelligent people dismiss this as nonsense, without support for it. But the ignorant are free, in America, to believe nonsense, if they wish.

II. Slavery Reparations
Dawn Onley's argument for the payment of slavery reparations is probably as good an argument as can be made, but it is feeble and

unpersuasive. The legal obstacles to a law suit to recovery such reparations are so substantial, that Johnny Cochran would have to pull a rabbit out of the hat to succeed. Of course, Mr. Cochran did just that in getting the acquittal of O. J. Simpson. But the reparations suit is even more daunting. Perhaps a better analogy would be that of pulling an elephant out of a hat. For starters, the statute of limitations ran out on this law suit about 137 years ago. Secondly, the specific proof of damages to particular people is virtually impossible. And, finally, the reparations movement seeks to recover from those who have absolutely no culpability for enslaving people over 140 years ago. Of course, Ms. Onley does not mention these problems. But I must highlight some of the absurd things she does address.

If the law suit includes allegations dating back to 1619—this was 155 years before the founding of the United States of America. And I believe it was at least that many years prior to the founding of FleetBoston Financial, Aetna and CSX. Only if illogic, error and stupidity govern the legal process, could wrong doing from the year 1619 become the basis for recovering damages today.

Ms. Onley argues that receiving damages from FleetBoston Financial, Aetna and CSX would "right America's wrongs." This is nonsense. Such a recovery would not be from America. It could not "right" anything that America did.

Ms. Onley claims that obtaining such a recovery is "needed so that African-Americans can finally heal." This is an assertion that cannot withstand scrutiny. Who can say with a straight face today that he or she is wounded today because America suffered slavery to exist over 135 years ago? I know there are some who can do this, but they cannot establish the proximate cause for such pretended injuries. Where there are race-based wounds today, we have laws to address many of them, and other means can be used to address other injuries. But frankly, some

people today develop victim attitudes, where they see themselves as the victims of racial discrimination where such does not exist. This attitude prevents healing, and not until individuals can separate real injuries from the perceived but non-existent injuries, will these individuals ever be able to heal. Obtaining a slavery reparations award will not facilitate this healing.

Ms. Onley claims that a reparations award would bring about a "truce in race relations." This is nonsense. First of all, our laws have long established equal rights for minorities—a "truce," if you will. But good laws cannot eliminate all bad conduct of all individuals. We cannot expect to eliminate all evil, as long as we give people the freedom to think and act and speak. Neither would a reparations award change this. At best, Ms. Onley's thinking is just wishful; it is not precise and soundly reasoned.

But from here, Ms. Onley's argument degenerates into ignorance. She equates "affirmative action" with the notion that: "The best person should get the job regardless of his or her color." That is not affirmative action; affirmative action is that many minority individuals will get the job because of his or her color. Affirmative action is a discriminatory policy whose purpose is to attempt to correct past acts of discrimination. But as an enduring policy it violates the very principle it was invented to correct.

Then Ms. Onley goes totally off the wall in her characterization of the monies now being made available to families of holocaust survivors. Ms. Onley states that Swiss banks are making payments to compensate Jews for their "slave labor." This is totally false. The Swiss banks paid funds to survivors of account holders—this was not pay for slave labor. [1]

_____
[1] Perhaps she confuses the Swiss banks payments with ICHEIC payments. But ICHEIC payments are not for slave labor either.

ICHEIC stands for the International Commission on Holocaust Era Insurance Claims. ICHEIC was funded by

Ms. Onley frankly does not know what she is talking about.

And finally, Ms. Onley warns us that in the future we may expect her to lead the charge for reparations for the ancestors of those women who were denied the right to vote in federal elections until August 26, 1920. It is clear to me, that Ms. Onley will be the right person to bring that suit. We'll look forward to reading about that later.

III. False Bias Accusations

Denise Branch, the head of a local chapter of the NAACP—apparently sees racial prejudice in virtually everything—whether or not it actually exists. This is another manifestation of the "victim's attitude" that seems to infect some minorities. I speak up against it because it can create the very problem it seeks to eliminate; it can be as invidious and as wrong as the very racism that it opposes. If someone wrongly accuses me of being a racist, when I am not, then this false accusation fosters the very problem it attempts to eradicate. Minorities must be careful not to fall prey to the inclination to misjudge and prejudge. When leaders of the NAACP are possessed of this victim's attitude, they can cause much damage and create additional racial discord. The example of Martin Luther King, Jr. was not tainted by this impatience and prejudice. Minority leaders will be more effective if they avoid this flaw.

Ms. Branch states that "we are treated differently because of the color of our

---

five major insurance companies, some funding by the German government and some funding by some European businesses. Payments are made to heirs of holocaust victims who had not previously been able to prove their entitlement to benefits. The insurance companies had contractual liability to make payments. The expansiveness of the holocaust would have resulted in a windfall to these insurance companies at the expense of victims who were deprived of the ability to prove claims. ICHEIC has provided a remedy for this. These funds are being released now through the use of relaxed standards to prove the existence of policies.

skin....For certain racial and ethnic groups, being arrested and locked up is a given." This categorical condemnation of the entire American society is both wrong and harmful to improving the racial problems that do exist. It is counterproductive to deny the work and motives of good people and the good that does exist. Sufficient legal and institutional changes have now taken place so that correcting the wrongs that continue to happen must be done on an individualized, specific basis. The continued cries of extremist militant minorities to make a wholesale condemnation of America is no longer productive; it is divisive and counterproductive to the advancement of rights for minorities.

Ms. Branch may have coined a phrase, when she decried the "criminalization of poor people and people of color." The implicit accusation in this phrase is that of blaming American society for making criminals of "people of color." This, again, is another manifestation of the "victim's attitude"—that always seeks to blame someone else for one's problems. As a generalization, this attitude prevents one from taking responsibility for one's own actions, and becoming one who blazes his own trails, seeks and accomplishes his own goals, and determines his own success. Leaders who attempt to instill this "victim's attitude" do their followers a great disservice.

Finally, Ms. Branch makes the false statement that she wishes or thinks were true. If true it would perhaps sustain her "victim's attitude". She states:

> "In almost every state in this country, African American and Hispanic American children are being locked up at a disproportionate rate and given harsher sentences than their Caucasian peers, though they commit crimes at roughly the same rate and proportion."

This is just not true. Many educated black leaders and scholars are well aware of this myth that those of the "victim's attitude" like to believe. Two examples will demonstrate the folly of this statement. First, a recent study in

New Jersey showed that a higher rate of blacks speed than do whites. Second, Professor Walter Williams, a prominent black economist at George Mason University, specifically refutes this notion and this attitude. He states:

> Most violent crime in our country is committed by blacks. According to U.S. Department of Justice statistics, blacks commit 54 percent of murders, 42 percent of forcible rapes, 59 percent of robberies, and 38 percent of aggravated assaults. For the most part, the victims are black. Ninety-three percent of murdered blacks were murdered by a black....
>
> Part of doing something requires the recognition that politicians, black elite and civil rights organizations are virtually useless. If anything, their excuse-making gives aid and comfort to criminals.

Walter Williams, *More Liberty Means Less Government*, Hoover Institution Press, 1999, at 21 & 22 (quoting from a column he wrote September 24, 1997). In Dr. Williams' tongue-in-cheek column, "White People Are Divine," (written January 10, 1996), Dr. Williams said this:

> What else, other than racism, can explain how blacks, who are 13 percent of the population, are 66 percent of professional football players and 80 percent of basketball players? Some people might try genetic explanations like white men can't jump .... I don't buy it; it's racism.

Williams, 7.

It is difficult for a society to function on an enlightened and informed level, if ignorant and foolish ideas are recognized and honored. There are enough problems to correct, and enough information needed to keep society busy correcting and informing for a long time. Fostering and promoting falsehoods only complicates things. Freedom and justice must be based upon truth. There is no virtue in well-intended but ignorant accusation. Falsehood and stupidity tends to enslave rather than to liberate.

91

CONSTITUTIONAL

LAW

UPDATES

III:i   May 2003   No. 6

News Items through December 31. 2002—

2002 National Elections Report—

CONSTITUTIONAL LAW UPDATES is a quarterly newsletter edited and published by C. Paul Smith, J.D.
Subscription cost is $25.00 per year (plus $1.25 tax in MD). To subscribe, send a check or money order to
CONSTITUTIONAL LAW UPDATES. P. O. Box 1204. Frederick MD 21702-0204. For further information, visit
Paul Smith's web site at www.cpaulsmith.com.

Metropolitan Washington, D. C. Area Is Terrorized and Petrified by Snipers in October, 2002

On Thursday, October 24, 2002, at approximately midnight, police arrested John Allen Muhammad (41) and John Lee Malvo (17) at a Rest Area on Interstate 70 in Frederick County, Maryland. This brought to an end the reign of fear that Muhammad and Malvo had brought to millions of people from Richmond, Virginia to Baltimore, Maryland.

Between October 2nd and October 19th, 2002, there we fourteen separate sniper incidents in the Washington, D.C. metropolitan area—resulting in ten deaths and three wounded. Each incident was unprovoked. The victims were randomly targeted and shot with the same, .223 Bushmaster rifle, from a long distance away.

To give this a personal perspective, the first five murders took place in a five-mile radius of the home where I grew up—my mother still lives there; and my brother lives in a condominium in the same radius. I have been to the Shopper's Food Warehouse in Glenmont, where James D. Martin was killed at 6:04 p.m. on October 2nd. I regularly drive by the Fitzgerald Auto Mall in Rockville where James Buchanan was shot and killed at 7:41 a.m. on October 3rd. I've been to the Mobil gas station in Aspen Hill where Premkumar Walekar was killed at 8:12 a.m. on October 3rd. Conrad Johnson was shot and killed outside his bus a half-mile from here at 5:56 a.m. on October 22nd. I've shopped at the Leisure World shopping center where Sarah Ramos was shot and killed at 8:37 a.m. on October 3rd, and I've bought gas at the Shell gas

station in Kensington, where Lori Rivera was killed at 9:58 a.m. the same day.

Subsequently, the duo killed one man in Washington, D. C., and three people in Virginia.

The two suspects have yet to be convicted. (Although the trial of the 17-year-old, Malvo, is currently under way in Virginia. Virginia was given the first shot to try the younger defendant because Virginia law provided the possibility of the death penalty for the 17-year-old.)

While it does not yet appear that there is a formal connection between these criminals and the Al Qaeda, they nevertheless are terrorists, and there is evidence that the older one, Muhammad, had sympathies with anti-American terrorist groups. Muhammad received marksman training in the U. S. military, before being discharged. Malvo, for his part, is an illegal alien. The duo left messages for the police, saying, "Call me God," and "Your children are not safe anywhere at any time." The latter note was left after a 13-year-old boy was shot while entering middle school in Bowie, Maryland on October 7th. Fortunately, the boy is recovering from the bullet he took to the chest.

One of the effects of this sniper ordeal is the cold realization of how helpless we are to defend against terrorism like this. After Muhammad and Malvo were arrested, police reported that they had checked the suspect's license plates at least ten times in October before making the arrest. But until October 24th, the police did not have information that linked that license tag with the ten murders.

Another effect of the sniper ordeal may have been the building of support for President Bush, in his efforts to eradicate the principal terrorist cells around the world.

Imminent War with Iraq Dominates All Political Issues in the Fall of 2002

After the terrorist attacks of 9/11/02, President Bush singled out Iraq as one of the three evil empires in the world that must be dealt with. (Iran and North Korea were the others.) Despite world-wide condemnation of terrorism, Saddam Hussein defiantly applauded and encouraged terrorism against Israel by promising to give $25,000 to the surviving family of each suicide bomber who terrorized people in Israel. By September of 2002, the United States had all it could take from Saddam Hussein. President Bush demanded that Iraq either disclose and surrender all its weapons of mass destruction, or else the U.S. would do it for them. This threat was understood by both Americans and Iraqis to mean "war."

On September 12, 2002, a year and a day after 9/11/01, President Bush challenged the United Nations to back up the U.S. in forcing Iraq to comply with the conditions of its surrender in 1991, or else face its own irrelevance, as the U.S. would, by itself, if necessary, force Iraq to comply. The U.N. obliged the U.S. and issued Resolution 1441, which warned Iraq to disclose, disarm and comply OR ELSE be forced to do so. On October 10, 2002, the House of Representatives voted 296 to 133 to authorize the President to "use the armed forces of the United States as he determines to be necessary and appropriate in order to defend the national security of the United States against the continuing threat posed by Iraq." Senate approval followed, thereby authorizing the President to use military force against Iraq.

In late October the U. S. military dropped 180,000 leaflets over Iraq, warning them not to fire on U.S.-led troops if a conflict developed. On November 21st, NATO offered its full support of the U.S. in this standoff. Later in November, the U.S. military dropped thousands of additional leaflets warning Iraqis to not fight.

In early December, Iraq issued a 12,000-page report accounting for its weapons of mass destruction. But on December 19th, the United States rejected the report and declared Iraq to be in material breach of Resolution 1441. A day earlier, the Bush administration set late January as the time when it would decide whether to go to war with Iraq.

The American nation understood that President Bush was threatening war, and a large majority of the nation fully backed him in this. 9/11 changed everything for most Americans. The hatred of some for America had reached intolerable levels, as manifest by the mass terrorist murders of 9/11. America could no longer sit back and ignore the anti-America hatred that was spawning the terrorism that now threatened us.

The national resolve to address the international terrorism issue was not without appreciation of the fact that American lives would be risked. As the 2002 November elections were held, a solemn nation threw its support behind President George Bush to continue the course he outlined—including forcing Saddam Hussein to comply or be removed.

Your editor announces the publication of—

The State of the Constitution

In February, 2003, the writing and publication of The State of the Constitution was completed. This beautiful, annotated book on the Constitution is a now available for purchase. It is the book for which the Constitutional Law Updates (CLU) are written. The CLU inserts are made to provide up-to-date supplements for the book.

The State of the Constitution is a loose-leaf book that explains the meaning of the principal provisions of the Constitution. Particular attention is given to current issues and political developments. It comes in an attractive, three-ring notebook (8 ½ x 11) with section dividers to assist in locating subject areas. The book has both a Table of Contents and an Index, in addition to a fully annotated Constitution. Together, these resources make this an excellent reference system for quick retrieval of information. The book also features over forty color photographs of places that are important in our American history and government. The book's subtitle describes its helpful function— CITIZEN'S HANDBOOK.

To order—

    Mail your order and check to: CLU
                                                 P. O. Box 1204
                                                 Frederick, MD 21702-0204

    Or FAX your order to: (301) 762-0285

    Or call the law offices of C. Paul Smith toll-free at 1 (866) 268-5982

The cost of the book is $39.95 (+ $2.00 sales tax for Maryland residents). Make checks payable to "Constitutional Law Updates." VISA, Master Card and American Express are accepted.

REPUBLICANS MAKE BIG GAINS IN 2002 MID-TERM ELECTIONS

President George W. Bush and the Republican Party scored a big win in the 2002 mid-term elections. This was only the third time in the last one hundred years that the party of the incumbent President gained seats in Congress. Those gains were slight, but they were enough for the Republican Party to regain control of the Senate, giving the Republican Party control of both Houses and the Presidency. The Republican Party also increased its lead in the control of state executive branches—winning gubernatorial elections in the Democratic strongholds of Maryland, Massachusetts and Georgia.

Pundits will debate the reasons for this Republican victory for years to come. President Bush has been popular—he has governed with a positive, inclusive tone. His conservative politics did not seem to hurt him. Perhaps the most significant factor to turn the public tide in his favor was his foreign policy—standing up against international terrorism that had reached our own shores on 9/11/01. Bush led the world in standing up against Saddam Hussein, who had mocked America for ten years, and had ruled ruthlessly over Iraq for over twenty years. Bush called on the United Nations to take a stand for liberty, rather than to merely give cheap lip service to liberty. These strong stances were what America wanted, and Bush's leadership in this certainly helped to give him the unusual mid-term election victory.

For a summary of some specific, significant elections results around the nation, see "2002 National Elections Highlights," beginning on the next page.

House Democrats Elect First Woman as Party Leader

Following the Republican victory in the mid-term elections, House Democratic Leader Dick Gephardt resigned that post, and the party elected Representative Nancy Pelosi (D-Cal.) as its party chair. She is the first woman to be elected national leader of her party in Congress.

Republicans Foresee Approval of Judgeships, Now that They Have Won Control of Both Houses of Congress and the Presidency

Having reclaimed control over the Senate in the November elections, the GOP began to relish the thought of finally obtaining the confirmation of many of the judgeships that the Democratic-controlled Senate had been able to block during the first two years of the Bush administration. (As it turned out, the realization of this desire was not to come easily.) During the fall of 2002, there existed widespread consensus that the Senate's judicial confirmation process had become flawed. Various proposals are now being debated to correct this. (See next issue of *CLU* for further discussion of the judicial confirmation process.)

Senator Lott Loses It in Celebrating Strom Thurmond's 100th Birthday

On December 5, 2002, Senator Strom Thurmond was wheeled into a party to celebrate his 100th birthday—making him the oldest senator, as well as the longest-serving senator in the history of the United States (48 years). But the celebrating turned out to be quite costly for Senate Majority Leader-to-be Trent Lott, who lauded Strom a little bit too much, in observing that Strom had been the unsuccessful Dixiecrat Presidential candidate in 1948. In his excessive exuberance, Senator Lott said that the nation would have been better off had it elected him. The problem is, however, that the Dixiecrats were outspoken segregationists. So as word trickled through the media of what Senator Lott had said, a hue and cry arose against Lott, which ultimately led to his resignation from his party's highest leadership post.

2002 National Elections Highlights

I. Congressional Elections
A. House

1. **Florida.** Republican Katherine Harris was elected to a congressional seat in Florida. Ms. Harris gained national recognition for her role as Secretary of State in certifying the Florida votes that gave George Bush all of Florida's electoral votes in 2000. There was no crippling backlash against Ms. Harris, who is riding the tide of her national recognition.

2. **Maryland.** Democrat Christopher Van Hollen (51%) defeated the incumbent (8-term) Republican Connie Morella (48%) for the 8th District seat in the House of Representatives. While Maryland, including Montgomery County is strong Democratic territory, the charming Connie Morella had held the congressional seat there for 16 years. However, following the 2000 Census, the Democratic-controlled State of Maryland redrew the congressional district boundaries to specifically increase the Democratic base in the 8th District—the state took away a rural Republican section of the 8th district and replaced it with a Democratic urban section. This was enough to give Van Hollen the victory.

B. Senate

1. **Georgia.** Republican challenger Saxby Chambliss defeated incumbent Vietnam veteran Democrat Max Cleland. This is seen as a strengthening of the Republican Party in Georgia.

2. **Missouri.** Republican Jim Talent defeated incumbent Democrat Jean Carnahan. This race drew a lot of national attention because it was the special election to see who would fill the remaining four years of the Mel Carnahan term. Mel Carnahan, was the Democratic former governor of Missouri who ran against and defeated incumbent Republican John Ashcroft in the 2000 election. Mel Carnahan died prior to that election. But undaunted by this setback, the stubborn Missourians elected Mr. Carnahan anyway. The governor of Missouri appointed Mr. Carnahan's surviving wife to take his seat until a special election could be held to select a permanent replacement.

3. **New Jersey.** When incumbent Democratic Senator Robert Torricelli suddenly announced that he was withdrawing from the Senate race in New Jersey, as he was trailing in the polls. Charges of corruption were hurting Torricelli. The Democrats immediately installed former Senator Frank Lautenberg to be the party's senatorial candidate in the election. Republicans sued to block Democratic-controlled New Jersey from ignoring the New Jersey law which prohibited the adding of a new candidate's name to the ballot after the legal deadline. The court ruled that New Jersey could ignore its law and accommodate the late change in the ballot. Ultimately, Lautenberg was elected.

4. **Minnesota.** Rep. Norm Coleman (50%) defeated Dem. Walter Mondale (48%). Former Vice President Mondale stepped in at the last minute to run after incumbent Paul Wellstone died in a plane crash. Coleman attributed the victory to his conservative views. Democratic National Comm. Chair, Terry McAuliffe attributed the victory to the popularity of President Bush. There was some criticism of how the Democratic party seemed to use the funeral services of Senator Wellstone for political purposes. Governor Jesse Ventura, for one was upset; as a consequence he appointed an independent, Dean Barkley (rather than a Democrat) to complete the remaining two months of Senator Wellstone's term.

5.   Louisiana. Louisiana's election laws provide that if neither senatorial candidate receives a majority of the popular vote in an election, then a run-off election is held between the two candidates with the most popular votes. In November, neither of the parties' candidates received a majority of votes; accordingly, a run-off election was held on the first Tuesday in December. Incumbent Democratic Senator Mary Landrieu defeated Republican challenger Suzanne Terrell (52-48).

II.   State Governors Elections

1.   Florida. Incumbent Republican Governor Jeb Bush defeated Democratic challenger Bill McBride in an election campaign that drew strong national participation of both major parties. Because the 2000 presidential election was so close in Florida, both parties looked at the 2002 gubernatorial election as an indicator of whether the Democratic party could take control of Florida, or whether the Republican control would be strengthened. It turned out to be the latter.

2.   Georgia. Republican Sonny Perdue defeated incumbent Democrat Roy Barnes in Georgia gubernatorial election. Perdue is the first Republican governor of Georgia since the carpetbagger Governor Rufus Bullock was chased out of the state in 1871. Perdue's victory is attributed to many to be the result of a backlash against former Governor Barnes for his reducing the large Confederate emblem on the state flag to a tiny dot. Similar backlash effects had previously occurred in South Carolina and Mississippi.

3.   Maryland. Republican Robert Ehrlich (52%) defeated Democrat Kathleen Kennedy Townsend (48%), making Mr. Ehrlich the first Republican governor of Maryland since Spiro Agnew won the governor's mansion in 1964 when Democratic in-fighting caused that party to split its votes among two candidates. Speculation abounds as to why Ms. Townsend (the incumbent Lt. Governor) lost and why Mr. Ehrlich won. Some have blamed Ms. Townsend's campaign and her campaign manager. Some criticized the vicious tone of her campaign against Mr. Ehrlich. But some other factors may have also contributed. Mr. Ehrlich selected Michael S. Steele for his Lt. Governor running mate. Mr. Steele is a very impressive black leader; his influence was certainly critical. Ms. Townsend may have also been hurt by her record with out-going Governor Glendening for taking a fiscally sound state government and taking it into the red, building a large deficit. The popular state Comptroller of the Treasury, William Donald Shafer (Dem) was critical of the Glendening-Townsend administration for fiscal irresponsibility. Finally, the Glendening-Townsend administration opposed the Inter-County Connector highway that would form an outer beltway in Maryland around Washington, D. C. During her election campaign, Ms. Townsend changed her mind and said she was in favor of the Connector.

4.   Massachusetts. Republican Mitt Romney defeated Democrat Shannon O'Brien (who was seeking to be the first woman governor) in the Massachusetts gubernatorial campaign. Four years earlier, Mr. Romney was defeated by Edward Kennedy in the senatorial election. But in the meantime, Mr. Romney had gained some national prominence in chairing the 2002 Salt Lake Winter Olympics. Massachusetts has been a strong Democratic state, but the people's fear of a further tax increase is reported to have helped Mr Romney win the race. Mr. Romney recently stated that he would not draw a governor's salary at this time.

House Expels
Congressman Traficant

On July 24, 2002, by a vote of 420-1, the House of Representatives voted to expel Congressman James A. Traficant, Jr. (D-Ohio) from his seat in the House. This action was taken following Traficant's conviction in April for racketeering, bribery and mail fraud.

Traficant was one of the most colorful speakers in the House, and he was fiercely independent. For example, he dared to differ from his party and supported Republican Dennis Hastert for Speaker of the House. He was often outspoken and refreshingly blunt—you could always get a great quote from him. On occasion he could be heard to quote Captain James Kirk while speaking on the floor of the House: "Beam me up, Scotty," he would say, to express dismay at a particular matter under debate.

But in April, a federal court in Cleveland convicted him of:

* Receiving free labor and materials from construction businesses in exchange for seeking favors for them from federal regulators;

*Requiring a staff member to turn over a $2,500 from his monthly paycheck;

*Seeking to persuade the staff member to destroy evidence and provide false testimony;

*Using staff members to do work on his boat and on his farm;

*Filing false tax returns; and

*Related bribery & mail fraud offenses.

Representative Traficant fought his expulsion to the very end. After the felony conviction in April, as his future expulsion became apparent, Traficant threatened his colleagues in the House that they would be stricken with some species of crotch rot if they dared to vote to expel him. Traficant's bombastic style was present to the bitter end, as he railed against the establishment during the 3-hour debate that preceded his expulsion vote. Not withstanding Mr. Traficant's bold defense and his foreboding prophecy, the House voted 420–1 to expel him. The lone vote in support of Traficant was cast by lame duck congressman Gary Condit, who was not successful in regaining his party's nomination, following the discovery of his relationship with intern (Chandra Levy) who had suddenly disappeared and was found murdered a year later.

The expulsion of members of Congress (Senators and Representatives) is rare, but not without historical precedent. Members convicted of felonies usually have the sense to resign. The most recent House member convicted of a felony who refused to resign was Michael "Ozzie" Myers, who was expelled by the House in 1980 by a 376-30 vote, after being convicted of bribery and conspiracy.

Under Article I, Section 5 of the Constitution, each House of Congress is empowered to make rules with respect to the qualifications of its members. The power of each House to exclude or expel members is not without limits. In 1969, the Supreme Court reversed the House's vote to exclude Representative Adam Clayton Powell, Jr. *Powell v. McCormack*, 395 U.S. 486 (1969).

Both the House and the Senate have used their power under Article I, Section 5 to prevent some Senators and Representatives from even taking a seat in Congress. Utah Representative Brigham Roberts (late 1890's) and Senator Reed Smoot (early 1900's) were both denied seats in Congress pursuant to this power. This was Congress' retribution for the Mormon practice of plural marriage that the Church discontinued prior to Utah's becoming the 45th State in 1896.

Homeland Security Department Approved by Congress—New Cabinet Post Created

On November 19, 2002, the Senate eventually approved the new Homeland Security Department, together with the new cabinet post, to be filled by former Pennsylvania Governor, Tom Ridge. The main purpose of this new department and post is to coordinate, unify and consolidate all of the various national security agencies to optimize the security of the nation.

GAO Suit Against Vice President Cheney Is Dismissed

On December 9, 2002, United States District Judge John D. Bates ruled that the Government Accounting Office (GAO), an arm of Congress, does not have standing to sue the Executive Branch, including Vice President Cheney. *Cheney v. GAO*, ___ F.Supp.2d ___ (D.C. 2002).

Months ago, Democratic Congressmen John Dingell (Mich.) and Henry Waxman (Calif.) sought to have Vice President Cheney identify the individuals with whom he had consulted in fashioning the administration energy policy. Both President Bush and Vice President Cheney have prior connections with the oil industry. And Democrats were concerned that the administration would have anti-environment leanings.

In dismissing the GAO suit, Judge Bates noted that absent a congressional subpoena, that GAO had no standing to sue. But even if a congressional subpoena had been employed, it is not clear that such a suit could be entertained because it would pit the competing rights of two equal branches of the government.

Australian Court Claims Jurisdiction in Libel Suit for Internet Publication Originating in United States

In early December, 2002, Australia's highest court ruled that Dow Jones & Co. (publisher of Wall Street Journal) must defend itself in Australian courts for an alleged libel that it published on the Internet.

This ruling has set off chilling reverberations around the globe.

In the United States, the Fourth Circuit Court of Appeals has held that two Connecticut newspapers could only be sued in Connecticut provided that they did not aim their publications at a specific, non-Connecticut audience. *The Washington Post* (December 16, 2002) contends that the Fourth Circuit rationale should apply internationally to internet situations.

Iraq Democracy-- Hussein Wins 100 Percent of Votes in Election

The Iraq government announced on October 16, 2002, that its beloved dictator Saddam Hussein was elected to a seven-year term in a landslide--receiving 100 percent of all votes. Hussein's victory this year even surpassed the results he received in 1995, when he received 99.96 percent of the vote. Of course, no one who desires to live dares to run against Hussein. Nevertheless, Hussein hailed his "democracy" as a model for the world.

5.2

5.3

Settlement Reached in Microsoft Antitrust Suit

On November 1, 2002, a settlement was reached in the government's antitrust suit against Microsoft.

The suit began in 1998, when the Justice Department and 19 states had sued Microsoft, alleging that it was a monopoly that used its position illegally to stifle competition. In 2000, U.S. District Judge Thomas Jackson ruled that Microsoft had violated the Sherman Antitrust Act and various state antitrust laws. On June 28, 2001, a United States Court of Appeals overturned that part of Judge Jackson's ruling that would have ordered the break up of Microsoft. Finally, on remand to District Court, Microsoft agreed to several changes in its policies and practices that led to this final settlement.

Discovery of Rare Fly Stops Construction of Sports Complex in California

The building of a $12 million sports complex in Colton, California was put on hold following the discovery of a Delhi Sands flower-loving fly that is an endangered species, protected by the Endangered Species Act.

The maximum penalty for harming or killing an endangered species is $100,000 for an individual and $200,000 for a corporation, and up to one year in jail.

If a construction worker had swatted and killed one of those flies, he could be looking at a fine of up to $100,000 and a year in jail.

Construction was forced to stop for 45 days, waiting a report and recommendation from the Fish and Wildlife Service.

The economic effects from protecting this rare fly could be gigantic. In addition to pulling the plug on the $12 million dollar building, the town of Colton stands to lose $35 million in taxes if the facility is not built. Discovery of the fly also held up sewer and flood-control projects and the construction of a middle school.

(From *The Washington Times*, 14 September, 2002.)

9.2

Ten Commandments
in the News

On December 24, 2002, Frederick City sold a small piece of land on which stands a granite monument engraved with the Ten Commandments. The sale of this small parcel for $18,000 induced the ACLU to drop its lawsuit against Frederick City, Maryland. The ACLU had alleged that because the Ten Commandments monument was on city property that this violated the Establishment Clause of the First Amendment. The sale left the monument where it has been for many years at the memorial park, but it changed the ownership of the few square feet of land on which the monument stands.

Frederick Mayor, Jennifer Dougherty, refused to fight the ACLU on this issue—much to the displeasure of many of her constituents. Supporters of the monument pointed out that the monument was part of a war memorial park where there were a half-dozen memorials to veterans who had given their lives in national wars. The monument was not in front of city hall or a court or any governmental building.

This was a victory for the ACLU, who avoided the risk of losing in court. If the ACLU had really thought they would win, then they would not have approved of the sale as a settlement of their case because in similar situations around the country the ACLU has challenged local governments which have sought to avoid litigation with the ACLU by selling small parcels of land rather than moving monuments away.

In another Ten Commandments case, on November 19, 2002, a federal appeals court panel ruled 2-1 to uphold a federal judge's decision in June to remove granite Ten Commandments monuments from four public schools in Ohio.

In still another Ten Commandments case, in late 2002 in Alabama, State Chief Justice Roy Moore, who had installed a 5,300-pound Ten Commandments monument in the State Judicial Building, was ordered by a federal court to remove the monument.

CLU 05/03

Hate Speech--
The Hatred of Some People
for America
Reaches Intolerable Levels

In 2001 and 2002 national headlines included numerous reports of peoples in America and around the world who proudly proclaimed their hatred for America and Americans. Several Muslim groups openly advocated terrorist acts against America. These groups and others blamed America for the suicide missions that killed 3,000 people at the Pentagon and the World Trade Center on 9/11/01.

While the U.S. recognizes and protects some speech, the First Amendment does not protect speech that incites acts of terror and murder. And American tolerance for speech that criticizes and derides us has reached a limit when that speech contributes to the death and terrorizing of innocent people in our homeland.

The American determination to either bring the regime of Saddam Hussein in line, or to remove it, is in great measure a result of 9/11. President Bush recognized the consensus of most Americans that we can no longer stand by idle and silent, as we watch people who hate us, lie about us and attempt to build international disdain for us. 9/11 has led the nation to take a stand—to refute the lies, to withhold benefits from those who seek to defame us, and to expose the hypocrisy of the evil dictators who malign us.

But the American resolve to do something about Saddam Hussein is more than a matter of national defense; it is also a duty we owe to the entire world. America has the moral obligation to take a stand against evil regimes that threaten peace-loving peoples. Regimes that reign with terror and hatred, and which advocate and incite mayhem and murder can no longer be ignored, if we have the power to deal with them. America's own survival as well as the protection of good people around the globe requires that the strongest nation in the world take appropriate action against speech that creates a clear and present danger to the lives of innocent people. At the very least, appropriate action means refuting the lies that endanger Americans around the globe. It also includes pressing criminal charges against those who aid and abet others to commit crimes.

We cannot force people to not hate us. But we need not tolerate excessive hateful speech that harbors, incites and causes acts of terrorism at home and abroad. The U.S. action to overthrow Saddam Hussein was a courageous act of love for the entire world. Now that the Iraq war appears to have been successfully conducted, the world is rid of one more evil tyrant.

CLU 05/03

C. PAUL SMITH

Attorney at Law
110 North Washington Street
Suite 402
Rockville, Maryland 20850
(301) 762-0033
FAX NO.: (301) 762-0285

June 20, 2002

Maryland State Board of Education
200 West Baltimore Street
Baltimore, MD 21201

Attention: Joyce Smith

Re: Multicultural Education Regulations

Dear Sirs and Madams:

My wife and I live in Frederick County, Maryland, and we are the parents of five children who are currently enrolled in public schools in that county.

I understand that the State Board of Education is proposing to make "sexual orientation" one of the "cultural groups" about which public school children will be educated. I understand that such a proposal is being made in order to protect gay students from harassment. I have several comments and suggestions to make regarding this matter.

1. I object to the public schools becoming the vehicle for social engineering in our State. I do not believe it is the proper role of the Board of Education to push the agenda of philosophies and programs that advance controversial moral viewpoints. Once the schools enter into such moral debates, there will be inevitable problems and controversies. Public school curricula should avoid engaging in social debate on controversial moral issues, of which homosexuality is certainly one.

2. If the schools ignore the wisdom of engaging in the debate of moral/social issues, then they should at least scrutinize their programs, their conduct and their language to be sure that there is sound and scientific support for official school words and actions. And in applying this standard to current proposals to educate public school children (grades K through 12) about protecting gay students from harassment, scientific studies demonstrate that there is a serious problem that would be created by such a program. The problem is that the very act of identifying students as gay in their formative school years has been shown to be totally unreliable and prone to encourage homosexual conduct, the latter of which causes serious physical and mental health problems.

Maryland State Board of Education
Page Two
June 20, 2002

A 1992 Minnesota study of 35,000 youth reported that 25.9% of 12-year-olds are uncertain if they are heterosexual or homosexual, whereas other studies show that only 2-3% of the adult population identifies itself as homosexual. (See page 5 of the enclosed NARTH brochure, "Homosexual Advocacy Groups & Your School." NARTH stands for the National Association for Research and Therapy of Homosexuality.) This demonstrates that any school program that would involve the **identification** of gays would run the risk of misidentifying almost 25% of the students as gay. And while the gay activists may want this misidentification, it can have an adverse affect on the misidentified students because of the implicit endorsement it would give of homosexual conduct, despite the acknowledged health and safety risks that accompany the homosexual lifestyle.

While the risk of serious disability and death from AIDS is well known, there are other serious health and social problems that come with homosexual conduct. A recent study by Garofalo (NARTH, p. 4) documents that the following high health risk behaviors are significantly greater for gay, lesbian and bisexual (GLB) high school students than for non GLBs:

Alcohol use before age 13	-	twice as high for GLBs
Cocaine use before age 13	-	14 times as high for GLBs
Use of inhalants	-	2 1/2 times as high for GLBs
Ever had sexual intercourse	-	twice as high for GLBs
Sexual contact against will	-	three times as high for GLBs

Additionally, the suicide rate is acknowledged to be higher among gay teens than other teens. Studies also show that there are more psychiatric disorders found among homosexually-oriented people (NARTH, pp. 3-4).

The overwhelming results of scientific studies further demonstrate that homosexuality develops through a combination of family, biological, and social influences, reinforced by a series of choices made by each individual over the years. Some gay researchers seek to dispute this, but even the renowned Dr. Robert Spitzer, who was responsible for removing "homosexuality" from the list of psychological disorders, now acknowledges that some people do change their sexual orientation. And there is no reputable scientific study that proves that gays are born that way. In the early 90's, Hamer and LaVay suggested that their studies showed that there may be a genetic cause of homosexuality, but neither their studies nor any subsequent studies have proved such a link. To the contrary, studies have demonstrated that multiple factors, including environment, behavior, exposure to early sexual stimulation and choices are significant factors in developing homosexual orientation.

Thus, if the State School Board is to use reputable, scientific data to support the action it takes with regards to teaching about homosexuality, it would be derelict to do anything that would encourage homosexual identification or homosexual conduct.

I will shortly send the Board a packet with additional reports and studies that support the representations I am making in this letter. However, initially, I am enclosing

Maryland State Board of Education
Page Three
June 20, 2002

the brochure from NARTH that I previously identified, as well as an article I wrote in
Constitutional Law Updates on this issue.

If you are interested, I would be happy to discuss this matter with the board.
Furthermore, I am friends with Dr. A. Dean Byrd, a psychologist who has treated
approximately 300 males who wanted to repress or eliminate the same-sex erotic
attraction that they were experiencing. I believe that Dr. Byrd would be happy to
communicate with you directly about these issues, if you would choose to seek his input.

3. Having said all of the above, this does not mean that the harassment of any
school youth should be condoned. Harassment of students should not be condoned or
tolerated. The ridiculing of one who is struggling with homosexual issues is not the right
thing to do. But teaching that homosexual orientation is acceptable is not the answer,
either. There is no reason to encourage homosexual conduct. Harassment can be
addressed without embracing the cause of the gays to encourage the debilitating and
dangerous lifestyle that homosexual conduct is.

Very truly yours,

C. Paul Smith

Encl.

CONSTITUTIONAL LAW UPDATES

III:ii   September 2003   No. 7

News Items through June 30, 2003

--See next page for a complete listing of reports in this issue--

CONSTITUTIONAL LAW UPDATES is a quarterly newsletter edited and published by C. Paul Smith, J.D.
Subscription cost is $25.00 per year (plus $1.25 tax in MD). To subscribe, send a check or money order to
CONSTITUTIONAL LAW UPDATES, P. O. Box 1204, Frederick MD 21702-0204. For further information, visit
Paul Smith's web site at www.cpaulsmith.com.

This issue of **Constitutional Law Updates** reports on several significant developments in constitutional law. The war to oust Saddam Hussein from power in Iraq and the continuing war against terrorism has resulted in several new, court rulings governing the rights of those accused in times of war. On the domestic front, two recent Supreme Court rulings are very significant—the Court has identified for the first time a liberty to engage in adult, consensual homosexual conduct; and the Court has identified the state interest in "diversity" as an interest that justifies extending affirmative action for another twenty years. And the balance of power between the three branches of the federal government is being contested, as the minority party in the Senate has waged a filibuster to prevent a full Senate vote on the President's judicial nominees—this tactic has never before been employed to prevent a full-Senate vote on nominees. These and other recent developments in our law are reported and discussed in this issue.

Articles in this issue—

CLU 08/03

Chief Judge Roy Moore of the Alabama Supreme Court— A Principled Stance May Cost Him His Judgeship

In late August, 2003, Judge Roy Moore was suspended from his position as Chief Judge of the Alabama Supreme Court because he refused to obey the order of a federal court judge to remove the 2 ½ ton Ten Commandments monument from the State Courthouse. The U. S. Court of Appeals for the Eleventh Circuit ruled that Judge Moore's keeping the monument in the State Courthouse violated the Establishment Clause of the First Amendment.

There have been and still are a number of Ten Commandments cases throughout the United States, in which parties are seeking for the Supreme Court to clarify, reshape, correct, change or review the Court's current position on freedom of Religion issues. But what makes Judge Moore's case so compelling is the prominence of his position (Chief Judge) and because he has taken such a strong stance in support of keeping the Commandments. (In fact, he is the one who had the monument put there in the first place.) The national publicity around this battle has been extensive. Perhaps this battle can stir up sufficient national interest to help bring about a return to the initial meaning of the Establishment Clause.

Judge Moore is appealing his suspension, and others are appealing the removal of the Ten Commandments from the State Courthouse. **CLU** will follow the developments in this case in future editions.

****

Supreme Court Recognizes a Personal Liberty to Engage in Private, Homosexual Conduct

by C. Paul Smith

On June 26, 2003, the Supreme Court in *Lawrence v. Texas*, 539 U.S. ___ (2003), struck down (6-3) the Texas law that criminalized private, consensual, adult, homosexual conduct. In so ruling, the Court specifically overturned its 1986 ruling in *Bowers v. Hardwick*, 478 U.S. 186 (a 5-4 decision), that upheld the conviction of one Mr. Hardwick for engaging in a sexual act with another man in violation of Georgia law. The result of this ruling is that the Constitution now recognizes and protects the liberty of individuals to engage in sexual acts with persons of the same sex, and the States cannot proscribe such conduct as long as it is private and between consenting adults.

This ruling is a tremendous victory for the militant gays, who have waged an unrelenting fight to overturn *Bowers* for the last seventeen years. On the other hand, this is a ruling that presents grave concerns for many because the Court's rationale, if extended to its logical conclusion, can undermine moral-based laws in all of the fifty states with respect to such matters as bigamy, same-sex marriage, prostitution, adultery, bestiality and obscenity.[1]

The *Lawrence* case will certainly become one of the most well-known cases of our time, paralleling *Roe v. Wade* in its fame.

One unusual aspect of the majority ruling is that the majority not only overturns the 1986 *Bowers* case, but they went out of their way chastise, lambaste and denigrate the

opinion of the Court whose personnel has changed in the intervening 17 years. The current majority criticized the *Bowers* court for failing to recognize the personal liberty to engage in consensual homosexual sodomy. While the majority in *Lawrence* repeatedly said that the result reached in *Bowers* was wrong, the majority never did assail the validity of the "fundamental rights" analysis that the Court used in *Bowers*. But curiously, despite its repeated criticism of the result in *Bowers*, the 2003 majority never did declare the new "liberty" to be a "fundamental right."[2] Instead, the *Lawrence* Court invalidated the Texas sodomy law based upon its violating a "liberty" found in the Due Process Clause of the Fourteenth Amendment. The result of this is to leave intact the very rationale that the 2003 majority criticized in *Bowers*.[3]

To understand the full significance of *Lawrence* one must read both the majority

---

[2] The Supreme Court resorted to a totally new rationale to obtain the result it wanted to reach in *Lawrence*; and this rationale is that a "liberty" exists under the Due Process Clause to engage in private, homosexual conduct. Apparently this "liberty" is distinguishable from a "fundamental right," although the majority never explained what the distinction is.

[3] While this may be confusing, it is clearly not an oversight. The majority, concurring and dissenting opinions are all circulated among all the Justices well in advance of the issuance of their rulings to make sure that there are no surprises and to give all sides the opportunity to consider all arguments and to revise their written opinions accordingly. Thus, one must conclude that the majority knew what it was doing and did not inadvertently fail to address an issue. The question for analysts, therefore, is why did the Court choose to label the newly protected personal right as a "liberty" protected under the Due Process Clause rather than one of the "fundamental rights" protected under the Constitution?

---

[1] Justice Scalia stated his concern that "[t]his effectively decrees the end of all morals legislation." (Slip opinion, p. 15.) However, the majority intimated that its ruling would not undermine state marriage laws; it wrote that this case "does not involve whether the government must give formal recognition to any relationship that homosexual persons seek to enter." (Slip opinion, p. 18.)

opinion (by Justice Kennedy—joined by Justices Stevens, Souter, Ginsburg and Breyer), Justice O'Connor's concurring opinion, and Justice Scalia's dissenting opinion (joined by Chief Justice Rehnquist and Justice Thomas).

I. Justice Kennedy's Majority Opinion

The Court held that the right of an individual to engage in sexual conduct with another person of the same sex is a "liberty" that is protected under the Due Process Clause of the 14th Amendment. The Court characterized this right as a part of the right to privacy that the Court identified in *Griswold v. Connecticut*, 381 U.S. 479 (1965); *Eisenstadt v. Baird*, 405 U.S. 438 (1972); and *Roe v. Wade*, 410 U.S. 113 (1973). The Court in *Lawrence* did not characterize the newly recognized right as a "fundamental right."

The Court held that the personal right to engage in private sexual conduct that was recognized in *Griswold v. Connecticut*, 381 U.S. 479 (1965), and which was specifically extended to conduct outside of marriage in *Eisenstadt v. Baird*, 405 U.S. 438 (1972), should have been recognized by the Court in *Bowers* (1986). The majority quoted a statement in *Eisenstadt* which it said should have been controlling in *Bowers* (slip opinion, p. 11) and which now has become the controlling principle:

"If the right of privacy means anything, it is the right of the *individual*, married or single, to be free from unwarranted governmental intrusion into matters so fundamentally affecting a person as the decision whether to bear or beget a child." 405 U.S. 453.[4]

The majority also cited *Cary v. Population Services Int'l*, 431 U.S. 678 (1977), as additional support. (In *Cary*, the Court

---
[4] The logic behind this new, controlling principle is suspect, since homosexual conduct has nothing to do with the decision of whether to bear or beget a child.

invalidated a New York law forbidding the sale of contraceptives to individuals under the age of 16.)

The Court criticized the majority in 1986 for failing to find a history and tradition that warranted recognition of an individual right to engage in sexual conduct with one of the same sex. The majority opinion pointed out that other nations around the world recognize an individual right to engage in homosexual acts (slip opinion, p. 16). The majority stated that "[t]his emerging recognition should have been apparent when *Bowers* was decided." (Slip opinion, p. 11.)

The Court held that the "right to liberty under the Due Process Clause gives them [homosexuals] the full right to engage in their conduct without the intervention of the government." (Slip opinion, p. 18.)

The Court declined to decide the case under the Equal Protection Clause, although it implied that it could have. But the Court declined to rule on that basis because it said that such a ruling would have averted the more important question of whether a right to engage in homosexual conduct exists under the Constitution. (Slip opinion, pp. 14-15.)

II. Justice O'Connor's Concurring Opinion

Justice O'Connor would not have overturned *Bowers*, a case in which she joined with the majority. She would have invalidated the Texas law for violating the Equal Protection Clause of the Fourteenth Amendment. Citing *Eisenstadt v. Baird*, she said that just as a state law that "discriminated between married and unmarried persons" in the distribution of contraceptives was invalidated by the Court, so should the Texas law that discriminated between heterosexuals and homosexuals be invalidated by the Court. (Slip opinion, p. 2.) She said that the Texas statute violated the Fourteenth Amendment because it banned "homosexual sodomy, but not heterosexual sodomy." (Slip opinion, p. 4.)

As pointed out above, the majority did not join with Justice O'Connor because her holding was too narrow to accomplish their purposes.

Justice Scalia (joined by Chief Justice Rehnquist and Thomas) found no violation of the Equal Protection Clause in the Texas law because it applied equally to men and to women. Justice Scalia pointed out that the O'Connor rationale was nothing more than circular reasoning. To illustrate he wrote:

"Of course the same could be said of any law. A law against public nudity targets 'the conduct that is closely correlated with being a nudist,' and hence, 'is targeted at more than conduct'; it is 'directed toward nudists as a class.' Be that as it may. Even if the Texas law does deny equal protection to "homosexuals as a class," that denial *still* does not need to be justified by anything more than a rational basis, which our cases show is satisfied by the enforcement of traditional notions of sexual morality." (Slip opinion, p. 17.)

III. Justice Scalia's Dissenting Opinion

Justice Scalia takes the majority to task for three things: (1) Creating a new basis for identifying unenumerated rights—i.e., as a part a the "liberty" within the Due Process Clause of the Fourteenth Amendment; (2) Failing to explain how the newly identified "liberty" squared with "fundamental rights" rationale of *Bowers*, the result of which the majority severely criticized; and (3) Departing from the Court's long-standing principles of *stare decisis*.

A. The new liberty identified by the Majority is based upon an archaic and distorted version of Substantive Due Process and is a departure from the Court's established principles for recognizing unenumerated rights.

The rationale invoked by the majority as a basis for the newly recognized liberty to engage in adult, consensual, homosexual conduct is a new species of "substantive due process" under the Fourteenth Amendment. This rationale was articulated in the early twentieth century in *Pierce v. Society of Sisters*, 268 U.S. 510 (1925) and *Meyer v. Nebraska*, 262 U.S. 390 (1923) as a basis for identifying and recognizing rights that were not specifically articulated in the Constitution.

However, as the Supreme Court began to recognize new rights in the mid-twentieth century, it began to distance itself from the "substantive due process" rationale, and in its place the Court began to formulate its "fundamental rights" rationale, which became the basis for recognizing the right of married couples to use contraceptives (*Griswold v. Connecticut*, 381 U.S. 479 (1965)); the right of unmarried couples to use contraceptives (*Eisenstadt v. Baird*, 405 U.S. 438 (1972)); and the right to privacy, including the limited right of a woman to control her own body (*Roe v. Wade*, 410 U.S. 113 (1973). In none of these three landmark cases (*Griswold, Eisenstadt* and *Roe*) did the Court base its ruling on the "substantive due process" rights under the Fourteenth Amendment. Rather, as Justice Scalia points out in his dissent, the Court "expressly disclaimed any reliance on the doctrine of 'substantive due process'" in *Griswold* and in *Eisenstadt* (Slip Opinion, p. 10). Rather, those opinions were grounded on a "right to privacy" found "in the penumbras of constitutional provisions other than the Due Process Clause." *Id.* In *Roe v. Wade* the Court adopted the "fundamental rights" rationale to which the Court had adhered ever since that case in deciding whether or not to recognize unenumerated rights. In other words, the majority in *Lawrence* misstates the rationale of the cases that it cites as precedent for its holding.

Based upon this background, when the Supreme Court dealt with the *Bowers v. Hardwick* case in 1986, the Court properly applied the "fundamental rights" principles, and appropriately declined to find and recognize a right to engage in homosexual conduct.

The majority opinion, misrepresents the rationale that its predecessor Court employed in all three of these cases (*Griswold, Eisenstadt* and *Roe*). The majority in *Lawrence* reaches the result it wants by citing these three cases as supportive; but the majority ignores and/or distorts the rationales that the Court used in each of those cases. What the Court has done in *Lawrence* is to resurrect a new brand of "substantive due process," even though for over thirty years the Supreme Court has abandoned that rationale as a legitimate basis for recognizing unenumerated rights.

Nevertheless, whether the Court's reasoning was correct or not, since a majority has now spoken, we now have a new basis for recognizing unenumerated rights.[5] The new basis is that the Supreme Court can identify and recognize certain "liberties" under the Due Process Clause of the Fourteenth Amendment. So, while the logic employed by the majority in citing *Griswold, Eisenstadt* and *Roe* as a basis for its action in *Lawrence* is flawed,[6] the result is nevertheless now the law.

B. The Majority did not explain why it opted not to apply "fundamental rights" principles in determining whether or not to recognize a new liberty.

Perhaps Justice Scalia's most important observation about the majority's opinion in *Lawrence* is a discussion of what kind of right or liberty it had just created. He points out that the majority did not call it a "fundamental right" (which would entail certain tests and principles to both establish it and to apply it to other situations). But instead, the Court identified it as a "liberty" protected under the Due Process Clause. In so-doing, the majority established a new basis for identifying unspecified rights protected under the Constitution. Albeit the new "liberty" is a part of the right to privacy first articulated in *Griswold*, but the Court had previously opted to refer to such rights as "fundamental rights." At first glance it is unclear why the majority in *Lawrence* avoided elevating this "liberty" to the status of a "fundamental right."

Some people will have difficulty following Justice Scalia's analysis of "fundamental rights," the "right to privacy," and the "liberty" protected under the Due Process Clause. Justice Scalia understands the technicalities of these principles as well as anyone in the world. But for many people, the rationale doesn't matter—only the bottom line: Homosexual conduct is now protected under the Constitution. But for those who wish to understand the Court's reasoning, to analyze whether the holding is based on sound reasoning, further analysis is necessary, and a review of Justice Scalia's dissent is essential to this understanding.[7]

Had the majority identified the right to engage in homosexual sodomy as a "fundamental right," then a state law that impinges upon that "fundamental right" must be invalidated unless the state has a

---

[5] I presume this new basis is in addition to the "fundamental rights" rationale, rather than in replacement of it.

[6] Justice Scalia characterizes the majority's reasoning as "manipulative" (Slip Opinion, at 2) and that their motives were "result-oriented" (Slip Opinion, at 7).

[7] Some have characterized the Scalia dissent as "angry," excessive and whiny. I submit that such glib criticisms come from uninformed and biased people. To the contrary, the dissent is most enlightening. The *Lawrence* holding is quite peculiar, and it cannot be comprehended without studying the Scalia dissent.

"compelling interest" to override the right. But since no "fundamental right" has been identified, a mere "rational" basis for a state law would be sufficient to sustain that law in restricting the newly identified "liberty." The meaning of this is that state marriage laws will not be invalidated by this newly identified "liberty."

But there is a pervasive contradiction in the majority's reasoning that is perplexing. On the one hand, it should be easier for a state to articulate a "rational" basis than a "compelling reason" to support a law that would impinge on a protected liberty. However, the Court's reasoning in *Lawrence* undermines and invalidates the very type of moral bases that have been upheld by the Court as sufficient "rational" bases for state laws (such as marriage laws) for the last two centuries. Thus, Justice Scalia rightly expresses grave concern that the *Lawrence* ruling is likely to jeopardize other moral laws that have been upheld ever since the ratification of the Constitution—laws regarding marriage, bigamy, prostitution, adultery, bestiality, and obscenity. And the next battle in the gay rights agenda is already underway—the legalization of same-sex marriages. Within a week after the *Lawrence* ruling, *The Washington Post* (July 5, 2003) called for the States to recognize same-sex unions (whether called "marriages" or not).

Not one word was spoken in the majority's opinion in *Lawrence* about the serious and debilitating health and societal side effects of homosexual relations. Not one mention of AIDS; not one mention of the increased physical and mental problems that plague homosexuals; not one mention of the lack of long-term stable relationships and of the high levels of promiscuity with multiple sex partners that attend same-sex unions; not one mention of how the traditional marriage with a father and a mother is the best environment in which to raise children in

order for them to become healthy, happy, educated, responsible and productive citizens.

C. Departure from *stare decisis.*

Stare decisis is the Latin phrase that stands for the principle that prior rulings should be upheld except for very weighty reasons in order to promote certainty and consistency in the law, and in order to put an end to litigation. Justice Scalia points out that the majority in *Lawrence* departed from the traditional tests that it has applied before reversing prior Court rulings. [8] He points out how the majority is applying a different standard to overturn *Bowers* than it applied in refusing to overturn *Roe v. Wade*. Justice Scalia said the majority was "manipulative in invoking the doctrine." (Slip opinion, p. 2.) Later, Justice Scalia stated: "The Court has chosen today to revise the standards of stare decisis," transforming it into a "result-oriented expedient." (Slip opinion, p. 7.) It is undoubtedly because of this departure that the majority devoted a major portion of its opinion to denounce the Court's ruling in *Bowers* only 17 years earlier. The majority makes the obligatory argument to support its decision, but it does not withstand honest intellectual review. And frankly, this probably does not matter to the majority, who acknowledged that it was because they perceived an "emerging recognition" of homosexual rights that they overturned *Bowers.* (Slip opinion, p. 11.)

Justice Scalia points out that the majority has departed from its role of neutral protector of the Constitution, and "has largely signed on to the so-called homosexual agenda . . . directed at eliminating the moral

---

[8] The traditional, three requirements to overturn a prior ruling are: "(1) its foundations have been 'eroded' by subsequent decisions . . . ; (2) it has been subject to 'substantial and continuing' criticism, . . . ; and (3) it has not induced 'individual or societal reliance' . . ." (Justice Scalia's slip opinion, p. 3.)

opprobrium that has traditionally attached to homosexual conduct." (Slip opinion, p. 18.) Justice Scalia accused the majority of inventing a "brand-new 'constitutional right' by a Court that is impatient of democratic change."" (Slip opinion, pp. 19-20.)

Despite the majority's attempts to rationalize how it disregarded the principle of *stare decisis*, the result is that the Court's actions now relegate *stare decisis* to a mere principle to invoke to reach a desired result—the invocation of *stare decisis* in *Lawrence* turns the principle into hollow rhetoric, to be discarded when it gets in the way of the majority's personal agendas. Specifically, the Court is saying that because it now disagrees with *Bowers*, it will not apply *stare decisis*, but because it still agrees with *Roe* it will apply *stare decisis* to it.

It remains to be seen whether *Lawrence* will become a ruling that undermines the moral fabric of our state and federal laws. This can be avoided if subsequent courts limit their application of *Lawrence* to its facts—i.e., the state cannot burst unannounced into the home of two consenting adults engaged in homosexual acts and then criminalize the adults for such actions. The majority holds, at the very least, that a right to privacy liberty precludes this. If the courts do indeed follow this limiting application of *Lawrence*, then the States will nevertheless remain free to enforce their laws respecting marriage, prohibiting same-sex marriages, prohibiting prostitution and obscenity. But it is certain that the militant gays will test the limits of *Lawrence* as they seek to secure more recognition and greater protection for their same-sex conduct.

*   *   *   *   *   *   *

Amendment Proposed to Restrict Marriage to the Union of One Man and One Woman

Both Senate and House bills are being drawn up that would amend the U. S. Constitution to restrict marriage to the union of one man and one woman. A House bill was introduced in May, titled "The Federal Marriage Amendment." Subsequently, Senate Majority Leader, Bill Frist, also advocated such an amendment.

However, since late June when the Supreme Court announced its ruling in *Lawrence v. Texas*, there has been a waning of some of the popular support for such an amendment.

Marriage laws have been primarily the domain of the States ever since the founding of this nation. However, as the federal government, including the judiciary, is beginning to assume authority over matters that should have been left to the states (e.g., finding a right to engage in homosexual conduct that overrides the power of the states to proscribe it), a constitutional amendment would be most appropriate.

California Requires Judges Affiliated with Boy Scouts to Disqualify Themselves from Cases with Homosexual Discrimination Issues

On June 20, 2003, *The Washington Times* reported new ethics standards drafted by the California Supreme Court that require its state judges who belong to the Boy Scouts of America (BSA) to disqualify themselves from cases in which they appear to be biased because of the BSA policy of excluding homosexuals. This new standard was a compromise standard, in place of a proposed rule that would have forbidden judges from belonging to the BSA. Several state judges who were affiliated with the BSA argued that the prohibition would have interfered with their First Amendment association rights. Nevertheless, the new rule would require a judge with BSA affiliation to disqualify himself from a case involving homosexual discrimination or homosexual adoptions.

A New Standard for Politically Correct Speech—Don't Criticize Gays or Lesbians

In April 2003, Senator Rick Santorum (R Pa.) angered some gay rights people and drew the criticism of many liberals for his making of the following comments in an interview with the Associated Press about the then pending Supreme Court case of *Lawrence v. Texas*:

"If the Supreme Court says that you have the right to consensual [gay] sex within your home, then you have the right to bigamy, you have the right to polygamy, you have the right to incest, you have the right to adultery. You have the right to anything."

Of course Senator Santorum was not advocating that our laws legalize bigamy, polygamy or incest. Rather he was pointing out that the legalizing of consensual homosexual conduct would undermine the existing laws that prohibit bigamy, polygamy and incest.

But much criticism was immediately leveled at Senator Santorum for making this comment was the subject of numerous editorials and pundit commentaries for a couple of weeks. The main criticism being that Senator Santorum was bigoted and mean because he dared to compare homosexual conduct with bigamy, polygamy and incest.

The Republican Party defended Senator Santorum. Senate Majority Leader Bill Frist (R-Tenn.) stated that Santorum was a voice for "inclusion and compassion" *(The Washington Post,* April 24, 2003). Senator Arlen Spector also came to his defense by stating that Santorum "is not a bigot" *(Id.)*. The White House also came to Santorum's defense, calling him an "inclusive man" *(The Washington Post,* April 26, 2003). However, the defensive nature of these statements of support—the fear of offending homosexuals that they display—are quite troubling.

It appears that the politically correct standard in much of our society today prohibits one from expressing any disapproval of the practice of homosexual sex. Any anyone who dares to criticize it becomes labeled a bigot and a homophobe, and a hater of gays and lesbians. Of course, this labeling is not necessarily true, and in fact it is totally false in many instances. This labeling is nothing more than a propaganda tactic that is used to promote the homosexual lifestyle by stifling open discussion of the issue.

This pro-gay attitude was strengthened by the Supreme Court's ruling in June that confirmed Senator Santorum's concerns. The Court's ruling in *Lawrence v. Texas* has given gay activists increased boldness and confidence in proclaiming the legitimacy of their proclivity. And there has been a silencing of some voices in opposition to homosexual conduct.

Does no one dare mention any more the world AIDS crisis and the fact that homosexual relations is a principal cause of its spreading? Does no one dare to point out the promiscuity that is rampant among gay sex partners? Does no one dare to point out the higher rates of drug abuse, child abuse, suicide, and other mental and health problems that attend homosexual conduct?

The silence on these important health issues is most curious in an era where we condone the government's enforcing of seat belt laws and anti-smoking campaigns.

Those who truly love homosexuals will do all they can to encourage them to forsake the self-destructive gay lifestyle.

PAUL & TERRY SMITH

103 Fairview Avenue
Frederick, Maryland 21701
(301) 694-2744
July 13, 2003

Frederick County Human Relations Commission
Winchester Hall
Frederick, MD 21701

Dear Commissioners:

    I am writing to express to you my concerns about an issue that I understand you will be addressing on or about July 14—that is whether "sexual orientation" should be added as a new "protected class" to the Frederick County anti-discrimination regulations. For the reasons stated below I oppose making sexual orientation a protected class. I believe this will be harmful to our community and will promote and encourage a lifestyle that is dangerous and unhealthy.

    In the wake of the recent Supreme Court ruling in *Lawrence v. Texas*, I expect there will be considerable public sentiment to acquiesce somewhat to the gay activist agenda for ever-increasing benefits and governmental endorsement of their lifestyle. However, I believe that such an attitude of capitulation would do our children and our entire society a disservice.

    I recognize that many governmental bodies in America have codified their opinions that "sexual orientation" should be included as one of the protected classes in statutes that prohibit discrimination in employment, housing and other public accommodations. However, unlike race, nationality and sex, one's sexual orientation can be influenced and often changed through a person's choices and behavior. Scientific studies confirm the role of choices, behavior and environment in both the causation of homosexual attraction and in the therapy that facilitates one's changing it. The "politically correct" notion that many people believe today is that one is born that way and that one cannot change. But scientific studies refute this. In support of this, it is important to note that Dr. Robert Spitzer (who spear-headed the movement that removed "homosexuality" from the APA's list of mental disorders in 1973) has recently completed a study of 200 gays who were successfully treated by psychologists in "conversion therapy." Dr. Spitzer's conclusion, which is scheduled for publication this fall, confirms that homosexual-oriented people can change.[1]

    The point is, if gay men and women have the power to become free of their same-sex attractions, then this argues against any moral imperative to make sexual orientation a "protected class." If homosexual orientation is a result of behavior, choices and environment, then there is no good reason to make this orientation (which is laden with physical and mental health problems) a protected class. Since "gays" are not born that way, and since they can change, and since homosexual conduct promotes both health problems and other societal ills,[2] our community should not promote this conduct, as would result from making sexual orientation a protected class.

---

[1] My information comes from Dr. A. Dean Byrd, a clinical psychologist, who, himself, has treated over 300 men who sought psychological assistance to help them change their erotic attraction to other men. Enclosed are several summaries of studies that Dr. Byrd has shared with me relative to this.

[2] Attached are recent studies that conclude the following: (a) There is a link between same-sex attraction and self-harm. Skegg, Nada-Raja, Diskson, Paul & Williams (March, 2003). (b) Suicide rates are significantly higher among homosexual men than heterosexual men. See e.g., "Is Sexual Orientation Related to Mental Health Problems and Suicidality in Young People? Fergusson, Horwood, Beautrais (1999). (c) Homosexual people are at a substantially higher risk for some forms of emotional problems, including suicidality, major depression, and anxiety disorder. Bailey (1999). (d) Homosexual women have a higher prevalence of substance use disorders than heterosexual women. Sandfort, de Graaf, Bijl and Schnabel (2001). (e) Gay unions, especially male companionships, are notoriously short-lived. Promiscuity, rather than fidelity, is the norm in homosexual relations.

8.4.5
13.3.3

Frederick County Human Relations Commission
Page Two
July 13, 2003

The *Lawrence* ruling did not establish a "fundamental right" to engage in homosexual conduct; rather the Supreme Court found that there was a constitutional "liberty" that protected from criminal prosecution consenting adults engaged in homosexual conduct in the privacy of their home.[3] The Supreme Court did not rule on how this newly recognized liberty would fare if pitted against an important state interest, such as the state interest to promote traditional families through marriage laws.

For the sake of our children and for the health and well-being of our community, the Human Rights Commission should do nothing to promote and encourage a lifestyle that brings many health risks and societal ills and which denies the blessings and beauties of traditional family relations to those who become trapped in its powerful grip.

My strong feelings should not be construed as hatred for gays, though I have observed that many gays seek to label any opposition to their lifestyle as hate-based. My feelings are motivated by the desire for my government to have the courage to speak up for the lifestyle that is best and to affirm that it is better to encourage gays to change than to encourage their engaging in practices that lead to physical and mental health problems and other ills for them and society. Scientific studies affirm the hope that I have expressed, even though the uninformed masses often acquiesce in the politically correct (though erroneous) notion that people are born that way and cannot change. In this regard, it is worthy again to note that Dr. Robert Spitzer's recently completed a study confirms that gays can change. This is the message of hope that is needed. The Commission should not unwittingly take an action that enables and encourages those who have same-sex attractions to become entrenched in a lifestyle that harms and enslaves them. Rather the Commission should lovingly discourage such debilitating behavior. It is certainly our constitutional right to make such a value judgment.

Very truly yours,

C. Paul Smith

---

[3] The distinction between the "liberty" recognized by the Court in *Lawrence* and a "fundamental right" is very significant. The militant gays have long sought to have the Court declare that they have a "fundamental right" to engage in homosexual conduct. The Supreme Court rejected this contention in *Bowers v Hardwick* in 1986. And while the Court overturned the result of *Bowers* in its opinion in *Lawrence*, the Court specifically declined to base its opinion upon the existence of a "fundamental right" to engage in such conduct. The Court declined to use that language, and instead identified it as a privacy "liberty" protected under the Due Process Clause. Consequently, the Court left open the right of states to limit the exercise of this "liberty" when it has a "rational basis" to restrict it. Thus, leaving intact the right of states to promote heterosexual marriage and to not promote homosexual unions. The problem with the Texas law, according to the Supreme Court, was that it criminalized adult consensual homosexual acts in the privacy of one's home without the presence of any competing state interest. Future cases will certainly clarify the extent of the newly identified "liberty" that the Court recognized in *Lawrence*.

Three years ago, in *Troxel v. Granville*, the Supreme Court ruled that parents have a "fundamental right" to rear and raise their children. This is the perfect example of a right that can be classified as "fundamental" because it has been universally recognized in American society for over two hundred years. Conversely, our society has never universally recognized a right of individuals to engage in homosexual conduct. This distinction was not lost on the Court, who declined to elevate the privacy "liberty" it recognized to that of a "fundamental right."

Judicial Appointments Crisis—
Senate Minority's Use of Filibuster Thwarts Constitution; Senate Should Change Rule XXII, the Filibuster Rule

by C. Paul Smith

In 2003, for the first time in our nation's history, United States Senators have invoked Rule XXII to filibuster presidential nominees for positions on United States Circuit Courts of Appeal.[1] Specifically, a Senate vote to confirm or reject the nominations of Judge Pricilla Owens [2]to the U. S. 5th Circuit Court and Miguel Estrada to the U. S. Court of Appeals for the District of Columbia have been blocked by a Democratic filibuster. Senators Tom Daschle (D-S.D.), Patrick Leahy (D-Vt.) and Charles Schumer (D-NY) have been the principal proponents of the filibuster. They accuse Judge Owens and Estrada of being unqualified and unfit because of their conservative political views and their beliefs on abortion.

Never before has the Senate used its filibuster rule to block the vote on a circuit court nominee. But the Democrats are apparently gearing up for the looming battle for Supreme Court nominees. It was anticipated that there might be a couple of vacancies this summer (2003), but neither the Chief Justice (age 79), Justice Stevens (age 83), Justice O'Connor (age 73), nor Justice Scalia (age 67) has announced his/her retirement. (They may be waiting for a time when they believe the selection of their successors may be more favorable.) In the meantime, the ongoing filibuster against judicial nominees clearly thwarts the constitutional mandate for the Senate to consider and vote on judicial nominees.

There is a simple way for the Senate to correct this abuse, but the Republicans dare not do it—The current Senate can, **by a majority vote**, dispense with or modify Rule XXII so that the Senate cannot use a filibuster to prevent an up-or-down vote on judicial nominees.

The legal issue behind this simple solution is whether an earlier Senate can make a rule that governs subsequent Senates without their consent. To my knowledge, there is no case law on this, but common sense dictates that each Senate can make its own rules. If the Senate prefers to be governed by tradition—recognizing the rules of prior Senates—that is fine, if that's what the current Senate wants. But the Supreme Court will not bind the Senate in 2003 to be bound by a rule made by another Senate, whether a Senate of the previous session or of a session one hundred years ago. A second issue is whether by Senate rule, the Senate can require a super majority vote for certain actions for which the Constitution only requires a majority vote. The answer to this issue is "Yes, but only if the current majority allows it."

---

[1] Rule XXII is the Senate rule that the Senate imposes on itself pursuant to Article I, Section 5, that gives any Senator the right to unlimited debate on any measure, unless 60 percent of the Senators vote for closure of that debate. This is the Senate filibuster rule.

[2] Pricilla Owens has the singular distinction of being the first judicial nominee that was re-nominated for a judgeship the next year after the Senate Judiciary Committee rejected her nomination. Despite her sterling qualifications, in 2002 the Senate Judiciary Committee voted her down 10-9 on a party-line vote. However, since the Republicans regained control of the Senate in the 2002 mid-term election, the President re-nominated her in 2003. This time she won the approval of the Judiciary Committee. But the Democrats resorted to its unprecedented use of the filibuster to prevent her coming to a vote before the full Senate, where her approval would have been certain.

The proposal to change Rule XXII to alter the filibuster rule has been called "the nuclear option," because it would destroy the tradition-honored filibuster rule and because it could make the once congenial Senate into a rancorous, partisan chamber—kind of like the House of Representatives. Well, this fear is laughable—the Senate is already engaged in an all-out political war; it has already become a rancorous, partisan chamber. But apparently the Republicans hadn't gotten word of this. Whatever congeniality does remain is in large measure a façade, behind which hostile, political back-stabbing is the norm.

Republicans have been reluctant to attempt the "nuclear option." After all, the Democrats have accused them of throwing a "temper tantrum." (*The Washington Times*, June 25, 2003). Apparently this is all it took to stop the Republicans in their tracks. For a time, the Republicans thought that the Democrats might suffer some negative repercussions from Hispanics in the next election for filibustering Estrada, an Hispanic. But polls showed that most Hispanics were not following what was going on—there is certainly no Hispanic outrage over how Estrada is being treated. Still, the Republicans refuse to act—except to try to wait out the Democrats, hoping to eventually get enough votes to defeat the filibuster. But the 21st Century filibuster just ain't what it used to be—there is no true "filibuster" any more. Whereas Senator Strom Thurmond took the Senate floor and spoke (filibustered) for over 24 hours in 1957, and Senator William Proxmire talked for over 16 hours in 1981, and Senator Alphonse D'Amato spoke for over 15 hours in 1992—today's filibusters don't require anyone to talk. Why? Because the Republicans have a gentlemen's agreement with the Democrats that there "would be" a filibuster, so that no one need actually waste any time on the Senate floor actually doing it. How generous that is of the Republicans! Why are they so tepid? Perhaps they fear being perceived as partisan and uncongenial and perhaps unfair. But they don't seem to fear being perceived as wimps. Linda Chavez says the problem with Republicans stems from the fact that "Republicans play by gentlemen's rules," while "Democrats play to win." They need to recall the words sung by Kenny Rogers, "Sometimes you have to fight to be a man."

Senate Majority Leader Bill Frist (R-Tenn.), blames the Democrats for abusing the confirmation process: "It's the Democrats right now who are engaged in a nuclear option, attempting for the first time in the history of this country to change the operating precedent of the United States Senate." (*The Washington Times*, June 25, 2003). What Mr. Frist is referring to is the fact that until 2003 the Senate had never invoked Rule XXII to impede the vote on a judicial nomination because it was understood that this would be improper. In fact, what the filibuster does to a nominee is to give the minority party the power to control the confirmation of nominees. Clearly the Constitution was never intended to require a super-majority vote to approve presidential nominees. Only the Senate's own rule—Rule XXII—has created this problem. And now that the current Senate chooses to use the rule to block judicial appointments, it's time for the current Senate to exercise the so-called nuclear option.

To demonstrate how ridiculous the filibuster rule is when applied to judicial nominations, one should simply examine the flimsy reasoning—the illogic—being invoked in its support.

Democrats accuse Republicans of seeking to disrupt the balance of power between the President and the Congress when the Republicans threaten to change Rule XXII. But just the opposite is true: **The filibuster rule is used only to block a full Senate vote; it is to prevent majority rule; it is to enforce the will of a minority on the Senate and on the United States.** Democratic Senator Zell Miller (Ga.) characterizes the current use of the filibuster against judicial nominees as a "perversion of the Senate rules." (*The Washington Post*, June 6, 2003.)

Senate Minority Leader Tom Daschle (D-S.D.) argued that diminishing the Senate's ability to block judicial nominees would undermine the Senate's obligation to provide "advice and consent" in presidential nominations. But just the opposite is true. The Senate's power is vested in a majority of Senators; the Constitution does not vest this power in a minority of Senators. Senator Daschle's comments are ludicrous! His party's use of the filibuster prevents the Senate from doing its constitutional duty to confirm or reject judicial nominees.

Senator Daschle also justifies his parties' blocking a vote on Owens and Estrada because it is necessary to keep ideologues and "extreme" judges off of the bench. (*The Washington Times,* May 12, 2003.) Nat Hentoff reports that Senator Daschle made this accusation in particular against Judge Owens: "Her record is so egregious that we have no choice but to filibuster." (*The Washington Times,* May 12, 2003.) One of the main objections the Democrats have to her is that she is on record as being conscientious about the right of parental consent to abortion by teenagers. But Mr. Hentoff points out that recent polls showed that the majority of Americans, including Democrats, were of the same opinion. *Id.* The result of this is that the filibuster empowers a minority to reject a judge whose ideology is shared with a majority of the nation, not to mention a majority of the Senate.

The lamest argument that the Democrats want to give is that they are doing nothing more than what the Republicans had done. But with the Democrats' resorting to the filibuster, this argument is not true. Previous to the Democrats' resorting to the filibuster, it had become the Senate's practice that the party in power would delay the scheduling of full Senate votes on the opposing party's nominees. In fact, many nominees never even made it out of the Senate Judiciary Committee. That is what happened in 2002 to Pricilla Owen and to a number of other of President Bush's nominees. This practice has been properly criticized by *The Washington Post.* But while both parties could accuse the other of some abuses in this practice, the Republicans never resorted to filibustering a Senate vote on a nominee. There is no precedent for this.

In 1998, Senator Patrick Leahy soundly criticized the notion of a Senator's waging a filibuster to block the vote on a judicial nominee: "I would object and fight against any filibuster of a judge, whether somebody I opposed or supported. If we don't like somebody the president nominates, vote him or her down." (Quoted by Terry Eastland, "Filibuster Benchmarks," *The Washington Post,* February 27, 2003.) But not only has Senator Leahy abandoned his principled, 1998 position, but he is now the leading politician who, for purely partisan purposes, uses the very perverse procedure he once condemned.

To top it all off, in addition to the litany of specious arguments that the Democratic leadership offers as an attempt to justify their filibuster, Senator Schumer has the audacity to justify his use of the filibuster out of respect for "the sacredness of the Constitution." *Id.* This is outrageous! Senator Schumer is clearly a fighter. But he is not a fair fighter; neither is he fighting in harmony with the Constitution. His use of the filibuster stands the Constitution on its head. His actions make a mockery of the Constitution, for the filibuster only serves to prevent the majority in the Senate from voting to confirm or reject the president's nominees. His party's use (abuse) of the filibuster rule (Rule XXII) is being used to contravene the clear mandate of the Constitution.

The greatest objective of the Democrats is to prevent the confirmation of any judge, and especially any nominee for Supreme Court Justice who has ever dared to criticize the abortion manifesto, that bedrock of the modern right to privacy—the *Roe v. Wade* decision of 1973. Democrats live in fear of this case being overturned or modified. Anyone who dares to speak ill of it is promptly labeled by the Democrats to be an "ideologue," a "radical," an "extremist"—one who is out of step with the mainstream of America, and one who must be rejected for any judicial nomination.

One of the ironies of this Democratic fear of ideologues is manifest in how the Democrats treat pro-lifers differently from pro-gay advocates; to them, one who would reverse *Roe v. Wade* is a terrible judicial activist, whereas one who works for the recognition of gay rights is a hero and a model of judicial wisdom and courage. For these Democrats, it's okay to invalidate state laws in order to create a heretofore unknown constitutional "liberty" to engage in homosexual relations; but it's wrong to criticize the judicial activism that eliminated the long-recognized power of the states to protect the fetal right to life. Distilled to its bare essence, for them it's okay to be a judicial activist who favors liberal causes, but its not okay to oppose the judicial activism that hurts the liberal agenda. This is what the Democratic filibuster is all about; it is nothing more than a cut-throat political debate. The Democratic attempt to clothe their extremism in words that claim to uphold the Constitution is nothing more than pure hypocrisy.

The Democratic Party's action to prostitute the Senate's judicial confirmation process by using filibusters to prevent a full Senate vote has made the nuclear option the right thing to do. Eliminating the use of a filibuster to block a Senate vote on a judicial nominee will restore the majority rule to the confirmation process. Now is the time to get rid of the Senate filibuster rule with respect to judicial and executive nominees. Failure of the Republicans to employ the nuclear option, if necessary, to correct this serious perversion will be a disgrace to Republicans and a disaster for the fundamentals of democracy and republicanism in America.

2.22
13.4

Supreme Court upholds extension of copyrights from 50 to 70 years

On January 15, 2003 the Supreme Court ruled 7-2 in Eldred v. Ashcroft, 537 U.S. 186, 123 S.Ct. 769 (2003), that the Sonny Bono Copyright Term Extension Act of 1998 was a valid exercise of Congressional power in giving artists and writers exclusive rights to profits from their works for limited periods of time. The Court held that Congress had the power to extend that exclusive use period from 50 to 70 years.

Victoria's Secret trademark was not violated by Victor's Little Secret

On March 4, 2003, the Supreme Court ruled unanimously in *Moseley v. V. Secret Catalogue*, 537 U.S. 418, 123 S.Ct. 1115 (2003) that Victor Moseley's use of the trade name "Victor's Little Secret" for the name of his sex-toy store in Elizabethtown, Kentucky did not violate the "Victoria's Secret" trademark. Justice Stevens wrote that Mr. Moseley's use of the phrase "Victor's Little Secret" "neither confused any consumers or potential consumer, nor was likely to do so." ... "[T]he mere fact that consumers mentally associate the junior user's mark with a famous mark is not sufficient to establish actionable dilution." Trademark owners must prove that they have lost capacity to identify and distinguish their goods and services.

Legal analysts think that this ruling will make it more difficult in the future for owners of famous trademarks to win trademark dilution cases.

Internet music-swapping services not liable for copyright infringements by users, federal judge rules

On April 25, 2003, a federal district court judge in California ruled that Internet music-swapping services are not liable for copyright infringement acts of their users. This ruling clears Internet systems like Grokster and Morpheus, who provide information on where music can be found on-line. This ruling is seen as break from the legal trend in protecting the rights of copyright holders that reached its height with the closing of Napster in 2001.

Grokster and Morpheus argued successfully that no protected information was transferred through their computers, and that their information-providing systems were valid for a host of legal activities, and that they should not be penalized for someone's illegal use of this information.

The federal judge cited the 1984 Sony Betamax case as controlling in the Morpheus and Grokster case. The Sony Betamax case held that companies that make and sell VCRs and photocopiers are not liable for what consumers do with those products.

Music and movie industries plan to appeal this ruling to the U. S. 9th Circuit Court of Appeals.

2.3

2.4

Supreme Court Upholds Redistricting Map Drawn by Federal Judges

On March 30, 2003, the Supreme Court announced its ruling in *Branch v. Smith*, 538 U.S. ___, 123 S.Ct. 1429 (2003) upholding the Mississippi congressional redistricting plan drawn up by a panel of three Republican-appointed federal judges. A unanimous Supreme Court found that that the federal judges were correct in blocking the state court redistricting plan. The Court found that in the absence of authorization by the state legislature, the state courts had no authority to draw congressional boundaries. The redrawn district that the state court judges had drawn resembled the funnel of a tornado; its unusual configuration was drawn to boost the number of Democratic voters in that district.

Amendment Proposed for Appointing Congressional Replacements in the Event of Catastrophic Attack on Congress

On June 4, 2003 a bipartisan commission of former members of Congress recommended that a new constitutional Amendment be passed to allow states to make immediate, temporary appointments to fill vacancies in the House and in the Senate in the event of a catastrophe that would kill or incapacitate a majority of Congress. The terrorist attacks of September 11th have given increased impetus to prepare for an act that could disable our government. House and Senate Rules Committees will consider such proposals that members of Congress may submit before any specific proposal will be voted on and sent to the States.

Lybia and Cuba work together on the U. N. Human Rights Commission

In case you're doing a double-take after reading the above headline, you are demonstrating the appropriate response to this news item. Of course, while these two nations are working together, no one can be sure of what they will be working for, nor whether they will continue their historic courses of action of suppressing human rights, notwithstanding they may now becoming hypocritical advocates for such rights.

On April 29, 2003, the United States Economic and Social Council unanimously (54-0) reelected Cuba to the U. N. Human Rights Commission.

The Washington Post reported (April 30, 2003) that Ari Fleischer, the spokesman for President Bush, made the obvious objection to this reelection: "Cuba does not deserve a seat on the Human Rights Commission. Cuba deserves to be investigated by the Human Rights Commission." The *Post* reported that even in the last month Cuba rounded up and imprisoned approximately 75 dissidents and gave them prison terms of up to 28 years.

Considering that Lybia chairs this U. N. commission, it is only fitting that Cuba should also have a seat on this commission to make the sham complete. For 30 years Lybia has not permitted freedom of speech and has been responsible for numerous acts of terrorism.

Belgium scraps its war crimes law

On July 12, 2003, Belgian officials announced that they would scrap their controversial war crimes law by which they asserted jurisdiction over war crimes committed anywhere and everywhere in the world. Their law had most recently come under criticism after war crimes prosecutions were launched against Israeli Prime Minister Ariel Sharon, against United States General Tommy Franks for his role in Operation Iraqi Freedom, and against President George Bush.

In the case against General Tommy Franks, ten Iraqis had gone to Belgium and filed a complaint against him.

No other civilized country in the world claims to exercise such universal jurisdiction. The Bush administration was angered by the complaints filed and by the Belgian presumption that it would provide a forum for the politically motivated prosecution of Americans.

The Washington Times pointed out (May 2, 2003) that this type of ridiculous legal action is the very reason why the International Criminal Court (ICC) is a very bad idea for the world and for America.

7.5 7.6 7.7
3.5.1 3.10

United States, Britain and Australia Oust Saddam Hussein from Iraq

Historically, the biggest news item of the first six months of 2003 is the operation Iraqi Freedom, in which the United States, Great Britain and Australia invaded Iraq and expelled the Saddam Hussein regime from control of Iraq. The U.S. had been building its military forces around Iraq for six months, waiting to invade Iraq if the President and Congress concluded that Hussein was not complying with U.N. Resolution 1441, which required Iraq to disarm and to disclose information about its weapons of mass destruction. The U.S. and Britain determined that Hussein did not comply, that he continued to defy the U.N. resolution and the U.S. and Britain. Finally, on March 20, 2003, the U.S. began bombing Baghdad, and U.S. British and Australian troops entered Iraq and began the campaign to take over control of Iraq. Six weeks later, on May 1, 2003, President Bush proclaimed victory, as the coalition forces had taken control of all major cities in Iraq.

Newspaper reports showed a grateful people celebrating in the streets, toppling the many statues of Saddam throughout the country. But there were also some rioting and plundering of businesses by Iraqis that accompanied the military victory. And for the next several months after victory was declared, there has continued to be widespread terrorist attacks on coalition forces, resulting in continued sporadic deaths and injuries to Americans. The attacks are believed to be from Hussein loyalists who are desperately hoping for Hussein to reappear and/or hoping to discourage the Americans. Coalition forces bombed the place where Hussein was believed to be, but his body was not recovered. So it is not certain that he is dead, although his regime has been replaced.

In the aftermath of the pronouncement of victory, the search for weapons of mass destruction (WMD) has continued in earnest. To date, little has been discovered. Evidence has been discovered of mobile biological weapons labs, and abundance evidence of the mass murders of hundreds by Hussein's regime, as it brutally killed any who dared to challenge Saddam's power. While the search continues, the Democrats have used the fact that the suspected WMD have not been found to attempt to malign President Bush and to gain a political advantage in the 2004 presidential election. Mounting American casualties are causing increased discontent with Operation Iraqi Freedom. This is testing the resolve of Americans to pay the price to rid the world of the terrorism that threatens us and our neighbors around the world.

For the time being the victory over Iraq has been a political plus for President Bush because the nation backed him in the effort and because there were relatively few casualties. But his dad can tell him that sometimes the polls can change quickly.

President Invokes War Powers Act and Wages War to Free Iraqi People

On March 21, 2003, President Bush formally declared to Congress his authority under the War Powers Act to use American forces to disarm and oust Saddam Hussein and his regime in Iraq. Congress promptly responded by approving of Operation Iraqi Freedom.

The 1973 War Powers Act allows presidents to dispatch troops to conflicts for up to 60 days, but requires congressional approval for longer conflicts.

Despite what Sentate Minority Leader Tom Daschle called a "dismal" failure of diplomacy (*The Washington Post*, March 22, 2003), he nevertheless joined a unanimous Senate (99-0) in voting to authorize the President's sending 250,000 troops to carry out his war plans in the Persian Gulf region (*The Washington Post*, March 21, 2003). On March 22, 2003, the House of Representatives voted 392-11 to similarly support the President's leading American troops in Operation Iraqi Freedom (*The Washington Post*, March 23, 2003).

Earlier in March, the United Nations declined to pass a new resolution authorizing the use of force against Iraq. But President Bush said that a new resolution was not necessary—that U. N. Resolution 1441 (passed six months earlier) already authorized the use of force. President Bush said that the United States was acting to enforce what the U. N. Security Council would not.

A Washington Post/ABC News poll conducted on March 17, 2003, showed that 71% of Americans supported a war to topple Saddam Hussein, while other nations disapproved of U. S. military action against Iraq (*The Washington Post*, March 19, 2003).

The result of Congressional votes supporting Operation Iraqi Freedom is that the war against the Saddam Hussein regime in Iraq is constitutionally legal. It was done in compliance with the War Powers Act and with the requirement that Congress declare war. The Constitution does not require Congress to use the specific words "declare war" in giving the President the necessary authorization to prosecute a war. (Article I, Section 8.)

Secret Detention of Individuals in Terrorist Investigations Is Upheld

On June 17, 2003, a three-judge panel of the United States Court of Appeals for the District of Columbia ruled (2-1) that terrorism investigations justify the withholding of information that might otherwise be discoverable under the Freedom of Information Act. The case is *Center for National Security Studies v. U. S. Dept. of Justice*, 331 F.3d 918 (D. C. Cir. 2003)..

The names of over 700 individuals are being kept secret by the federal government in ongoing investigations into terrorist threats. *The Washington Post* called the actions "dreadful," and urged the Supreme Court to review and clarify the appellate court ruling.

Supreme Court Rejects ACLU Challenge to Spy Laws

On March 24, 2003, the Supreme Court rejected a request by the American Civil Liberties Union (ACLU) to submit briefs in an appeal from a ruling by the Foreign Intelligence Surveillance Court (or "spy" court) that had refused to issue a warrant requested by the government. The ACLU sought to have a say in this appeal, but the Supreme Court would not let them become involved. *ACLU v. U. S.*, 538 U.S. ___, 123 S.Ct. 1615 (2003). (No written opinion accompanies this Order.)

In 1978 Congress passed the Foreign Intelligence Surveillance Act (FISA) and established the Foreign Intelligence Surveillance Court ("spy court"), which is authorized, among other things, to issue secret wiretapping warrants where the suspect is a "foreign power or agent of a foreign power." "Probable cause" (which is normally required to obtain search warrants) is not required to obtain a spy court warrant. Following the 9/11 terrorist attacks, there has been a sharp increase in the number of emergency warrants requested. In May of 2003, the spy court issued a ruling that limited the powers of the government under the USA Patriot Act. Attorney General Ashcroft appealed that ruling to the FISA Court of Review. The government is the only party allowed to participate in this review. But the

ACLU sought to intervene in the review, arguing that the closed, secret proceedings should be monitored. The Supreme Court ruled against the ACLU, holding that secrecy is indispensable for anti-terrorism investigations.

Supreme Court Upholds Federal Immigrant Custody Law

On April 29, 2003, the Supreme Court ruled (5-4) in *Denmore v. Kim*, 538 U.S. ___ (2003), upholding the constitutionality of a seven-year-old federal law that the government may detain and keep locked up immigrants who have committed certain "aggravated" offenses can continue to be detained by immigration authorities if deporting proceedings are pending.

Immigrant rights groups had urged the Court to give such immigrants the right to a bail hearing to consider whether they would be likely to commit another crime or jump bail. But the Court ruled that no bail hearing was required, and this treatment of convict immigrants did not violate their right to due process of law. The Court ruled that the right to bail does not apply to non-citizens and that Congress can make laws that apply differently to aliens than to citizens.

Fourth Circuit Upholds Detention of U. S. Citizen as "Enemy Combatant"

On January 8, 2003, a three-judge panel of the Fourth Circuit U. S. Court of Appeals, upheld the federal government's detaining of American citizen Yaser Esam Hamdi (age 22) during wartime without affording him the constitutional protections normally afforded criminal defendants. *Hamdi v. Rumsfeld*, 316 F.3d 450 (4th Cir. 2003).

Mr. Hamdi was captured in Afghanistan while fighting against U.S. forces and fighting alongside Taliban guerrillas and al Qaeda terrorists. The court said that because Hamdi was captured in a "zone of active combat in a foreign theater of conflict," the President's constitutional war powers authorized the detention of Hamdi.

Supreme Court Rules that Pro-life Protesters Are Not "Extortionists"

On February 26, 2003, the Supreme Court ruled 8-1 in *Scheidler v. NOW* and *Operation Rescue v. NOW*, 537 U.S. 393, 123 S.Ct. 1057 (2003) that pro-life protesters outside abortion clinics cannot be prosecuted as extortionists and racketeers under the federal Racketeer-Influenced and Corrupt Organizations Act (RICCO). RICCO was enacted for mob-fighting purposes, and eight Justices declined to extend that law to make it applicable to political protests. Chief Justice Rehnquist wrote for the majority that the acts of protesters in disrupting an abortion clinic did not constitute extortion because the protesters did not "obtain property."

Had the RICCO applied, the protesters could have been liable for treble damages to the abortion clinics they disrupted. The lower court had found 92 violations of federal and state laws and had awarded $85,926 in damages. Applying RICCO, these damages had been multiplied by three, resulting in $257,780 in damages. However, the Supreme Court ruling nullified the damage award by ruling that RICCO was inapplicable.

While RICCO does not apply to protesters who may disrupt the business of an abortion clinic, another federal law does protect the clinics—the Freedom of Access to Clinic Entrances Act (FACE) of 1994. This law, however, does not include the strong civil damage provision.

Bush Administration Asks Supreme Court to Reverse Ninth Circuit Ruling on the Pledge of Allegiance

On April 30, 2003, the Bush Administration filed a petition asking the Supreme Court to reverse the ruling of the Ninth Circuit Court of Appeals in *Nedow v. United States Congress*, 292 F.3d 597 (9th Cir. 2002), in which that federal appeals court ruled unconstitutional a California law that required daily patriotic observances in public schools that may include the Pledge of Allegiance. The Ninth Circuit stated: "The statement that the United States is a nation 'under God' is an endorsement of religion." And that, according to the Ninth Circuit, violates the Establishment Clause of the First Amendment. The plaintiff in the law suit, Mr. Newdow (an atheist) said that his daughter's religious liberty was violated simply by her hearing the Pledge recited in school as a part of the official daily program of the state school system.

Attorney General John Ashcroft promised to "spare no effort to preserve the rights of all our citizens to pledge allegiance to the American flag," and to defend centuries of tradition in which "our government and people can acknowledge the important role religion has played in America's foundation [and] history."

In the petition filed by the United States, Solicitor General Theodore Olson said that Congress' addition of the phrase "under God" to the Pledge in 1954 does not amount to the promotion or "establishment" of religion that is forbidden by the First Amendment.

The dissenting judge on the three-judge panel stated that the majority's reasoning would also condemn the Gettysburg Address, the Constitution, the Declaration of Independence and the fourth verse of "The Star-Spangled Banner."

Fourth Circuit Upholds Ban on VMI Dinner Prayer

On April 28, 2003, a three-judge panel of the U. S. Court of Appeals for the Fourth Circuit upheld a lower court ruling that the Virginia Military Institute (VMI) tradition of school-led dinner prayers is unconstitutional. *Mellen v. Bunting*, 327 F.3d 355 (4th Cir. 2003).

The panel wrote that "[t]he supper prayer has the primary effect of promoting religion, in that it sends the unequivocal message that VMI, as an institution, endorses the religious expressions embodied in the prayer." The Court went on to state: "While the First Amendment does not in any way prohibit VMI's cadets from praying before, during, or after supper, the Establishment Cause prohibits VMI [a state run university] from sponsoring such a religious activity."

Virginia Attorney General Jerry Kilgore argued that the prayer did not violate the Establishment Clause, and that prayers such as these are precisely the sort of prayers recited in the United States military on ships at sea and before Lunch at the United States Naval Academy.

Nonprofit Advocacy Corporations Barred from Making Political Contributions

On June 16, 2003 the Supreme Court ruled in *Federal Election Commission v. Beaumont*, 539 U.S. ___, 123 S.Ct. 2200 (2003) that the federal law barring corporations from making direct contributions to candidates for federal office applies to nonprofit advocacy corporations as well as to for-profit corporations, and that such a law does not violate the First Amendment rights of the advocacy corporations.

The North Carolina Right to Life group had argued that it should not subject to the law banning federal campaign contributions because of its First Amendment right to be free from federal regulation of protected speech; the right to life group felt that it was exempt from any governmental speech regulation because it was a tax-exempt organization that was funded by private monies. But the Supreme Court disagreed, ruling (7-2) that profit and non-profit corporations alike are prohibited from contributing to federal campaigns.

This ruling will affect powerful advocacy groups such as the AARP, the NRA and the Sierra Club.

Experts do not see any insights in this case to foreshadow how the Supreme Court is expected to rule on the constitutionality of the McCain-Feingold Campaign Finance Reform Act within the next year.

Appeals Court Strikes Portions of the Campaign Finance Reform Act— All Now Wait for the Supreme Court to Review It

On May 2, 2003, a three-judge panel of the United States Court of Appeals for the District of Columbia Circuit ruled (2-1) that important sections of the McCain-Feingold Campaign Finance Reform Act were unconstitutional. *McConnell v. Federal Election Commission*, 251 F.Supp.2d 919 (D. C. Cir. 2003). This sets the stage for the case to be appealed to the Supreme Court, which is expected to rule on the case before the end of 2003. On June 5, 2003, the Supreme Court ordered an expedited review of the case. Four hours of oral arguments are scheduled for September 8, 2003.

The lower federal court upheld some portions of the law, but the ruling is not seen as having any great significance since all parties know that the Supreme Court will have to weigh in on the law before either party will be able to know what, if anything, is left of the Campaign Finance Reform Act.

Virginia Cross Burning Statute Ruled Unconstitutional

On April 7, 2003, the Supreme Court ruled (7-2) in *Virginia v. Black*, 538 U.S. ___, 123 S.Ct. 1536 (2003), that a Virginia statute that made cross burning a crime was unconstitutional because the law treated any cross burning to be prima facie evidence of intent to intimidate. The Court held that some uses of cross burning are protected symbolic speech, and that the Virginia law was overly broad in criminalizing all cross burnings.

There was no majority opinion supporting one rationale for the holding, thus, the opinion of Justice O'Connor that announced the ruling of the Court is called a "plurality" opinion. But only Justices Scalia and Thomas would have upheld the statute.

Seven of the Justices agreed that cross burning can be symbolic, expressive speech that is protected by the First Amendment. Therefore, the Virginia statute that prohibited such speech based upon its content violated the First Amendment. Justice O'Connor's plurality opinion (jointed by Justices Rehnquist, Stevens and Breyer) felt that the Virginia law's presumption of wrongful intent made the statute invalid. The statute provided that "any such burning of a cross shall be prima facie evidence of an intent to intimidate a person or group of persons." Because this provision subjects a person to be convicted of having a wrongful intent without any evidence other than the cross burning itself. Justices Souter, Kennedy and Ginsburg felt the statute to be invalid whether or not the presumption of wrongful intent provision were to be corrected.

Court Upholds Law Requiring Pornography Filters at Libraries

On June 23, 2003, the Supreme Court upheld (6-3) the requirement of the Children's Internet Protection Act (CIPA) which forbids libraries to receive federal funds for internet assistance unless they install filters that prevent minors from accessing pornographic materials. *United States v. American Library Association, Inc.*, 539 U.S. ___, 123 S.Ct. 2297 (2003).

Seventh Circuit Confirms Conviction of Man for Possessing Child Pornography on His Computer

On January 7, 2003, the U. S. Court of Appeals for the 7th Circuit affirmed the conviction and 33-month prison sentence of George Kelly for possessing on his computer child pornography, i.e. pictures of real children engaged in sex acts. Mr. Kelly's defense that he was an innocent recipient of unsolicited material was unsuccessful. In January 2002, Mr. Kelly had visited a sex chat room that the government was regulating and from which he arranged to receive material.

Last year, on April 16, 2002, the Supreme Court ruled in *Ashcroft v. Free Speech Coalition*, 535 U.S. 229, 122 S.Ct. 1389 (2002) that "virtual pornography," computer-generated images of younger children may not be outlawed, and to that extent invalidated that portion of the Child Pornography Prevention Act of 1996. But other parts of this law remained in effect and were used in prosecuting Mr. Kelly.

Redneck Humor T-Shirt Held Not to Constitute Harassment or Intimidation

On May 19, 2003, the Supreme Court refused to review a case from the 3rd U.S. Court of Appeals that allowed a public school student to wear to school a T-shirt with a "Top 10 Reasons You Might Be a Redneck Sports Fan," followed by comedian Jeff Foxworthy's list that included,

"You wear a baseball cap to bed" and "You know the Hooters' menu by heart."

School officials in Warren County, New Jersey had suspended the teenager for three days for wearing the T-shirt, but the federal appeals court ruled that school had overstepped its bounds and that there was nothing intimidating or harassing about the message on the humorous shirt.

Supreme Court Allows States to Take Private Property without "Just Compensation" through Lawyer Trust Accounts

In April, the Supreme Court ruled in *Brown v. Legal Foundation of Washington*, 538 U.S. ___, 123 S.Ct. 1406 (2003), that States may make and take interest on the funds of individuals that are held in escrow by attorneys, when that interest is used to support legal services programs.

For the last quarter century, many states have adopted programs to consolidate the escrow funds of its attorneys and to make and collect interest on them. Such accounts are called Interest on Lawyer Trust Accounts (IOLTA). The states use this interest to fund state legal service programs for the poor.

Since this escrow (or trust account) income was clearly owned by private individuals, it would normally be subject to the requirements of the Fifth Amendment—that the government must give those individuals "just compensation" for the property taken. However, the Court carved out an exception to this general rule because the escrowed monies would not otherwise have earned any interest (state regulations prohibit it). The majority reasoned that because there would not have been any income on the funds without the special dispensation of the states to allow it in the case of IOLTA, that therefore the individuals actually suffer no loss, and therefore no compensation to them is required.

Southwestern Arroyo Toad Stops Development in Rancho Viejo, California

On April 1, 2003, the United States Court of Appeals for the District of Columbia upheld government action in San Diego County, California in stopping a real estate development project that would have jeopardized an endangered species of toad, the Southwestern Arroyo Toad.

The federal government halted the real estate project by the authority of the Endangered Species Act. The developer sued, arguing that the government action had overstepped the boundaries of the commerce clause. But the federal judge disagreed, and the three-judge appeals panel unanimously upheld the lower judge's ruling.

Apparently the Fifth Circuit Court of Appeals has rejected the reasoning used by the D. C. Circuit in this case. This split in the circuits may lead to a Supreme Court review of the Endangered Species Act.

Environmental Laws Impede Training of U. S. Military

On January 13, 2003, *The Washington Post* reported that the Pentagon planned to ask Congress for relief from environmental protection laws that impeded crucial military training. The Pentagon urged a "common sense" solution to how the major environmental laws were interpreted and administered so as not to interfere with important defense training. Military training bases at Ft. Lewis, Washington; Camp Pendleton, California; Eglin Air Force Base, Florida; Norfolk Naval Station, Virginia; and Massachusetts Military Reservation in Cape Cod have all been affected by environmental regulations.

30th Anniversary of the Endangered Species Act marked by misuse

2003 marks the thirtieth anniversary of the Endangered Species Act of 1973. Although the law specifically provides for the federal government to "take into account the economic impact of specifying any particular areas as a critical habitat," those enforcing and interpreting the law have most frequently used the law to economically hinder and harm communities around the nation. For example, in an op-ed piece by Joseph Perkins in *The Washington Post* (February 20, 2003), Mr. Perkins stated that the Act was used to stall the construction of an 8-lane, $260 million highway proposed for San Diego because of a claim that the highway would destroy the habitat of the Quino Checkerspot butterfly. Mr. Perkins also reported that the southern California regional economy would be hurt by as much as $5.5 billion, if the environment-alists succeeded in preventing a half-million acres from development in order to save the coastal California gnatcatcher and the San Diego fairy shrimp. *Id.*

But in addition to fanatical interpretation and administration of the Endangered Species Act, a recent study by the U. S. Fish and Wildlife Service reported earlier this year that there is "no clear statistical evidence" that the medium-size brown owl is declining and requires federal protection. *Id.* Joseph Perkins concludes that the Endangered Species Act has been misused by the federal government, and that Congress should revise the law.

Court Rules that States Are Subject to the Federal Family and Medical Leave Act

On June 1, 2003, the Supreme Court ruled (6-3) in *Nevada v. Hibbs*, 539 U.S. ___, 123 S.Ct. 1972 (2003) that the State governments can be sued for violation of the federal Family and Medical Leave Act (FMLA). This case is significant because in recent years the Supreme Court has interpreted the 11th Amendment to restrict the applicability of federal laws against the States. However, a majority of the Court distinguished the FMLA from other federal laws.

Mr. Hibbs, who was an employee of the State of Nevada, had sought leave under the FMLA to attend to his ill spouse. When Nevada denied him the relief he sought, he filed suit. Nevada's initial defense was that it was immune from suit by virtue of the 11th Amendment.

Chief Justice Rehnquist, writing for the majority, stated that the 14th Amendment provides an exception to the 11th Amendment's prohibition against individual suits against states. He said that Congress had specifically provided for the FMLA to address gender-based discrimination in the workplace, and that therefore Mr. Hibbs' suit was proper and that the Court would apply "heightened scrutiny" to the state interest that was pitted against the FMLA. In Mr. Hibbs' case, the state interest could not withstand the scrutiny, and therefore Mr. Hibbs' suit against the state based upon the federal law could go forward.

Supreme Court Rules That States Can Force HMOs to Accommodate All Doctors and Hospitals

On April 2, 2003, the Supreme Court ruled unanimously in *Kentucky Association of Health Care Plans, Inc. v. Miller*, 538 U.S. ___, 123 S.Ct. 1471 (2003) that states have a right to force health maintenance organizations (HMOs) to afford all doctors and hospitals the right to participate, provided they agree to abide by the HMO's terms.

This ruling upheld Kentucky's "any willing provider" (AWP) law that challenged the HMO's power to create limited networks of health care providers who would agree to accept lower fees in return for a higher volume of business.

In this case the HMO had argued that the Kentucky AWP law was invalid because it was preempted by federal law that regulated this area (i.e., by the Employee Retirement Income Security Act of 1974 [ERISA]). However, the Court ruled that ERISA grants an exception to this preemption for state laws that "regulate insurance, banking or securities."

Supreme Court Carves Out Exception to Rule That States Cannot Be Sued by Individuals

On April 23, 2003, the Supreme Court ruled in *Franchise Tax Board of California v. Hyatt*, 538 U.S. ___, 123 S.Ct. 1683 (2003), that a Nevada man could sue the State of California for invasion of privacy and fraud the state's violation of Nevada law in Nevada courts. The California officials had sought to apply California law in Nevada.

This case is significant because it articulates another exception to the general rule that the Supreme Court has reinforced during recent years that the Eleventh Amendment precludes an individual from suing a state.

Supreme Court Overturns Excessive Punitive Damages Award

On April 7, 2003, he Supreme Court, in a 6-3 ruling, overturned a Utah jury verdict for awarding excessive punitive damages against State Farm Insurance Co. for how it handled a couple's accident claim. *State Farm Auto. Ins. Co. v. Campbell*, 538 U.S. ___, 123 S.Ct. 1513 (2003).

In this case, a couple had sued and obtained a $2.6 million judgment (that was reduced later to $1 million) against State Farm Insurance for improperly handling their accident case. But the Court could not tolerate the additional punitive damage award of $145 million dollars, which the Court found to be "grossly excessive."

Writing for the dissent in this case, Justice Scalia admitted that the jury had "run wild" in awarding excessive punitive damages, Justice Scalia (writing the dissent) argued that this did not bestow on the courts the right to legislate; he argued that the states should correct these problems, not the courts.

Retrial of Defendant because jury deadlocked in first trial over whether to sentence defendant to death or to life imprisonment does not violate the Double Jeopardy Clause

On January 14, 2003, the Supreme Court ruled 5-4 that the retrial of a defendant in order to reach a unanimous verdict on the sentence did not violate the defendant's Fifth Amendment right to not be tried twice for the same crime. *Sattazahn v. Pennsylvania,* 537 U.S. 101, 123 S.Ct. 732 (2003). The five-judge majority ruled that the double jeopardy protection only applies if a defendant is acquitted.

Supreme Court Rules That State Cannot Retroactively Alter Statute of Limitations to Prosecute Child Molestation Cases

On June 26, 2003, the Supreme Court, by a 5-4 ruling in *Stogner v. California,* 538 U.S. ___, 123 S.Ct. 2446 (2003) overturned the 1994 California law that retroactively extended the already-expired statute of limitations in child molestation cases. This ruling will affect an estimated 800 cases in California (including convictions that will be overturned and other cases will be dropped).

California had sought to prosecute a man for sex-related child abuse occurring 25-43 years earlier, but California law barred prosecutions brought more than one year after a victim's report to police.

Supreme Court upholds bringing conspiracy charges after government has acted to prevent a conspiracy from being achieved

On January 21, 2003, the Supreme Court unanimously ruled in *United States v. Jimenez Recio,* 537 U.S. 270, 123 S.Ct. 819 (2003), that the government may charge defendants with conspiracy even if the government has infiltrated the crime ring and made it impossible for the alleged conspirator to achieve its goal. In so doing, the Court overturned a ruling of the U. S. Court of Appeals for the 9th Circuit.

The Bush administration successfully argued in this case that such charges should be allowed in order to prosecute not only drug conspiracies, but also terrorist plots.

Supreme Court establishes guidelines for forcing defendants to take medication

On June 16, 2003, the Supreme Court ruled 6-3 in *Sell v. United States,* 539 U.S. ___, 123 S.Ct. 2174 (2003), that lower courts had improperly ordered St. Louis dentist Charles T. Sell to take antipsychotic drugs in order to stand trial on charges of Medicaid fraud, mail fraud and money laundering. Justice Stephen Breyer wrote for the majority that medication may be forced on a defendant only if doing so would significantly further any important government objective (such as being substantially likely to make him/her competent to stand trail) and if doing so would be "substantially unlikely" to produce side effects that would the fairness of the defendant's trial.

California's '3-Strikes' Law Upheld

On March 5, 2003, the Supreme Court ruled 5-4 that California's "three strikes and you're out" law (the toughest in the nation) did not violate the Eighth Amendment's prohibition against cruel and unusual punishment. *Ewing v. California*, 538 U.S. ___, 123 S.Ct. 1179 (2003). (The Supreme Court also decided a companion case on this issue, *Lockyer v. Andrade*, 538 U.S. ___, 123 S.Ct. 1166 (2003).

Defendant Gary Ewing had appealed his sentence of 25 years in jail for stealing three golf clubs. He argued that the sentence was excessively harsh for the nature of the offense. But the majority held that the harsh sentence did not violate the Constitution and in particular did not violate the prohibition against cruel and unusual punishment. (Justice Scalia wrote separately, that the Eighth Amendment only banned certain methods of punishment.)

In his dissenting opinion, Justice Stephen Breyer said that Ewing's sentence was two to three times longer than what other states would have imposed, and that this was disproportionate to the crime. But Justice O'Connor pointed out that Ewing's sentence was not grossly disproportionate in light of his "long history of felony recidivism," including three burglaries and a robbery.

Supreme Court Upholds Megan's Laws

On March 5, 2003, the Supreme Court ruled in a Connecticut case and an Alaska case that Megan's laws are constitutional. These laws provide the public with information about potential sexual predators based upon prior records. A unanimous Court ruled in *Connecticut Dept. of Public Safety v. Doe*, 538 U.S. ___, 123 S.Ct. 1160 (2003) that names, pictures and other information about convicted sex offenders can be published on the World Wide Web. By a 6-3 vote, in *Smith v. Doe*, 538 U.S. ___, 123 S.Ct. 1140 (2003), the Court also upheld an Alaska law requiring quarterly reporting by ex-convict sex offenders of their addresses and license numbers for 15 years after leaving jail.

The ex-convict sex offenders unsuccessfully argued that these laws constituted punishment and imposed onerous reporting requirements and made it harder to find and keep employment. They also argued that the laws were unfair because in their cases, their crimes were committed before the reporting laws were passed.

10.8.2
9.6

Denial of visitation privileges in prison for 2 years does not violate the Constitution

On June 16, 2003, the Supreme Court ruled in *Overton v. Bazzetta*, 539 U.S. ___, 123 S.Ct. 2162 (2003) that a ban on having visitation with individuals outside of prison for two years for an inmate with at least two substance-abuse violations did not violate the Constitution; it was not cruel and unusual punishment under the Eighth Amendment; neither did it violate the inmate's First Amendment free association rights.

Supreme Court Embraces New, Diversity Rationale to Extend Affirmative Action

On June 23, 2003, the Supreme Court announced its ruling in the two University of Michigan affirmative action cases. *Grutter v. Bollinger*, 539 U.S. ___, 123 S.Ct. 2325 (2003) and *Gratz v. Bollinger*, 539 U.S. ___, 123 S.Ct. 2411 (2003). The gist of the two rulings is that it is okay to make race a factor in college admissions, as long as it's not too big a factor (*Gratz*), and that the Court (for the first time) declares that a state's interest in "diversity" has now become a "compelling state interest" that is sufficient to trump the Equal Protection Clause of the the Fourteenth Amendment (*Grutter*). Both of these rulings suspend the requirement of the Fourteenth Amendment that States cannot discriminate on the basis of race.

In *Gratz*, the Court ruled (6-3) that the University of Michigan policy that gave an applicant for admission 20 points (one-fifth of the points needed to guarantee admission) on the basis of race violated the Equal Protection Clause of the 14th Amendment because the policy was not sufficiently narrowly tailored "to further a compelling state interest."

However, in *Grutter*, the Court ruled (5-4) that the University of Michigan Law School admissions policy that aspires to achieve racial diversity in its student body is narrowly tailored to achieve a compelling state interest to promote diversity in education, and therefore it does not violate the Equal Protection Clause. Heretofore, diversity has not been recognized as a basis for suspending the application of the Equal Protection Clause. Previously, the Court had justified certain racial preferences (affirmative action) because of the state interest in compensating for years of disadvantage that blacks had suffered from governmental and societal discrimination. But just as the life of this temporary remedial

exception was expiring, the Supreme Court has now recognized a new rationale for further extending racial preferences under affirmative action.

Justices Sandra O'Connor and Stephen Breyer were the two swing votes in these two cases. The other justices voted either against the validity of both admissions programs (Rehnquist, Thomas, Scalia & Kennedy) or for the validity of both programs (Stevens, Souter & Ginsburg).

It is worthy of note that the lone black Justice, Clarence Thomas, felt that no state interest in diversity should displace the strict demands of the Equal Protection Clause. Quoting Frederick Douglass 140 years ago, Justice Thomas wrote in his dissent in *Grutter*: "What I ask for the negro is not benevolence, not pity, not sympathy, but simply *justice.*"

In a most interesting statement of limitation by Justice O'Connor (who wrote the majority opinion in *Grutter*), she stated that the state's interest in racial diversity would lapse in 25 years. This is a remarkable statement. On the one hand it confirms that "affirmative action" is but a temporary remedy for the existence of vestiges of discrimination that are found to remain in our society, despite the presence of the Equal Protection Clause and 130 years of legislation to enforce it. The Supreme Court's pronouncement of a temporary remedy for society's shortcomings is constitutionally offensive because it constitutes a legislative act on the part of the Supreme Court that is not the Court's prerogative, but results from judicial impatience with the legislature to correct what the Court deems a legislative flaw.

Commission on Civil Rights Is Liable for Discriminating against Employee

It is a compelling irony that the U. S. Commission on Civil Rights has been found liable for discriminating against one of its own employees. Yet that is what happened. On May 1, 2003, *The Washington Post* reported that the Equal Employment Opportunities Commission (EEOC) found that the U. S. Commission on Civil Rights had retaliated against and wrongfully demoted Emma Monroig after she had initiated a complaint against the Commission. The EEOC ordered that Ms. Monroig be reinstated and that the Commission must pay her $165,000 in damages.

143

CONSTITUTIONAL

LAW

UPDATES

| IV:i | May 2004 | No. 8 |

News Items through December 31. 2003

CONSTITUTIONAL LAW UPDATES is a semiannual newsletter edited and published by C. Paul Smith, J.D.
Subscription cost is $13.00 per year (plus $0.65 tax in MD). To subscribe, send a check or money order to
CONSTITUTIONAL LAW UPDATES, P. O. Box 1204, Frederick MD 21702-0204. For further information, visit
Paul Smith's web site at   www . cpaulsmith . com   Copyright C. Paul Smith 2004.

Major News Items from July - December, 2003

Arnold Schwarzenegger Is Elected Governor of California

On October 7, 2003, foreign body builder-turned actor-turned U. S. citizen, Arnold Schwarzenegger, was elected governor of America's largest state, California. Who would have thought twenty years ago, after watching Arnold banter about in only a loin cloth in *Conan the Barbarian*, that he would some day be elected the governor of California, or of any other state?

Arnold's lines in those early films were always limited and short--usually just a word or two at a time. Sometimes he would get a longer line, such as, "Hasta la vista, baby!" We knew is accent was heavy, and we figured that he might not be very bright. Wrong! Not only is he well disciplined, but he is also well educated; in fact, he's even smart.

As the drive to recall Governor Gray Davis went forward and the first televised debate between the several replacement candidates approached, Arnold was already the front-runner. His popularity as a candidate was simply remarkable; his box office appeal appeared directly related to voter appeal. So, as the night of the televised debate approached two weeks before the election, the whole nation tuned in to see how Arnold would manage in a pressure-filled, intellectually challenging, political debate.

Arnold was very impressive in the debate. Not only did he give good answers to the questions, but he had quick and witty responses to the verbal attacks made at him. For days after the debate people chuckled when they thought of his reply to Ariana Huffington, that he had a part for her to play in his next terminator movie. The headline in *The Washington Post* summed it up nicely: "Arnold Steals Show in California Debate; deflects hits with humor, levels criticism at Bustamonte" (September 25, 2003). Any question that may have existed about Arnold's *gravitas* was more than satisfied. Arnold's performance at the debate sealed the victory for him at the polls two weeks later.[1]

---

[1] A news article in *The Washington Post* on September 26, 2003, incorrectly analyzed the impact of

On October 7, 2003, the election played out as though it was a Hollywood script. California voters terminated the governorship of Gray Davis and voted in Arnold Schwarzenegger.

The Governor Davis total recall election was fascinating for some other reasons, as well. It was only less than a year earlier that California reelected Governor Davis. But just months into his second term, the people became fed up with the rising state budget deficits and the energy crisis that happened because the State refused to build new power facilities to provide for its growing population. Extremist environmentalists became so powerful in California that they too contributed to the state's fiscal problems. So too, the state's penchant to deliver taxpayer-funded social entitlements to a flood of illegal immigrants and to other non-contributors eventually brought the state's debt to an unacceptably large amount. Energy shortages and blackouts and the prospect of increased taxes to fix the state's deficits eventually made the people mad. The result was a grass roots recall petition that yielded a million signatures (if I recall correctly). And eleven months after California reelected Governor Davis to be Governor, the voters put him out of office, and voted Arnold Schwarzenegger in.

I almost forgot to point out that Arnold is a Republican, whereas ex-Governor Davis is a Democrat. Now, as the presidential election draws near, Republicans are salivating over the possibility of winning in California this November. But the rejection of Governor Davis may not be a rejection of the Democratic Party. And while the Democratic Party seemed to self-destruct in uncertainty during the recall campaign,[2] that scenario is not likely to unfold again in November.

---

the September 24th televised debate: "Davis Seen as Debate's Winner." Not so.

[2] The Democrats couldn't decide whether to campaign against the recall or whether to abandon Gov. Davis and campaign for Lt. Governor Bustamonte, in the event the recall succeeded. The Democrats pinned their hopes on Lt. Gov. Bustamonte, but the voters did not seem to distinguish Bustamonte from Davis. The political dilemma left a huge opportunity for the Republicans.

Democratic Senators Filibuster For 39 Hours

From November 12th through 13th, 2003, Republican Senators sought to bring four judicial nominees for a full Senate vote for confirmation. However, the Democratic Senators blocked the confirmation vote by filibustering for 39 hours, until the Republicans gave up.

The judicial nominees were William H. Pryor, Jr. (Alabama Attorney General);[1] U. S. District Court Judge Charles W. Pickering;[2] Texas Supreme Court Justice Priscilla R. Owen; and District of Columbia attorney, Miguel A. Estrada.

The previous edition of **Constitutional Law Updates** (Sept. 2003) included an article on the filibuster dilemma. I would point out that the Republicans are hoping that the nation will be incensed with the obstructionism of the Democrats in refusing to allow Senate votes on judicial nominees. There is some doubt that the nation really cares about this issue, but they should. Ultimately at stake is the political, philosophical and moral make-up of the Supreme Court. At least three replacements are expected in the next four years.

President Bush Signs Law Banning Partial Birth Abortion

On November 5, 2003, President George Bush signed a federal law banning partial birth abortion. Former President Clinton had vetoed a similar bill passed by Congress during his term.

Some claim that banning partial birth abortion violates the *Roe v. Wade* decision. This is not so. *Roe v. Wade* specifically provided that states had

---

[1] Coincidentally, Mr. Pryor was the one who led the prosecution in Alabama to remove Chief Justice Roy Moore for his failure to remove the Ten Commandments monument from the State Court Building.

[2] Subsequently, President Bush made recess appointments of Judges Pryor and Pickering, as authorized in Article II, Section 2. But those appointments will terminate at the end of this session of Congress. Subsequent to this, on May 18, 2004, President Bush agreed with the minority, Democratic Senators to make no more recess appointments until his first term expires on January 20, 2005 in return for their agreement not to block prompt confirmation votes on 25 non-controversial judicial nominees. *The Washington Post* and *The Washington Times*, May 19, 2004.

the right to prohibit abortions in the last trimester because of the states' interest in the potential life of the fetus.

Democrats attempt to paint as extremists those judicial nominees who oppose partial birth abortion. This is a gross distortion. The majority of the nation is opposed to partial birth abortion, as is evidenced by passage of this law.

Endangered Species Act Marks Its 30th Anniversary

On December 28, 2003, the Endangered Species Act (ESA) turned 30 years old. President Richard M. Nixon signed it into law in 1973.

The ESA has been criticized as both ineffective in protecting endangered species and as deleterious to economic growth. Michael De Alessi, "The Endangered Species Act; It Should Be Dead as the Dodo," *The Washington Times*, December 26, 2003. The ESA has also been criticized for being used by the government to take private lands without compensation. *Id.*

This issue's strange-but-true environmental protection story involves the ESA and took place in August, 2003. A federal judge in Minnesota order the Army Corps of Engineers to lower the water level of the Missouri River to protect the habitat of three endangered species—two birds (the Great Plains piping plover and the least tern) and a fish (the pallid sturgeon). The problem with lowering the river level is that it makes the level lower than needed for navigational purposes. The federal judge ruled that the ESA must take precedent over shipping, flood control and other considerations. This ruling conflicts with court rulings in Nebraska and the District of Columbia. *The Washington Post*, August 7, 2003.

9th Circuit Rules Citizens Have No Right to Own a Gun

On December 1, 2003, the U. S. Supreme Court declined to review a ruling by the Ninth Circuit U. S. Court of Appeals, holding that U. S. citizens have no Second Amendment Right to own a gun. By refusing to review this case, the Supreme Court lets stand a conflict between the 9th and 5th Circuits. The Fifth Circuit held that citizens do have a Second Amendment right to own a gun. *The Washington Times*, December 2, 2003.

2004 Presidential Election--
Brace for an Ugly Campaign

The election campaign for President of the United States will proceed this year while the nation continues at war in Iraq. This will pose some difficult issues for the challenging party; the Democrats will have difficulty resisting the urge to politicize every item of negative news that will come from Iraq.

The recent publication of photographs showing American soldiers treating Iraqi prisoners in humiliating and degrading ways has served to fuel the hatred and energy of our enemies against us, and thereby endangering the lives of our troops and of our citizens around the world. How politicians address these problems and others that may come to light is extremely important--they do not want to embolden our enemies through criticizing our management of the war. Senator Kerry must make it clear that America will defeat any and all who fight against us in Iraq. If Senator Kerry's criticism of President Bush's war effort is excessive, he could end up giving comfort, support and encouragement to our terrorist enemies. Specifically, Senator Kerry's dilemma is that if he does not sufficiently criticize President Bush, then the voters will not see a need to elect him to replace President Bush. But if Senator Kerry's criticism goes too far--and he is deemed by the voters as having given aid and comfort to your enemies--then the voters will reject him for this. The safety of our troops must not be compromised by the desire to challenge and criticize the President.

Senator Kerry is aware of this dilemma. He will acknowledge it, and he will insist that he always acts in a way to protect our troops. But the voters will decide how well he balances his need to criticize President Bush with the need to present a united front to our enemies.

It will be extremely difficult for Senator Kerry to know exactly where to draw the line in deciding when and how to criticize President Bush. And the Democratic Party has a vocal faction that has no compunction to bash and criticize Bush for virtually everything. If Senator Kerry is guided by this excessive animosity for President Bush, he could both bring harm to our troops and ruin his election chances. He will likely pick up more moderate voters if he adopts the position of Democratic Senator Joe Lieberman on the war.

Senator Lieberman is pretty much in harmony with the Bush administration on war issues.

During the next six months, if Senator Kerry errs on the side of being excessively critical of President Bush, then this will make the campaign especially ugly--as it threatens the safety of troops abroad.

The Beheading of American,
Nicholas Berg--
A True Hate Crime

The barbaric and heinous act of the anti-American terrorists in cutting off the head of Nicholas Berg has disgusted and infuriated Americans. It will steel our resolve to defeat terrorists wherever they are found. The gruesome, tortuous killing reveals the dark evil of the terrorists, who cannot be reasoned with any more than wild animals can be reasoned with. They are a blight to humanity. They respond to relatively minor acts of abuse with retaliatory acts that are grossly disproportionate to the wrongs for which they seek retribution. They are so consumed in their hatred for Americans that they inflict pain, torture and death on innocent people, such as Nick Berg, who was in Iraq seeking to help the Iraqis, and to rebuild the country. And while the terrorists perform their despicable evil, they invoke the name of God, as though He is honored by it. One need not condemn all of Islam in order to condemn these murderers. These terrorists are the embodiment of evil.

The image of the horrific murder of Nicholas Berg puts a personality and an image to the face of terrorism. This image confirms the necessity and the rightness of the war on terrorism, a cause that should be joined by all civilized nations around the globe.

Coalition Forces Capture Saddam
Hussein, Hiding in a Hole

On December 14, 2003, American forces captured Saddam Hussein hiding in a hidden hole, accessible from the court yard to a home in Dawr, Iraq. Saddam's capture is important because it is proof that he has been defeated. He is scheduled to be tried for the murders and atrocities he committed against his people.

The Campaign Finance Reform Case--
An Ephemeral and Costly Decision

McConnell, et al. v. Federal Election Commission, et al., 540 U.S. _____ (2003)

by C. Paul Smith

On December 10, 2003, the United States Supreme Court (by a 5-4 vote) upheld the Bipartisan Campaign Reform Act of 2002 (BCRA). *McConnell v. Federal Election Commission,* 540 U.S. ___ (2003). Senator Mitch McConnell, the National Rifle Association, the Republican National Committee, the American Civil Liberties Union, and several others had sued to block the BCRA because they contended that it violated the First Amendment Freedom of Speech. But the Supreme Court disagreed-- leaving the BCRA intact for the 2004 presidential election campaign.

McConnell v. F.E.C. is one of the most important Supreme Court decisions in the last ten years because of its impact on political speech in our democratic-republican system. In upholding the BCRA, the Supreme Court has put its support behind Congress in its attempt to prevent political parties and big corporations from having a corrupting influence on federal campaigns through large injections of money. However, the price for this ephemeral benefit is too high. The BCRA will not keep money out of federal politics any more than one can dig a hole in water. And, in its over-zealous attempt to cleanse politics from the influence of money, the Supreme Court had to diminish and undermine some of the most important principles of free speech that our Constitution has heretofore protected.

The Supreme Court gave this case expedited review because the Court's resolution of this case would affect the 2004 presidential election campaign. The Supreme Court convened in Washington to hear oral

arguments in the case in September, 2003 (approximately three weeks prior to their normal return date.) The Court issued its extensive, complex ruling on December 10, 2003.

Many experts had predicted that the Supreme Court would hold the BCRA to be unconstitutional. But, by a narrow 5-4 ruling, the Court upheld all the major parts of the BCRA. (Only the prohibition against contributions from minors to political parties was struck down.)

McConnell v. F.E.C. signals a movement on the part of the Supreme Court to give Congress increased latitude in regulating election campaign speech. This is hailed by some as a great victory because of the concern that elections are being bought by big money. However, others are deeply concerned that the Court has succumbed to popular pressures to improperly regulate the most important speech of all--election campaign speech--in a mistaken belief that the regulation of soft money campaign expenditures will cleanse political campaigns of some corruption.

The Court's ruling on Titles III and IV of the BCRA were nearly unanimous. But its ruling on the key issues in *McConnell* was decided by a narrow, 5-4 vote. The liberal block of Justices (Stevens, Souter, Ginsburg and Breyer) were joined by Justice Sandra Day O'Connor. Justice O'Connor is frequently the swing vote in close cases. Here she sided with those who have voted to empower Congress to restrict certain political speech.

In this article, I will first summarize how the Supreme Court ruled in *McConnell* and explain the basic rationale in support of

Voting of the Justices

Title of the Bipartisan Campaign Finance Act	Court Ruling	Rehnquist	Stevens	O'Connor	Scalia	Thomas	Kennedy	Souter	Ginsburg	Breyer

Titles I & II

Court Opinion on Titles I & II was written by Justices Stevens & O'Connor

Title I
(Political Parties cannot use soft money in local campaigns; restricts electioneering ads immediately before elections)

	Upheld	D	O	O	D	D	C part D part	O	O	O

Title II
(Corporations & Labor unions cannot use soft money in local campaigns; restricts electioneering ads immediately before elections)

	Upheld	D	O	O	C part D part	C part D part	C part D part	O	O	O

Titles III & IV

Court Opinion on Titles III & IV was written by Chief Justice Rehnquist--the Court was nearly unanimous in ruling that plaintiffs lacked standing to challenge Titles III & IV

Title III	Upheld	O	O	O	O & C	C	O	O	O	O
Title IV										
Sec. 304	Upheld	O	O	O	O & C	O & C	O	O	O	O
Sec. 305	Upheld	O	D	O	O & C	O & C	O	O	D	D
Sec. 307	Upheld	O	O	O	O & C	O & C	O	O	O	O
Sec. 311	Upheld	O	O	O	O & C	D	O	O	O	O
Sec. 316	Upheld	O	O	O	O & C	O & C	O	O	O	O
Sec. 318 **	Invalidated	O	O	O	O & C	D	O	O	O	O
Sec. 319	Upheld	O	O	O	O & C	O & C	O	O	O	O
Sec. 403(b)	Upheld	O	O	O	O & C	O & C	O	O	O	O

Title V

Court Opinion on Title V was written by Justice Breyer

Title V	Upheld	D	O	O	D	D	D	O	O	O

Key:

O = Opinion of the Court
C = Concurring Opinion
D = Dissenting Opinion

* The Court ruled that Senator McConnell and other plaintiffs lacked standing to challenge that part of the BCRA which would restrict or prohibit them from running certain campaign ads within 60 days of a general election because there was not yet a real case or controversy that was ripe for adjudication. This issue will undoubtedly be raised in the future.

* * The only provision of the BCRA that was struck down was Section 318, which prohibited minors from making campaign contributions. The Court ruled that this limitation violated the First Amendment speech rights of minors.

that decision. Second, I will point out what I perceive to be the flaws that the Supreme Court has created and imbedded in our constitutional jurisprudence through the *McConnell* decision.

I. What the Supreme Court Did in *McConnell v. F.E.C.*

There are eight different written opinions in the *McConnell* case, taking up 279 pages. Because of this it is difficult to make a short, concise analysis of the ruling. The complexity of the case led the Court to assign four different Justices to write the opinion of the Court on five different parts (Titles) of the law. This is a most unusual procedure that was required because of the many issues involved. Justices Stevens and O'Connor jointly authored the Court's opinion with respect to Titles I and II; Chief Justice Rehnquist authored the Court's opinion with respect to Titles III and IV; and Justice Breyer authored the Court's opinion with respect to Title V. The chart on the previous page gives a breakdown of how the Justices voted on the various issues in the case.

The BCRA deals primarily with "soft money" and "electioneering communication." Soft money is money that is not specifically earmarked to support a particular federal candidate. "Electioneering communication" is campaign speech that advocates the election of a specific, identified candidate. Those communications that do not fall under the definition of "electioneering communication" are often referred to as the "issue ads."

The precise definition of "electioneering communication" is central to understanding the meaning and effect of the BCRA. Section 201 of the BCRA defines "electioneering communication" to be communication which--

"(I) refers to a clearly identified candidate for Federal office;
(II) is made within--
(aa) 60 days before a general,

special, or runoff election for the office sought by the candidate; or
(bb) 30 days before a primary or preference election, or a convention or caucus of a political party that has authority to nominate a candidate, for the office sought by the candidate; and
(III) in the case of a communication which refers to a candidate for an office other than President or Vice President, is targeted to the relevant electorate."

The two principal parts of the BCRA are covered in Titles I and II of the Act. Title I prohibits political parties from running issue ads. Title II, in general, prohibits corporations and labor unions from running issue ads immediately before election day.

Title I applies to political parties and prevents them from soliciting, receiving or spending money that is not specifically earmarked to support a particular federal candidate (soft money) (Opinion of the Court, JJ. Stevens and O'Connor, p.23[1]). This prohibits parties from using issue ads and limits their communications to those that identify specific candidates and which are funded by hard money (i.e., money that is earmarked to support a particular candidate).

Title II applies to corporations and labor unions, and prohibits them from using issue ads within 30 days of a primary election and within 60 days of a general election. Corporations and labor unions remain free to run ads that support identified candidates through political action committees (PACs)[2] (Opinion of the Court, JJ. Stevens and O'Connor, p.98). An exception to this

---

[1] Note that all page references in this article refer to the slip opinion pages of the respective Justices in the original published opinions of the Court. When published in the official reporting publications, these citations will have different page numbers.

[2] But a corporation's contributions to an individual candidate through a PAC can total no more than $5,000 per election. This is a relatively small amount that a corporation can spend in support of a candidate, and even then it can be done only through a PAC. Thus, the BCRA does severely limit the speech of corporations and labor unions in support of federal candidates.

restriction is given to those corporations that are in the broadcast business; during the restricted periods they remain free to broadcast news stories, commentaries and editorials that could constitute "electioneering communication." (Opinion of the Court, JJ. Stevens and O'Connor, p.102).[3]

There were four major challenges to the constitutionality of the BCRA: (a) That the contribution limits were invalid; (b) that the expenditure limits were invalid; (c) that the BCRA exceeded Congress' authority to regulate elections under Article I, Section 4 of the Constitution; and (d) that the BCRA violated the Equal Protection Clause of the Fourteenth Amendment. How the Court resolved each of these constitutional attacks is summarized below.

A. Contribution Limits--FECA Sec. 323(a). The heart of the majority's opinion in *McConnell* is that when the Supreme Court reviews the propriety of campaign contribution limits set by Congress, the Court does not apply the "strict scrutiny" review standard to determine whether those limits violate protected speech, but rather that the Court applies a less stringent standard, called "closely drawn" scrutiny. (Opinion of the Court, JJ. Stevens and O'Connor, p.27.) The Court found that the government's interest in preventing both actual corruption in campaign contributions **and** the appearance of corruption, justified minimal restrictions on citizens' free speech rights. (Opinion of the Court, JJ. Stevens and O'Connor, p.75.) By applying this more lenient standard, a majority of the Court found that the BCRA did not violate protected speech. The Court held that campaign expenditures have only a "marginal restriction upon the contributor's ability to engage in free communication," (Opinion of the Court, JJ. Stevens and O'Connor, p. 9) and

that "limiting contributions served an interest in protecting the integrity of our system of representative democracy" (*Id.*). Based upon this, the Court upheld the right of Congress to limit such contributions.

B. Spending Limits--FECA Sec. 323(b). The BCRA prohibits the use of federal campaign contributions for state and local candidates. The Court ruled that these soft money spending limits do not violate the First Amendment free speech and association rights because Section 323(b) is closely drawn to match the important governmental interest of preventing corruption and the appearance of corruption in federal elections. Hard money contributions are not affected by this. Restrictions of Section 323(b) are "closely drawn" to match government objectives. (Opinion of the Court, JJ. Stevens and O'Connor, p.27.)

C. Article I, Section 4 Authority to Make Election Rules. The Court held that the BCRA does not exceed Congress' authority under Article I, Section 4 to "make" or "alter" rules governing federal elections. (Opinion of the Court, JJ. Stevens and O'Connor, pp. 79-80.)

D. Equal Protection Issue. The Court ruled that the BCRA does not violate the Equal Protection Clause of the Fourteenth Amendment by favoring special interest groups over political parties. Congress is entitled to take into consideration differences between the two. Prohibiting political parties from raising and using soft money does not violate the First Amendment. And interest groups remain free to raise and use soft money provided it is not used for "electioneering communications." (Opinion of the Court, JJ. Stevens and O'Connor, p.80).[4]

---

[3] In response to this, the NRA announced that it is looking into buying a television or radio station to free itself from the BCRA restrictions that prohibit it from saying what it wants about political candidates. John R. Lott, Jr., "The NRA's Announcement," *The Washington Times*, December 22, 2003.

---

[4] This writer is frankly stunned at the paucity of reasoning offered by the Court in support of this significant restriction on political speech.

II. How the Supreme Court Went Astray in *McConnel v. F.E.C.*

The BCRA did more than just expand existing campaign expenditure laws--it redefined the rules and definitions with respect to coordinated expenditures (soft money), introducing vagueness and ambiguity to the law. For example, under the BCRA, issue ads within 30 days of a primary election and within 60 days of a general election are now prohibited if they "refer[] to a clearly identified candidate for Federal office." (Sec. 201). But "clearly identified" is not clear and unambiguous; the unanswered question is whether a candidate can be "clearly identified" by implication and without the specific use of his/her name. And to make matters worse, the BCRA introduced harsh penalties (imprisonment and fines) for the violation of the ambiguous rules.

The BCRA seems to give an advantage to incumbents--which could bode well for Republicans in the November 2004 elections. The BCRA is not likely to adversely affect this year's presidential campaign of George Bush, who appears to be a premier fund raiser of "hard money" which is not limited by BCRA.[5] But regardless of which party may be the beneficiary of BCRA regulations, this writer finds the BCRA to be an unwise and improper departure from traditional First Amendment freedom of speech principles.

Passage of the BCRA by Congress indicates that a majority of Americans favor this new regulation of campaign finances. So these people will be happy that the Supreme Court upheld the BCRA. And even many of those who opposed the BCRA will not be unduly concerned that it was upheld--it's just not a big deal to many people. Nevertheless, because of the profound effect that the BCRA is expected to have on federal elections, including the 2004 presidential campaign, it is important to review what the Supreme Court

did in *McConnel v. F. E. C.* And what the Court did was restrict important free speech rights in election campaigns, and give broadcast and publishing media preferential treatment over political parties, corporations and labor unions in addressing election issues.

In *McConnell*, the Supreme Court has adopted a position that gives Congress increased authority to restrict and prohibit the expenditures of all of these on issue ads that cross over the line and "refer" to a "clearly identified" federal candidate. That is the principal point that should be recognized in analyzing *McConnell*; the development of the Court's position from *Buckley v. Valeo* (1976) to *McConnell v. F.E.C.* should not be overlooked. In *Buckley*, the Supreme Court upheld the placing of limitations on federal campaign contributions, but struck down a regulation on campaign expenditures. Justices Rehnquist, Scalia, Thomas and Kennedy continue to argue (in *McConnell*) that even the limitations on campaign contributions violate the First Amendment. The Court upheld such limitations in *Buckley* by ruling that a less restrictive standard of review should be applied to campaign finance regulations. Then, in 2001, the Supreme Court ruled *in F.E.C. v. Colorado Republican Federal Campaign Committee*, 533 U.S. 431, that Congress can also regulate a political party's "coordinated" expenditures (i.e., soft money) as well as contributions to the party. Now, two years later (in *McConnell*), the Court is giving increased authority to Congress to limit expenditures of parties, corporations and labor unions if federal candidates are clearly identified.

Despite the Court's rhetoric that this does not impinge on Freedom of Speech, I am quite uncomfortable with such a notion. And the Court has not acknowledged that it is changing its position--giving more and more latitude to Congress to pass laws that restrict the speech of American citizens in election campaigns.

The one aspect of the BCRA that seemed most vulnerable to this writer was the

---

[5] Except that the BCRA requires disclosure of the names of those who contribute $10,000 or more.

provision in Title II that prohibits all corporations and labor unions, except news media, from publishing issue ads within 30 days of a primary election and within 60 days of a federal election. This bestowal of preferred status on news media in addressing core political issues, but barring corporations and labor unions from doing so at election time is troubling. Justice Kennedy's dissenting opinion complained that in enacting Title II of the BCRA, Congress violated speech rights that are some of the most basic or a free society. Justice Thomas, in a separate dissent, pointed out that Congress has now opened the door to regulation of the media--a precedent, which may henceforth be used to control the media, just as easily as bestowing upon it a preferred status.

The following excerpts from the dissenting opinions of Justices Rehnquist, Scalia, Thomas and Kennedy succinctly state grave concerns about the effect of the BCRA on political speech in America:

A. The Justice Scalia Dissent.

Justice Scalia wrote that there were three fallacious propositions that were responsible for creating the mindset that now supports BCRA--(1) that money is not speech; (2) that pooling money is not speech, and (3) that speech by corporations can be abridged. Justice Scalia disputes the validity of all three of these propositions.

1. Money Is Not Speech.

"Until today, however, that view [that the regulation of money does not impinge on speech rights] has been categorically rejected by our jurisprudence. As we said in Buckley, 424 U.S., at 16, 'this Court has never suggested that the dependence of a communication on the expenditure of money operates itself to introduce a nonspeech element or to reduce the exacting scrutiny required by the First Amendment.'" (J. Scalia Dissent, p. 5.)

"The right to speak would be largely ineffective if it did not include the right to engage in financial transactions that are the incidents of its exercise." (J. Scalia Dissent, p. 7.)

"But where the government singles out money used to fund speech as its legislative object, it is acting against speech as such, no less than if it had targeted the paper on which a book was printed or the trucks that deliver it to the bookstore." (J. Scalia Dissent, p. 7.)

2. Pooling Money Is Not Speech.

"Another proposition which could explain at least some of the results of today's opinion is that the First Amendment right to spend money for speech does not include the right to combine with others in spending money for speech. Such a proposition fits uncomfortably with the concluding words of our Declaration of Independence: "And for the support of this Declaration, . . . we mutually pledge to each other our Lives, *our Fortunes* and our sacred Honor." (Emphasis added.) The freedom to associate with others for the dissemination of ideas--not just by singing or speaking in unison, buy by pooling financial resources for expressive purposes--is part of the freedom of speech." (J. Scalia Dissent, p. 10.)

3. Speech By Corporations Can Be Abridged. As late as 1978, the Supreme Court treated corporate speech on par with the speech of individual people. *First National Bank of Boston v. Bellotti*, 435 U.S. 765 (1978). In this case the Court said: "It is the type of speech indispensable to decision-making in a democracy, and this is no less true because the speech comes from a corporation rather than an individual. The inherent worth of the speech in terms of its capacity for informing the public does not depend upon the identity of its source, whether corporation, association, union, or individual." (J. Scalia Dissent, p. 12.)

B. The Justice Thomas Dissent.

"In response to this assault on the free exchange of ideas and with only the slightest consideration of the appropriate standard of review of the Court's traditional role of protecting First Amendment freedoms, the Court has placed its imprimatur on these unprecedented restrictions. The very "purpose of the First Amendment [is] to preserve an uninhibited marketplace of ideas in which truth will ultimately prevail." *Red Lion Broadcasting Co. v. FCC,* 395 U.S. 367, 390 (1969). Yet today the fundamental principle that "the best test of truth is the power of the thought to get itself accepted in the competition of the market," *Abrams v. United States,* 250 U.S. 616 , 630 (1919) (Holmes, J., dissenting), is cast aside in the purported service of preventing "corruption," or the mere "appearance of corruption." *Buckley v. Valeo,* 424 U.S 1, 26 (1976) (per curiam). Apparently, the marketplace of ideas is to be fully open only to defamers, *New York Times Co. v. Sullivan,* 376 U.S. 254 (1964) nude dancers, *Barnes v. Glen Theatre, Inc.,* 501 U.S. 560 (1991) (plurality opinion); porno-graphers, *Ashcroft v. Free Speech Coalition,* 535 U.S. 234 (2002); flag burner, *United States v. Eichman,* 496 U.S. 310 (1990); and cross burners, *Virginia v. Black,* 538 U.S. ___(2003)." (J. Thomas Dissent, p. 3.)

"Although today's opinion does not expressly strip the press of First Amendment protection, there is no principle of law or logic that would prevent the application of the Court's reasoning in that setting. The press now operates at the whim of Congress." (J. Thomas Dissent, p. 25.)

C. The Justice Kennedy Dissent.

"Today's decision upholding these laws purports simply to follow *Buckly v. Valeo,* 424 U.S. 1 (1976) (per curiam), and to abide by *stare decisis,* see ante, at 27 (joint opinion of STEVENS and O'CONNOR, JJ. (hereinafter

Court or majority)); but the majority, to make its decision work, must abridge free speech where *Buckley* did not. *Buckley* did not authorize Congress to decide what shapes and forms the national political dialogue is to take. To reach today's decision, the Court surpasses *Buckley's* limits and expands Congress' regulatory power. In so doing, it replaces discrete and respected First Amendment principles with new, amorphous, and unsound rules, rules which dismantle basic protections for speech." (J. Kennedy Dissent, p. 3.)

"To the majority, all this is not only valid under the First Amendment but also is part of Congress' "steady improvement of the national election laws." *Ante,* at 6. We should make no mistake. It is neither. It is the codification of an assumption that the mainstream media alone can protect freedom of speech. It is an effort by Congress to ensure that civic discourse takes place only through the modes of its choosing. And BCRA is only the beginning, as its congressional proponents freely admit." (J. Kennedy Dissent, p. 4.)

"The majority says it is not abandoning our cases in this way, but its reasoning shows otherwise." (J. Kennedy Dissent, p. 11.)

D. The Chief Justice Rehnquist Dissent.

"No doubt Congress was convinced by the many abuses of the current system that something in this area must be done. Its response, however, was too blunt. Many of the abuses described by the Court involve donations that were made for the "purpose of influencing a federal election," and thus are already regulated. See *Buckley, supra.* Congress could have sought to have the existing restrictions enforced or to enact other restrictions that are "closely drawn" to its legitimate concerns. But it should not be able to broadly restrict political speech in the fashion it has chosen. Today's decision, by not requiring tailored restrictions, has significantly reduced the protection for political speech having little or nothing to do with corruption or the appearance of corruption." (Chief Justice Rehnquist Dissent, pp. 9-10.)

III. Conclusion

For now, few seem to care whether and to what extent the BCRA impinges on protected speech. The attitude of the majority of the Supreme Court reflects a fear of any speech that might come from big corporations; existing campaign finance laws already punished criminally those who bribed candidates and government officials. But the BCRA authorizes the restricting of political speech by corporations even if the speech merely "appears" to be corrupting. This "appearance" standard is quite troubling; it is amazing to see that it survives any "closely drawn scrutiny" by the Supreme Court; it is amazing that the Court found that the mere

"appearance" of corruption is a legitimate government interest that warrants the prohibition and limitation of such speech.

The Court has clearly dismantled the protection of Free Speech that the First Amendment has provided for 213 years. Indeed, the majority's fear of the influence of big business on politics has grown so much that they just don't care that the BCRA impinges on speech that has historically been jealously protected.

James O. E. Norell, a writer for the National Rifle Association got it right, when in 2001 he wrote this about the BCRA:

> "Campaign finance reform is not about big dollars influencing elections. . . . It is about who will control information to the electorate. . . . It is about a television/radio blackout of truth, opinions and beliefs of individual Americans who pool their power by choosing to belong to organizations like the NRA--organizations that give them the collective clout they need to reach millions of voters through paid issue advocacy."[6]

---

[6] James O. E. Norell, "The McCain-Feingold Bill: Putting a Muzzle on the First Amendment," *America's First Freedom* (official journal of the National Rifle Association), June 2001 (p.33).

6.1   6.3
13.4 13.3.3

A Federal Marriage Amendment--
Let the Debate Begin

by C. Paul Smith

Emboldened by the Supreme Court's decision in *Lawrence v. Texas*, 539 U.S. ___, 123 S.Ct. 2472 (2003) that established a constitutional "liberty" to engage in homosexual conduct, pro-gay activists in Massachusetts, California and New Mexico have acted to change laws in order to give recognition to same-sex marriages. Although the *Lawrence* decision did not specifically legitimize same-sex marriages, some contend that implicitly it did. Justice Antonin Scalia, in his dissent, predicted that *Lawrence* signaled that barriers to same-sex marriages would soon start coming down.

In November 2003, by a 4-3 vote ruling, the Massachusetts Supreme Court struck down the Massachusetts law that prohibited same-sex marriages. *Goodridge v. Department of Public Health*, (Mass., No. 08860, Nov. 18, 2003) U.S. Law Week, Vol. 72, pp. 1306-1307. The majority applied the rational basis test to the law, and stated that there was no rational basis for prohibiting same-sex marriages, and stated that denial of marriage licenses to same-sex couples violated the Equal Protection Clause of the Fourteenth Amendment.[1] Thereafter, in February 2004,

the county clerk's office in San Francisco issued 2,800 marriage licenses to same-sex couples, defying California laws that prohibited this. (*The Washington Times*, February 20, 2004, and *The Washington Post*, February 21, 2004.)[2] Also in February 2004, county clerks in New Mexico issued at least 66 marriage licenses to same-sex couples, defying New Mexico laws that prohibited it. (*The Washington Post*, February 22, 2004.) Similar legal battles are unfolding in New Jersey and Oregon. (Bruce Fein, "Contemporary Consensus Amendment," *The Washington Times*, March 16, 2004.) The legal battles to resolve these conflicts will continue for some time.

---

[1] The majority stated that "the State's action confers an official stamp of approval on the destructive stereotype that same-sex relationships are inherently unstable and inferior to opposite-sex relationships." 72 U.S. Law Week, at 1307. The majority based its ruling on *Romer v. Evans*, 517 U.S. 620 (1996), in which the Supreme Court struck down a Colorado amendment to its constitution which would have prohibited that state from ever making homosexuals a protected class. The Massachusetts Courts misinterpreted *Romer*, basically turning a shield into a sword. The Court ruled in *Romer* that although Colorado did not have to make homosexuals a protected class, the State could not

amend its constitution to provide that it could homosexuals could never be made a protected class. This distinction was lost on the Massachusetts Supreme Court. *Romer* was never intended to require any state to recognize same-sex marriages.

The Massachusetts Court has implicitly adopted the point of view that the two sexes must be treated absolutely equal. The U. S. Constitution does not require this. This is an argument that might have had some validity if the Equal Rights Amendment (ERA) had been ratified. But one of the reasons that proposed amendment was not ratified by sufficient states was because of the concern that it would lay the groundwork to eliminate all the legal bases for distinguishing men from women. Thus, while the nation wanted more rights for women, including equal pay for equal work, the nation rejected the notion that men and women should be equal and interchangeable in marriage laws. The Equal Protection Clause was not intended and has never been interpreted by the Supreme Court to mandate the extremist view that the Massachusetts Supreme Court has now embraced.

[2] A gay couple from Maryland was one of those who sped to San Francisco to get in on the action. *The Washington Post*, February 20, 2004.

With this backdrop, in early 2004, the Bush administration reiterated its plan to spend $300 million a year to promote healthy marriages.[3] In the meantime, marriage-related issues are also being addressed through the Defense of Marriage Act (1996) and the proposed Federal Marriage Amendment (FMA).

1. The Defense of Marriage Act.
The Defense of Marriage Act (DOMA) was passed by Congress and signed into law seven years prior to the Supreme Court's ruling in *Lawrence v. Texas*.[4] The DOMA says that the states do not have to recognize same-sex marriages made in another state. Of course, this law won't help Massachusetts escape the activism and edicts of its own Supreme Court.[5] And it is not known yet whether DOMA or the Full Faith and Credit Clause of the Constitution (Article IV) will prevail when the two inevitably clash. The Full Faith and Credit Clause requires states to recognize the validity of official acts of sister states unless those laws are repulsive to those of the other state. But there is plenty of uncertainty in this

exception, making it impossible to predict which principle would trump the other.

2. The Federal Marriage Amendment. In May of 2003, Colorado Republican Marilyn Musgrave introduced in the House of Representatives a proposed Federal Marriage Amendment.[6] Subsequently, an identical amendment was proposed in the Senate. On February 24, 2004, President Bush announced his support for a FMA.[7]

It is difficult to predict whether Congress and the States will be able to pass a federal marriage amendment restricting marriage to heterosexual couples. For while in recent polls a majority of Americans are opposed to recognizing same-sex marriages,[8] not all of these people favor a constitutional amendment to mandate it. Conservatives are divided on this issue. The very foundation of conservatism is that state rights should be recognized and that federal laws must not encroach on the domain of the states. Thus, a federal amendment defining marriage would infringe on the historical power of states to define and regulate marriage.[9] Of course the problem with this strict conservative approach is that it fails to acknowledge that the Supreme Court has long ago (beginning in 1965) pre-empted the regulation of the rights and

---

[3] The Bush administration first announced this initiative in 2002, and its purpose was not directed at the same-sex marriage issue. The plan is to promote two-parent families and to discourage parents from having children out-of-wedlock. The administration believes that strengthening the traditional family is a good way to reduce many social ills, including crime and poverty. *The Washington Times*, January 15, 2004; and Matt Daniels, "Marriage, Society--Building Blocks for Both," *The Washington Times*, April 15, 2004.

[4] Congress passed the DOMA in response to a ruling by the Hawaii Supreme Court that recognized same-sex marriages. (Subsequently, an Alaska court made a similar ruling.) By large majorities in the House (342-67) and in the Senate (84-14) Congress passed, and President Clinton signed the DOMA in 1996. Subsequently, Hawaii amended its constitution to specifically prohibit same-sex marriage. Currently 38 states specifically prohibit same-sex marriages. *The Washington Times*, February 25, 2004; and John Leo, "Judicial End-Run," *The Washington Times*, November 27, 2003.

[5] 70% of the people of Massachusetts oppose legalizing homosexual unions. Armstrong Williams, "Marriage Rites and Civil Rights," *The Washington Times*, February 2004.

[6] It states: "Marriage in the United States shall consist only of the union of a man and a woman. Neither this Constitution or the constitution of any State, nor state or federal law, shall be construed to require that marital status or the legal incidents thereof be conferred upon unmarried couples or groups." *The Washington Times*, February 25, 2004.

[7] *The Washington Times*, February 25, 2004.

[8] Recent polls by "The New York Times" and CBS News and one by "USA Today" and CNN all found that more than 60% of Americans oppose legalizing homosexual unions. Armstrong Williams, "Marriage Rites and Civil Rights," *The Washington Times*, February 2004.

[9] Conservative commentator Morton Kondracke opposes amending the Constitution with a federal marriage amendment. He compares such an amendment with the national mistake of attempting to enforce a certain level of morality through Prohibition. *The Washington Times*, February 19, 2004.

157

relationships incident to marriage, through its famous cases of *Griswold v. Connecticut* (1965) (the right of married couples to use contraceptives), *Eisenstadt v. Baird* (1968) (the right of adults to use contraceptives), *Roe v. Wade* (1973) (the right to an abortion), and *Troxel v. Granville* (2000) (the right of parents to raise their children). Thus, the states have already lost whatever powers they once had to regulate these incidents of marriage. Therefore, since the states have no authority to regulate these incidents of marriage, the states' rights argument that a constitutional amendment should not define marriage is hollow rhetoric. The fact is that because the Supreme Court has legislated so extensively in controlling the incidents of marriage, it is folly to consider this to any longer be a matter subject to state control. The genie is out of the bottle and will not be put back in. Purist conservatives must acknowledge this, and move on. The strength and reach of federal constitutional rights has now come to be so great that a federal solution through constitutional amendment is a preferred way to deal with the same-sex marriage issue; and it is a good way to prevent activist judges from attempting to establish same-sex marriage in society through radical interpretations of existing constitutional law. A constitutional amendment can reign in these social reformers.

The most fundamental of all societal relationships the male-female union. It is of unsurpassed importance. The rights incident to it are paramount and not to be made subject to erosion or dilution or obliteration by the actions of different states. Just as the rights to bear and beget children and the right to rear children are protected by the Constitution, so too, the scope and parameters of the right to marry or not may also be governed by the federal Constitution. Conservatives who resist a federal marriage amendment effectively acquiesce in federal control of marriage. An amendment prohibiting same-sex marriage would not return marriage to state control, but it would correct and/or

prevent activist courts from recognizing same-sex marriages.

Why is it better for America to allow the Supreme Court to write our national laws with respect to all these incidents of marriage, than to have these matters resolved through the democratic processes in amending the Constitution? There is nothing wrong with amending the Constitution to resolve a matter of such supreme importance. And, in doing so, if *We the People* should modify any of the court-crafted rules, then that's just fine. Amending the Constitution is difficult, but it is clearly a proper way to correct the courts who go astray.

James Madison and the founders of the Constitution did not initially seek to establish the federal rights contained in the Bill of Rights. But their subsequent establishment in the Constitution by amendment in 1791 has not been a mistake; to the contrary, the inclusion of these rights in the first Ten Amendments to the Constitution has come to be revered and cherished by virtually all Americans.

Several Democratic members of Congress have decried the FMA as being "based in intolerance and divisiveness,"[10] and as an attempt to "write bias back into the Constitution."[11] Rosie O'Donnell, criticized President Bush for supporting an FMA, calling the President's words of support to be "vile" and "hateful."[12] Although some people may be of this opinion, I find this view to be totally in error. It erroneously imputes vile and hateful motives where none exists; it is a defensive smear tactic, to attempt to intimidate and scare good people from speaking up for virtue. It is good and proper to uphold the traditional value that marriage is only for heterosexual couples and is the preferable

[10] Steny H. Hoyer (D-Md.), House Minority Whip, *The Washington Post*, February 25, 2004.
[11] Senator Edward M. Kennedy (D-Mass.), *The Washington Post*, February 25, 2004.
[12] Maggie Gallagher, "Are You a Bigot?" *The Washington Times*, March 5, 2004.

relationship in which to bear, raise and rear children, and that it is right and proper for society to make and enforce laws that promote this lifestyle. This is not a bigoted position; it is loving; it is in the best interest of children and of our whole society; and it is supported by scientific and historical evidence.[13]

The Washington Post has gone on record condemning a federal marriage amendment, arguing that it would debase the Constitution. *The Washington Post,* February 25, 2004. This is a specious argument. There would be nothing debasing about such an amendment. As pointed out, above, for forty years the Supreme Court has gradually pre-empted the states from legislating the basic incidents of marriage--in effect divesting the states of the authority to define and control marriage. If a majority of three-quarters of the states ratified the Federal Marriage Amendment, this would not debase the Constitution. Such an amendment would merely be an act of the people to take back from the Supreme Court an area of the law that the Court had usurped from the states. Any "debasing" that occurred, was done by the Supreme Court in failing to exercise judicial restraint and by its judicial legislating of various aspects of marriage for forty years. A federal marriage amendment would only serve to correct some of this usurpation.

The nation is ready for a full debate of a federal marriage amendment. It could be valuable in reigning in maverick judges, such as the majority of the Massachusetts Supreme Court. It would block radical judges around the country from mischief by attempting to establish gay marriage in defiance of established law. It would support the important societal value of reserving marriage for prospective father-mother couples who can give their children the blessing of being raised by both a father and a mother.

---

[13] The bias accusation is founded on the false assumption (albeit a widely held view) about the nature of individuals who experience erotic, same-sex attraction. The false assumption is that these people are born that way and that they cannot change. But scientific studies do not support this belief. Scientific studies have found no causative genetic link; rather they have proven that behavior and environment are key causative factors; and studies have shown that some people can and do change. Some of these studies are cited in C. Paul Smith, "Creating Special Rights for Gays Threatens America," *CLU* I:i (April 2001) and in a reprint of a letter to the Frederick County Human Relations Commission in *CLU* III:ii (September 2003).

159

Ten Commandments Monument on Grounds of Texas Capitol Does Not Violate Constitution

On November 12, 2003, a three judge panel of the Fifth Circuit U. S. Court of Appeals unanimously upheld the placement of a six-foot high granite monument of the Ten Commandments on the grounds of the Texas State Capitol. *Van Orden v. Perry,* 5th Cir., No. 02-51184. The Circuit Court confirmed and upheld the ruling of a district court judge.

The Court found that the placement of the monument complied with the three-part test under *Lemon v. Kurtzman,* 403 U.S. 602 (1971): (1) It has a secular purpose; (2) Its primary effect neither advances nor inhibits religion; and (3) It does not foster excessive entanglement with religion. (Only the first two tests were in dispute in this case.)

1. Secular Purpose. The court found that the monument was placed on the state grounds "to recognize and commend a private organization for its effort to reduce juvenile delinquency." Additionally, the court was found to have a record of honoring the contributions of donors and those they represent. The Fifth Circuit disagreed with the ruling of the Seventh Circuit in *Books v. Elkhart, Indiana,* 235 F.3d 392 (7th Cir. 2000), noting that the commandments have a "secular dimension as well as religious meaning." [The Seventh Circuit had basically ignored this.] The Fifth Circuit also distinguished the Texas monument from that in Elkhart, Indiana because in that case the state had adopted a secular purpose for its display on the eve of trial, and there was no religious service attending the acceptance of the Texas monument in 1961.

2. Primary Effect. The court found that the Ten Commandments have both secular and religious messages. The court did not find the primary purpose of the monument to be to advance or inhibit religion. The monument was one of 17 monuments on the state grounds that honor "people, ideals and events that

compose Texan identity." The court found that a reasonable viewer would not view the display as a state endorsement of religion. In addition, the court noted that the monument had stood for 42 years without the filing of any legal complaint; the court found this to be supportive of the secular purpose of the monument.

Analysis and Comment. Courts in the United States continue to be split over allowing Ten Commandment monuments to remain on state property. A national battle continues to be fought--not only to decide whether such monuments can remain, but to determine whether even the mere acknowledgement of God must be excised from all aspects of our state and federal governments, or whether the Constitution will continue to accommodate religion and the belief in God. The resolution of this battle continues to hang in the balance.

Other Ten Commandments Litigation.

Pennsylvania--On August, 2003, the Third Circuit U.S. Court of Appeals ruled that a Ten Commandment plaque that had been on the wall of a Chester County, PA courthouse since 1920 did not violate the First Amendment, and could remain. *The Washington Times,* Aug. 23, 2003.

Montana--Miles City agreed to move a Ten Commandment monument from government land to a private museum. This settled a six-year dispute. *The Washington Times,* Sept. 25, 2003.

Kentucky--The Sixth Circuit U. S. Court of Appeals blocked Kentucky Governor Paul Patton from taking a Ten Commandments marker out of storage and installing it next to its Flower Clock on the state capital grounds. *The Washington Times,* August 23, 2003.

Georgia--The Eleventh Circuit U. S. Court of Appeals allowed Richmond County, Georgia to continue using its 130-year-old court seal featuring the Ten Commandments tablet. *The Washington Times,* August 23, 2003.

Alabama--The Eleventh Circuit U. S. Court of Appeals made Justice Roy Moore remove the 5,300 Ten Commandments monument from the state supreme court building. *The Washington Post,* July 2, 2003.

Alabama Chief Justice Roy Moore's Legal Battle to Keep the Ten Commandments Monument

Alabama Chief Justice Roy Moore placed a 5,300-pound granite Ten Commandments monument in the rotunda of the Alabama State Supreme Court building. When suit was brought to have the monument removed, the case eventually made its way to the Eleventh Circuit U. S. Court of Appeals in Atlanta, Georgia. On July 1, 2003, that Court ruled that the monument must be removed because it violated the Establishment Clause of the First Amendment. *The Washington Post,* July 2, 2003. Justice Moore then filed a petition with the U. S. Supreme Court, asking them to review his case. Justice Moore argued that the federal courts had no jurisdiction over a state chief justice. But on November 3, 2003, the Court announced that it would not review Justice Moore's case, which in effect affirmed the ruling of the Eleventh Circuit that the monument would have to be removed. *The Washington Times,* November 4, 2003.

Justice Moore took an untenable position in his case; no right-minded jurist has ever argued that the federal courts has no jurisdiction to rule on whether a state officer's actions violated the federal constitution.

When Justice Moore continued to defy federal court orders, the rest of the Alabama Supreme Court removed him from office. *The Washington Post,* November 14, 2003. While Justice Moore's acts of defiance cost him his job, they also made him an instant celebrity. He has had many speaking engagements around the country, and he is even viewed as a possible candidate to challenge Republican Senator Bob Riley in the next election for that position. *Id.*

Justice Moore's actions have won the acclaim of many who are upset with the current trend of the courts to interpret the First Amendment in a way that is antagonistic to God. However, Justice Moore's legal tactics were extreme and without solid legal support.

Occasionally the United States Supreme Court can create new law and get away with it. But Justice Moore did not.

Constitutional Law Updates

IV:ii November 2004 No. 9

The 2004 Presidential Election— What Does It Mean for the Future?

By C. Paul Smith

As projected, the 2004 Presidential Election was very close. When I retired at 2:00 a.m. Wednesday morning, the re-election of President George W. Bush looked certain. The next day, at 11:00 a.m., Senator Kerry conceded defeat, acknowledging that a count of the 145,000 provisional ballots in Ohio would not give him enough votes to overcome his 130,000-vote deficit.

President George W. Bush won the electoral vote 286 - 252 (as compared with 271-267 in 2000). But this time President Bush also received a majority of the popular vote (by 3 1/2 million votes). While the victory was narrow, it nevertheless gives President Bush some vindication and a majority popular approval of his policies on the war on terror, Iraq, tax cuts, the economy, and support of traditional marriage.

There are, however, some less obvious, but extremely important observations to be made about the 2004 Election; they relate to the following matters, which will be discussed briefly below:

CONSTITUTIONAL LAW UPDATES is a semi-annual newsletter edited and published by C. Paul Smith, J.D. Subscription cost is $13.00 per year (plus $0.65 tax in MD). To subscribe, send a check or money order to CONSTITUTIONAL LAW UPDATES, P. O. Box 1204, Frederick MD 21702-0204. For further information, visit Paul Smith's web site at www.cpaulsmith.com   Copyright C. Paul Smith 2004.

I. Major Media Bias

Like many Americans, as we watched the election returns Tuesday evening, we switched from network to network to compare how and when they were announcing their projections. The most obvious difference was the protracted delays on the part of ABC, CNN and CBS in announcing their projections as to the winner in Ohio. Whereas FOX News and NBC both announced, shortly after midnight their projections that Bush had won in Ohio, ABC, CNN and CBS all refused to admit the obvious--that Kerry could not win--until mid-day on Wednesday. By 2:00 a.m. on Wednesday morning, it was abundantly clear that Kerry could not win Ohio, and therefore that Bush would win the presidency. With this in mind, I went to bed and rested assured. But the next morning, when I checked the different networks, ABC, CNN and CBS continued to insist that Ohio was too close to call. But their reasoning in support was pathetic--it demonstrated that they were desperately, emotionally, clinging to the hope that somehow Kerry would pull it out and win in Ohio. But there was no basis for the hope. This failure to call Ohio for Bush, just highlighted the bias of ABC, CNN and CBS for Kerry.

Despite the multiple revelations of the pro-Kerry/pro Democrat bias in October, CBS and Dan Rather continue to operate in a manner oblivious to their prejudice that all can plainly see. In case you forgot, the timing of the 60-Minutes broadcast casting aspersions on President Bush's National Guard Service of 30 years ago, was intended to hurt Bush in the polls, and was based upon a forged document. When the forgery was made manifest, CBS insisted that its report was valid, even though it was based upon the forged document. And then, just a week prior to the November 2nd Election, CBS was planning to run another 60-Minutes program (on Sunday evening, October 31st) that would accuse the Bush administration of (18 months earlier) allowing a cache of 380 tons of explosives in Al Qaqaa, Iraq to slip out of its possession during the war in Iraq. But the CBS attempt to ambush the Bush campaign backfired when *The New York Times*, normally a CBS ally, ran the story a week before CBS wanted the accusation aired. This gave the Bush administration enough time to refute the accusation before Election Day--and they did; they presented evidence showing that the explosives were gone before we got there.[1] By the time the dust settled on this story, CBS had once again proved its anti-Bush bias--a bias so strong that CBS had again rushed to judgment against Bush without supporting evidence. The polls showed that the allegations of neglect initially caused Kerry to pick up a few points and to pull ahead of Bush in the polls. But by Election Day, after the Bush people had exposed the allegations, Bush regained his slight lead in the polls.

Conservatives are infuriated at Dan Rather and CBS. The perfect punishment for them would be to allow them to continue to broadcast their biased material, as a living monument to not only the bias of CBS and Dan Rather, but also to their patent desires to put the advancement of their own political agendas ahead of objective news coverage.

But let's not forget the ABC anti-Bush bias, either. On the eve of the second

---

[1] The International Atomic Energy Agency (IAEA) reported that Saddam Hussein had 380 tons of explosives at Al Qaqaa. The IAEA reported that it had marked these explosives for identification. However, by the time American troops arrived at Al Qaqaa, these explosives were already gone. On April 10, 2003, the 101st Airborne found no IAEA-marked explosives when they arrived in Al Qaqaa. And a few days prior to this, when the Third Infantry Division arrived in Al Qaqaa, they had also searched and found no IAEA-marked explosives. *See The Washington Post*, October 28, 2004 and *The Washington Times*, October 26 and 28, 2004.

presidential debate, ABC News Political Director Mark Halpern issued a memo to his news people, including Charles Gibson, who would moderate that debate, with a clear, implicit message to be tougher on Bush than on Kerry. The memo said this: '[T]he current Bush attacks on Kerry involve distortions and taking things out of context in a way that goes beyond what Kerry has done." Therefore, Mr. Halpern wrote that ABC News has "a responsibility to hold both sides accountable to the public interest, but that doesn't mean we reflexively and artificially hold both sides 'equally' accountable when the facts don't warrant that . . . It's up to Kerry to defend himself, of course. But as one of the few news organizations with the skill and strength to help voters evaluate what the candidates are saying to serve the public interest [sic]. Now is the time for all of us to step up and do that right." "ABC's memo problem," *The Washington Times*, October 12, 2004.

Neither let us forget Michael Moore's propaganda film, *Fahrenheit 911*, that masqueraded as a documentary film. Senator Kerry received a significant boost in election support from this film that portrayed President Bush as an inept, blundering figure. Many viewers accepted and continue to accept this rendition as factual. In fact, there is talk that it may be nominated for an academy award for the best documentary of the year. If this happens, it will be further proof of how deeply infected Hollywood is with its anti-Bush/anti-conservative bias.

And all of this background, of course, just sets the stage for the Election night coverage. Thus, after we watched FOX News and NBC News project Ohio for Bush, we had to laugh when we saw Dan Rather, Wolf Blitzer and Judy Woodruff sweating bullets and frantically insisting that Ohio was too close to call. The irony of their bias is that they don't seem to see it-- they don't seem to recognize their pro-Democrat/pro-Kerry/anti-Bush bias.

II. Reliability of Most Polls

Except for the exit polls, and for the polls that were taken and published on Halloween weekend just prior to Election Day, the American pollsters appeared to have produced fairly reliable results. (The exit poll problems are discussed below.) There were two principal reasons that the Halloween weekend polls were slanted in favor of Kerry.

First of all, expert pollsters tell us that weekend polls are not reliable because their weekend participants tend to be skewed--usually in favor of Democrats. In spite of this, the pollsters took and reported polls to attempt to gauge the positions of Bush and Kerry as Election Day approached. These polls showed a slight lead for Kerry. Of course, the pollsters did not announce the inherent "weekend weakness" of these polls. But, conservative talk shows did provide this limitation, to those who tuned in to hear it.

But this year, there was also a second flaw in these polls--the major pollsters gave 2-3 points to Kerry in their final polls because they said that the undecided voters tend to vote against the incumbent and because there were many first-time voters who (although unreachable in their polling data) should be projected as voting for the challenger. As it turns out, the evidence does not bear out either of these presumptions.

The bottom line is that most of the polls from the Sunday and Monday preceding Election Day showed Kerry with a slight lead. But, from the Election Day results on Tuesday, it was President Bush who had the slight lead.

III. Unreliability of the Exit Polls

Closely related to, if not actually another part of, the major media bias against President Bush and Republicans is what happened with the exit polling on Election Day 2004.

Random, written questions were submitted to voters Tuesday after they cast their votes. (Actually, there is some question as to how "random" these were.) But, in any event these questionnaires sought to elicit the thinking of voters as to why they voted the way they did. This year, I happened to have been asked to complete such a questionnaire--so I did.

Later that evening, in watching the news coverage of returns, I listened to several commentators talking about and analyzing the results of this exit polling data. Wow! What a startling experience! I was astounded at the conclusions the commentators were trying to make from these questionnaires. To give one example of how flawed these questionnaires were, consider the following: One question was for me to select from a group of a dozen possible issues, what to me were the two, most important issues in the 2004 presidential election. The list included all the main issues--health care, gun control, the economy, tax cuts, etc. I selected "terrorism" and "moral values." However, another possibility was "Iraq." Now, in my thinking, Iraq is intricately a part of the war on terrorism; I selected "terrorism" since it was broader and "included" the war in Iraq. Later, I heard a commentator reporting on findings from the exit polls that showed that those voters who saw Iraq as the main issue in this election, tended to vote for Kerry by a 4-to-1 margin, whereas voters who saw terrorism as the main issue in this election tended to vote for Bush by a similarly large margin. I was appalled that the commentators sought to extrapolate voter intent from questions in a way that I found to be misleading. The poll-takers sought to oversimplify voter intent. The question upon which their analysis was based was unsuitable to support the conclusions for which the questions were used.

But, of course, the major problem with the exit polls this year, was that they were cited to show that Kerry was winning big--bigger in virtually every state where they were used. They showed Kerry winning by 18 points in Pennsylvania. (Kerry eventually won in Pennsylvania, but by a much narrower margin.) They showed Kerry winning in North Carolina, Florida and Ohio, and they showed him competing in Virginia--to name a few states. As the results of these exit polls were made available around noon on Tuesday, the Kerry camp was feeling quite good about things--in fact, it looked like he could win in a landslide.

However, before midnight on Tuesday, all analysts, and all of the nation who were tuned in to the news, realized that the exit polling data was unreliable; those charged with determining whether and when to project a state for Bush or Kerry had to disregard the exit polling data.

So bad was this exit polling data, that there has arisen universal curiosity to find out why it was so bad. In 2008 the effect of this colossal botch-up is that no one will rely on exit polling data in a close election. It will take a yet-to-be demonstrated track record of accurate exit polling, before those polls will again have legitimacy in the eyes of America.

IV. Release of the Osama bin Laden Video on Election Eve

One week before Election Day, a purported videotape of and from Osama bin Laden surfaced, in which Osama checked in on the Presidential Election. Analysts concluded that it was indeed Osama, and that it had been recently made.

Osama's 18-minute video echoed the Democrat Party's talking points in criticizing President Bush. For example, Osama blamed George Bush for causing problems, and he pledged to bankrupt America in its efforts to fight terrorism. For example, he

3.1

even criticized President Bush for reading to elementary school kids for a few minutes after learning of the jet crashing into one of the World Trade Center towers on September 11, 2001. I mention this criticism because it is such an insignificant matter. I am not suggesting any collusion between Osama and the Democrats; but the video does show that the terrorists listened to the criticisms made by Senator Kerry and others against America and the President. In the heat of the election campaign, Mr. Kerry and his supporters, did say things that encouraged the terrorists. The Osama video proves this.

In response to the Osama video, both President Bush and Senator Kerry denounced bin Laden and promised to defeat the terrorists.

The effect of the video on the Election did not appear to be major. But in a close election, sometimes small things can tip the scales in one direction or another. Democrats discounted any effect that the video might have for either party. But it may have given the President a slight lift. While the video was a reminder that Bush has failed to capture bin Laden, it nevertheless was a reminder of the continuing threat that the terrorists pose to America. And since Osama aimed his criticisms at Bush, and not Kerry, the American reaction may have been to increase support for Bush.

It appears that the Osama video was timed to be an in-your-face, defiant statement to mock America for being unable to capture Osama or to stop terrorism. It seems to be a reflection of Osama's inflated feeling of importance, rather than an attempt to affect the outcome of the election. If Osama did intend to help Senator Kerry with his video, he failed. Perhaps in his training he never learned the story of Br'er Rabbit and the briar patch.

V. Effect of Conservative Media

There is no question that George W. Bush would not have won the 2004 election without the conservative talk shows, especially Rush Limbaugh and Sean Hannity, and without the "fair and balanced"[2] news reporting of FOX News.

---

[2] The mainstream media regard FOX News as being biased towards conservatives. They further decry the condition of a nation that now can select to receive its news information from a source that has a conservative bias. However, this is ill-informed, condescending and erroneous. As one who does tune in to FOX News with some regularity, I find that it includes biased discussion from both liberals and conservatives. But their news programs often covers news stories for which the liberal media refuses to give time. For example, the mainstream press refused to give fair treatment to the Swift Boat Vets, who were infuriated with Senator Kerry for the false and exaggerated testimony that he gave to Congress in 1971 about the atrocities that he and other American soldiers committed in Vietnam. In attempting to ignore the Swift Boat Vets, the mainstream press attempted to characterize these vets as attempting to discredit Kerry for not being worthy of his purple hearts. But that was not the main thrust of what the Swift Boat Vets were saying--they felt Kerry was "Unfit for Command" because his testimony before Congress betrayed his fellow veterans, including those who were being held captive in Vietnam **because** his testimony gave aid, comfort and encouragement to our enemy, the Viet Cong, at the very time when we were at war against them. This, to the Swift Boat Vets, was unforgivable, and was a valid issue in the presidential campaign, as a factor in whether or not Senator Kerry is fit to be Commander-in-Chief. And this charge is also pertinent because Senator Kerry's on-going criticism of President Bush's handling of the war in Iraq crossed over the line of propriety, as Kerry said the U.S. should not have attacked Iraq ("the wrong war, at the wrong place, at the wrong time"); that President Bush misled the nation and went to war for bad reasons; that President Bush and his leaders were responsible for the atrocities at Abu Ghraib; and that President Bush was responsible for alienating our allies. Thus, John F. Kerry, ended up doing in the presidential campaign of 2004, the very thing he had done before the Congressional committee in 1971--he was falsely criticizing his country and its president **in time of war** for wrongly waging a war.

It is amazing that President Bush never stated this case against Senator Kerry. But it was

3.1

These organizations and programs aired the Bush side of issues that were not covered by the mainstream media. Those who have not read and listened to the news from both sources will likely be unable to acknowledge this bias.

Almost every day I compare the treatment of issues in *The Washington Post* to the treatment in *The Washington Times*. Regularly, the treatment is different. And the liberal, mainstream media, just doesn't get it. For example, I recently read a letter in *The Washington Post* where its chief editorial writer defended the newspaper by stating that *The Post*'s opinion pages operated independently from the news pages

---

clearly relevant, and the refusal of the mainstream press to give any meaningful air time to this is proof of its liberal bias.

And with regard to the Abu Ghraib matter, by the time we reached October, 2004, it was manifestly clear that the abuse of Iraqi prisoners was not directed by the policies of President Bush, but was the result of the repulsive, illegal acts of a few individuals. The responsible American guards were being prosecuted and punished. Nevertheless, on October 15, 2004, as *The Washington Post* was sensing that the public was no longer sufficiently angry at President Bush for these abuses, it made its lead editorial, "Remember Abu Ghraib?" *The Post* did this for blatant partisan reasons; *The Post* was not satisfied that the nation had now sorted out this problem and was moving on to other issues without blaming President Bush. Determined to do all it could to make the President suffer in the polls for Abu Ghraib, *The Post* saw fit to resurrect the story to attempt to slam the President. The primary effect of this partisan act was to again confirm the bias of *The Washington Post*.

Finally, while the mainstream media may find FOX News to have a dangerous conservative slant, I often find that some of its programs are still weighted too much to the left--both through the time given to liberal guests and because some of its news anchors and talk show hosts have a liberal bias; three examples are Shepherd Smith, Gretta Van Susteren and Geraldo Rivera.

Based upon my observations, those who complain that FOX News has a conservative bias, don't know what they are talking about. The fact that the network does not have a pro-liberal bias does not give the network a conservative bias.

of the paper, such that while the editorial page might support John Kerry, this did not affect how the news pages treated Kerry and Bush. Once again, I had to laugh--they just don't get it! The fact that the opinion pages are run independent of the news pages does not mean that the two are not both biased. In fact, it is the news pages that are more infected with bias than the editorial pages. At least when you read an editorial, you know that it is in the "opinion" section. By definition, the two pages of opinion pieces are all acknowledged to be such. But the biases in *The Washington Post* that I find most offensive are (i) the selection of stories, (ii) the omission of stories, (iii) the location of stories (whether on the front page or inside pages), and (iv) the headlines and article captions.

VI. Effect of the Bipartisan Campaign Finance Reform Act

The 2004 Presidential Election has made a farce of the Bipartisan Campaign Finance Reform Act (BCFRA). It did not keep money out of the campaigns. The Section 527 loophole was so big that it made a joke of the BCFRA expenditure restrictions.

Both parties and their supporters learned how to get around the BCFRA limits, and we ended up with a campaign that attracted more spending than ever before.

VII. Effect of Presidential Debates

As a Bush supporter, I was frustrated at some of the President's performance in the debates with Senator Kerry: Specifically, his failure to respond to accusations that (a) he fired General Shinseki because he requested that too many troops be sent to Iraq; (b) that the war in Iraq was a "diversion" from the war on terrorism, and that this caused the U.S. to take away troops that were needed in Afghanistan and to send them to Iraq; and (c) that the President botched an opportunity to capture Osama bin Laden in Tora Bora. I was frustrated at the President's failure to promptly respond and refute these allegations. Nevertheless, I believe the President was right and Kerry was in error on most of the substantive issues in the debates.

President Bush's re-election has now proven that a candidate (at least the incumbent president) can lose the debates and still win the election. This is reassuring because it proves that many of the people can see through the limitations of debates as being the best indicator for which candidate would be best for the nation.

By saying this, I do not mean to disparage President Bush. I believe he did fine, especially in the latter two debates. But Senator Kerry clearly won the first debate. And Senator Kerry proved that he is not only a capable, but a very eloquent speaker. Frankly, Senator Kerry was very impressive in the debates--and a better debater than President Bush. But I found Kerry wanting--and in many instances wrong on the substance of his words. The Presidential debates of 2004 shows that the nation is capable of using the debates as *one* factor, but not necessarily the *deciding* factor in assessing who should be the President.

VIII. Effect of Third-Party Candidates

The 2004 Presidential Election marked the first election since 1988 where a third-party candidate did not have a major impact on the results. The Nader vote did not prevent Senator Kerry from carrying any state. However, in 2000, it is quite obvious that if Nader had not been on the ballot in Florida, then Al Gore would most probably have picked up the extra 538 votes he needed to win Florida and the election. Similarly, in both 1992 and 1996, third-party candidate Ross Perot took votes from Republican candidates Bush (1992) and

Dole (1996) to give those election victories to Bill Clinton.

To this day, President Bill Clinton is regarded by his party as having extraordinary charisma and magic as a politician. It is easy to overlook the Perot factor. And remember, Clinton never did win a majority of the popular vote in those elections.

IX. Myth that High Voter Turnout Is Better for Democratic Candidates

Going into Election Day, Senator Kerry's camp believed that a large voter turnout would take him to victory. He and the pollsters and the main stream media all believed that high voter turn out would work to Kerry's favor. However, that is not what happened. Oh, the turnout was very high-- approximately 60%--an increase from the 2000 turnout of 56%. But the additional votes were going for Bush more than for Kerry. The Republican Party never did buy into the traditional thinking that a high turn out favored Democrats. The Republicans beat the bushes and energized its base, bringing in a record turnout that made Bush victorious.

X. Why Did Kerry Fail to Win?

This is the question that the Democrats are asking themselves in analyzing the election results. But to me, it was an incredible feat for him to even make it close. In order for him to get his party's nomination, he had to abandon his recently acquired pro-war stance and adopt the stance of the left wing of the Democratic Party to oppose and criticize the war. Howard Dean was activating the Democratic base by vehemently denouncing Bush and the Iraq war; in order for Kerry to win his party's nomination, he had to revert back to his anti-war stance and get out in front of that movement. This he did; he out-maneuvered Dean and dethroned Dean as the party spokesman against the war, proclaiming that this was "the wrong war, at the wrong place, at the wrong time." Of all the candidates for the Democratic nomination, only Senator Joe Lieberman had the courage to defy the radical left wing of his party, as he continued to insist that the war in Iraq was right. After capturing the nomination, Senator Kerry had to change his stance to the Lieberman position in order to be competitive in the race for the White House. The Bush campaign rightly criticized Kerry with flip-flopping on this, the most critical issue of the election.

Thus, after winning the nomination as an anti-war candidate, Kerry had the almost impossible task of having to flip-flop to become pro-war and to make the case that President Bush's handling of the war was inept, was responsible for the loss of American troops, and was alienating the world. Kerry almost succeeded. The anti-Bush sentiment is so strong (close to one-half of the voters), that these people were happy to overlook not only Kerry's unprincipled political life, but also Kerry's over-the-top criticisms of America's efforts in Iraq.[3]

When American troops claimed military control over Iraq in May of 2003, we had lost approximately 250 troops. This was an impressive victory, and the nation could stomach these losses. However, in the

[3] In this regard, Kerry's 1971 testimony before the Senate Committee, in which he accused his fellow Americans of committing horrendous atrocities on the people in North Vietnam, turned a large segment of the nation against him. This black mark from his path, showed that Kerry was excessively aggressive in pursuing his own political agenda at the expense of betraying his fellow soldiers. It was the outrageousness of his testimony that drew attention to him in 1971, and which perhaps helped him to achieve early political victories. But the facts caught up with him in 2004. And Kerry could not shake the disdain and anger of military veterans and others, who saw his a parallel between his anti-American statements in 1971 and his statements against the war in Iraq in 2004.

18 months since, we have lost approximately nine hundred troops to continual suicide bombings and attacks by terrorists/insurgents. These losses do not sit well with the nation; neither were these losses foreseen by the nation. Although President Bush was careful not to guarantee either a quick victory or a low casualty victory, many did not anticipate the extent of the terrorist attacks that have occurred since we dethroned Saddam Hussein. Nevertheless, both Bush and Kerry were united in asserting that America had to stick it out and prevail in Iraq. Kerry sought to distinguish himself by asserting that he would do better in directing the war--but he did not articulate a specific plan that differentiated himself from President Bush on this. And, frankly, President Bush had been steadfast and resolute on Iraq--he has never flinched or wavered.

On Election Day, Americans re-elected President Bush. Kerry came close; but he was not able to overtake Bush. In retrospect, it is amazing that Senator Kerry did as well as he did. In 2003, following the quick and decisive military victory in Iraq, President Bush's popularity was high, and no one gave much of a chances for any Democrat to succeed in November 2004. Senator Kerry's relative success was in large part due to his superb political skills.

XI. The Great Divide--A Polarized Nation

One thing that the 2004 Election demonstrates is the great political divide that exists in America. It consists of a number of divisions superimposed over one another. There continues to be a sharp divide between whites and blacks. (Over 85% of the black vote went to Senator Kerry.) There is an urban-rural divide--virtually all rural areas voted for Bush, while virtually all urban areas voted for Kerry. The nation is also divided in its support for traditional marriage vs. gay unions. And the Democrats continue to attempt to divide

America into the "Haves" and the "Have Nots."

Now that the Presidential Election is over, we may have a short period of good will and unity. Historically, the nation often comes together immediately following an election, despite the divisiveness and even viciousness of the campaign. And both President Bush and Senator Kerry have said the customary things about working together as a nation. But I don't think any reasonable spectator of American politics believes that any lenthy period of political unity will be inaugurated by President Bush's victory and Senator Kerry's defeat. Any period of peace is just the eye of the hurricane. Before long Congress and the nation will be embroiled in debating some important and divisive issues. I hope that the war on terror, including the war in Iraq, will not be one of these divisive issues. The nation must unite to defeat the forces of terrorism in Iraq and help the new Iraqi government to get off the ground.

But some of the divisive issues that will soon take center stage include the following:

- Federal Marriage Amendment
- Continuing the tax cuts
- Fixing Social Security
- National health care issues
- Partial-birth abortion
- Stem cell research
- Confirmation of federal judges, including nominees to the Supreme Court

President Bush characterized Senator Kerry as being "gracious" in his call conceding defeat and acknowledging the President's victory. But, as I listened to Senator Kerry's concession speech, I also heard his statements that the fight for their causes most go on and that "the President" should work to unify the country. Already some of the liberal commentators are predicting that Bush won't be able to unite the nation, claiming that despite his

promises to unite the nation in 2000 that he acted to alienate and divide the country. Well, the conservatives take issue with this accusation. Perhaps we can all agree that right now the nation is sharply divided on a number of issues. But if the recent Election means anything, it is the predominant consensus that it is the Democrats that are more divisive than the Republicans. And as evidence of the continuing efforts by liberals to divide and blame the nation, listen to the words of columnist E. J. Dionne, Jr. in *The Washington Post* on November 5, 2004:

Let's be honest: We are aghast at the success of a campaign [the Bush campaign] based on vicious personal attacks, the exploitation of strong religious feelings and an effort to create the appearance of strong leadership that would do Hollywood proud. We are alarmed that so many of our fellow citizens could look the other way and not hold Bush accountable for the utter incompetence in Iraq and for untruths spoken in defense of the war. We are amazed that a majority was not concerned about heaping a huge debt burden on our children just to give large tax breaks to the rich.

And we are disgusted that an effort consciously designed to divide the country did exactly that--and won. With all his failures, Bush could not count on a whole lot more than 51 percent. Karl Rove and company calculated perfectly, organized painstakingly, greatly increased conservative turnout and produced a country divided just their way.

The opposition should not crawl into a hole or be silent about these things. A decent respect for the outcome of an election never requires free citizens to cower before a temporarily dominant majority. There is, on the contrary, an obligation to stay engaged in a battle that, as John Edwards says, rages on.

. . . But the burden for achieving national unity is on a president who could manage a narrow victory only by savagely trashing his opponent.

While I disagree with most of Mr. Dionne's conclusions, I do believe that the tone of his opinion piece correctly describes the political posture that the Democrats will take in the coming months; it is not one of cooperation and conciliation.

XII. The Next Political Battle-- the Nomination and Confirmation of Justices to the Supreme Court

Perhaps the most important issue for this country during the next four years will be the appointment of two to four new Justices to the Supreme Court. The Democrats live in fear that the President will select Justices who would overturn *Roe v. Wade*, 410 U.S. 113 (1973), in which the Court established a woman's right to have an abortion. This fear is what underlies the Democratic filibusters of President Bush's judicial nominees during the past two years.

And while Republicans will control 55 our of 100 seats in the Senate in 2004, this is 5 seats short of what is needed to block a filibuster. The editorial pages will be filled with opinion pieces about this ideological battle during the next couple of years. While President Bush was able to put off this fight during his first term, it cannot be avoided this term.

If Democrats continue to use the filibuster to prevent Senate votes on judicial nominees, then the Republican Senate will have to change their rules to eliminate the use of filibusters to block votes on judicial nominees.

There is already some building intensity on this issue, manifest by Senator Arlen Spector's warning that President Bush should not submit any nominee that would overturn *Roe v. Wade*. Senator Spector's comments may result in his fellow Republicans not voting him to be chair of the Judiciary Committee.

A. About "Strict Constructionists." Democrats fear all critics of *Roe v. Wade* and all "strict constructionist" judicial nominees. This phrase instantly evokes hysterical panic whenever liberals ever hear the phrase; and they fight for all they're

worth to block any such nominees. But a word of education is in order regarding "strict constructionists." Few of them exist, and there is no reason President Bush would have to nominate one. First of all, to be a "strict constructionist" means that one opposes the Court's recognizing any right except those specifically enumerated in the Constitution. Thus, a "strict constructionist" would not have voted to recognize the right to an abortion (*Roe v. Wade*), nor a couple's right to have access to contraceptives (*Griswold v. Connecticut* and *Eisenstadt v. Baird*), nor the parents' right to rear their children (*Troxel v. Granville*).[4] Of course, the problem with not being a "strict constructionist" is that there are no limits on what new rights the court can recognize or on what rights the court might refuse to recognize. For example, in the case of *Roe v. Wade*, the Court chose to recognize the woman's right to control her body, but the Court chose not to recognize the right of a fetus to continue to live, even though many states had recognized such a right. But on the other hand, the problem with true "strict constructionists" is that they reject the Ninth Amendment, which states: "The enumeration in the Constitution of certain rights shall not be construed to deny or disparage others retained by the people."

But having said all this about what a true "strict constructionist" is, the fact is that there is none on the Supreme Court--some Justices are merely "stricter" than others.

Leaving aside the technical meaning of "strict constructionist," the term is loosely used with different meanings by Republicans and Democrats. Republicans use it to mean one who is reluctant, cautious or stingy in identifying new constitutional rights. And in this sense, Republicans would identify Justices Scalia and Thomas

---

[4] The citations for these cases are: *Roe v. Wade*, 410 U.S. 113 (1973); *Griswold v. Connecticut*, 381 U.S. 479 (1965); *Eisenstadt v. Baird*, 405 U.S. 438 (1972); *Troxel v. Granville*, 530 U.S. 57 (2000).

as "strict constructionists," even though neither is. On the other hand, Democrats use the term to mean someone who would overturn the sacred right to an abortion, established in *Roe v. Wade*; to Democrats the term is more of a label of horror than a term of any technical meaning.

But having now been educated on the true meaning of a "strict constructionist," let us move on to the present national problem of getting good judicial nominees for the Supreme Court and the appellate courts.

There is no reason why President Bush should nominate a true "strict constructionist" to be a Supreme Court Justice. What is needed is a non-activist judge who has the wisdom and courage to stand up against the growing tide in America of judges who legislate and abandon established interpretations of the Constitution. This abandonment has occurred with respect to the Establishment Clause (e.g., Ten Commandments monument cases), the meaning of which has been changed by the Supreme Court during the last 50 years. Similarly in the recent case of *Lawrence v. Texas*, 539 U.S. ___ (2003), a majority of the Court embraced judicial activism and discarded its traditional principles of *stare decisis* in order to embrace the new-found "liberty" under the Due Process Clauses to engage in private, consensual, adult homosexual conduct.

The nation does not need, and this writer does not want a "strict constructionist" Supreme Court Justice. We just need Justices who will uphold the Constitution and stop the activism and legislation and unwise creation of new rights.

B. About Roe v. Wade. Some words of instruction are also in order regarding *Roe v. Wade*. There were several problems with the Court's ruling in this case:

(1) The Court legislated,[5] rather than merely ruled on a case; (2) The Court extended the power of the federal government to a new extreme by prohibiting states from protecting the fetal right to life, except in the last trimester of pregnancy; (3) The Court held that a fetus is not a "person" within the meaning of the Due Process Clauses of the Fifth and Fourteenth Amendments; and (4) The Court established a woman's right to privacy and to control her own body, and the Court held that this right included a limited right to have an abortion-- a right that is virtually unlimited in the first two trimesters of a pregnancy.

In my opinion, one part of the *Roe v. Wade* ruling is good--the identification and upholding of a woman's right to control her own body. But this right should not be an "absolute" that can always extinguish the right to life of the child with whom she is pregnant. The Supreme Court erred, in my opinion, by extinguishing the fetal right to life. The Court could have ruled that both rights should be recognized. Had they so ruled, the two would have to be balanced if the mother would want an abortion.

But one of the problems we face today is that *Roe v. Wade* has now been extended beyond what it was in 1973. At least one court today has invalidated the law recently passed by Congress banning partial-birth abortions. These radical judges have tried to eliminate the states' right (recognized in *Roe*) to prohibit abortions in the last trimester in order to protect potential human life.

The overturning of *Roe v. Wade*, was desirable 30 years ago. Several fetal right to life amendments were proposed to do this. But none has succeeded. At this point, however, it makes no sense to exert political

---

[5] The Court established a pregnancy trimester scheme to determine when a woman would have a right to an abortion and when a state could have the power to prohibit an abortion because of its interest in potential human life.

3.1

effort to overturn *Roe v. Wade*. But we certainly need Supreme Court Justices who will stop the courts from further extending the right to have an abortion at the expense of fully-developed, unborn babies who are capable of surviving outside the womb. Partial-birth abortion is totally unnecessary, and the law banning it is good. The theoretical argument is a fiction that an exception should exist in any ban against partial-birth abortion in order to protect the life of the mother--this objection is a fiction! Obstetricians have refuted the claim that a partial birth abortion either saves the life of pregnant women or provides any significant benefit to their health.

What is needed in the judiciary are judges who are not activists--who will neither improperly expand nor contract the Constitution. We need Justices who will Return the law-making function of the government to Congress and to the States,

and re-establish the Courts as merely the interpreters of the Constitution.

XIII. Education--the Key to the Future

The closeness of the 2004 election highlights the need to educate society--to refute the many myths and lies about conservatives, and to expose the bias and hatred of extremist left. Education is the antidote for the ignorance that breeds and sustains the anti-conservative firebrands. And the key to a lasting education is to educate the rising generation, which is now in our nation's schools. This is a formidable task, with liberals in control of most of our universities and many of our states' school systems. But as daunting as the task may be, we must tackle it and pursue it diligently until truth prevails.

Cheney Case Strengthens Executive Branch

On June 24, 2004, the Supreme Court ruled (7-2) in *Vice President Dick Cheney v. United States District Court for the District of Columbia*, 542 U.S. ___, that private groups seeking to compel the Executive Branch to disclose information pertaining to advisory committee meetings have the burden to show that such disclosure does not interfere with the Executive Branch's duties and privileges.[1]

This case strengthens the power of the Executive Branch, and it is a victory for the Bush Administration. It gives the Executive Branch protection from information-seeking law suits brought by private individuals. It expands and strengthens the executive privilege. Politically, it has upheld Vice President Cheney's refusal to disclose the names of some individuals attending the meetings conducted by Vice President Cheney regarding the fashioning of a national energy policy.

Mr. Cheney, who has previously worked for or invested in oil and energy companies, was suspected of having received input at these meetings from some of his former business associates. Sierra Club and Judicial Watch sought to find out what influence was given by whom at these meetings. But the Supreme Court now ruled that the executive privilege puts a burden on those seeking information in civil litigation discovery against the Executive Branch to show that requiring the Executive to produce specific materials would not impinge on the constitutional duties and privileges of the Executive.

For most people, further discussion and analysis of what happened in this case may not be interesting. However, lawyers and students of the Constitution will find this to be a fascinating case.

The specific facts and findings in this case involve a rather complex, technical discovery dispute in the case brought by the Sierra Club and Judicial Watch against Vice President Cheney,[2] in which the former sought to force the Vice President to disclose documents introduced and the names of people attending the advisory committee meetings related to the development of recommendations for a national energy policy.

Under the Federal Advisory Committee Act (5 U.S.C. App. Sec. 2, hereafter FACA), advisory committees are subject to various open-meeting and disclosure requirements. However, such committees that are "composed wholly of full-time, or permanent part-time, officers or employees of the Federal Government" are exempt from the disclosure requirements (5 U.S.C. App.

---

[1] Note that the U. S. District Court is the party (opposing the Vice President) in this case and not Sierra Club and Judicial Watch, the two organizations who sued the Vice President. The reason for this is because the Vice President is seeking to obtain from the Circuit Court of Appeals a writ of mandamus against the District Court. There will be further discussion of this unusual procedural issue later in this article.

[2] Initially there were other parties in the case, including the advisory committee itself, the National Energy Policy Development Group (NEPDG) and alleged non-government participants. The NEPDG was eventually dismissed from the case because it had already been dissolved. The alleged non-government participants were dismissed, since the Federal Advisory Committee Act (FACA, 5 U.S.C. App. Sec. 2) did not create a private cause of action. The suit against the Vice President and other government officials went forward. Their legal position in this case is the same as that of Vice President Cheney, therefore this article merely focuses on the Vice President.

Sec. 3). Sierra Club and Judicial Watch alleged that the attendance of some non-federal employees at these meetings made them *de facto* members and therefore removed the exemption from disclosure obligations. The Vice President disputes this. But the case went forward on a "discovery" dispute; the courts have not, and probably will not ever address the ultimate issue.

I. The Discovery Dispute

In litigation, "discovery" is the pre-trial investigation and preparation that parties undertake to prepare for trial. It can include the taking of depositions, requesting answers to written interrogatories, and requesting the production of documents and things. In this case, Sierra Club and Judicial Watch [hereafter petitioners] sent a request for production of documents (a discovery request) that sought the exact information the production of which was the ultimate relief they sought in their law suit.

II. Procedural Steps to Block Discovery

In response to the discovery requests, compliance with which would have produced the very information that the Vice President contended could not be legally required, the Vice President filed a motion to dismiss the case and objected to providing requested documents until there was a final ruling on that issue. The District Court deferred ruling on the motion to dismiss and allowed some "tightly reined discovery"; the District Court was preparing to hold a hearing and determine whether the Plaintiffs' *de facto* argument did require the Vice President to disclose information.

Thereafter, Petitioners immediately sent the Vice President a broad, far-reaching discovery request for documents. Before responding to the discovery request, the Vice President (a) filed a petition for a writ of mandamus with the same Court of Appeals, asking the Court to order dismissal of petitioners' complaints.[3]

The Court of Appeals (by a 2-1 vote) dismissed the writ of mandamus, stating that the case of *United States v. Nixon*, 481 U.S. 683 (1974),[4] requires that the Vice President must first assert with particularity those matters which he seeks to protect from intrusion (Slip Opinion, p. 5).

The Vice President then filed a Petition for Writ of Certiorari, asking the Supreme Court to review the case. The Supreme Court granted review. Thereafter, on June 24, 2004, the Supreme Court vacated the judgment of the Circuit Court of Appeals and remanded the case for further consideration.

As will be shown, the Supreme Court's opinion, which sets the guidelines to be followed by the Circuit Court, appears to guarantee that either the case will be dismissed by the Circuit Court or at least that the Vice President will be ultimately insulated from providing the requested information.

---

[3] The Vice President also filed an appeal to the Court of Appeals. No resolution has been made of that appeal, but the Supreme Court's ruling on the writ of mandamus probably makes the appeal moot.

[4] This is the case that precipitated President Nixon's resignation, as he was ordered by a unanimous Court to turn over the audio tapes that provided evidence that he obstructed justice in connection with the prosecution of the Watergate break-in.

III. The Writ of Mandamus

A writ of mandamus is an order from a higher court, ordering a lower court to do something. It is similar to an appeal, but it can be obtained quickly. It is referred to as a "drastic and extraordinary remedy" (Slip Opinion, p. 9), and is intended to allow one to tap into the court's broad powers to deal with unusual situations for which the usual rules are inadequate. There are three prerequisites to obtaining a writ of mandamus: (1) There must be no other adequate means for relief; (2) the right to the writ must be clear and indisputable; and (3) the writ must be appropriate under the circumstances.

In denying the Vice President's request for a writ of mandamus, the Court of Appeals said that the Vice President had the burden to invoke the executive privilege with specificity as to each discovery request that it contends to be improper. The Court of Appeals went on to hold that because the Vice President did not do this, therefore he did not meet the first requirement to obtain a writ of mandamus; the Court of Appeals said that the Vice President had not done all that he could have done, and therefore his petition for a writ of mandamus was premature. (Slip Opinion, p. 12.)

But the Supreme Court disagreed with this approach.[5] The Court pointed

out that it has previously issued such a writ "to restrain a lower court when its actions would threaten the separation of powers by 'embarrass[ing] the executive arm of the Government,' [citations omitted]" (Slip Opinion, p. 10). The Court said that the Court of Appeals had misread the *United States v. Nixon* case. The *Nixon* case, being a criminal matter, carried with it more stringent disclosure requirements. Second, the information sought in Nixon was not for discovery, but involved subpoenas that were "required to satisfy exacting standards of '(1) relevancy; (2) admissibility; (3) specificity.'" (Slip Opinion, p. 16.) Finally, the Court found in Vice President Cheney's case that this was not a routine discovery issue, and that special considerations existed because of "the Executive Branch's interests in maintaining the autonomy of its office and safeguarding the confidentiality of its communications." (Slip Opinion, p. 14.)

IV. Supreme Court Recognizes, Expands the Executive Privilege

The Court found that the discovery requests were "anything but appropriate," and that the *Nixon* case did not support the proposition that the Executive Branch should have the burden to specifically invoke executive privilege

---

[5] The Opinion of the Court was written by Justice Kennedy (joined by Chief Justice Rehnquist, Justice O'Connor and Justice Breyer). Three additional Justices concurred in the result.

In a concurring opinion, Justice Stevens said that in a case where the ultimate relief sought is the same matter sought by discovery, then those seeking discovery have the burden to show the need for specific discovery requests.

In another concurring opinion, Justice Thomas (joined by Justice Scalia) wrote that only if Sierra Club and Judicial Watch had demonstrated their right to the documents by "clear and undisputable evidence" would they be entitled to the documents. Justice Thomas said they failed to demonstrate this and therefore issuance of a writ of mandamus would be proper.

Justices Ginsberg and Souter dissented. They felt the government should have the burden to object to intrusive discovery by making specific objections and specifically asserting executive privilege in order to avail itself of that privilege.

3.9

by "making particularized objections."
(Slip Opinion, p. 17.) The Court called
this a "real burden." (Slip Opinion, p.
18.) The Court said that a mandamus
writ could be proper to protect the
Executive Branch from "unnecessarily
broad subpoenas." (Slip Opinion, p. 19.)
The Court said that the Court of Appeals
has an obligation to determine whether
the lower court "actions constituted an
unwarranted impairment of another ranch
in the performance of its constitutional
duties," and that the assertion of
executive privilege is not "a necessary
precondition to the Government's
separation-of-powers objections." (Slip
Opinion, p. 20.)

The case remanded back to the
Court of Appeals for the District of
Columbia. This should ultimately lead to
the termination of petitioners' case, but
as of this writing, the case continues,
albeit only on life-support.

3.5.1 & 3.10 & 2.8

Supreme Court Rules Hamdi Has Right to Challenge Designation as Enemy Combatant

On June 28, 2004, the Supreme Court ruled (5-4) in *Hamdi v. Rumsfeld*, 542 U.S. ___, that the government's detention of Yaser Esam Hamdi was proper, but ruled (8-1) that Hamdi now has the right to challenge the Government's designation that he is an "enemy combatant."

I. Hamdi's Capture and Detention

One week after the terrorist attacks in the United States on September 11, 2001, Congress passed a resolution, Authorization for Use of Military Force (AUMF), which authorized the President to use military force in Afghanistan to subdue al Qaeda and to topple the Taliban regime there. Later that year, Yaser Esam Hamdi (age 21) was seized by military groups with whom the United States was allied. It was reported that Hamdi belonged to troops that were fighting the United States and our allied forces. Hamdi was transferred to the control of U. S. troops, and in January 2002, he was transferred to the U. S. Naval Base in Guantanamo Bay. In April, 2002, after it was learned that Hamdi was an American citizen, he was transferred to a brig in Norfolk, Virginia. Later he was transferred to a brig in Charleston, South Carolina.

The Government contended that Hamdi is an "enemy combatant," and that accordingly the United States could hold him indefinitely, without formal charges or proceedings.

II. The Habeas Corpus Proceedings

In June, 2002, Hamdi's father, Esam Fouad Hamdi, filed a petition for a writ of habeas corpus in the United States District Court for the Eastern District of Virginia. That proceeding invoked the jurisdiction of the federal courts to determine whether or not Hamdi's detention was proper. The District Court ordered that counsel be provided for Hamdi. The government appealed, and the Fourth Circuit reversed the District Court. On remand, the habeas corpus proceeding continued, and the Government produced an affidavit from Michael Mobbs, which asserted that Hamdi had been fighting with Taliban forces against the U.S., that Hamdi's unit surrendered, and that Hamdi himself surrendered an assault rifle to Northern Alliance forces. (Slip Opinion, pp. 4-5.) The District Court then ruled that based upon the generic and hearsay nature of the affidavit there was insufficient evidence to detain Hamdi. (Slip Opinion, p. 5.) The Government again appealed, and the Fourth Circuit again reversed, upholding the Government's position— that Hamdi was captured in a zone of active combat in a foreign theater of conflict, and that "[o]ne who takes up arms against the United States in a foreign theater of war, regardless of his citizenship, may properly be designated an enemy combatant and treated as such." (Slip Opinion, p. 8, and 316 F.3d at 475.) Hamdi then filed a petition for certiorari, and the Supreme Court agreed to review the case, and has now upheld the Government's right to detain Hamdi (by a 5-4 vote), but held (8-1) that Hamdi now has the right to challenge his detention as an "enemy combatant."

This ruling defeat's the Bush administration's assertion of unassailable authority to detain individuals captured abroad who are found with forces fighting against the United States.[1] However, the ruling nevertheless establishes broad powers favorable to the Government in handling "enemy combatants." Specifically, when an individual is afforded the chance to challenge his designation as an "enemy combatant," the Court stated that the government can use hearsay to establish its claim and that there is a presumption that the government's designation is correct. This puts on the individual detained the burden to prove that the designation was in error.

The Court's ruling does not address the issue of how long and under what circumstances the government can postpone giving a detainee the opportunity to challenge his designation. In Hamdi's case, the wait of approximately 2 ½ years was not held to be unlawful; there was no government argument that security exigencies made it imprudent for the government to have to deal with the issue at this time.

III. Hamdi's Right to Challenge His Designation as an "Enemy Combatant"

Only Justice Thomas sided with the Government in its position that Hamdi had no right to challenge his detention as an enemy combatant. Justice Thomas argued that the detention is authorized by the Executive's war powers in Article I of the Constitution.

The other eight justices all agreed that Hamdi has the right to challenge his enemy combatant status, but they differed sharply as to whether his detention should be continued.

A. Justice O'Connor's Opinion.

The Court's judgment was announced by Justice Sandra O'Connor (joined by Chief Justice Rehnquist, Justice Kennedy and Justice Breyer).[3] The Court ruled that Hamdi had the right to challenge his detention as an "enemy combatant" through the habeas corpus petition; that the Government can use hearsay evidence as a basis for detention, and that there is a presumption that the Government's evidence is correct.

B. The Scalia-Stevens Dissent.

It is not very often that Justices Scalia and Stevens find themselves on the same side of difficult issues. But Justice joined in Justice Scalia's dissent here.

Basically, Justice Scalia argued that unless Congress suspends the writ of habeas corpus, then Hamdi must be freed. Article I, Section 9, clause 2 of the Constitution gives Congress the power to determine when the writ of habeas corpus should be suspended because of national emergency. Since Congress did not suspend the writ, Hamdi should go free.

C. The Souter-Ginsberg Dissent.

Justices Souter and Ginsberg contend that Congress' Authorization for the Use of Military Force, passed in September, 2001, did not empower the military to detain Hamdi.

IV. Postscript

In late September, 2004, the Government released Hamdi, allowing him to fly to Saudi Arabia, where he will then renounce his U. S. citizenship and never again be allowed to enter the United States.

---

[1] After his capture in Afghanistan, and after learning that Hamdi was an American citizen, he was eventually brought to the United States. This case does not address what Hamdi's rights would be if he were being detained overseas.

[3] Justice O'Connor's ruling represents a majority of the Justices (5) because Justice Thomas concurred in the legality of Hamdi's detention.

Non-Custodial Parent Lacks Standing to Challenge the Constitutionality of "Under God" in Pledge of Allegiance

On June 14, 2004, the U. S. Supreme Court ruled 5-3[1] that Michael Newdow lacked standing to bring suit to challenge the California public school policy that required teachers to lead the students in a daily, voluntary recitation of the Pledge of Allegiance, including the words, "one Nation under God." *Elk Grove Unified School District v. Newdow*, 542 U.S. ____. This means that the Supreme Court and the nation will have to wait until another day to find out whether the reference to "God" in the Pledge of Allegiance violates the Establishment Clause of the First Amendment.

The First Amendment (passed in 1791) begins: "Congress shall make no law respecting the establishment of religion." A national Pledge of Allegiance was adopted by Congress in 1942. In 1954, Congress added the phrase "one Nation under God" to the Pledge.

Michael Newdow, a confirmed atheist, a divorcee, and the father of a California school girl, took umbrage over the fact that his daughter was required by law to be present when her teacher and fellow students participated in a recitation of the Pledge of Allegiance at the beginning of each school day. The daughter--who is not atheist, but is a Christian--was not bothered by the practice; neither was the child's mother, Sandra Banning, who had sole legal custody of the child. Mr. Newdow's position conflicted with that of his child and the child's custodial parent. The Supreme Court then had to first decide whether Mr. Newdow had "standing" to challenge the wording in the Pledge. The Court concluded he did not, and thereby put off the Establishment Clause issue until another day.

Historically, Justice Rehnquist has taken the lead in declining to review cases because of a parties' lack of standing. In this, case he concluded that Mr. Newdow did have standing to challenge

the California law, but a majority of the Court concluded otherwise.

I. Standing to Sue

Article III of the Constitution empowers the Supreme Court (and those courts inferior to it) to resolve "cases" and "controversies." Conversely, the Court's power does not extend to giving advisory opinions about matters that "could" some day become a "case" or a "controversy." The Court's power is further limited to those actual parties who have a direct interest in a case or controversy. For example, if my neighbor punches his wife in the nose, I cannot sue and recover damages against my neighbor for the damages he caused his wife to suffer. Why? Because I am not a party in interest; I, myself, did not suffer any direct injury from the assault--I do not have **standing** to bring such a suit.

Through the years Supreme Court has formulated some principles for testing whether a particular litigant has standing. In Mr. Newdow's case there were two general principles that the Court applied to determine whether the non-custodial parent could challenge the state action: Article III Standing and Prudential Standing.

A. **Article III Standing.** This refers to Article III of the Constitution, the one that establishes the Judicial Branch of the Government. Article III standing exists if the subject matter of a suit is a "case" or a "controversy." All eight Justices agreed that Mr. Newdow satisfied this criteria. No one doubted the sincerity of his complaint that the phrase "under God" bothered him and that he disliked his daughter's having to be exposed to the daily recitation of this phrase.

B. **Prudential Standing.** This refers to judicially self-imposed limits, such as declining to find standing if one attempts to litigate another's rights or generalized grievances, which should more appropriately be addressed through legislation than a court ruling. In applying this standard, the Court decided that Mr. Newdow should not be allowed to challenge the California Pledge of Allegiance policy. The Supreme Court has historically deferred to state and local courts on domestic relations issues. In Mr. Newdow's case, the U. S. District Court, in applying California law, decided that Mr. Newdow had no right to sue on behalf of his daughter--as a "next friend." In other words, he lacked standing. The Ninth Circuit

[1] Justices Stevens, Kennedy, Souter, Ginsberg and Breyer were in the majority. Chief Justice Rehnquist, Justice O'Connor and Justice Thomas were in the minority. Justice Scalia took no part in the decision--he recused himself because he had previously spoken out on this issue.

Court of Appeals reversed the District Court on the standing issue. But (as has so often happened), the Supreme Court reversed the Ninth Circuit.

II. The Dissenters Address the Substantive Issue, Laying the Groundwork for the Next Appearance of the "Under God" Issue.

The three dissenting Justices agreed that the Ninth Circuit against the Pledge should be reversed. But the three dissenters wanted to reach the substantive issue rather than to overturn the Ninth Circuit merely on the basis of Mr. Newdow's lack of standing. The Chief Justice, Justice O'Connor and Justice Thomas argued that the majority had misapplied the case of *Ankenbrandt v. Richards*, 504 U.S. 89 (1992), in denying Newdow standing to challenge the "under God" phrase in the Pledge. Their three dissenting opinions were undoubtedly intended to help lay the groundwork to defeat the Newdow claim whenever it should return.

A. Chief Justice William Rehnquist. Justice Rehnquist laid out the long history of God in American government. He said that having a teacher lead a class in the voluntary recitation of the Pledge of Allegiance, including the words "under God" "does not impermissibly coerce a religious act (Chief Justice dissenting, Slip Opinion, 14), but that it is a "commendable patriotic observance" that was commended by popular laws enacted by the national and state governments. *Id.*, at 16.

B. Justice Sandra O'Connor. Justice O'Connor pointed out that the Supreme Court has a variety of tests and principles that it applies to Establishment Clause issues depending on the category of Establishment Clause issue. She said that two principal tests are the "coercion" test and the "endorsement" test. She said that the Ninth Circuit wrongly applied the "coercion"[2] test to the "under God" issue, and that the proper test to apply was

the "endorsement"[3] test. Further, she said that the Court has to make a "reasonable" interpretation of the challenged governmental action. Justice O'Connor's concluding comments on this issue are quite persuasive:

[T]he Constitution does not guarantee citizens a right entirely to avoid ideas with which they disagree. It would betray its own principles if it did; no robust democracy insulates its citizens from views that they might find novel or even inflammatory.

Michael Newdow's challenge . . . to "one Nation under God," however sincere, cannot be the yardstick of our Establishment Clause inquiry. Certain ceremonial references to God and religion in our Nation are the inevitable consequence of the religious history that gave birth to our founding principles of liberty. It would be ironic indeed if this Court were to wield our constitutional commitment to religious freedom so as to sever our ties to the traditions developed to honor it.

(Justice O'Connor dissenting, Slip Opinion, 12-13.)

C. Justice Clarence Thomas. Justice Thomas addressed the substantive issue and argued that the Court should overturn its 1992 ruling in *Lee v. Weisman*, 505 U.S. 577. This was the case where the Supreme Court held that it violated the Establishment Clause for a public school system to have a prayer delivered at a high school graduation. In the case of Mr. Newdow, the Ninth Circuit had relied on *Lee v. Weisman* in ruling in Mr. Newdow's favor. Justice Thomas said that that case was bad law and should be overturned. He also stated that the Establishment Clause (which does not protect individual rights) should not be incorporated (through the Due Process Clause of the 14th Amendment) to apply to the states (Justice Thomas dissenting, Slip Opinion, 6-7).

---

[2] *Santa Fe Independent School District v. Doe*, 530 U.S. 290 (2000) and *Lee v. Weisman*, 505 U.S. 577 (1992) are the principal cases that set forth the "coercion" test. The gist of the "coercion" test is that the public schools must not take actions that may coerce the highly susceptible, impressionable school children who by law are required to attend school.

[3] The "endorsement" test was used by the Court in *County of Allegheny v. ACLU*, 492 U.S. 573 (1989). The controlling principle is that the government must not convey a message "that religion or a particular religious belief is favored or preferred." *Id.* Justice O'Connor would apply a reasonable approach in applying the "endorsement" test because "adopting a subjective approach would reduce the test to an absurdity. Nearly any government action could be overturned as a violation of the Establishment Clause if a "heckler's veto" sufficed to show that its message was one of endorsement." (Justice O'Connor dissenting, Slip Opinion, 2-3.)

Supreme Court Upholds Injunction Baring Enforcement of the Child Online Protection Act

On June 29, 2004, the Supreme Court ruled (5-4) in *Ashcroft v. American Civil Liberties Union*, 542 U. S. ____ that a District Court had properly enjoined (blocked) the enforcement of the Child Online Protection Act (COPA) because the law was likely unconstitutional.

This case is not that unusual. However, recent developments make this case noteworthy.

In 1973, in the case of *Miller v. California*, 413 U.S. 15, the Supreme Court announced the principles that have provided the basis for most obscenity legislation ever since. Basically the Court held that obscenity is not protected speech under the First Amendment, but that to be "obscene" the speech must appeal to the prurient interest, be patently offensive according to community standards, and that it must depict sexual conduct the prohibition of which is specifically defined by applicable law.

Non-obscene speech which is deemed harmful to minors can be restricted as to them, but not if the restrictions are overly broad (interfering with the right of adults to have access to such speech[1]). *Ginsberg v. New York*, 390 U.S. 629 (1968).

The advent of the internet has brought with it a proliferation of both obscene and non-obscene pornographic speech. Congress has sought to pass laws prohibiting the dissemination of such speech to minors, but without a lot of success.

In 1996 Congress passed the Communications Decency Act, which was intended to protect minors from obscenity and pornography on the internet. But the Supreme Court struck down major portions of this law because it was not narrowly tailored to serve a compelling state interest and because less

restrictive alternatives were available. *Reno v. ACLU*, 513 U.S. 844 (1997).

In 2004, in another attempt to regulate internet pornography, Congress passed the Child Online Protection Act [hereafter COPA]. This law imposes a fine of up to $50,000 and up to six months in prison for the knowing posting for "commercial purposes" of content that is "harmful to minors." Material that is "harmful to minors" includes obscenity (as defined in the *Miller* case) and lewd nudity. The law provided an exemption from prosecution for those commercial purveyors who employ reasonable measures to restrict access to the material by minors (including the use of credit card numbers and adult access codes). This exemption is very broad.

Nevertheless, the Supreme Court still ruled that the statute "likely"[2] amounts to an improper restriction on protected speech. The Court reasoned that since a less restrictive technological alternative exists to shield offensive materials from minors (filters), therefore the more restrictive measures enacted by COPA would not likely survive strict scrutiny by the Court.

Comment and Analysis

The fact that this was a 5-4 opinion, indicates that Congress almost succeeded in passing an internet pornography regulation law. The exemption provision is so broad, that it is difficult to envision a worthy purveyor of pornography that might be wrongfully prosecuted. Four of the Justices (the Chief Justice, Justice O'Connor, Justice Scalia and Justice Breyer) saw it that way.

The case itself is still alive—the Supreme Court only addressed the injunction issues. But the ruling is clearly an indication that COPA will ultimately be struck down later.

---

[1] It is this right of adults to have access to non-obscene pornography that leads to the invalidation of most laws aimed at protecting minors from exposure to pornography.

[2] "Likely" is a key word here because the Court only addressed whether the statute is "likely" to be held unconstitutional later. Remember, this case is about an injunction, where the ACLU successfully asked the Court to block the enforcement of COPA until a final hearing because the law is "likely" to be held unconstitutional.

Hiibel v. Sixth Judicial District Court of Nevada

On June 21, 2004, by a 5-4 ruling, the Supreme Court upheld a Nevada law that required individuals to stop and identify themselves in the course of investigatory stops under suspicious circumstances. *Hiibel v. Sixth Judicial District Court of Nevada*, 542 U.S. ___ (2004).

The Supreme Court said that this brief interrogation is proper under *Terry v. Ohio*, 392 U.S. 1 (1968), and that the brief investigatory stop does not violate Hiibel's Fourth Amendment rights to be free from unreasonable searches and seizures.

The Court said that the compelled disclosure of Hiibel's name and identity presented no reasonable danger of incrimination, and that therefore the Nevada law did not violate the Fifth Amendment's prohibition against compelling one to give incriminating testimony against oneself.

Since 1966, these brief "Terry stops" have been legal. However, until now, the Court has never resolved whether an individual can be charged and convicted, in a Terry stop situation, for refusal to disclose his name. We now have an answer: States can criminalize an individual's failure to do this.

Missouri v. Seibert

On June 28, 2004, the Supreme Court ruled (5-4) that Ms. Seibert's incriminatory testimony was inadmissible where the police intentionally withheld giving Ms. Seibert the Miranda warning prior to interrogating her, and where the police then used that information to get an incriminatory statement from Ms. Seibert in a second interrogation a short time later that was preceded by a Miranda warning.

Accordingly, the law now is that intentional delay by the state to give an accused the Miranda warning violates the rights of the accused, and can result in excluding testimony obtained thereby.

The facts of this case make the law a little less palatable. Ms. Seibert feared being charged with neglect in connection with the death of her son, afflicted with cerebral palsy, who died in his sleep. So Ms. Seibert then conspired with her sons and some friends to conceal the circumstances of her son's death by burning down their mobile home, and causing an unrelated mentally ill 18-year-old young man to die in the fire, to give the appearance that Ms. Seibert's son had not been left unattended. Ms. Seibert and company then carried through with the plan.

United States v. Patane

On June 28, 2004, the Supreme Court ruled (5-4) in *United States v. Patane*, 542 U.S. ___, that the failure to give *Miranda* warnings to a suspect does not require suppression of physical evidence obtained following voluntary statements by the suspect. Mr. Patane (a convicted felon) was convicted for unlawfully possessing a pistol.

Statements made by an accused who has been detained but has not received his *Miranda* warning is not admissible. (This is the exclusionary rule that operates pursuant to the law established in *Miranda v. Arizona*, 384 U.S. 436 (1966). But what about physical evidence found by the police as a result of statements made by an accused after his detention but before he was given the Miranda warning, and where the accused interrupted the police from giving the warning by stating that he knew his rights? In *United States v. Patane*, the Supreme Court ruled such physical evidence to be admissible.

This ruling seems inconsistent with the Court's contemporaneous ruling in *Missouri v. Seibert*. The Justice who was the swing vote in these two cases is Justice Kennedy. In his concurring opinion in *Patane*, Justice Kennedy concluded that so long as the unwarned statements themselves were not introduced at trial, the physical evidence should be admissible

On the one hand, this seems like splitting hairs. On the other hand, so what? What does it hurt? Guilty people should have the freedom to say things that contribute to their prosecution for crimes.

CONSTITUTIONAL LAW UPDATES

| V:i | July 2006 | No. 10 |

May a State Prefer and Promote One Type of Family over Another?

by C. Paul Smith

May a state give preferences to one type of family over another? This question is at the heart of the legal battle being fought in the State of Maryland in 2006. For over 200 years Maryland and every state in the Union had answered this question with an unequivocal "Yes." But today this answer and the underlying bases for it are being challenged. Throughout the nation a war is being waged to create a new right to marry someone of the same sex. This effort would undermine traditional marriage as the preferred institution in society for the rearing of children. This battle has now come to the State of Maryland.

Background. In 1972, the Maryland Legislature passed a state Equal Rights Amendment (Article 46 of the Maryland Declaration of Rights). The next year (1973), the same Legislature passed a statute that states: "Only a marriage between a man and a woman is valid in this State" (Section 2-201, Family Law Article, Maryland Code). The clear intent of the Maryland Legislature was that its passage of an Equal Rights Amendment was not intended to change the definition of marriage in Maryland so as to authorize same-sex marriage. In recent years the Maryland Legislature has passed laws that have extended additional rights and protections to gays, including the Antidiscrimination Act of 2001 which bars discrimination on the basis of sexual orientation in public accommodations, employment and housing. But this law, and the others like it, specifically provide that they are not to be construed to validate same-sex marriage. [1] Thirty-one years later, a suit was brought asking the Court to declare Section 2-201 to be unconstitutional.

---

[1] See, e.g., Chapter 340 of 2001, Section 2. This same caveat was also put in Senate Bill 796 in the 2005 Legislative Session. For a thorough discussion of this legislative history, see the "Memorandum in Support of Defendants' Motion for Summary Judgment," filed in *Deane v. Conaway* by the Maryland Office of the Attorney General, dated June 15, 2005.

CONSTITUTIONAL LAW UPDATES is a newsletter edited and published by C. Paul Smith, J.D. To order copies ($5.00 per issue), write CLU, P. O. Box 1204, Frederick, MD 21702-0204. For further information visit www.cpaulsmith.com . Copyright C. Paul Smith 2006.

Case History. On July 7, 2004 Gitanjali Deane and her partner Lisa Polyak, and 17 other individuals filed a law suit in the Circuit Court for Baltimore City, asking the Court to declare unconstitutional the Maryland law that prohibits same-sex marriage. The Defendants in the law suit are Frank Conaway (Clerk of the Baltimore City Circuit Court) and Clerks from four additional County Circuit Courts. The name of the law suit is *Deane v. Conaway*. The Office of the Attorney General of the State of Maryland is defending this suit. The ACLU is one of the principal organizations representing the plaintiffs.[2]

Because there are no material disputes about the facts that give rise to this case, both sides filed motions for summary judgment in early 2005. Briefs and reply briefs were filed, including briefs by several parties that requested an opportunity to be heard as *amicus curiae* (friends of the court).[3] Judge Brooke Murdock heard oral arguments in this case on August 30, 2005. On January 19, 2006, Judge Murdock issued her ruling and accompanying opinion. She held that Section 2-201 of the Family Law Article "violates Article 46 of Maryland Declaration of Rights because it discriminates, based on gender against a suspect class; and is not narrowly tailored to serve any compelling governmental interests" (Memorandum, p.2). The State of Maryland appealed Judge Murdock's ruling. Judge Murdock has stayed the effect of her ruling pending appeal to the Maryland Court of Special Appeals. The State's (Appellant's) brief must be filed by August 20th; Appellees' brief must be filed by September 22nd; the State's Reply Brief must be filed by October 20th; and oral argument will be held in November.

Exhibit 1 lists some of the principal issues that are involved in this case. This article focuses on the rational basis issue because it is the most critical one. However, I should initially address two other important findings of Judge Murdock--both of which, in my opinion, are legally flawed. Judge Murdock found that the Maryland law prohibiting same-sex marriage violated plaintiff's "fundamental right" to marry, and that it discriminates against a "protected class" based upon gender. The quick response to these findings is this: First, there is no fundamental right to marry someone of the same sex; Judge Murdock's ruling departs from existing law in making this conclusion. Second, because the Maryland marriage law impacts both sexes equally, it does not discriminate against one sex over another. With the exception of Massachusetts and Hawaii, the Courts around the country have rejected the rational used by Judge Murdock.[4] Most importantly, Judge Murdock's ruling departs from the settled interpretation of this issue in the State of Maryland. By not discussing these legal issues in depth here, I don't wish to diminish their importance. The State of Maryland very aptly addressed them in its memoranda. But I am addressing the rational basis argument because I felt that it has not yet been adequately covered.

---

[2] Plaintiff's are represented by (1) Andrew H. Baida and Caroline D. Ciraolo, of the Baltimore law firm, Rosenberg Proutt Funk & Greenberg, LLP; (2) Arthur B. Spitzer of the American Civil Liberties Foundation of the National Capitol Area; (3) Kenneth Y. Choe and James D. Esseks of the American Civil Liberties Union Lesbian and Gay Rights Project; and (4) David R. Rocah of the American Civil Liberties Union Foundation of Maryland.

[3] The author submitted such a brief on behalf of an organization called Citizens for Traditional Families (CTF). CTF has also filed an *amicus* brief with the appellate court, asking the court to reverse Judge Murdock's ruling.

[4] But in July 2006, the Massachusetts Supreme Judicial Court approved a proposed constitutional amendment that would end same-sex marriages in that State. *The Washington Times*, July 15, 2006 (page A-1).

Exhibit 1

Issues before the Court of Special Appeals
in the case of *Deane v. Conaway*

Issues	Plaintiff's Position	Maryland's Position
Is there a fundamental right to marry someone of the same sex?	Yes	No
Does one have a right under the Equal Protection Clause to marry someone of the same sex?	Yes	No
Are gays a protected class in Maryland, such that they, as gays, are entitled to equal protection under the law?	Yes	Not with respect to the right to same-sex marriage
Is the Maryland law that prohibits same-sex Marriage subject to strict scrutiny?	Yes	No
Does Maryland have a compelling interest that justifies prohibiting same-sex marriages?	No	Yes
Is there a rational basis to support the Maryland law?	No	Yes
Under the Maryland Constitution and laws, by Definition marriage is and has always been a Civil contract between a man and a woman.	Yes, but marriage laws have evolved to address inequities based upon sex.	Yes
Does the Maryland marriage law violate the Maryland Equal Rights Amendment?	Yes	No
Is there a rational basis that supports the position that traditional, heterosexual couples raise children better than gay couples?	No	Yes
Is there a genetic cause of homosexuality? Or, are people born that way?	Yes	No

Deane v. Conaway is destined to make its way to Maryland's highest court, the Court of Appeals. Because of the importance of the issues now before Maryland's Court of Special Appeals, some thought that the higher court might *sua sponte* (of its own initiative) take jurisdiction over the case. However, this has not happened. Perhaps the higher court wishes to have the case analyzed, argued and developed as fully as possible before it gets the case.

At the heart of this law suit is the issue of whether or not a state can prefer one type of family over another without violating the due process and equal protection rights of individual citizens. Maryland's laws respecting marriage and divorce have traditionally favored heterosexual couples as the preferred type of family. (Laws that regulate marriage and divorce and other laws prohibiting adultery and fornication codify this preference.) But with the advent of contraception and with laws in Maryland that allow single individuals and gay couples to adopt, gay couples argue that there is no longer any governmental interest that justifies prohibiting same-sex marriage. Ultimately, the State of Maryland must articulate a rational basis for giving preferential treatment to traditional marriage over same-sex marriages, or else the Court of Special Appeals will uphold Judge Murdock's ruling.

The Maryland Attorney General's Office made excellent arguments in its memoranda to Judge Murdock, but in my opinion, the State did not effectively argue that the social benefits of traditional marriage were important and that they were better than those offered in same-sex marriage. It would be a mistake if the State should not submit a strong argument on this issue before the Court of Special Appeals. George A. Rekers, Ph.D., points out that states that have litigated and opposed same-sex marriage and who have made the *social benefits argument* have prevailed, whereas those who have declined to make this argument have failed.[5]

I. Issues Before the Court of Special Appeals in *Deane v. Conaway.*

In *Deane v. Conaway*, the gay plaintiffs (appellees) will argue that their studies prove that gay couples raise children just as well as heterosexual couples; they will present scientific studies that support this, and they will dispute whatever studies the State presents that prove otherwise. Appellees will seek to turn the legal debate into a contest between psychological studies. But if the argument does go in this direction, then the State should have the upper hand; it should argue that empirical data is not required to support a state's rational basis for preferring traditional marriage. The State should also point out that the gay's studies are not conclusive and that they are contradicted by other studies, and that therefore the state legislature has the right and power to make the policy decision as to whether it wishes to promote traditional heterosexual marriage for its citizens. Under traditional principles of legal analysis, the State should prevail on this issue.

Most appellate cases involve only a few issues, but as Exhibit 1 indicates, there are multiple big issues in the Deane v. Conaway case. In addition to the issues listed in Exhibit 1, consider the following six aspects of this case that make it both interesting and polarizing.

---

[5] George A. Rekers, Ph.D., "Review of Research on Homosexual Parenting, Adoption and Foster Parenting," University of South Carolina School of Medicine (2004), p. 1.

A. **Redefining "Marriage."** The lynchpin in plaintiffs' argument is their need to redefine marriage. Plaintiffs seek to redefine marriage so as to eliminate any distinction between males and females. Of course, the traditional definition of marriage has always been that marriage is only between a man and a woman; and implicit in this definition is the acknowledgement that men and women are different. Plaintiffs attempt to use Maryland's Equal Rights Amendment (ERA) to invalidate the state law that prohibits same-sex marriage. Never mind the fact that the Legislature never intended for the ERA to have such applicability. It is indeed interesting to observe what strong arguments the plaintiffs make to prove that there are no significant differences between men and women. The plaintiffs ignore and discount the fact that only women can bear children. The plaintiffs would deny that mothers have any special aptitude for nurturing children that is better than what a man can offer. The plaintiffs would certainly either ignore or discount any benefits that a baby could receive by being nursed. Similarly, the plaintiffs would deny that there are any significant physical and emotional differences between men and women.

B. **Effects from Redefining Marriage to Include Same-Sex Marriage.** The plaintiffs presume in their argument that by broadening the meaning of "marriage" to include gay partnerships, that this will not have any effect on traditional marriages. But this presumption is short-sighted at best; in fact, it is actually a failure to consider and evaluate what those effects will be. The redefinition of marriage will ultimately destroy marriage as an important asset to a healthy, prosperous and happy community. Why? Because henceforth the State will not be able to encourage or promote traditional marriage--because this would discriminate against same-sex marriage. The State, including the schools, will not be allowed to endorse any type of marriage as the preferred one for its people; instead the State will increase the amount of materials in its school curricula in order to educate and promote all types of families as equally valuable; single-parent families, parentless families and gay couple families--all will be taught to be equally valuable. We'll be headed down this road if Deane and her friends win their case.

C. **Broad Societal Effects vs. Individual Effects.** A gay couple may ask, "How does it hurt heterosexual couples to allow a gay couple to marry and receive the benefits of marriage?" Again, on an individual comparison basis, it is possible that a particular gay couple could do well in many aspects of parenting--providing food, clothing, shelter and an education. This is the principal argument that the plaintiffs make in *Deane v. Conaway*; they argue that in their particular cases they (as gays) could raise children as well as heterosexual couples, and that therefore the State cannot possibly have a rational basis for limiting marriage to heterosexual couples. But there are several flaws in this reasoning. First, the State preference for heterosexual marriage is based upon broad societal concerns and effects.[6] Even if two gay plaintiffs could prove that they could raise children well, such specific, anecdotal evidence does not invalidate the broader rationale and policy. Second, there are some rational bases for preferring heterosexual marriage. (See Section II, below.)

D. **Silence the Opposition Through Name-Calling.** Those who attack the states' preference for traditional marriage attempt to silence their opposition by smearing them. For example, anyone who would dare to oppose gay marriage is labeled a "gay-basher," a

---

[6] Monte N. Stewart articulated this point very well in the "Petition and Brief of Amicus Curiae, Citizens for Traditional Families, Family Leader Foundation, and United Families International in Support of Defendants-Appellants," June 22, 2006, pp. 15-19, filed in Conaway v. Deane, case no. 02499 before the Maryland Court of Special Appeals.

"homophobe," one who is "prejudiced," "ignorant" and "hateful." This tactic has been working very well in Maryland. Militant gays have learned to openly take offense when their lifestyle is criticized; and they use this tactic to silence much of their opposition.

E. **Not All Discrimination Is Bad.** It is true that preferring and promoting traditional marriage over all other relationships is a form of discrimination. It is the proper endorsement of one particular lifestyle as the one that the State selects as being most likely to lead to the betterment of society by fostering the health, happiness, wealth and good citizenship of its people. But this is not unlawful nor improper discrimination. Not all discrimination is bad. Furthermore, I would point out that scientific studies do not prove that people were born that way--i.e., that being gay has a genetic cause.[7] In fact, the studies show that experience and environment are key factors in causing this.[8] Furthermore, studies show that some of those who are gay can change and repress their erotic same-sex attraction. (See, e.g., footnote 11, study by Robert Spitzer.). This mutability characteristic differentiates sexual orientation from other protected classes, such as race, color, national origin and sex.

F. **Studies Show That Traditional Marriage Is Better for Society.** Admittedly, there are scores of studies by gays that attempt to elevate the quality of their lifestyle while they seek to ignore its deleterious affects. Some of these studies are seriously flawed, as is pointed out by Wright and Cummings (footnote 10) and others. But the better science is on the side of traditional marriage. There are excellent, scientific studies that conclude that traditional marriage is better for society than same-sex marriage. (See Section II, below.) For traditional marriage to prevail in Maryland, this argument must be made to the Court of Special Appeals.

II. The 2006 New York Case That Should Guide the Maryland Court of Special Appeals.

In early July (2006) New York State's highest court, the Court of Appeals, ruled *in Hernandez v. Robles* (the first of four cases comprising 44 different gay plaintiffs), that the New York law prohibiting same-sex marriages was valid, and did not violate the State's Constitution.

---

[7] There is no study to cite for this because no study has shown such a causative relationship, although many have hoped that such a link could be should. A 1991 study by Simon LeVay and a 1993 study by Dean H. Hamer suggested that there could be a genetic link to sexual orientation. (The citation for these studies are given on Exhibit 2, at footnotes 15 and 16.) But these studies do not even purport to prove such a linkage. And neither study has yet to be replicated, although attempts had been made. Thus, even the "suggestion" of a linkage is nothing more than a wish. If you are asking why you should believe my perspective on this issue, I encourage you to review Exhibit 2, at the end of this article. This two-page document reproduces pages 4, 5, 6 and 7 of the *amicus curiae* brief filed by the American Psychology Association (APA) with the U. S. Supreme Court in the case of *Boy Scouts of America v. Dale* 530 U.S. 640 (2000), and then analyzes what the APA said and did not say in its brief. A review of this exhibit will demonstrate the veracity of my analysis and the desperation of the APA to find a causative genetic link even though there is no scientific support for it.

[8] See, e.g., Gerard van den Aardweg, Ph.D., "Homosexuality and Bodily Factors: Real Evidence: None; Misleading Interpretations: Plenty. Holland (2005). See also William Byne & Bruce Parsons, *Human Sexual Orientation: The Biologic Theories Peappraised,* 50 Archives Gen. Psychiatry 228 (1993); Ruth Hubbard & Elijah Wald, *Exploding the Gene Myth* (1993); Richard C. Friedman & Jennifer Downey, "Neurology and Sexual Orientation: Current Relationships, *Journal of Neuropsychiatry,* Vol. 5, No. 2 (Spring 1993); and George Rice, Carol Anderson, Neil Risch & George Ebers, "Male Homosexuality: Absence of Linkage to Microsatellite Markers at XQ28," *Science,* Vol 284 (April 1999). Additional studies that support the findings of Byne and Parsons include Jeffrey Santinover, M.D. (1996) and Consiglio & Ferre.

Both the holding and rationale in this case should be extremely persuasive in Maryland.[9] The reasoning of the New York Court of Appeals for upholding the prohibition against same-sex marriage is simple and straight-forward. The Court said:

> We conclude, however, that there are at least two grounds that rationally support the limitation on marriage that the Legislature has enacted. . . . First, the Legislature could rationally decide that, for the welfare of children, it is more important to promote stability, and to avoid instability, in opposite-sex than in same-sex relationships. . . . [And second] The Legislature could rationally believe that it is better, other things being equal, for children to grow up with both a mother and a father. [Slip Opinion, pp. 5-6.]

If the Maryland judges apply the "rational basis" test in *Deane v. Conaway* the way the U. S. Supreme Court has traditionally applied it, then Maryland's traditional marriage law will also be upheld. The New York Court held firm on this principle, whereas Judge Murdock misapplied the "rational basis" test; she converted that test into a "strict scrutiny" test, and then she refused to recognize the important governmental interests that are furthered by preferring and promoting heterosexual marriage as the best type of family.

It is of special interest to note how the New York Court of Appeals dealt with the gays' arguments that studies show that gay couples do as well at raising children as heterosexual couples. The plaintiffs in *Hernandez v. Robles* argued that "a home with two parents of different sexes has no advantage, from the point of view of raising children, over a home with two parents of the same sex" [Slip Opinion, p.7]. The New York Court said that plaintiffs *could* be right, but the Court said that "the Legislature could rationally think otherwise." *Id.* The Court went on to explain:

> To support their argument, plaintiffs and amici supporting them refer to social science literature reporting studies of same-sex parents and their children. Some opponents of same-sex marriage criticize these studies, but we need not consider the criticism, for the studies on their face do not establish beyond doubt that children fare equally well in same-sex and opposite-sex households. What they show, at most, is that rather limited observation has detected no marked differences. More definitive results could hardly be expected, for until recently few children have been raised in same-sex households, and there has not been enough time to study the long-term results of such child-rearing. [10]
>
> Plaintiffs seem to assume that they have demonstrated the irrationality of the view that opposite-sex marriages offer advantages to children by showing there is no scientific evidence to support it. Even assuming no such evidence exists, this reasoning is flawed. In the absence of conclusive scientific evidence, the Legislature could rationally proceed on the common-sense premise that children will do best with a mother and father in the home. . . . And a legislature proceeding on that premise could rationally decide to offer a special inducement, the legal recognition of marriage, to encourage the formation of opposite-sex households. [Slip Opinion, pp. 7-8.]

---

[9] Within days of the New York decision, the 8th Circuit Court of Appeals made a similar holding that the State of Nebraska had legitimate state interests that justified the state's limiting marriage to heterosexual couples. This holding overturned the ruling of a federal district court judge, who had ruled otherwise. *The Washington Times*, July 15, 2006, pp. A-1 & A-4.

[10] This rational preserves for another day, another challenge to laws that prohibit same-sex marriage.

13.3.3

Perhaps the most important part of the above analysis is the sentence in the last paragraph above: **"In the absence of conclusive scientific evidence, the Legislature could rationally proceed on the common-sense premise that children will do best with a mother and a father in the home."** In other words, as long as a scientific debate continues with regard to this issue, the courts will defer to the legislatures on the issue of whether a state can prefer and promote heterosexual marriage over same-sex marriage. However, an important element in this debate is the need to present the court with studies that conclude that traditional, heterosexual marriage is better for the children. Therefore, those who wish to defend traditional marriage both in the courts and in arena of public opinion, must continue to present the studies that conclude that traditional, heterosexual marriage is best.

III.   The Social Benefits Argument

There is more to be said about the social benefits that support a state preference for traditional marriage. But before I develop this a little more, let me again draw your attention to **Exhibit 1**, which lists a number of legal issues involved in the same-sex marriage debate. One reason we will not take the time and space to address these issues in depth here is because even if plaintiff should prevail on some of them, the final resolution of the case still hinges on whether or not there are social benefits (either a rational basis or the stronger, compelling state interest) that support a state preference for traditional marriage over same-sex marriage. The opinion of the New York Court of Appeals cut right to the chase, and dealt with the rational basis issue.

A. The Bias of the APA. The American Psychological Association (APA) consists of many psychologists who have published studies that purport to show that gay couples can do as good a job at raising children as heterosexual couples. Because of this, some of those who favor traditional marriage are reluctant to enter into such a debate; they seek to win the same-sex marriage debate on other legal grounds. But I think this is a mistake. I am willing to make all the arguments that support state preferences for traditional marriage, but I think that it is also best to make the "societal effects" argument--to articulate the reasons why it is best for the state to promote traditional families as the one that is best geared to rear children. As I proceed to make this argument, I recognize that I will be forced to take issue with the APA and with many of its members. But I am prepared to do so.

B. The APA Bias Has Been Exposed. Not all psychologists agree with the APA; in fact not all psychologists who belong to the APA agree with official positions of the APA; in fact, two prominent psychologists, Rogers Wright and Nicolas Cummings (one of whom is a former president of the APA), have written a book that criticizes the APA for allowing itself to become the spokesman for various causes (including gay rights causes) at the expense of sacrificing their integrity as scientists.[11] The APA has become so polarized in its support of gay rights that it has taken an official position opposing what is called "conversion therapy," by which an individual who is experiencing erotic same-sex attraction can voluntarily receive psychological therapy to seek to repress or if possible eliminate this attraction. Drs. Wright and Cummings decry the APA's rejection of the right of an individual to make choices for himself/herself with respect to

---

[11] Rogers H. Wright and Nicolas A. Cummings, *Destructive Trends in Mental Health: The Well-Intentioned Path to Harm.* New York, Routledge (2005).

sexual orientation. The APA position is diametrically in opposition to the recent study published by Dr. Robert Spitzer[12] that confirms that people with an erotic same-sex orientation can change. In summary, the book by Wright and Cummings is important in exposing the unscientific bias that has taken hold of both the APA and many of the psychologists who are its members.

C. The Social Benefits of Heterosexual Marriage. The importance of this revelation could be tremendous in the case of *Deane v. Conaway*, because the appellees (the gay individuals) will be presenting studies that will purportedly show that gay couples do as good as or better than heterosexual couples in raising children. It is possible that same-sex couples can teach their "children" the academic subjects as well as heterosexual couples can. But the benefits of traditional marriage are much broader and more powerful than mere academic study. Here is a summary of some reasons why it is best for the state to prefer and promote traditional families for the rearing of children.

1. It is best for children to be raised by their natural parents in order for the children to best **understand who they are**--how they are a part of a family, including grandparents; and to help the children understand what and who their individual heritage is, and how it has helped to mold their parents and each of them individually. An individual's private heritage can be a strength and a positive motivation in his/her life. No institution better fosters this benefit than traditional marriage.

2. It is best for children to be raised by their married, natural parents who love each other so that the children can have the benefit of observing the loving relationship of the man and the woman, and so that the children can observe how their parents regard children as the sweetest and most important fruit of a loving relationship. Traditional marriage is the institution that provides the best model for children so that they can learn firsthand the important connection between sexual relations and children. Neither single-parent families nor gay couples can model this ideal relationship.

3. It is best for children to be raised by a man and a woman so that the children can learn the differences between men and women, and so that they can learn how a man and a woman can make valuable complementary contributions to a marriage relationship. A traditional heterosexual relationship can model the wide range of differences between men and women. As children grow older, it is desirable for adolescent girls to have a female mother to talk to about what they are experiencing physically, emotionally and socially. It is also valuable for adolescent girls to have a male father close in order to get his feedback and guidance during the critical teenage years. Similarly, adolescent boys need the opportunity to receive the complementary guidance of both a man and a woman as they are growing.

4. Studies show that those who are healthiest, happiest and wealthiest tend to be those who are in a traditional marriage.[13]

---

[12] Study by Robert L. Spitzer, M.D., published in *Archives of Sexual Behavior*, Vol. 32, No. 5, Oct. 2003, 403-417.

[13] See A. Dean Byrd, "Gender Complementarity and Child-rearing: Where Tradition and Science Agree." *Journal of Law & Family Studies*, University of Utah (2005). See also, George A. Reckers, "Review of Research on Homosexual Parenting, Adoption and Foster Parenting." University of South Carolina School of Medicine (2004). See also, Dale O'Leary, "Why AMA Policy is Not in the Best Interest of Children or Families," NARTH BULLETIN, Vol. 10, No. 3 (December 2001), pp. 3-5 [in which Ms. O'Leary cites numerous findings from the study by Garofalo et al (1998)].

5. Traditional marriage helps and promotes both parents to have enduring ties to the children that they bring into the world.

6. Studies show that there are fewer incidences of juvenile delinquency, crime, drug abuse, alcohol abuse, welfare need, mental and emotional problems, suicide, depression and HIV and AIDS among those who were raised in traditional families than in other types of families.[14]

7. Heterosexual couples can best model the appropriate way for a heterosexual couple to interact with one another, and can best model the appropriate way for people of the same sex to interact with one another. Children raised by a gay couple have less of a chance to learn these important relationship skills.

8. Traditional marriage is the best way to help men to break away from the selfishness of adolescence and to convert themselves to responsible, loving beings who begin to put the needs of others before themselves--as they learn to love, cherish and support their wives and children.

IV. Conclusion

Favoring the Maryland law that prefers heterosexual marriage is not a position of hatred or animosity towards gays; rather it is a positive preference for the traditional family institution as the one that is best geared to promote the health, welfare and happiness of the entire society.

State governments have a right to make laws that prefer and promote certain conduct, while at the same time discouraging other conduct. Definitive empirical proof is not required to support such laws. Unless a "protected class" or a "fundamental right" is involved, only a rational basis is required to sustain a state's preference to promote traditional marriage as the only type of marriage it recognizes.[15] This is the most basic issue at stake in *Deane v. Conaway*. Not only is there a rational basis for such a law, but there are multiple compelling state interests that support this law. Therefore, the Court of Special Appeals should reverse Judge Murdock and uphold the Maryland law that prefers and promotes traditional heterosexual marriage as the only valid marriage in Maryland.

---

[14] (a) There is a link between same-sex attraction and self-harm--Skegg, Nada-Raja, Diskson, Paul & Williams (March 2003). (b) Suicide rates are significantly higher among homosexual men than heterosexual men. See, e.g., Fergusson, Horwood, Beautrais, "Is Sexual Orientation Related to Mental Health Problems and Sucidality in Young People?" (1999). (c) Homosexual people are at a substantially higher risk for some forms of emotional problems, including suicidality, major depression, and anxiety disorder--Bailey (1999). (d) Homosexual women have a higher prevalence of substance use disorders than heterosexual women--Sandfort, de Graaf, Bijl and Schnabel (2001). (e) a study by Garofalo et al (1998) documents that gay, lesbians and bisexual high school students have higher incidences of alcohol use, cocaine use and illegal inhalant use. See also, Timothy J. Dailey, "The Negative Health Effects of homosexuality," *Insight*, No. 232, Family Research Council (March 2001).

[15] There is no "protected class" involved in this case, despite the fact that Judge Murdock found that there was. Neither does there exist a "fundamental right" to marry someone of the same sex. Judge Murdock similarly found that there was such a "fundamental right." I submit that these two findings by Judge Murdock's are legally flawed. It is not within the purview of this writing to examine those issues. If the Court of Special Appeals were to agree with Judge Murdock on these issues, then the State would have to prove that it has a "compelling state interest" that justifies its giving preferential treatment to heterosexual marriage over same-sex marriage. The purpose of this paper is to give those arguments.

religion, or gender. Further, the research provides considerable support for anti-discrimination legislation, such as N.J.S.A 10:5-1 to 5-49, as a means to reduce prejudice in addition to reducing overt discrimination, by increasing interpersonal contact between members of the majority and minority groups.

Conferring broad-based organizations with a readily available means to insulate themselves from anti-discrimination legislation thwarts state policy aimed at alleviating the potentially significant negative psychological, as well as physical and economic, effects of discrimination and prejudice.

ARGUMENT

I. THE NATURE OF SEXUAL ORIENTATION

A. What Causes a Particular Sexual Orientation?

[1]

Scientific research and clinical experience indicate that sexual orientation is not "voluntary" for most people. Most people – especially men – do not experience their sexual orientation as the result of conscious choice.[9] The available studies of gay men indicate that the core feelings and attractions that form the basis for adult sexual orientation

---

9/   For example, 80% of the 60 gay men in one community sample said they had "no choice at all" about their sexual orientation. *See* Gregory M. Herek, J.C. Cogan, J.R. Gillis & E.K. Glunt, *Correlates of Internalized homophobia in a community sample of lesbians and gay men*, 2 J. Gay and Lesbian Med. Ass'n 17-25 (1998). In a larger, not-yet-published study, the same researchers found 72% of the 898 gay men studied reported having "no choice," and another 13% reported "very little choice" (on file with the APA). Summarizing the prevalent view, one researcher explained: "The concept of voluntary choice is as much in error here as in its application to handedness or native language." John Money, *Sin, Sickness or Status? Homosexual Gender Identity and Psychoneuroendocrinology*, 42 Am. Psychologist 384 (1987).

-6-

[4] [5] [6]

molecular studies of one aspect of DNA have reached inconsistent conclusions with respect to a linkage with sexual orientation.[15] Another study, as yet unreplicated, reported differences between heterosexual and gay men in the volume of a cell group in the anterior hypothalamus, a brain structure involved in sexual behavior.[16] Results of a study of women suggests that women who were exposed to certain prenatal estrogens are more likely to be lesbian or bisexual.[17] Other researchers, critical of this research, have proposed an "interactionist" model, in which genetic factors are

---

Michael Bailey, Richard C. Pillard, Michael C. Neale & Yvonne Agyei, *Heritable Factors Influence Sexual Orientation In Women*, 50 Archives Gen. Psychiatry 217 (1993); J. Michael Bailey & Deans S. Benishay, *Familial Aggregation of Female Sexual Orientation*, 150 Am. J. Psychiatry 272 (1993), Frederick L. Whitam, Milton Diamond & James Martin, *Homosexual Orientation in Twins: A Report of 61 Pairs and Three Triplet Sets*, 22 Archives Sexual Behav. 187 (1993).

15/   *See* Dean H. Hamer, Stella Hu, Victoria L. Magnuson, Nan Hu & Angela M.L. Pattatuci, *A Linkage Between DNA Markers on the X Chromosome and Male Sexual Orientation*, 261 Science 321 (1993) (study of 76 gay males and 40 gay brother pairs); Stella Hu *et al*., 11 Nature Genet. 248 (1995) (follow-up study of 33 additional gay brother pairs); William J. Turner, *Homosexuality: Type I An Xq28 Phenomenon*, 24 Archives Sexual Behav. 109 (1995); *but see* George Rice, Carol Anderson, Neil Risch & George Ebers, *Male homosexuality: Absence of linkage to microsatellite markers at Xq28*, 284 Science 665-667 (1999) (attempting, but failing, to replicate the Hamer *et al* results with a sample of 52 gay sibling pairs).

16/   Simon LeVay, *A Difference in Hypothalamic Structure Between Heterosexual and Homosexual Men*, 253 Science 1034 (1991), *see also* Simon LeVay, *The Sexual Brain* (1993).

17/   *See* Heino F.L. Meyer-Bahlburg, Anke A. Ehrhardt, Laura R. Rosen & Rhoda S. Gruen, *Prenatal Estrogens and the Development of Homosexual Orientation*, 31 Developmental Psychology 12 (1995).

---

typically emerge by early adolescence.[10] For some people, adult sexual orientation is predictable by early childhood.[11] "By the time boys and girls reach adolescence, their sexual preference is likely to be already determined, even though they may not yet have become sexually very active."[12]

[2]

Scientific investigation into developmental precursors of adult sexual orientation has not yet consistently identified those factors for the population as a whole.[13] It is not yet clear to what extent and in what way genetic, other biological traits, or early childhood experience may contribute to its development. Studies of identical twins have found that "heritabilities were substantial under a wide range of assumptions."[14] However,

---

10/   *See* Alan P. Bell, Martin S. Weinberg & Sue Kiefer Hammersmith, *Sexual Preference: Its Development in Men and Women* 186-87 (1981); Richard R. Troiden, *The Formation of Homosexual Identities*, 17 J. Homosexuality 43, 43-73 (1989) (reviewing research literature).

11/   *See* J. Michael Bailey & Kenneth J. Zucker, *Childhood Sex-Typed Behavior and Sexual Orientation: A Conceptual Analysis and Quantitative Review*, 31 Dev. Psychol. 43 (Jan. 1995); Richard Green, *The Immutability of (Homo)sexual Orientation: Behavioral Science Implications for a Constitutional (Legal) Analysis*, 16 J. Psychiatry & L. 537 (1988); Richard Green, *The "Sissy Boy Syndrome" and the Development of Homosexuality* 370 (1987).

12/   Bell *et al.*, *supra* note 10, at 186.

13/   *See* Bell *et al.*, *supra* note 10, at 193-211.

14/   J. Michael Bailey & Richard C. Pillard, *A Genetic Study of Male Sexual Orientation*, 48 Archives Gen. Psychiatry 1089 (1991). Bailey and Pillard's study, which has since been replicated, found: where one identical twin was gay, the other was gay in 52% of the cases; where one fraternal twin was gay, the other was also gay in 22% of the cases; and where one brother by adoption was gay, his adoptive brother was gay in just 11% of the cases. *Id.* at 1089. *See also* J. Michael Bailey & Khytam Dawood, *Behavioral Genetics, Sexual Orientation, and the Family*, in *Lesbian, Gay, and Bisexual Identities in Families* 3 (Charlotte J. Patterson and Anthony R. D'Augelli eds. 1998) (reviewing research); J.

[3]

-7-

conceptualized as indirect influences on the development of sexual orientation.[18]

B. Can Sexual Orientation Be Changed?

[7]

Once established, sexual orientation is highly resistant to attempts to change it.[19] Although some therapists report that their clients changed their sexual orientation in treatment, no scientific comparison with a control group has been reported. Closer scrutiny has shown that such changes were more likely among bisexuals who were highly motivated to reject a homosexual behavior pattern. Many interventions aimed at changing sexual orientation have succeeded only in reducing or eliminating homosexual behavior rather than in creating heterosexual attractions. One scholar concluded upon review of reports on "conversion therapy" that there is no reliable evidence that "sexual orientation is amenable to redirection or significant influence from psychological intervention."[20]

18/   William Byne & Bruce Parsons, *Human Sexual Orientation: The Biologic Theories Reappraised*, 50 Archives Gen. Psychiatry 228 (1993).

19/   *See* Douglas C. Haldeman, *The Practice and Ethics of Sexual Orientation Conversion Therapy*, 62 J. Consulting & Clinical Psych. 221 (1994) [hereinafter Haldeman, *Practice*]; Douglas C. Haldeman, *Sexual Orientation Conversion Therapy for Gay Men and Lesbians: A Scientific Examination*, in *Homosexuality: Research Implications for Public Policy* 149-60 (John C. Gonsiorek & James D. Weinrich eds. 1991) [hereinafter *Homosexuality*]; A. Damien Martin, *The Emperor's New Clothes: Modern Attempts to Change Sexual Orientation*, in *Innovations in Psychotherapy with Homosexuals* 23-58 (E.S. Hetrick & T.S. Stein eds. 1984).

20/   Haldeman, *Practice*, *supra* note 19, at 224. Moreover, attempts to change someone's sexual orientation runs a risk of causing depression, anxiety, and self-destructive behavior. *See* American Psychiatric Ass'n, No. 98-56, *Position Statement on Psychiatric Treatment and Sexual Orientation* (Dec. 11, 1998) (opposing psychiatric treatment based on the assumption that a patient should change sexual orientation) <http://

Comments on APA Brief, pages 4-7

[1] That most people do not make a conscious choice of their sexual orientation is just stating the obvious; most people are instinctively attracted to the opposite sex. The fact that sexual attraction does not typically emerge in an individual until early adolescence does not support a finding that homosexual orientation is innate; rather it highlights the fact that there are years of opportunities for influences on impressionable children that can shape or distort their orientation at adolescence.

[2] This statement is significant because it is an admission that even the militant gays cannot say that homosexual orientation is genetically determined. The clever thing about this APA brief is that while on the one hand they acknowledge there is no proof that a gay person is born that way, the APA nevertheless argues that one is. They make every argument they can to support what they wish were true. But the plain language they use admits that there is no scientific evidence to prove what they desperately hoped to prove. Their language, however, acknowledges that their best argument is that only "suggestions" exist where they need "proof."

[3] The studies of identical twins do not support any genetic causation or "linkage" with homo-sexual orientation. The study by Rice, Anderson, Risch and Ebers (discussed in note 6, below), specifically refutes Hamer's conclusions that studies of identical twins show any genetic "linkage" with sexual orientation. The APA brief does not account for the environmental and interactional factors that could easily account for the findings of Bailey and Pillard.

[4] This is an incredible sentence; it shows how desperate the APA is to drum up support for its hypothesis that gays are born that way: The APA states that scientific studies "of DNA have reached *inconsistent conclusions* with respect to a linkage with sexual orientation." In other words, there is no proof of the linkage they were hoping to find. And the study by Dean H. Hamer that they cite has been criticized in the scientific community for improper methods.

[5] Again, in the APA's desperation to cite anything to support its hypothesis that gays are born that way, they cite the study by Simon LeVay, which they acknowledge has not been "replicated." In other words, it is not yet reliable. In fact, the study by Byne and Parsons (which is discussed below, and which is referenced in an APA footnote) specifically refuted LaVay's findings. Byne and Parsons pointed out that a man's experiences and behavior could account for the differing volume in that part of the brain.

[6] A comment must be made about the APA's reference to "other researchers" who have "proposed" an "inter-actionist" theory as to what factors may cause a person to be homosexually oriented. The APA brief cites only one study—the study by Byne and Parsons; however, there are several studies that support the Byne and Parsons conclusions; and the critical aspects of the Byne and Parsons conclusions **have been replicated.** (See e.g., Ruth Hubbard and Elijah Wald, *Exploding the Gene Myth* (1993); Richard C. Friedman and Jennifer Downey, "Neurobiology and Sexual Orientation: Current Relationships, *Journal of Neuropsychiatry*, Vol. 5, No. 2 (Spring 1993); and George Rice, Carol Anderson, Neil Risch, and George Ebers, "Male Homosexuality: Absence of Linkage to Microsatellite Markers at XQ28," *Science*, Vol. 284 (April 1999). Satinover (1996) and Consiglio, Ferre have also published studies that support the findings of Byne and Parsons. Further, the APA puts its own slant on the Byne and Parsons study that makes it sound like even their study concludes that "genetic factors are . . . indirect influences." This statement is misleading because it mentions only the genetic factor; in fact the Byne and Parsons study specifically refuted the LeVay study that had "suggested" a genetic causation of homosexual orientation. Byne and Parsons concluded that homosexuality results from an interaction between the environment and personality characteristics; that biologic factors may affect a person's personality does not mean they cause homosexuality. Byne and Parsons found that an individual's interaction with others appears responsible for one's developing a homosexual orientation.

[7] This particular statement is such a grave distortion that it approaches outright dishonesty. The APA cites "one" scholar who criticizes what they call "conversion therapy" as being ineffective and as having the potential to cause "depression" and "self-destructive behavior." What the APA does not tell you is that the conclusions of this "one" scholar are vehemently disputed by many psychologists who have successfully worked with hundreds of men with same-sex attractions to help these men change. Dr. A. Dean Byrd has treated approximately 300 such men and has achieved a 70% success rate in helping these men to manage, repress and lose the desires they want to change. Other therapists have success ratios in excess of 50% around the nation. (See study by Satinover, 1996.) The APA has a well documented bias against those who attempt "conversion therapy"; according to Dr. Byrd, at one time the APA condemned and prohibited such therapy; however, they later rescinded this condemnation, in part because of the large number of individuals who were plagued with same-sex attractions and who sought psychological help. This put the APA in the position of turning its back on these individuals, until they rescinded their condemnation stance.

CONSTITUTIONAL

LAW

UPDATES

VI:i	October 2007	No. 11

Special Presidential Primaries Campaign Edition

With the key Republican and Democratic Presidential primaries coming up in January 2008, the campaigns of the hopefuls of each party are in full swing. It is likely that within the next four months, each party's nominee will be identified, and the longest presidential campaign in the history of our nation will be under way.

On the Democratic side, Senator Hillary Rodham Clinton appears to have her party's nomination all but locked up. Senator Barack Obama trails by a large margin. Senator Al Gore, who just won a Nobel Peace Prize for his documentary film on global warming, *An Inconvenient Truth*, is hoping to get enough bounce from this prize to bring a united Democrat party calling at his door, asking him to be the party's new leader. But I don't think that will happen. And the campaign of Senator Edwards doesn't appear headed anywhere either. So on the Democrat side, the two remaining issues are (1) Who will be Hillary's vice presidential nominee? and (2) Can Hillary get elected? As to the former, that is anybody's guess. For my part, I would suggest Al Gore as the perfect candidate. He served Bill well enough, and if we're going to have former President Bill Clinton as the new First Man, to accompany a first woman President, it just seems that the threesome should be reunited for old times' sake. As to the latter question, there is serious question as to whether Hillary can get elected because she has been a polarizing figure. She seems to get some sympathy support because she is kind of a victim to her husband's sexual escapades, but she is also seen as one who disparages the traditional role of being a devoted wife and mother.

--continued on next page

CONSTITUTIONAL LAW UPDATES is a newsletter edited and published by C. Paul Smith, J.D.
To order copies ($5.00 per issue), write *CLU*, P. O. Box 1204, Frederick, MD 21702-0204.
For further information visit www.cpaulsmith.com. Copyright C. Paul Smith 2007.

3.1

from the cover page--

On the Republican side, a Fox News poll has Mayor Giuliani leading with a 29% rating. Behind him is Senator Fred Thompson at 16%, Senator McCain at 12%, Governor Romney at 11%, Governor Huckabee at 5%, Representative Tancredo at 2%, Representative Paul at 2%, and Representative Hunter at 1%. All of the candidates except Ron Paul are supportive of the war effort in Iraq. But the Republican nomination is clearly up for grabs. While Mayor Giuliani is regarded as a strong and effective leader, and one who has the strength to lead the nation in war, he is rejected by many conservatives because of his positions on abortion, gun control, immigration and gay rights. Conservative evangelicals find Giuliani's social policies to be unacceptable—so their support will go elsewhere in the primaries. And, of course, Dr. James Dobson has indicated that he and his supporters would not be able to support Giuliani if he gets the Republican nomination. This could perhaps open the door for either McCain, Thompson or Romney. But Senator McCain brings a track record with him that is unacceptable to many Republicans—his support of the campaign finance reform law alienates some Republicans; and his position on immigration alienates other Republicans. Fred Thompson is a well-respected spokesman of conservative principles, but he appears old and tired. Romney is right on most issues, and he seems bright, energetic and competent; his track record as a successful businessman and leader has earned him some solid support. Perhaps his biggest disadvantage may be that he is a Mormon. You would think that in a nation that celebrates diversity that this would no longer be a political liability. But, we shall see. Which of these four candidates will prevail will likely be determined by the end of January 2008. At this point, it is hard to predict who that will be. But most Republicans would be happy with any of the candidates (except Ron Paul) as either presidential or vice presidential candidates.

Well, moving on from the leading contenders to the campaign issues—this issue of **CLU** provides several writings on some of the important issues of the 2008 campaign: The Iraq War, the SCHIP Bill, the Hate Crimes Bill, Same-Sex Marriage, Freedom of Speech, Campaign Finance Reform, Freedom of Religion, and Affirmative Action. Reading and understanding the material in this issue will help both the candidates and the electorate to understand key issues in the 2008 Presidential Campaign.

HATE CRIMES BILL SHOULD BE VETOED

On September 27, 2007, the Senate passed S. 1105, the Hate Crimes Bill, or as it is officially named, "The Matthew Shepard Local Law Enforcement Hate Crimes Prevention Act of 2007." The House version was passed May 3, 2007. The bill is now before President Bush, who has said he would veto it. He should.

The Hate Crimes Bill is a bad piece of legislation, and it should be defeated/vetoed for the following reasons. First, the area of crimes that S. 1105 attempts to regulate is an area of State concerns, in which Congress does not have authority to legislate. Second, "hate crimes" legislation is philosophically flawed and counter-productive. And third, S. 1105 is an attempt to control and criminalize certain thoughts, opinions and speech.

1. Crime legislation belongs to the States. The type of crime which S. 1105 seeks to regulate is in an area which has been reserved to the States under the Constitution from the beginning. Police power is reserved to the States through the Tenth Amendment. The U. S. Supreme Court recently confirmed this interpretation of the Constitution when it struck down the Violence Against Women Act. In *United States v. Morrison*, 529 U.S. 598 (2000), the Court struck down this law because the acts and crimes that the law sought to regulate were exclusive State matters, and the Constitution did not confer on Congress the authority to legislate in that area. The drafters of S. 1105 are fully aware of the *Morrison* case, and they have attempted to draft S. 1105 to circumvent the holding of *Morrison*. As will be explained below, the drafters of S. 1105 included several special provisions in an attempt to overcome the hurdles that led to the demise of the Violence Against Women Act.

These remedial, jurisdictional provisions include the following: (i) In the law's preamble, it asserts that incidences of hatred pose a "serious national problem"; (ii) that the States need federal help to address these incidences of violence caused by hate; (iii) that "violent crime motivated by bias" "devastates not just the actual victim," but also "savages the community"; (iv) that it affects interstate commerce; (v) that "Federal jurisdiction over certain violent crimes motivated by bias enables Federal, State and local authorities to work together as partners in the investigation and prosecution of such crimes"; and (vi) that "[t]he problem of crimes motivated by bias is sufficiently serious, widespread, and interstate in nature as to warrant Federal assistance to States, local jurisdictions, and Indian tribes." Clearly, the intent of making these various statements is to make the case that the situation warrants federal crime legislation. But I am not convinced that these six stated reasons warrant federal legislation. By what authority does Congress tell the States that Congress is taking over a particular area of legislation that has traditionally belonged to the States. I don't think Congress can do this, except to the extent authorized in the Constitution. Thus, with respect to reason "iv," above, to the extent that interstate commerce is involved, federal legislation would be appropriate—in interstate kidnappings, for example. But the intent of the Hate Crimes bill is to make it much broader than just interstate kidnappings.

The law attempts to provide a mechanism for States to request federal grants to address hate crimes. This "opt in" procedure is also something that appears geared to address the concern that the law might be viewed as encroaching on States' rights. Finally, the bill also provides that a certification is required from the Attorney General that the federal participation in the hate crime prosecution is agreeable to the state.

3

After these technical, jurisdictional issues are addressed, the bill defines hate crimes: it is to willfully hurt someone because of the person's "actual or perceived race, color, religion, national origin, gender, sexual orientation, gender identity or disability."

2. Hate crime legislation is philosophically flawed and counter-productive.
Hate crimes legislation is ill-advised and is philosophically a mistake for several reasons. **First**, it necessarily discriminates against certain types of intent and certain types of hate. The inclination to discriminate against types of hatred is unnecessary and unhelpful. The types of "hate" that the bill makes federal crimes is so under-inclusive that the bill is manifest as nothing more than an attempt to gain special protections for a few, select classes of people. **Second**, the law is unnecessary because criminal laws can already address the wrongs that are done with appropriate penalties. For example, in the case of Matthew Shepherd, who was killed because he was gay, States can pass and enforce law to put away the perpetrator for life, if not to even execute him/them. Hate crime laws can add nothing to the severity of the available penalties. **Third**, adding penalties for specified types of "hatred" introduces a costly and unnecessary expense to our criminal justice system. It is sufficient to punish for the crime without having to add an element of proof with varying additional penalties depending upon the type of hatred that motivated the crime. It is an unnecessary and wasteful policy to go to the expense to prove certain types of hatred. The perfect equality of our laws had been based upon the premise that society would punish crimes for the hurt inflicted, without regard for the too many gradations of types of intent. With regard to unlawful killings, our laws already categorize them into First Degree Murder, Second Degree Murder, Voluntary Manslaughter and Involuntary Manslaughter. There is just no need to further categorize.

3. The Hate Crimes Bill is a back-door attempt to control and criminalize certain thoughts, opinions and speech.
This thought-control campaign is manifest by the types of "hatred" that are being identified as those meriting favorite or discriminatory treatment over other types of hatred. Hate crimes laws would be the tool of gay activists to insulate themselves from the ongoing debate in our society about whether gays are born that way, whether they can change, and whether governments should extend special rights to gays. While the bill lists other protected classes that one cannot hate, the driving force behind the law is to protect the gays from hate. But the effect of this law would be to stifle and/or punish legitimate speech at which an over-sensitive person (in any of the listed protected classes) may take offense. To give an example of this latter point, a child in high school in Frederick County, Maryland was recently threatened with expulsion because he called someone "gay." The Frederick County behavioral regulations for students are so strict, that even legitimate discussion of gay issues can be punishable; it's okay to speak supportively of the gay lifestyle, but a student better not speak disparagingly of that lifestyle, or else he could be expelled— because he would be guilty of "hate speech," which gays might perceive as threatening. The federal government already endorses a day of celebration each year for the gay lifestyle—this is approved. But if one would dare condemn the gay lifestyle, then that speaker would be guilty of "hate speech," for which he could be punished, fired, etc.

The Hate Crimes Bill is flawed and should be defeated. It is not a matter for the Congress to legislate. It is philosophically flawed, and it would be a tool to stifle legitimate political debate on important national issues.

Supreme Court Appointees, Roberts and Alito, Have Proven to Be Excellent Choices

On Thursday, June 28, 2007, the Supreme Court ended its term, by issuing several important rulings, five of which were extremely important, 5-4 rulings, in which Chief Justice John Roberts and Justice Samuel Alito combined with Justices Scalia, Kennedy and Thomas to bring narrow victories over the four more liberal Justices, Stevens, Souter, Ginsberg and Breyer. Each of these cases deals with important principles of Constitutional law.

The Constitutional issues involved and the names of these cases are as follows:

Affirmative Action – *Parents Involved in Community Schools v. Seattle School District No. 1.*

Freedom of Religion – *Hein v. Freedom From Religion Foundation, Inc.*

Freedom of Speech – *Morse v. Frederick.*

Freedom of Speech/Campaign Finance Reform – *FEC v. Wisconsin Right to Life.*

Federalism/Environment – *National Association of Home Builders v. Defenders of Wildlife*

By a narrow margin, the Court came out on the correct side of each of the key issues in these cases. This is good for the Constitution. The closeness of the vote in these cases highlights the importance of electing leaders who will appoint judges and Supreme Court Justices who will preserve and protect the Constitution.

Both Republicans and Democrats complain that the judicial appointees of the other party are undermining the Constitution by their rulings and opinions. But unless one becomes a student of constitutional law, he or she will not know who is right and who is wrong in this war of accusations. A review of these five, close cases that were decided in June 2007, will help one to understand the difference between conservative and liberal Justices. I believe that a review of these cases will also highlight the correctness and superiority of the point of view of the conservative Justices, which in turn will highlight the importance of electing leaders who will appoint judges and Justices of the mind-set and caliber of Justices John Roberts and Samuel Alito.

I think it can accurately be said that the Supreme Court is slightly more conservative now, with Justices Roberts and Alito, than it was with Justices Rehnquist and O'Connor. This is so because, although Justice Sandra Day O'Connor was a conservative on many issues, she nevertheless sometimes aligned herself with the more liberal Justices on some issues. Thus far, both Justices Roberts and Alito seem to be further to the right than was Justice O'Connor.

Just as the appointment of judges and Justices was an important campaign issue in the 2004 presidential election, so it continues to be important in the 2008 presidential campaigns. Had the Democrats won the White House in 2004, then every one of these five cases would have been decided differently because the Democrats would have appointed Justices of the same philosophical persuasion as Justices Ginsberg or Stevens; the composition of the Supreme Court would be a 6-3 liberal majority, instead of a 5-4 conservative majority.

There will likely be one or two additional vacancies in the Supreme Court during the next president's term in office. (Justice Stevens is in his 80s; Justice Ginsberg has been ill; and Justice Scalia has hinted at retirement.) Thus, for the 2008 presidential campaign, the question of which candidate would appoint the better Justices for the Supreme Court continues to be very important.

8.4.6

Affirmative   Action

Parents Involved in Community Schools v. Seattle School District No. 1

On June 28, 2007, the Supreme Court announced it ruling on an affirmative action issue that arose in Seattle, Washington and Jefferson County, Kentucky. By a 5-4 vote in *Parents Involved in Community Schools v. Seattle School District No. 1*, 551 U.S. ___ (2007), the Court struck down desegregation plans in both of these school districts because the plans were based purely on racial percentages and were not related to either of the two acceptable justifications for affirmative action, i.e., to remedy past racial injustices or to provide the benefits of a racially diverse student body. The Supreme Court has legitimized these two justifications for affirmative action, and the Court has stated that if a desegregation plan is narrowly tailored to accomplish one of these objectives, then the demands of the Fourteenth Amendment's Due Process Clause are satisfied. But neither the Washington nor the Kentucky plans even attempted to articulate such a connection with its racial percentage plans. Accordingly, the plans failed to survive the strict scrutiny that the Equal Protection Clause demands of any racially-driven, governmental plan.

This decision once again pitted the five more conservative Justices with the four more liberal Justices. But this ruling is likely to evoke more criticism and commentary than the other rulings announced this week for several reasons. This is primarily so because it pertains to race, and there are a number of outspoken leaders in the nation who do not hesitate to speak out against racism whenever they can, whether or not the particular facts justify such an allegation. The dissenting Justices implicitly called for such criticism in their long and emotional argument against the majority's opinions. But for all the protestations of the dissenters, Chief Justice Roberts and the majority correctly applied the law, and properly rejected the desegregation plans. If the dissenters' opinion had been in the majority, this case would have stood for a significant extension and expansion of the types of racially-motivated, affirmative action plans that the Court has chosen to permit under the Equal Protection Clause. The Roberts Court wisely drew a line in the sand and took a stand against further expansion.

It should be pointed out that the Parents Involved opinions are 185 pages in length. Few people will take the time to read them, let alone to understand them. I expect that the discussion of this case will be limited primarily to name-calling and superficial treatment. The Majority will be labeled as "racists" and the dissenters will be hailed as the heroes of the down-trodden. Neither is true. The plain language of the Equal Protection Clause and the clear language of the earlier cases on affirmative action all support the ruling of the Court on this important issue.

The pages of opinions generated by the Justices in addressing this case was multiplied because of the acerbic dissent of Justice Breyer, who spent numerous pages giving his account of historical events and stating his sociological arguments for upholding the Seattle and Jefferson County plans. Justice Thomas' concurring opinion devoted 36 pages to respond to Justice Breyer's argument. The Chief Justice's (the Majority) opinion, devoted thirteen pages to respond. But the Majority was not side-tracked; they got it right.

Freedom   of   Speech

Morse v. Frederick

On June 25, 2007, the Supreme Court ruled in *Morse v. Frederick*, 551 U.S. ____ (2007) that Deborah Morse, a high school principal in Alaska, did not violate the free speech rights of one of her students, Joseph Frederick, when she confiscated a 14-foot banner that Frederick displayed at a school event, which banner bore the phrase, "BONG HiTS 4 JESUS," and when she suspended Frederick for not complying with her directive to take the banner down. This case was another 5-4 ruling, with newly appointed Justices Roberts and Alito on the side of the majority.

The key fact in this case is WHERE the speech event occurred. In most places and circumstances, such speech is fully protected by the First Amendment. But certain limitations kick-in when it occurs as a part of a school event.

The dissenting Justices (Stevens, Souter, Ginsberg and Breyer) complain that the suspension of Frederick was unfair; that the displaying of the banner was not disruptive; that the phrase did not encourage the use of drugs; and that Frederick had no intent to promote the use of drugs—that he was just trying to get attention. But the unique situation of the public school setting justifies the actions taken by Principal Morse in this case. The majority got it right.

The situation would be different if the student were disciplined for something he had said in an in-class discussion about drugs or politics or some other relevant issue. But when a student seeks to use a school forum to make his own speech, for his own purposes, his speech rights are limited because he has no right to disrupt the school program or to use the other students to advance his agenda. And the Court's ruling affirms that "disruption" is broadly defined, and that the school authorities are given substantial latitude to make the spur-of-the-moment judgments that they feel are best for the school. Their discretion is not subject to review except for weighty reasons.

While I, for one, disapprove of some of the public school curriculum that my children are and have been subjected to, nevertheless, the greatest problem facing our public schools today is the lack of discipline of the students and the lack of control that teachers have over their students. The increased freedom of students has led to significant increases in disrespect in classrooms; and this has in turn had a serious, deleterious effect on our public education system. If the school system must subject itself to recognize and showcase every student who decides to exercise a freedom of speech right, this could lead to chaos. The Supreme Court's ruling in *Morse v. Frederick* is a step in the right direction, to help the schools regain control so that the education environment can be better for all students.

Now, having shared my social commentary on *Morse v. Frederick*, let me say a little bit about the legal issues involved. The guiding case with respect to this school speech issue is *Tinker v. Des Moines Independent Community School Dist.*, 393 U.S. 503 (1969). In that case the Supreme Court allowed students to wear black arm bands in protest of the Vietnam War. The Court ruled that unless the speech [the wearing of the armbands] would "materially and substantially disrupt the work and discipline of the school," then the conduct was protected under the First Amendment. In that case the students' conduct prevailed over the school administrators. But in the case of the "BONG HiTS 4 JESUS" banner, the principal said that the banner had to be taken down because she thought that it promoted illegal drug use. The student denied that this was his intent, and a close analysis of the wording yields uncertainty about what the phrase actually means. But the majority of the Supreme Court held (and correctly, in my opinion) that the principal's "on the spot" action to confiscate the banner was a "reasonable" action for her to take in controlling student expressions that could contribute to dangerous conduct (Roberts, C.J., slip opinion, at p. 15).

Public schools should not be made a stage for national debate on current social/political issues. Students should not be empowered to take over the education system at will by asserting freedom of speech rights at any time he or she chooses. To allow this would be to sew the seeds of disruption in the school. In fact, this disruptive effect has already been in operation for over 30 years. It has contributed to a decline in student discipline and to an increase in the widespread disrespect that now plagues public schools.

FEC vs. Wisconsin Right to Life

On June 25, 2007, the Supreme Court ruled 5-4 in *FEC v. Wisconsin Right to Life*, 551 U.S. ___ (2007) that the Federal Election Commission (FEC) erred in barring the Wisconsin Right To Life (WRTL) organization from broadcasting three issue ads during the 2004 election campaign. The three ads had addressed the concern of the WRTL to stop the Senate filibustering of the appointment of federal judges. The FEC had ruled that these ads were the "functional equivalent" of express advocacy because they implicated Senator Feingold, who was supportive of the filibusters and who was running for re-election. The U. S. District Court for the District of Columbia found in favor of WRTL, and overturned the ruling of the FEC; the court ruled that the three ads were not "express advocacy" ads and were not the "functional equivalent" of express advocacy. The Supreme Court affirmed the ruling of the District Court.

This is an important ruling because it effectively overturns part of the McCain-Feingold, Bipartisan Campaign Reform Act of 2002 (BCRA). Just three years ago, the Supreme Court ruled (5-4) in *McConnell v. Federal Election Commission*, 540 U.S. 93 that the BCRA was constitutional. For those who have followed this issue for some time, you may recall that after its passage in Congress, there was considerable disappointment among conservatives that President Bush did not veto the bill. Some thought that the President may have been counting on the Supreme Court to invalidate the law. This writer, for one, had predicted that the Court would find the BCRA to be an unconstitutional limitation on speech that is protected under the First Amendment. But, by the narrowest of margins (5-4) the Supreme Court upheld the BCRA.

The issue that was before the Court in *FEC v. WRTL* addressed one aspect of BCRA—issue ads that are aired by corporations during the blackout period, 30 days before a primary and 60 days before a general election. The WRTL wanted to run their three issue ads during the regulated period even though they acknowledged that the BCRA prohibited their broadcast. The WRTL argued that the issue ads were protected speech that must be permitted regardless of the prohibiting language of the BCRA. The Supreme Court agreed.

This case is so significant because it is very difficult to distinguish between issue ads (which are not barred by the BCRA) and express advocacy ads for or against specific candidates for election (which are barred by the BCRA). The difficulty to distinguish the two is demonstrated in the WRTL case. While the wording of the ad addressed an issue and did not directly encourage voters to vote for or against any candidate, the effect of the ad was to criticize Senator Feingold for supporting a filibuster of a Senate vote on the President's judicial nominees. Thus, the effect of the WRTL ads was to indirectly criticize a candidate. But five of the Justices upheld the right of WRTL to broadcast its issue ads regardless of whether the effect might be to help or hurt a particular candidate.

It should be noted that the Court was not unified in the reasoning for this ruling, and that makes the case even more intriguing. Chief Justice Roberts and Justice Alito reasoned that the McConnell ruling of three years ago had preserved for corporate speakers a right to broadcast issue ads during the blackout period so long as they were not "express advocacy" or the "functional equivalent" of express advocacy. Then, Justice Roberts reasoned that an issue ad should not be deemed the functional equivalent of express advocacy unless the ad "is susceptible of no reasonable interpretation other than as an appeal to vote for or against a specific candidate." This, of course, is an extremely broad test that would protect almost all issue ads from being found to "express advocacy." This, broad standard, that would immunize most issue ads from the reach of the BCRA is so protective of issue ads that all seven of the other Justices argued that it would effectively overturn the *McConnell* case. That's where Justices Scalia, Kennedy and Thomas come in; they wanted to specifically overturn that portion of the *McConnell* case; and for that reason they joined in a concurring opinion (authored by Justice Scalia) that ruled in favor of WRTL, but they would invalidate part of the *McConnell* ruling. This left the remaining four Justices complaining in their dissent (by Justice Souter) that the Court had erred by effectively overturning a major part of the *McConnell* case by invalidating Section 203 of the BCRA.

Where does that leave us as the 2008 Presidential Campaign is fast upon us? The BCRA remains good law, but the ruling in *FEC v. WRTL* effectively guts it with respect to corporate issue ads. Personally, I prefer Justice Scalia's reasoning, but the reasoning of Chief Justice Roberts is not bad either. And that's what you get with a plurality decision— more than one rationale in support of a specific ruling. In any event, this ruling is an important victory for fundamental freedom of speech rights.

Freedom of Religion   Establishment Clause

Hein v. Freedom From Religion Foundation, Inc.

On June 25, 2007, the Supreme Court ruled 5-4 in *Hein v. Freedom From Religion Foundation, Inc.*, 551 U.S. ____ (2007) that being a taxpayer is not enough to give an individual standing to bring a suit to challenge the Executive Branch's using faith-based programs for delivering social services as a violation of the First Amendment's Establishment Clause.

This ruling is important because it blocks law suits that challenges the government's accommodation of religion, including acknowledging religion and on occasion even working with religion in addressing social needs. The *Hein* ruling means that anti-religion zealots have no right to bring a law suit to challenge the work of the Executive Branch for involvement with religious organizations merely because this may hurt their feelings. The *Hein* ruling dictates that in order to have standing to challenge such Executive Branch action, the complaining party must show that it has suffered "injury in fact," not just "psychic injury."

The name of the complaining party indicates exactly what this law suit was all about. The complainant wants to eradicate all vestiges of religion from government. They are upset with the nation's long, constitutional tradition of accommodation of religion; they are madder still at the national motto, "In God We Trust" and at the statement in the pledge of allegiance that we are a nation "under God." They cringe every time a President says, "God bless America." Their stated goal is to change all of this. They wish to convert the meaning of the Establishment Clause of the First Amendment from a shield to a sword; they wish to change "freedom of religion" to "freedom from religion."

The *Hein* ruling is an important defeat for the anti-religionists. However, a review of the *Hein* ruling is interesting and important for some other reasons, too. Like the Court's ruling on the same day in *FEC v. Wisconsin Right to Life*, a majority of five conservative justices came to the same conclusion, but based upon different rationales. In fact, in both of these cases, the rationales of Justices Scalia and Thomas were in some respects closer to that of the dissenting Justices (Stevens, Souter, Ginsberg and Breyer), in that these six felt that the distinctions made by Chief Justice Roberts and Justice Alito were not logically sustainable—that there was no basis for limiting the application of *Flast v. Cohen*, 392 U.S. 83 (1968) to Congressional acts but not to Executive acts. But in both cases, Justices Scalia and Thomas voted with the Chief Justice and Justice Alito because the former felt that the Court should overturn an erroneously decided case rather than to try to carve out an exception to the cases. I find this to be intellectually intriguing.

In *Hein*, discussion centers on the case of *Flast v. Cohen*, in which the Supreme Court ruled that a mere taxpayer had standing to challenge in court the government's using funds allocated by Congress under the Elementary and Secondary Education Act of 1965 to support parochial schools. (J. Scalia's concurring opinion, p. 5.) But the Court in *Hein* distinguished *Flast* by pointing out that *Flast* dealt with a Congressional act whereas the expenditure in *Hein* was a discretionary expenditure of the Executive Branch. Justices Scalia and Thomas agreed with the Chief Justice and Justices Kennedy and Alito as to the result—they just felt that *Flast* was wrong in the first place, and that it should be overturned.

I am with Justices Scalia and Thomas on this case. The "psychic injury" test for standing is bad policy. The *Flast* case continues to recognize and endorse this ephemeral standard. To illustrate the application of the "psychic injury" look at some litigation that took place in my town, Frederick, Maryland just a few years ago. An eighteen-year-old student filed suit to remove a Ten Commandments monument from the city's war veterans' memorial park. In order for this young man to state a valid cause of action he first had to declare that by seeing the Ten Commandments monument in the park that this caused him emotional pain and grief. For if the young man could not say that the monument bothered him, then he would not be able to challenge the constitutionality of the city's harboring of the Ten Commandments monument. The young plaintiff contacted the ACLU to get the legal direction he needed, then he claimed that the monument disturbed him, and then—because of the *Flast* case—he got standing to suit the City in court.

The *Flast* case has served to open the flood gates to a host of litigation aimed at making people feel good, rather than addressing claims for actual injuries in fact. The nation has become obsessed with addressing touchy, feely mental and emotional matters. The penchant for hate crime laws is another manifestation of this same trend. It is not enough to punish a criminal for his wrongful acts of violence, but we have enacted laws to give increased punishment if we can prove that the criminal harbored certain, specified bad intents at the time. This exercise is unnecessary; it is the product of legislators having too much spare time on their hands; it costs more tax monies to administer; and it causes all parties more money to implement.

Justices Scalia and Thomas were right to call for *Flast* to be overturned. They were unsuccessful in this, but at least the conservative block was successful in limiting the bad effects of *Flast*.

The Iraq War—
The Most Important Issue of Our Day

by C. Paul Smith

Two driving forces for much of the national news at this time are the 2008 Presidential Campaigns and the war in Iraq. Because several key state primaries have been set for early 2008, the campaigns of the presidential hopefuls are in high gear. The war in Iraq is the centerpiece of every campaign, and tentacles of this issue are far-reaching.

In August and September, it became apparent that the Democratic approach to the war was shifting—Democratic contenders suddenly stopped their high-pitched screaming for the U. S. to get out of Iraq, and they began to take a different tact. Neither Senators Clinton nor Obama would commit when they would pull out all of our troops if she or he became president. The reason for this change in campaign strategy should be understood: It is the product of their acknowledgement that the U.S. will still be in Iraq when the next president takes office, and if one of them is president, she or he would then bear the responsibility of whether the pull-out from Iraq was a victory or a defeat. And even they seem to recognize that announcing a pull-out date is synonymous with defeat and surrender. Thus, the campaign rhetoric from both top Democratic contenders has stopped its previous, unceasing calls for an immediate withdrawal (or "redeployment" as the Democrats liked to call it).

Of course, one principal reason why the Democrats had to change their campaign strategies about the war is that in July, General Petraeus reported significant progress and success in Iraq after the implementation of his "surge" strategy for six months. When Democratic congressional leaders grilled and criticized General Petraeus, this did not play well in the nation's heartland. And the national indignation against this approach reached its peak when *The New York Times* gave a special, reduced rate to the Move-on.org full-page ad stating: "General Petraeus or General Betray us." (The Democrat penchant for rhyme over reason is demonstrated by this ad.)

But the Democratic campaign strategists are not rolling over, and their efforts that are hurting the war effort have not stopped. To be

clear, I do not believe the Democratic goal is to lose the war in Iraq—rather it is to put a Democrat in the White House in 2008. The problem is that the Democratic strategy to win the White House has centered on criticizing the Bush leadership of the war; and they have disregarded the safety and success of our troops in their excessive zeal to regain political power. A current, deplorable example of this is the insistence of the House Democrats to pass a resolution to condemn the Ottoman (Turk) massacre ("genocide") of Armenians in 1915. That's right—1915—92 years ago! The timeliness of this resolution could not be worse. Now is **not** the time to pursue this condemnation effort! We need Turkey's cooperation for the use of its air space as we conduct the Iraq war. And worse than that—on this very day (October 15, 2007) thousands of Turkish troops are poised on the border of Iraq, ready to attack the Iraqi Kurds. In case the Democrats had not thought this through—it is not in our national interest to open up a new war front against another nation. This Democrat-led effort to alienate Turkey is sabotaging our war effort, and it must stop.

But, back to the current campaign strategies—in 2004 there was a dramatic shift in the Democrat Party's criticism of the war after they nominated John Kerry to be their banner-carrier; the criticism shifted from blaming Bush for starting the war, to how to conduct the war. Before Kerry secured the nomination, every contender except Senator Lieberman (who was then ostracized and rejected by his party) railed incessantly at President Bush for mistakenly putting the U.S. in Iraq. But once Senator Kerry emerged with the nomination, his campaign tune had to be tempered by the truth—it would be a mistake to abruptly pull-out of Iraq. All Senator Kerry could offer was to run the war better than President Bush was running it—and Senator Kerry offered no specific plans that were much different from what President Bush was doing. In the end, the anti-war approach that appealed to the left wing of the Democrat Party, and which secured his party's nomination, ran out of air and failed to win over sufficient middle-of-the-roaders during the general election.

But, back to October 2007, while there are still war detractors in Congress who continue to call for the setting of a withdrawal date, there is a growing acknowledgement that setting a withdrawal date would be disastrous. This would be a declaration of defeat, which the Democrats had hoped to saddle the Republicans with, but the Republicans would not take the bait. And the Democrats certainly don't want to set themselves up to bear the responsibility of defeat if they should retake the White House. Therefore, Democrats are abandoning the "pull-out now" approach. But the newest Democratic tactic is to attempt to pit the war funding against the funding of health services—to try to make the case that President Bush is wasting money on the war that could be spent on other needed governmental services.

One example of this is the Democratic bill to expand SCHIP (the State Children's Health Insurance Program) that provides health insurance for households not poor enough to qualify for Medicaid, but not affluent enough to be able to afford their own health insurance. Thus, the SCHIP program has met a specific national need since 1997. Currently a family of four with income of $43,000 or less qualifies for SCHIP. But the current SCHIP bill proposes to make this program available to families of four with incomes or $63,000 or higher—150% - 200% higher than the prior income limit. This would make the SCHIP benefits available to numerous families that do not need the government benefit, and it would cause some people to cancel health insurance policies that they can afford in order to obtain the cheaper government health care. Thus, the current SCHIP bill is wasteful. President Bush had proposed a $5 billion increase for SCHIP over five years. But the Senate bill proposed a $35 billion increase, and the House bill had proposed a $50 billion increase. President Bush vetoed the bill that did pass because it was wasteful and counter-productive.

The dirty little secret is that the Democrats know full well that Congress is not likely to override the President's veto, but that's fine with them because the Democrats intend to use this as a weapon against the Republican candidate in the presidential campaign. They will pull out a tactic from their old "Smear the Republicans" play book. They intend to paint the Republicans as sacrificing the health of Americans in order to prosecute the war in Iraq. The right thing for Congress to do is to pare down the excesses in the new SCHIP legislation. Since the Democrats do not intend to do this, then the Republicans should reveal the Democrat strategy for exactly what it is—a cheap political tactic!

The national news on October 12th and 13th included broadcasting the criticisms on the Iraq war made by former three-star General Rick Sanchez, who led the war effort in Iraq in 2003. General Sanchez called the war effort a "failed policy," and he said the current surge was just a "desperate attempt" to win. The liberal media loves to drum up whatever war criticisms it can find. Of course, General Sanchez has a personal stake in this matter because it was at least partly his "failed direction" in Iraq that the Bush Administration eventually rejected in late 2006. The news reports I heard did not mention this factor.

Nevertheless, the fact is that negative news reports about the Iraq war have decreased drastically during the past two months—and the reason is that the war effort is now going much better, and insurgents are being defeated and driven out. This has led to a shift in focus on the war debate—the new question is how and when and to what extent will the U.S. withdraw our forces when we achieve the security goals for the new Iraq government. It is a welcome relief to be debating this, rather than a premature pull-out. The debate of details about the size and duration of the American presence in Iraq in the aftermath of the war is a debate based upon victory, so Democrats may find little incentive to bring it up, since their ultimate goal seems to be winning political power rather than winning the war in Iraq.

CLU 10/07

An Historical Perspective on the Iraq War

An historical review of the devastation that was wrought by evil extremists in the Twentieth Century is helpful to understand the importance of taking a stand against international terrorism in the Twenty-first Century.[1] This review validates the effort by the United States to attempt to establish a democratic government in Iraq.

The immediate cause of World War I was the assassination of Francis Ferdinand, the Archduke of Austria-Hungary in 1914. In response to this slaying, Austria-Hungary declared war on Serbia. This was followed by all of Europe becoming involved in the war because of the multiple entangling alliances that the nations had signed agreeing to come to the defense of one another in the event of war. Although millions of Europeans died from this war, the United States stayed out of the conflict until a German message was intercepted in which Germany asked Mexico and Japan to join them in war against the United States. As payment for their help, the German message promised to help Mexico recover some of the land it had ceded to the United States. The revelation of this secret message led the United States to declare war against Germany on April 2, 1917. By the time the war ended in 1918, there were 116,516 American deaths. But the death count of all military personnel was 9,180,233 (5,232,738 from the Allies, and 3,947,495 from the Central Powers), plus another 5 million civilian deaths.[2]

The American troops provided impressive strength and contributed to the decisive victory for the allies in eastern France in 1918. The Germans then asked for an armistice, and on November 11, 1918, Supreme Allied Commander Marshal Foch demanded the Germans to accept harsh conditions to end the strife, and the Germans were forced to accept.

Europe and the entire world had had its fill of war. In addition to the nearly 10 million people killed in the war, there were more than 20 million more who were wounded or missing. The horrors of war were so terrible, that the European nations were of a mind-set to avoid war again at almost all costs. But this mind-set played into the hands of Adolf Hitler.

Hitler took it personally that Germany surrendered to end World War I. Within weeks after he was elected to be Germany's Chancellor in 1933, he began ruling as a dictator. In 1936, Hitler took over the Rhineland, an area in eastern France. France did nothing. In 1938 Hitler's forces took over Austria. The world only watched. On September 1, 1939 German troops invaded and took over Poland. Britain and France then declared war on September 3rd. In November 1939, Germany invaded Finland. Most nations of the world still did nothing—being of the mindset to avoid war at all costs. In the spring of 1940, Germany attacked Denmark and Norway; in May Germany invaded Belgium, Luxembourg, The Netherlands and then the rest of France. (France surrendered in June.) In the spring of 1941 Germany invaded Greece and Yugoslavia, and then in June Germany invaded Russia—still the United States watched in silence.

After the bombing of Pearl Harbor by the Japanese, the United States declared war against Japan on December 8, 1941, and three days later the U. S. declared war against Germany and Italy. The evil of Hitler and Nazi Germany knew no bounds; it was not

---

[1] See, e.g., William J. Bennett, *America, The Last Best Hope* (Nashville: Thomas Nelson, Inc. 2007). William J. Bennett's best-selling, two-volume history of the United States (through 1989) is not only interesting, informative and well-written, but it is *timely* as well— timely because the mere recounting of the oppression and unmitigated evil of Nazi Germany and Communist Russia is an important reminder that the free world must work together to prevent ruthless tyrants from conquering free peoples through military might in the hands of evil extremists.

[2] By nation, these military death counts were as follows: Of the Allies: British Empire-942,135; France-1,368,000; Italy- 680,000; Russia-1,700,000; and the United States-116,516. Of the Central Powers:

Austria-Hungary-1,200,000; Germany-1,935,000; and the Ottoman Empire (Turkey)- 725,000. See "World War I," *The World Book Encyclopedia* (1969).

limited to conquering other nations. Hitler ordered and carried out the systematic annihilation of over six million European Jews before Germany was defeated.

U. S. involvement in World War II was key in freeing western Europe from Nazi Germany. But the U. S. involvement in this war was four times as long and cost four times as many lives (405,399) as did World War I. The total civilian and military deaths from World War II is estimated to be 55 million people,[3] and the non-fatal casualties must be at least that many more.

One of the sad commentaries on World War II is the fact that the enormous, Nazi global atrocity could have been lessened if the free people of the world had taken a stance against Nazi Germany earlier. But instead, out of a distaste for war, we stood by passively as Hitler boldly took over nation after nation, in his quest to rule the world. With the perspective of passage of time, the appeasement and pacifism of Britain's Prime Minister Neville Chamberlain has forever earned him the historical reputation of a weak leader, whose refusal to confront evil oppression resulted in disaster for millions of people.

But the evil oppression of one people over others did not end with the surrender of Germany. While the U. S. had been allied with Russia to defeat Germany, this was an alliance of convenience rather than one of principles and ideology. Stalin's leadership of his people was ruthless. When Russian soldiers were captured, Stalin treated them as traitors. And he didn't treat his other soldiers much better. His way to clear a mine filed was just to march his soldiers through it. The Russian military deaths in World War II are estimated to be 7,500,000. And as soon as the Germans surrendered to Russia and the United States, then Russia proceeded to occupy Germany and many surrounding nations. And then Russia imposed its communist government on the nations it occupied. Thus,

the U. S. occupation of France, Germany and other European nations was not just to rebuild and to make sure Nazi Germany was never resurrected—but it was to block the expansion of the world's newest wicked regime— Communist Russia. The U. S. presence in Korea, Vietnam and other nations was an attempt to protect those nations from being overtaken by new, despotic leaders and nations. The commitment and cost to do this has been expensive for America, but the protection and benefit this has afforded our friends of freedom around the world is invaluable.

All of this brings us to where we are today, in Iraq. The American lives that have been lost, while we have worked with the Iraqi people, to help them establish a government, have been precious; the sacrifices have been great. But the potential blessings of freedom and prosperity for the Iraqis, and for us and other nations of the world is worth the cost. The world continues to be burdened with evil, fanatical, extremists who do not value life, and who will happily kill and injure others as it suits their purposes to enslave and control others.

The joint American-Iraqi goal to help bring freedom, peace, prosperity and good government to Iraq and stability to the region is a noble, worthy cause. It appears to be within grasp. But it would be wrong to abandon the Iraqis, who have counted on and relied on America to see the struggle through to the end. To prematurely leave Iraq would expose those Iraqis who have relied on us to death and torture at the hands of terrorists and insurgents. It would be the height of selfishness and arrogance to abandon the millions of Iraqis who have put their hope in us and have risked their own lives and fortunes to take a stand for freedom in a troubled land. We cannot set up our friends for the death and destruction that will come to them if we suddenly give up because we decide it is no longer worth it to us to defend them. National love requires steadfastness and commitment. As long as the Iraqis want our help, we should not abandon them.

---

[3] See "World War II," *The World Book Encyclopedia* (1969).

MARYLAND COURT OF APPEALS UPHOLDS STATUTE LIMITING MARRIAGE TO OPPOSITE-SEX COUPLES

by C. Paul Smith

On September 18, 2007, the Maryland Court of Appeals issued the long-awaited ruling in the case of *Conaway v. Deane* (September Term, 2006, Case No. 44), upholding the constitutionality of the Maryland law that "[o]nly a marriage between a man and a woman is valid in this State" (Family Law Article, Section 2-201). The Court of Appeals by a 4-3 vote, rejected the plaintiffs' arguments that the Maryland law violated both the State Equal Rights Amendment (Article 46) and the Equal Protection Clause of the Fourteenth Amendment. The Court also rejected the argument that there is a "fundamental right" to same-sex marriage.[1]

Background. Around the country, those who follow the development of gay rights and the effort of gays to secure the right to same-sex marriage had been waiting anxiously for almost a year for the Court of Appeals to rule. Several other states have weighed in on this issue, and except for Massachusetts,[2] all have upheld state marriage laws that restrict marriage to opposite-sex couples. In late 2006, New York's high court ruled on this issue;[3] and the Maryland Court followed that court's marriage, but ordered its state legislature to create within 180 days a new law providing

holding on the main points. Also in 2006, the Supreme Court of New Jersey came down with a ruling that upheld traditional civil unions for gay partners.[4] But the vast majority of states that have addressed the issue, have resolved it much like the Maryland Court of Appeals. Judge Glen Harrell's majority opinion gives a thorough treatment of all the key issues.[5]

Even though Circuit Court Judge Brooke Murdock had ruled in favor of plaintiffs (Deane et al, appellees), it was still the plaintiffs who had the greater burden on appeal because the appeal was primarily based upon questions of law rather than questions of fact; and the established law was not on plaintiffs' side. If Deane et al were to prevail, the Court of Appeals would have to depart from traditional interpretations of the applicable law. Those around the country who have followed this issue saw the possibility that Maryland might depart from traditional interpretations because of its long history of recognizing and legislating rights and benefits for gays. But while Maryland was certainly at the forefront of such national trends, this history had a flip side that argued against the plaintiffs because for the last 30+ years, almost every time the Maryland Legislature would pass a law extending special rights to gays, the Legislature would also pass a disclaimer that specifically qualified the application of such rights—that the bestowal of new rights was not to be construed in any way to affect the Maryland

---

[1] It is not known at this time whether Deane and the other plaintiffs will petition the Supreme Court for a writ of certiorari, or whether such a petition would be granted.

[2] *Goodridge v. Dep't of Public Health*, 798 N.E.2d 941 (Mass. 2003).

[3] *Hernandez v. Robles* 855 N.E.2d 1 (N.Y. 2006).

[4] *Lewis v. Harris*, 908 A.2d 196, 200 (N.J. 2006). The Vermont Supreme Court had ruled similarly in 1999. *Baker v. State*, 744 A.2d 864 (1999).

[5] At the circuit court level, Judge Murdock had based her ruling on Article 46 (the state ERA) and on the Equal Protection Clause, but not on the basis of a "fundamental right." The Court could have declined to deal with any issues other than those that were addressed by Judge Murdock. But at the outset of the majority opinion, Judge Harrell explained that the Court would be addressing other issues that are relevant, including the fundamental rights issue.

law that limits marriage to only a man and a woman. Thus, while Maryland was at the forefront in recognizing rights for gays, the State also made it specifically clear from the outset that both the State ERA and the bestowal of state rights for gays did not extend to a right to same-sex marriage.

Maryland's ERA. With that background, when the case came before the Court of Appeals, the State's history of recognizing gay rights was of only limited value—it was a double-edged sword, so to speak. The Court first addressed whether the marriage statute's prohibition of same-sex marriages violated the State ERA. The Court had never before construed the ERA to invalidate the statute restricting marriage to opposite-sex couples. And the majority opinion again declined to do so.

Standard of Review. The next major issue addressed in Judge Harrell's opinion was which of the three levels of scrutiny to apply to the Maryland law—strict scrutiny, intermediate scrutiny, or rational basis review.[6] The Court made a lengthy analysis of and rejected plaintiffs' (appellees') arguments that gays were a protected class, that heightened or strict scrutiny was warranted, and that there existed a fundamental right to marry someone of the same sex. By a 4-3 vote, the Court found no "protected class," no "suspect criteria" and no "fundamental right"; and the Court therefore ruled that strict scrutiny was not proper. The Court also failed to find a basis to apply the intermediate (or heightened) scrutiny.[7] The Court held that the rational

basis standard was the proper one (*Conaway*, p. 96).

To satisfy the minimal, "rational basis" test, "a statute reviewed under the rational basis test enjoys a strong presumption of constitutionality, [and] can be invalidated only if the classification is without any reasonable basis and is purely arbitrary" *Conaway*, at 97, citing *Whiting-Turner Contract Co. v. Coupard*, 304 Md. 340, 352 (1985). As long as the court can find any conceivable reasonable basis for the statute, it will pass muster. Thereafter, predictably, the Court found that there existed a rational basis for the disparate treatment.[8] The Court held that "the State's legitimate interest in fostering procreation and encouraging the traditional family structure in which children are born" is an adequate and proper basis to supports limiting marriage to opposite-sex couples.[9] Judge Battaglia, in her dissent, argued that the statute should be subject to strict scrutiny (not rational basis scrutiny), and she further stated that she would have remanded the case for a thorough hearing on the issue of whether or not the State could meet the burden to show that it had a compelling interest to justify the discriminatory treatment.[10]

---

[6] *Conaway*, pp. 43-47. At these pages Judge Harrell identified the three types of scrutiny, and then proceeded to discuss which level of scrutiny was warranted to address the Maryland statute.

[7] With regard to the intermediate level of review, the Court addressed the issue of whether or not homosexuality was innate, and implied that if it were that the Court might apply either strict scrutiny or heightened scrutiny. But the Court, after examining various scientific studies on the issue, specifically

declined to find homosexuality to be an immutable characteristic. *Conaway*, pp. 66-70.

[8] Of the dissenting Judges, Chief Judge Bell and Judge Battaglia argued that strict scrutiny was warranted. Judge Raker agreed with the majority, that the rational basis test should be applied (*Conaway*, Raker, J., dissenting, at p. 5). However, Judge Raker went on to argue that the Maryland statute could not withstand rational basis scrutiny. While Chief Judge Bell argued that "strict scrutiny" applied, he nevertheless concurred with Judge Raker's analysis that the statute failed to meet the rational basis test. I would submit that Judge Raker's application of the rational basis analysis is a major departure from the traditional interpretation and application of that test.

[9] Conaway, pp. 98 and 109.

[10] *Conaway*, Battaglia, J., dissenting, at p. 80. Judge Battaglia correctly pointed out that the case had not yet fully developed and explored: "Neither party has explored this issue in the depth appropriate to an

The Equal Protection Clause. In determining whether the Equal Protection Clause has been violated, if a challenged law affects a "protected class," then the Maryland statute could be upheld only if the state had a "compelling interest" to justify the disparate treatment, and only if the court would "strictly scrutinize" the statute and the state interests to make sure that the stringent test had been satisfied. But, if no protected class and no suspect criteria is involved, then the Maryland statute need only satisfy the rational basis test (as explained above). Appellees' argument that strict scrutiny must be applied was based primarily upon the argument that the marriage law discriminated against a class of people; and they argued that *Loving v. Virginia*, 388 U.S. 1 (1967) supported this view.[11] But the majority disagreed and held that the Virginia law in *Loving* was blatant "anti-black legislation" and that the rule articulated in *Loving* was a prohibition from subordinate treatment of either women to men or men to women, *as a class*.[12] The majority applied the traditional, most widely accepted interpretation of *Loving*—that it prohibits classifying males or females as a class in the absence of a compelling state interest. Accordingly, because the Maryland marriage restriction applies to males the same way it applies to females, therefore the statute does not impinge upon the rights of any protected class.[13]

The Fundamental Right Argument. The remaining major issue in the case was whether or not there existed a "fundamental right" of one person to marry another person of the same sex. To start with, it was acknowledged by all that there is a fundamental right to marry. But the definition of that right was subject to dispute. Deane et al argued that the fundamental right to marry included the right to marry someone of the same sex. But the State countered that the fundamental right to marry has always been limited by the traditional meaning of marriage—that it is between a man and a woman, and that therefore the right to marry has always been limited to the right to marry someone of the opposite sex. The latter interpretation was adopted by the majority.

The Future. The majority opinion in *Conaway v. Deane* is 110 pages in length, and the three dissenting opinions added another 130 pages. (Judge Bell concurred with both Judge Battaglia and with part of Judge Raker's opinion; then Judge Bell added a brief dissent of his own for good measure.) With that many pages of reasoning and rhetoric, one could certainly

---

issue of such permanent, transcendent magnitude." *Id.* Of course, the case was decided on the basis of summary judgment motions, and the court had only been presented sparse evidence on sociological and societal impact of various child-rearing possibilities, and therefore the court was not in a position where it could properly rule on the compelling interest issue.

[11] *Conaway*, pp. 37-41. In *Loving* the Supreme Court held unconstitutional a Virginia Miscegenation statute that prohibited marriages between blacks and whites.

[12] Id., 41.

[13] Appellees argued that the Court of Appeals had previously ruled in *Giffin v. Crane*, 351 Md. 133, 716 A.2d 1029 (1998), that if a law makes sex a factor in a

legal distinction, then the state ERA is violated. However, Judge Harrell pointed out that a review of the reasoning of *Giffin* in its context made it clear that the Court was speaking of distinctions between men and women as classes. *Conaway*, at 27. Judge Harrell pointed out that his conclusion is supported by the majority of the federal and state courts that have addressed this issue, including the Court of Appeal of Washington, that stated in *Singer v. Hara*,522 P.2d1186 (Wash. App. 1974) that to interpret an ERA in a way that requires states to permit same-sex marriages "would be to subvert the purpose for which the ERA was enacted." *Id.*, at 1194. The three dissenting Judges (Chief Judge Bell, Judge Raker and Judge Battaglia) all agreed with Judge Murdock that this interpretation is erroneous; they argued that since the law prohibits someone from marrying another based upon the sex of the partner, that this is sexual discrimination that violates both the State ERA and the Equal Protection Clause of the Fourteenth Amendment.

identify other important parts of the opinions that I have failed to address. And it is not expected that this ruling will end all debate of this important social issue. I don't think anyone is predicting that the issue is now settled. In Maryland, I would predict that the next forum for this debate will be in the Legislature, where in 2008 I expect to see both a bill to amend the Constitution to restrict marriage to a man and a woman, and opposing bills to both legitimize same-sex marriage and to authorize civil unions for same-sex couples. On that point it is of interest to note that there is now pending before the Supreme Court of California, several "Marriage cases," which have been combined together, and in which that Court is being asked to rule on the constitutionality of California Referendum No. 22, where the voters rejected civil unions and voted to restrict marriage to only opposite-sex couples.[14]

---

[14] That case if both interesting and important. The State's Attorney General argued successfully against Referendum 22 at the first appellate level, where that court ruled that the Referendum was unconstitutional. The issue in California involves some of the same issues covered by the 2006 New Jersey case (*Lewis v. Harris*, 908 A.2d 196, 200 (N.J. 2006)) and the 1999 Vermont case (*Baker v. State*, 744 A.2d 864 (1999)).

TRADITIONAL MARRIAGE IS BEST FOR REARING CHILDREN

by C. Paul Smith

On September 18, 2007, the Maryland Court of Appeals issued the long-awaited ruling in the case of *Conaway v. Deane*, upholding the constitutionality of the Maryland law that "[o]nly a marriage between a man and a woman is valid in this State" (Family Law Article, Section 2-201). The Court of Appeals by a 4-3 vote, rejected the plaintiffs' arguments that the Maryland law violated both the State Equal Rights Amendment (Article 46) and the Equal Protection Clause of the Fourteenth Amendment. The Court also rejected the argument that there is a "fundamental right" to same-sex marriage.[1] It is anticipated that any future efforts to establish a right to same-sex marriage in Maryland will take place in the State Legislature.[2] When that debate takes place it will certainly include a debate of whether gay couples can raise children as well as heterosexual, married couples. Current studies demonstrate that married, heterosexual couples are better for raising children than other combinations, including both single-parents and same-sex partnerships.

The superiority of the traditional marriage relationship for the rearing of children is supported by both the advantages of marriage to the couple and to the children.

To begin with, the benefits to married partners are better than the benefits to single parents or co-parenting adults. Married men and women are more likely to be financially stable.[3] Married adults have greater longevity, less illness and disease, better health and health care, increased happiness, lower levels of mental illness (including depression), and less substance abuse than both single and co-habiting adults.[4] Homosexual people are at a substantially higher risk for some forms of emotional problems, including suicidality, major depression, and anxiety disorder.[5] Homosexual women have a higher prevalence of substance use disorders than heterosexual women.[6] Gay, lesbian and bisexual high school students have higher incidences of alcohol use, cocaine use and illegal inhalant use than others.[7] The benefits from traditional marriage help parents to be better at rearing children than single parents and co-habiting adults.

Studies also provide direct evidence that traditional marriage relationships are better for the rearing of children than either single-parents or cohabiting adults, including

---

[1] It is not known at this time whether Deane and the other plaintiffs will petition the Supreme Court for a writ of certiorari, or whether such a petition would be granted.

[2] During the last two sessions there were bills offered to amend the State Constitution to limit marriage only between a man and a woman. In light of the recent ruling, it is not certain whether such a bill would be forthcoming in 2008. But on the other side of this issue, it is anticipated that gay rights activists may introduce a bill to do legislatively what they were not able to accomplish judicially.

---

[3] Wilcox, W.B. et al. (2005). Why marriage matters: Twenty-six conclusions from the social sciences. 2d ed. New York: Institute for American Values. Cited in the testimony presented by A. Dean Byrd (February 1, 2007) "Dr. Byrd Provides Testimony in English Court Case Regarding Same-Sex Adoption" [hereafter referred to as "Byrd"], p. 1. A 13-page summary of Dr. Byrd's testimony is found at the website of the National Association for Research and Therapy of Homosexuality (NARTH) at www.narth.com. Most of the studies cited in this article come from Dr. Byrd's testimony summary.

[4] Waite, L. & Gallagher, M. (2000). The Case for Marriage. New York: Doubleday., cited in Byrd, p. 2.

[5] Bailey (1999).

[6] Sandfort, de Graaf, Bijl and Schnabel (2001).

[7] Timothy J. Dailey, "The Negative Health Effects of Homosexuality." *Insight*, No. 232, Family Research Council (March 2001).

same-sex couples.[8] Dr. A. Dean Byrd states that "Mothers and fathers contribute in gender-specific and in gender-complementary ways to the healthy development of children.[9] In support of this, Dr. Byrd referred to the following summary of Child Trends research:

> Research clearly demonstrates that family structure matters for children, and the family structure that helps children the most is a family headed by two biological parents in a low-conflict marriage.... There is thus value for children in promoting strong, stable marriages between biological parents.[10]

Dr. Byrd states that "extensive research spanning decades yields an overwhelming abundance of data supporting the importance of both mothers and fathers to the healthy development of children."[11] In 1982 Baumrind concluded that children of dual-gender parents are more competent, function better, and have fewer problems than other children.[12] In 1991 Baumrind found that the combined parenting from a mother and a father in the home provided complementary benefits to the children.[13] In 1984 Greenberger confirmed and bolstered Baumrind's 1982 study; Greenberger's study found that the optimal development of children requires gender-specific and gender-complementary contributions that a mother or a father cannot do alone.[14] The difference

between mothers' and fathers' parenting styles have been confirmed by studies, including studies by Rossi (1987)[15] and Shapiro (1994).[16] A study by Clarke-Stewart (1980) concluded that fathers' play and mothers' play with their children are different, and that each offers distinct benefits to the children.[17] Studies by Rohner and Veneziano (2001)[18] and by Diener (2002)[19] documented the unique contribution that fathers make in the development of a child. The absence of a father in the home has been linked to teenage pregnancy, child abuse, domestic violence and the need for psychiatric care.[20] The discipline styles of fathers and mothers also tend to be different, and it is beneficial to children to be exposed to both styles.[21] A study by Golombok, Tasker & Murray (1997) found that the deficits experienced by children in "father absent families" is no different than the deficits experienced by children raised in lesbian families.[22] The

[8] Popenoe, D. 1996. *Life without father.* New York: Mark Kessler Books, The Free Press. Pg. 176, cited in Byrd, p. 2.

[9] Byrd, p. 3.

[10] Moore, K. A. et al. (2002). Marriage from a child's perspective: How does family structure affect children and what can we do about it? *Child Trends Research Brief* (Washington D.C.: Child Trends) (June), cited in Byrd, p. 3.

[11] Byrd, p. 8.

[12] Baumrind, D. (1982). Are androgynous individuals more effective persons and parents? Child Development, 53, 44-75, cited in Byrd, p. 3.

[13] Baumrind, D. (1991). The influence of parenting style on adolescent competence and substance use. *Journal of Adolescence,* 11(11), 59-95, cited in Byrd, p. 3.

[14] Greenberger, E. (1984). Defining psychosocial maturity in adolescence. In P. Karoly & J.J. Steffans, (Eds.) *Adolescent behavior disorders: foundations and temporary concerns.* Lexington, MA: Lexington Books., cited in Byrd, p. 3.

[15] Rossi, A..S. (1987) Parenthood in transition: From lineage to child to self-orientation. In J.B. Lancaster, J. Altman, A.S. Rossi, and L.R. Sherrod, eds., Parenting across the life span: Biosocial dimensions. New York: Aldene De Gruyter, 31-81.

[16] Shapiro, J. L. (1994). Letting dads be dads. *Parents,* June, 165, 168.

[17] Clarke-Stewart, K.A. (1980). The father's contribution to children's cognitive and social development in early childhood. In F.A. Pedersen, ed., *The father-infant relationship: observational studies in the family setting.* New York: Praeger, cited in Byrd, p. 4.

[18] Rohner, R. P. & Veneziano, R.A. (2001). "The importance of father love: history and contemporary evidence," *Review of General Psychology* 5.4, 382-405, cited in Byrd, p.4.

[19] Diener, M.L., Mangelsdorf, S.C., McHale, J.L. & Frosch, C.A. (2002). *Infancy,* 3(2), 153-174; and Masser, A. (1989). Boys' father hunger: The missing father syndrome. *Medical Aspects of Human Sexuality,* 23(1), 44-50. Both of these are cited in Byrd, p. 5.

[20] Blankenhorn, D. (1995). *Fatherless America: Confronting our most urgent social problem.* New York: Basic, cited in Byrd, p. 5.

[21] Gilligan, C. (1994). *In a different voice.* Cambridge, MA. Harvard University Press, cited in Byrd, p. 5.

[22] Golombok, S., Tasker, F., & Murray, C. (1997). Children raised in fatherless families from infancy: Family relationships and the socioeconomic development of children of lesbian and single

adverse affects of the absence of a mother in raising children has also been documented. The 1998 study by Eisold confirmed this.[23] Research confirms that mothers and fathers are not interchangeable; each provides separate and distinct advantages for the raising of children.[24]

Advocacy groups insist that same-sex parents can raise children as well as opposite-sex parents. But Dr. Byrd says that "studies on same-sex parenting are quite limited and quite limiting,"[25] and that most studies that have been cited in support of this proposition have either serious research flaws or other limitations that affect their conclusions.[26] In 2000, Lerner and Nagai made a detailed analysis of 49 studies that purported to show that homosexual parents raise children as well as married biological parents. Lerner and Nagai concluded that all 49 studies suffered from "severe methodological flaws, plus other problems.[27] These conclusions were confirmed by Williams (2000),[28] Nock, a sociologist at the University of Virginia,[29] and Stacey and Biblarz (2001).[30] Wright and

Cummings also noted these serious flaws in their book, *Destructive Trends in Mental Health* (2005).[31] More recently, a study by Wainwright and Patterson refuted the claim of some gay activists that incidents of delinquency and substance abuse in adolescents raised by lesbian couples does not differ from those raised by heterosexual couples.[32]

Based upon this and other research, George A. Rekers concluded that children are better off raised by heterosexual parents than by gay couples.[33] A 2005 study by Dean Byrd also confirms this conclusion.[34]

Finally, I would make the obvious argument that a gay couple cannot model a healthy male-female relation between the parents. This statement is beyond the need for proof by scientific study, but its importance should not be overlooked. Over 99 percent of society's children have and will continue to marry in traditional opposite-sex marriages, where children will be conceived, born and

heterosexual mothers. Journal of Child Psychology and Psychiatry 38:783791, 788, cited in Byrd, p. 6.

[23] Eisold, B., (1998) Recreating mother: The consolidation of 'heterosexual' gender identification in the young son of homosexual men. *American J. of Orthopsychiatry* 8:3:433-442,cited in Byrd, p. 7.

[24] Biller, H. (1993). *Fathers and families: paternal factors in child development.* Westport, CT: Auburn House, cited in Byrd, p. 7.

[25] Byrd, p. 9.

[26] Byrd, pp. 9-12.

[27] Lerner, R. & Nagai, A.K. (2000). "Out of nothing comes nothing: Homosexual and heterosexual marriage not shown to be equivalent for raising children," paper presented at the Revitalizing the Institution of marriage for the 21st Century conference, Brigham Young University, March, Provo, UT, p. 1, cited in Byrd, p. 9.

[28] Williams, R. N. (2000). A critique of the research on same-sex parenting. In D. C. Dollahite, ed. *Strengthening Our Families,* Salt Lake City, Utah: Bookcraft, 325-355, cited in Byrd, p. 10.

[29] Nock Affidavit, Paragraph 3. Halpern v. Attorney General of Canada, No. 684/00 (Ont. Sup. Ct. of Justice), cited in Byrd, p. 11.

[30] Stacy, J. & Biblarz, T.J. (2001). (How) does the sexual orientation of parents matter? American Sociological Review, 66(2), 172, cited in Byrd, p. 11.

[31] The esteemed psychologists, Drs. Rogers H. Wright and Nicholas A. Cummings describe this blatant and embarrassing situation as a trend to sacrifice science for a popular social agenda. *Destructive Trends in Mental Health,* New York: Routledge (2005). Dr. Cummings is a former APA President and a recipient of five honorary doctorates. Dr. Wright served on the APA Board of Directors. One of the important erroneous beliefs that Wright and Cummings bring to light is the unfounded assertion that homosexuality is innate and immutable. In 2003 Dr. Robert L. Spitzer published his research and findings that many people have successfully changed and repressed same-sex attractions that had plagued them for many years. (See *Archives of Sexual Behavior,* Vol. 32, No. 5, Oct. 2003, 403-417.) The Spitzer study is especially significant because he is the very man who years ago took the lead in advocating to remove homosexuality from the list of psychiatric disorders.

[32] Wainwright, J. & Patterson, C. (2006). *Journal of Family Psychology,* 20,3,526-530, cited in Byrd, p. 11.

[33] George A. Rekers, Ph.D., "Review of Research on Homosexual Parenting, Adoption and Foster Parenting." University of South Carolina School of Medicine (2004).

[34] A. Dean Byrd, "Gender Complementarity and Childrearing: Where Tradition and Science Agree." *Journal of Law and Family Studies,* University of Utah (2005).

raised.[35] There is nothing more geared to the happiness and success of individuals than a happy, traditional family, where parents are able to meet the many and varied needs of male and female children. It is advantageous to the children to have both a male parent and a female parent, each of whom can supply different but important counsel and leadership. When a child is reared in a home with a mother and father who love each other, this is the supreme situation that society can elect to establish. Restricting marriage to opposite-sex couples establishes this preference.

     Scientific studies support the conclusion that biological parents are more likely to be better than single parents and same-sex partners in raising children

---

[35] Study of marriages in Sweden and Norway, where same-sex marriages are allowed, reveals that less than one percent of marriages taking place there (between 1993 and 2001, after same-sex marriage was legalized) are same-sex marriages. Gunnar Andersson, et al., "The Demographics of Same-Sex Marriage in Norway and Sweden," Demography 43 [2006]: 79-98, cited in World Congress of Families, "Homosexual Unions: Rare and Fragile,"
http://www.worldcongress.org/WCFUpdate/Archive08/wcf_update_816.htm .

218   3.1

CONSTITUTIONAL
LAW
UPDATES

| VII:1 | January 25, 2008 | No. 12 |

Mitt Romney for President

by C. Paul Smith

Mitt Romney is the best candidate for President of the United States.

As I write this,[1] Mitt Romney just won the Nevada caucuses in a landslide, taking 51% of the Republican votes. Ron Paul was a distant second with 14%. All the other Republican candidates were in the single digits. Also, today, McCain won the South Carolina Republican primary with 33% of the votes (again including independents). Huckabee placed a close second with 30%, followed by Thompson with 16% and Romney with 15%. The liberal media is crowning McCain with the front-runner jacket, and are pronouncing that he has taken the lead because the Republicans believe he is the candidate most likely to beat either Hillary Clinton or Barack Obama. I don't buy it. I don't think McCain is going to get the Republican nomination, and I don't think he is the Republican Party's best hope to beat the Democrats. And I am not ready to repudiate my principles to win the election, even if what the liberal pundits say is true. Furthermore, current polls in Florida have McCain, Romney and Giuliani running neck and neck (although the Rasmussen poll has Romney ahead 25% - 20%), and in California one poll has Romney in the lead.

I. WHERE WE STAND AFTER THE SOUTH CAROLINA PRIMARY—THE END IS NEAR FOR HUCKABEE, THOMPSON AND GIULIANI

---

[1] The first major draft of this article was written on January 19th and 20th, 2008, right after the results were announced from the South Carolina Republican Primary. Thereafter, it was revised several times, until it was completed on January 25, 2008.

CONSTITUTIONAL LAW UPDATES is a newsletter edited and published by C. Paul Smith, J.D.
To order copies ($5.00 per issue), write *CLU*, P. O. Box 1204, Frederick, MD 21702-0204.
For further information visit www.cpaulsmith.com. Copyright C. Paul Smith 2008.

Now that the South Carolina Primary is over—it appears that the race for the Republican nomination will be between Romney and McCain. The reason is clear: First, Romney currently has more delegates than any other candidate, including McCain. Second, because no Republican contender has more than 25-30% support at this time, it impossible to pick a winner at this point. Third, Romney is already in Florida, where he will campaign vigorously for the next 10 days— and he is expected to stress his economic message, which proved to be a winner in Michigan and elsewhere. The fact that the nation is currently facing the threat of a recession makes the economy the biggest issue for the nation. And Romney's experience and understanding of economic issues is superior to that of any other candidate. President Bush and Congress are at this very moment discussing a temporary stimulus package to revitalize the sagging economy.[2] All of this should play into Romney's hands and help him in Florida. And fourth, the other three main contenders are basically eliminated by the South Carolina results. [A Rasmussen poll on Tuesday had Romney with 25% support, trailed by McCain and Giuliani with 20%. Huckabee was a distant fourth.]

(a) **Huckabee** needed to win in South Carolina, but he failed to do so. Although he only lost to McCain by a slim margin (33%- 30%), still Huckabee did not win. A candidate has to win some primaries. Except for Arkansas (where he was governor), there is no other state where he can expect to find the evangelical support that he will need to win. Huckabee is a great communicator, and he talks a good talk, but his governing record—especially on taxes and immigration—belie his words. Huckabee still has a mathematical chance to win the nomination, but the probabilities are poor. While Romney and McCain both have excellent chances to win numerous additional primaries—that is not so for Huckabee. Huckabee has said so many things that will come back to haunt him, and he has flip-flopped on major positions during the campaign. This will cause Huckabee to slowly fade in the remaining primaries. Although there will certainly be some evangelicals who will not back a Mormon, I predict that most of them **will** because the evangelicals are mostly people of principle, who support the same principles that Romney advocates. For all the reasons I stated above, true conservatives will have a hard time supporting McCain. I predict that Romney will pick up most of the Huckabee supporters.

(b) **Thompson** was desperate to win in South Carolina, and he didn't. By finishing a distant third in a state that he believed to be the home of some of his most ardent supporters— this brought an end to the Thompson campaign.[3] He will continue to be respected for his loyal support of conservative principles, but he is not what the party is looking for in a candidate. His support will go elsewhere. I predict that most of his support will go to Romney, for the same reason that most of the Huckabee supporters will eventually back Romney—because he stands for the same principles that Thompson stands for.

(c) **Giuliani** has not had a good showing anywhere yet. He is counting heavily on doing well in Florida, where he, Romney and McCain are all polling at about 20-25%. Giuliani is literally desperate to win in Florida. If he does not win there, I believe he'll be out of

[2] On January 24th, the House passed the stimulus package on which it and President Bush had agreed. That measure now heads to the Senate, where quick approval is also expected.

[3] On January 22, 2008, Thompson announced that he was getting out of the race. He did not endorse any other candidate.

the running. Whereas Giuliani at one time had a lead in the national polls, McCain has now overtaken him. Both Giuliani and McCain draw support from the more moderate (liberal, if you will) parts of the Republican party. Both McCain and Giuliani are regarded as men with the leadership skills that would serve our nation well. But neither McCain nor Giuliani are regarded as strict conservatives. Giuliani is pro choice and supports gay marriage. Put all of this together, and what you get is: McCain is currently taking the support from those in the party that might otherwise support Giuliani. Thus, Giuliani is suffering most from McCain's resurgence, and it will lead to Giuliani's bowing out of the race after Super Tuesday.

The combination of all of this will be that Romney and McCain will be the only two Republican candidates left standing after Super Tuesday. The biggest question then becomes: Where will the Giuliani, Huckabee and Thompson supporters go? For the reasons stated below, I believe that most of this support will go to Romney.

II. THE PROBLEMS WITH McCAIN

The problem with McCain is very simple: He's not a conservative.[4] He is liberal on too many important issues. True, McCain has been strong on the war on terror, and this is important. But if he should win the Republican nomination, I, like his 95-year-old mother, would have to hold my nose in voting for him over the Democratic nominee. But at this point, I'm not ready to capitulate and support a Republican candidate whose political philosophy is too much like that of the liberals. McCain's political philosophy is more like that of Bill Clinton than that of a conservative; he listens to what the voters want, then he decides what position he will take. Either for this reason, or because he really does embrace liberal causes, too often on important issues McCain has sided with liberals, against conservatives. Here is a quick list of John McCain's serious political errors/flaws that make him unacceptable to me:

1. **Campaign Finance Reform**. McCain is one of the main proponents of this flawed law—the McCain-Feingold Campaign Finance Reform Bill.[5] This law imposed serious limitations on political speech in the name of seeking to keep "special interests" from having too much influence on national, political debate. The restrictions it imposes on precious political speech is significant; and the law gives increased influence and power to the media, which continues to be heavily slanted in favor of the liberal point of view. This is an assault on free speech. McCain's excessive zeal to curtail the speech of people who pay for advertising to advocate a political position is a serious error. His goal to keep money out of politics is naïve and unsound. McCain is the darling of the media, but his actions betray conservatism.

---

[4] McCain knows this is his weakness. So he has begun to run television ads in Florida with testimonials from some of his supporters that state that McCain is a conservative. While McCain will insist he is a "conservative," the problem is his well-known record, where he has consistently separated himself from the conservatives and sided with liberals.

[5] Because of the serious limitations that this has on free speech, I have previously addressed this issue in *CLU* three times: "Campaign Finance Reform Act—A Monument to the Ignorance of the American people and to the Phoniness of Congress," July, 2002; "The Campaign Finance Reform Case—An Ephemeral and Costly Decision" (*McConnell v. FEC*), May, 2004; and "*FEC v. Wisconsin Right to Life*," October, 2007.

McCain's excessive zeal for his ill-conceived campaign finance reform law led him to file a brief against the Wisconsin Right to Life group when that group challenged the constitutionality of the McCain-Feingold Campaign Finance Reform law. McCain didn't like the Right to Life group's issue ad that ran within 30 days of a general election in Wisconsin. Fortunately, the Supreme Court ruled in favor of the Right to Life in June of 2007 and struck down that part of the campaign reform law that prohibited issue ads just prior to a general election. This case is extremely important for two reasons. First it demonstrates that McCain's priorities are wrong; he sided with his campaign reform law over the fetal right to life. I disagree with his priorities. Second, his thinking is infected with the ill-founded and erroneous notion that you can take money out of political speech, and that doing so is a virtue. This thinking is naïve, and is a rejection of the most fundamental principles of freedom of political speech, which is the bedrock of all our freedoms in America. McCain's loses twice in this matter, and it demonstrates that he lacks the judgment to be our leader.

2. **Gang of 14**. McCain is one of those seven Republican Senators who undermined the effort of Republican Senate Leader Bill Frist, who was prepared to repeal that part of Senate Rule XXII (the filibuster rule) which empowered the minority in the Senate to block judicial nominations unless there existed a super majority (60%) in favor of a nominee. This Senate rule had come to be abused by the Democrats during administration of Bush (43); in essence, as practiced by the Democrats, they used this rule to control the approval of judicial nominees. This part of the rule—that is the use of filibustering to block nominees—should be eliminated. The filibuster can remain for legislation, as far as I'm concerned, but not for nominees. John McCain played a key role in preserving this abusive practice. He abandoned the Republican, conservative party when he exercised this power. This act of betrayal by McCain endeared him even more to the liberals. But it infuriates me. What kind of a leader is this? He's not my leader. He seems more concerned about appealing to the liberals than to fighting for the principles of conservative government.

3. **Immigration Reform.** McCain was one of the authors—along with Ted Kennedy—of the immigration bill that they and President Bush proposed in 2007—a bill that would have in essence granted amnesty to the 12 million illegal immigrants in America. This proposal was soundly rejected by the American people. This proposal was a repudiation of the rule of law in America, and it would have rewarded those who violated our laws; it would have been an insult to those people who have faithfully followed and complied with our immigration laws. While McCain demonstrated his flawed judgment in proposing this bill, he nevertheless did show that he is a disciple of the Bill Clinton school of leadership, for when he realized that the majority of Americans opposed the McCain-Kennedy Immigration Reform Bill, he eventually got in step with the majority. Well, that's partly good, because at least he has changed for the better. But, McCain demonstrated flawed judgment; he demonstrated the type of leadership we can expect from Democrats, but not the type of judgment and leadership that this nations needs. We can do better than settle for this in a candidate.

4. **He voted against the Bush Tax Cuts.** When McCain twice voted against Bush tax cuts he demonstrated that he does not subscribe to the economic theory that appropriate tax cuts stimulate the economy and actually lead to increased governmental revenues. McCain voted with a minority of Congress—he sided with the most liberal of the Democrats in opposing the tax cuts.[6] Fortunately for the nation, McCain's viewpoint was not successful. Those tax cuts

[6] McCain was one of only two to Republicans to vote against the tax cuts.

helped the national economy to recover from the brief recession that President Bush inherited from the Clinton administration, and those tax cuts helped keep the national economy strong despite the significant strains and demands of the war against terrorism. McCain's position on this is another reason why the nation does not need and should not want him at the helm. Once again, McCain fought against the principles of conservatism and sided with his liberal friends on the other side of the aisle.

5. **The Truth about McCain's "Truth" Campaign.** One of John McCain's chief political strategies is to promote himself as the "straight talk candidate," the candidate of truth, and at the same time to attack Mitt Romney as a liar and as a flip-flopper. In the first New Hampshire Debate, McCain attacked Romney for falsely labeling the McCain-Kennedy Immigration Reform Bill as an "amnesty" measure. He criticized Romney for running false attack ads to attempt to smear him. Well, so much for the truth; McCain himself had called the McCain-Kennedy bill a form of amnesty. Romney had correctly characterized McCain's position. McCain demonstrated that he is a great political counter-puncher, but to those who demand the truth—they will find McCain wanting in this quality. McCain's attacking Romney in New Hampshire does demonstrate McCain's intuitive ability to recognize the one candidate who will be his toughest competitor—Mitt Romney. But McCain's attempt to paint himself as the candidate of "truth" is actually an untruth. In Florida, McCain continues to accuse Romney of changing his positions with every new, changing wind. But McCain is himself the master flip-flopper. Most notably, he flipped on tax cuts, and he flopped on immigration. While he can aspire to be the candidate of truth, he has not earned the right to wear that title.

6. **Federal Marriage Amendment.** This amendment would mandate that marriage in the United States can only exist between a man and a woman. Senator McCain has opposed this amendment on the grounds that it violates the constitutional limits of federalism. This is usually an acceptable conservative response to legislation that tends to infringe on the rights of the states. However, because the federal government—through the courts—has already pre-empted the states in the regulation of all major aspects of marriage, the only way to recoup what has been lost by the states is to enact a constitutional amendment. This is perfectly in harmony with the Constitution; an amendment is needed to address this matter; and addressing the attack on the family by passage of a constitutional amendment is good, proper and necessary.[7] And to those who nevertheless cling to their conservative rationale and who refuse to acknowledge the critical nature of the threat to the family, I would point out that conservatism is not the only important principle of government. And in this particular case, the normal conservative approach that is sufficient to resolve most governmental questions must yield to the over-riding critical family value that is under assault in our society. Furthermore, the Courts have already pre-empted the regulation of marriage by its long string of cases that have usurped state regulation of marriage. By this I am referring to the following cases: *Griswold v. Connecticut* (1965), *Skinner v. Oklahoma* (1942), *Eisenstadt v. Baird* (1968), *Roe v. Wade* (1973), and *Lawrence v. Texas* (2003). Finally, I would note that Senator McCain does indeed find some protection in his citing "federalism" as a basis for not supporting the Federal Marriage Amendment. But what I see is that he is afraid to speak out on one of the most important issues of our day—he chooses to

---

[7] I previously addressed this issue in CLU, and explained the need for an amendment to correct the serious harm that court decisions have inflicted on the family. See "A Federal Marriage Amendment—Let the Debate Begin." May, 2004.

wait to see if a super majority of the nation ever becomes supportive of this amendment. When and if that happens, I have no doubt that he would fall in line, and then run to the front of the line. But that is not the leader I am looking for. Conversely, Governor Romney has spoken out strongly in support of this amendment and in support of other issues to protect and strengthen the traditional family as the foundation of peace, prosperity and liberty in America.

III. A DISCUSSION OF ROMNEY AND McCAIN ON OTHER ISSUES

The War on Terrorism, including Iraq and Afghanistan. All three Democratic candidates condemn every aspect of the war in Iraq; the three of them argue over who would lead the nation to retreat and withdraw the fastest. Except for Ron Paul, all the Republican contenders condemn the Democratic plan for announcing a retreat date, and for premature withdrawal without first securing victory. In January of 2007, Mitt Romney was beginning his campaign for the Republican presidential nomination. At that time, our military was suffering excessive deaths in Iraq, and President Bush was just announcing the beginning of the "surge." At that critical moment for the nation, I listened carefully to what Romney would say about what I regard as the most important issue of our day. Romney supported the surge 100%. He recognized that a premature withdrawal from Iraq would endanger the lives of millions of Iraqis who had relied on America to help them begin their new government. He recognized that a premature withdrawal from Iraq would be an invitation for the terrorists to take over that torn nation. He recognized that America could defeat the insurgents. He recognized that success in Iraq could bring a lasting stabilizing influence to that important region of the world. Six months later, when the evidence proved the "surge" to be successful, it was easy to support the continuing war effort in Iraq. But Romney stood up for the tough, but right approach when it was not popular to do so. This speaks very favorably for Mitt Romney.

McCain, of course, is also supportive of success in Iraq. He insists that America secure victory before leaving. He proudly reports that he was a vocal critic of the Bush administration's military strategy until it was changed (and the "surge" was announced) a little over a year ago. It seems that the economy has now replaced Iraq as the issue about which most people are concerned, but in my mind, the war on terror and the Iraq and Afghanistan military operations continue to be the most important issues for the nation. The billions of dollars that America has poured into this effort CAN bring the world important and lasting benefits. We cannot ignore the radical terrorism that brings death, destruction and fear to peaceful people around the world. The only issue of significance between Romney and McCain in this area is whether or not waterboarding is torture. There is no consensus among military experts that this is torture. McCain says it is and he denounces it, whereas Romney would not conclude that it was torture. Romney insisted that it was best for America not to spell out all of the details of what kinds of interrogation techniques the nation will and will not use. Despite McCain's vehement denunciation of waterboarding, Romney's position is better for the nation, and he did not back down in the face of McCain's condescending lecturing.

One final comment is in order following the Republican Presidential debate on MSNBC last night (January 24, 2008). In watching the debate, with many questions coming from Tim Russert, and in listening to Russert's comments after the debate—it is clear that Russert and the liberal media is attempting to resurrect the Iraq war as an issue to take down the Republican nominee when they get to the national election. Up until last night, the economy had become the most important campaign issue. But the problem for Democrats is that the Republicans, and

6

especially Romney, prevail on the debate of this issue. The Democrats are desperate to conjure a way to knock out the Republican nominee, whoever he might be. Thus, after the debate last night, Russert gleefully explained how he had painted all of the top Republican contenders in a corner, because they all supported going into Iraq, and they all supported leaving Iraq victorious. Russert could hardly contain himself as he chuckled that current polls show that six out of ten people today were opposed to initially going into Iraq and want to get out of Iraq immediately. What this means is that Iraq and the war on terror issues will continue to be important issues until the November election. Romney and McCain are on the same page on this issue.

Health Care. Health care is an important issue for most of the nation. Romney's approach makes sense and avoids drawing the federal government into the arena. Romney's plan keeps health care in the hands of private industry. Romney's plan is the perfect answer to the Democratic threat to put universal health care under the control of the government, where there is destined to be inefficiency, waste, increased health care costs, and increased taxes to cover all the newly created waste. Senator McCain has not made health care an important issue in his campaign.

No Child Left Behind. This is the one area where I believe Romney is mistaken in his support because I believe it best to leave education entirely in the hands of the states. I believe this to be the best approach, and it is certainly mandated by the Constitution. At least Romney is seeking to obtain more state control in the implementation of this program. McCain has not made education a key issue is his campaign.

Abortion—Pro Choice vs. Pro Life. Regardless of which nominees emerge from the two parties, this issue will be a clear point of difference between the two parties in November. But for now, on the Republican side, between Romney and McCain, both candidates are pro-life. Except for McCain's lapse in judgment in siding with campaign finance reform over life in the Wisconsin Right to Life case, McCain has been a long and consistent supporter of the right to life. Romney is a relatively recent convert to being a political supporter of the right to life. By that I mean that while he personally has been opposed to abortion, he nevertheless supported the right of the woman to choose. Romney admits he erred in this; he points out that he changed his position on this once he was elected Governor of Massachusetts, and that as governor he sided with the right to life in the official acts he took. Romney's recent conversion makes some conservatives suspect of how genuine his position now is. Romney points out that President Reagan had a similar conversion, and that he became a powerful advocate for protecting the unborn. I am satisfied that Romney's conversion is real.

The Economy. Mitt Romney has made economic growth a key part of his campaign, and he speaks on economic issues very effectively. Romney's experience in business for 25 years enables him to effectively present the conservative message on taxes, jobs, foreign trade and the myriad of other economic issues. No other candidate comes close to Romney in this important area, and Senator McCain is no exception. Huckabee tried to use Romney's experience in economic matters to disparage him, by asking, "Who would you rather have for President, the guy who works beside you, or the guy who laid you off?" But the truth is that America would rather have as president "the guy who can create jobs and who can make the economy stronger." That would be Mitt Romney.

If McCain were to win the Republican nomination, this would devastate the Republican Party because many of McCain's core principles are a repudiation of basic conservative values. While I might vote for him over the Democratic nominee, I would work with fellow conservatives to block him from undermining and changing the core principles of the party. McCain will never convince the conservative base to change their minds. The question is whether he can gain enough support of the more moderate Republicans. I believe that the majority of Republicans are of the same mindset as me in this regard. As a Republican, I have core principled beliefs that I embrace, and which guide me in my political actions and decisions. I will not repudiate my principles. I will exert all the influence I can to help the Party remain true to these principles. I believe that many, if not most Republicans are similarly committed to principles. This does not mean that the Party must be on the right side of every issue—for it is not. But McCain's position on multiple important issues is such a major departure from these principles that I cannot support him as a leader of conservativism. Thus, if he were to become President, I predict that it would cause great disruption and change in the Republican Party.

But this possible disruption need not occur. Mitt Romney's political philosophy is much more closely aligned with the party's conservative base, and would actually be an improvement from the philosophy of President George Bush. Republicans ask "What would Reagan do?" McCain comes up wanting when the question is put to him. Romney does much better.

IV. ROMNEY WILL WIN THE REPUBLICAN NOMINATION

Republicans tend to be people of principal—this is an advantage for Romney. Both men communicate well and have demonstrated good leadership abilities. Each man has personality qualities and deficits, but nothing of great significance, in my opinion. I think the Mormon factor will turn out to be a non-issue. I expect it will be virtually eliminated when some of the evangelical leaders speak up in support of Mitt. Finally, Mitt is younger, more energetic, better looking, and has an attractive family, and brings a noticeable record of business success—all of which will serve him well.

A final note should be made regarding the Republican debate last night on MSMBC. Romney was the clear winner last night. He was given more questions than any other candidate, and his responses were lucid, forceful and persuasive. He was very impressive. McCain did well, too, but Romney looked better. No one is better than Romney in quickly stating his position and then backing that position with facts and reasons. Romney is looking more and more polished. He presents himself as a practical man who understands and can fix the both "Washington" and the national economy. He looks very presidential.

I predict that the majority of Republicans will not be fooled by McCain's phony "Truth" campaign. I predict that the majority of Republicans will vote for their principles, and that they will reject the notion that they need to abandon their principles (and vote for McCain) in order to defeat the Democratic nominee. Thus, I predict that Romney will win the Republican nomination. And as long as we're making predictions, I predict that Romney will defeat the Democratic nominee (whether it's Clinton or Obama) in the November election. More about that later.

CLU 01/08

226

13.3.3

CONSTITUTIONAL

LAW

UPDATES

| VII:ii | March 2008 | No. 13 |

Re-defining "Family"—a way to destroy it

by C. Paul Smith

Those who seek to broaden the definition of "marriage" and "family" in order to secure for same-sex couples all the benefits that states confer on couples in a traditional marriages (between a man and a woman) are pursuing a course which will undermine marriage and which is geared to bring increased hardships and difficulties to children. Therefore, these efforts to redefine marriage should be defeated.

In October 2007, Maryland's highest court (the Court of Appeals) upheld a state law stating that marriage in Maryland can only be between a man and a woman. *Conaway v. Deane* (2007). (See the November 2007 issue of *CLU*.) This ruling is in line with that of virtually every other state in the nation, except Massachusetts, in holding (1) that limiting marriage to heterosexual couples DOES NOT violate the Equal Protection Clause of the Fourteenth Amendment of the Constitution; (2) that a rational basis exists for excluding same-sex couples from marriage; and (3) that there is no "fundamental right" under the Constitution to same-sex marriage.[1] However, while this battle is now over, the war continues. The next battle front issue in the gays' war to obtain special rights has moved to the Maryland State Legislature, where a handful of bills have been introduced that seek to have benefits conferred on gay couples through either establishing "civil unions" or "domestic partnerships," or through broadening the definition of marriage to include same-sex marriages. For states to pass such laws is certainly permissible, unless the Constitution should be amended to provide otherwise.[2] The key issue in this debate appears to be summed up by this line of thinking: **If we can pass a law extending to gay couples some of the benefits of "marriage" without hurting the institution of marriage, then I will do it.** I believe that the "If" clause in this statement is an impossibility, and that therefore the State should not broaden its definition of marriage to include same-sex unions.

There appear to be some undecided delegates on the Maryland House Judiciary Committee who are prepared to vote to preserve marriage, such that they would vote not to create "civil unions" nor "domestic partnerships" nor to broaden marriage to include same-sex couples **IF** they find evidence that extending marriage-like benefits to same-sex couples would have an adverse effect on families and children. But if they cannot find such a negative correlation, then they may vote to extend these additional rights to gay couples.

It is the purpose of this issue of *CLU* to articulate such an argument that can help this handful of legislators to see what the negative effects would be from extending these special rights to gay couples. There follows copies of two letters I submitted to the Judiciary Committee on February and March, which attempt to answer this important cause-effect inquiry. I offer them here because I believe they are helpful.

---

[1] This issue is now before the California Supreme Court, which challenges Proposition 22 (passed by the people of California in 2000, making marriage only between a man and a woman. The case arose from the actions by the City of San Francisco, that licensed approximately 4,000 gay marriages in 2004.

[2] A federal marriage amendment has been proposed that would establish a national standard. See *CLU*, May 2004.

CONSTITUTIONAL LAW UPDATES is a newsletter edited and published by C. Paul Smith, J.D.
To order copies ($5.00 per issue), write CLU, P.O. Box 1204, Frederick, MD 21702-0204.
For further information visit www.cpaulsmith.com. Copyright C. Paul Smith 2008.

C. PAUL SMITH

Attorney at Law
One Church Street, Suite 910
Rockville, Maryland 20850
(301) 762-0033
FAX NO.: (301) 762-0285

February 28, 2008

House Judiciary Committee
Maryland House of Delegates
Lowe Office Building
Annapolis, MD 21401

      Re: House Bill 1345
             Maryland's Marriage Protection Act

Dear Committee Members:

    I am a husband, a father and a grandfather. I reside in Frederick, Maryland, where I am currently one of the city's Aldermen. For over 35 years I have worked with youth as a parent, a baseball and basketball coach, a scoutmaster, the bishop of a church congregation, and in other capacities as well.

    I am writing in support of House Bill 1345, which would establish a state referendum in November for the voters to determine whether to amend the State Constitution to provide that in Maryland marriage is only between a man and a woman. This is not an anti-gay bill. It is a pro-child and pro-marriage bill. The bestowal of benefits on husbands and wives through Maryland marriage laws does not punish those who are not married. This bill is part of an important state policy to promote the traditional family as the preferred one for the bearing and rearing of children. I urge the passage of House Bill 1345.

    1. Resolving the issue by referendum. The provision in the bill to resolve this sensitive social issue by a state referendum is an excellent idea. The referendum approach to the issue is appropriate for an amendment to our Constitution on a matter of such great importance.

    2. Defining marriage as only between a man and a woman will strengthen families. Although the bill only calls for a referendum on the issue, its purpose is to achieve an amendment to our Constitution that does limit marriage to a relationship only between a man and a woman. For the reasons stated below, I believe that this would be a desirable improvement in our Constitution.

    First, although our state law (Section 2-201 of the Family Law Article of the Code of Maryland) currently provides that marriage is only between a man and a woman, by making this same provision a part of the Constitution would make the restriction stronger, and would be a protection to and promotion of marriage and of strong families.

CLU 03/08

House Judiciary Committee
Page Two
February 28, 2008

Second, the amendment would be a strong public policy statement that Maryland promotes and encourages traditional marriage as the best relationship for the bearing and rearing of children in the state. This is a policy that affects the vast majority of the people in the state. It is a policy that has been a part of Maryland law for over 200 years—a policy that discourages people from having sexual relations outside of marriage, and encourages couples to commit to love and care for one another in a legal (and often at the same time a religious) ceremony before beginning sexual relations with a partner. This is a good and wise standard. It is a policy that bestows certain legal benefits upon the married partners. All of this promotes marriage as the fundamental unit of society for the rearing of children, and to provide for the health, support, safety and well-being of people in the state. During the last 50 years, the increased incidences of drug use, alcoholism, crime, welfare needs, and various health problems can all be tied to the weakening of the family and a decrease in the number of families having both a father and a mother in the home. The proposed bill is a simple step that reinforces the important policy that our forefathers recognized when they first enacted marriage laws.

Third, scientific studies show that the traditional marriage relationship is best for the rearing of children. Most people believe that this is true, but many are not aware of the scientific studies that support this cause-effect relationship. Attached is a four-page article that I recently prepared and published in *Constitutional Law Updates*, October, 2007, which gives some of the primary studies that support this conclusion. I am aware that you will be (or may already have been) provided with materials that seem to contradict this. But if you wish to become fully informed about the scientific studies on this issue, then you should consider the books and studies referenced in the attachment. An honest scientific review of this issue will demonstrate that the superiority of traditional marriage for rearing children is borne out conclusively by the studies.

Fourth, a state has the right to prefer and promote one type of relationship for the bearing and raising of children in the state. As the Court of Appeals recently held in *Conaway v. Deane* (2007), as long as there is a rational basis for the state to promote traditional marriage, it may properly do so. The Court went on to find that such a basis does exist.[3] There will always be some families without both a father and a mother. But the existence of such situations does not diminish the need and the importance of establishing a state policy that promotes traditional marriage as the best and preferred relationship for the rearing of children. State laws set state policies. And House Bill 1345 would help set the policy that this state wishes to encourage traditional families, with both a mother and a father, for the rearing of children.

---

[3] It is of interest to note that in addressing the various arguments raised against the Maryland marriage law, the Court of Appeals found it significant that scientific evidence has not established what some have asserted—that homosexuality is innate. In fact, scientific studies refute this assertion. See, e.g., footnote 31 in the attachment.

House Judiciary Committee
Page Three
February 28, 2008

Fifth, that part of the bill that would not recognize civil unions and domestic partnerships is an important and desirable part of this bill because the giving of these relationships the same legal benefits as marriage would ultimately undermine the state policy to promote and prefer traditional marriage. This part of the bill does discriminate between the preferred, traditional marriage relationship and other relationships. But this differentiation is necessary in order for the state to have a policy that promotes the best interests of the children as a whole. Not only is there a rational basis for this disparate treatment, but the overwhelming evidence from scientific studies supports the state's having a policy that encourages traditional marriage as the best relationship for raising children in the state. This preference is not a punitive act against other relationships, rather it is an essential part of having a policy that prefers one relationship over others. The proposals before the Legislature to recognize civil unions and domestic partnerships are merely back-door attempts to eliminate the preference that Maryland law has long given to traditional marriage. The proposals to recognize civil unions and domestic partnerships are back-door attempts to redefine marriage. The effect of recognizing civil unions and/or domestic partnerships would be to repudiate traditional marriage as the best and preferred relationship. State law cannot be all things to all people; either it must make traditional marriage the preferred family relationship or not. If the State were to establish a preference for traditional marriage **and** to recognize civil unions and domestic partnership, then the State would be taking inconsistent positions. If the State chooses to continue to prefer and promote traditional marriage over other relationships, then it may do so, and it should do so. But the State cannot do both, for the bestowal of special legal rights on other relationships undermines the state effort to establish a policy and preference for traditional marriage as the best relationship for the bearing and rearing of children.

Thank you for your consideration of my comments.

Very truly yours,

C. Paul Smith

Encl.

C. PAUL SMITH

Attorney at Law
One Church Street, Suite 910
Rockville, Maryland 20850
(301) 762-0033
Fax No.: (301) 762-0285
March 4, 2008

Chairman Joseph Vallario and
House Judiciary Committee, Room 101
Lowe House Office Building
Annapolis, MD 21401

     Re: House Bill 1345 and related "marriage" bills

Dear Chairman Vallario and Members:

    I am submitting this to supplement the letter (with summary) and the oral comments I made to your committee on February 28th. These comments are to address this issue:

If the Legislature passes measures to recognize gay partnerships as "civil unions," "domestic partnerships" or "marriages" will this adversely impact traditional marriage?

For the reasons given below, the answer to this question is YES!

    If the State were to recognize gay partnerships as either "civil unions," "domestic partnerships," or "marriages," this would significantly undermine the State policy to promote traditional marriage as the preferred relationship for the bearing and rearing of children. The traditional policy would be undermined because the State would effectively be saying that there is no preferred relationship for the bearing and rearing of children.

    The purpose of having a state policy to promote traditional marriage is to set up a legal system and laws to encourage child-bearing to occur within the bonds of marriage between a man and a woman. The purpose of such a state policy is also to discourage the birth of children outside the bonds of marriage. If the State were to bestow the same benefits of marriage on any and all couples who have guardianship of a child, this will effectively repeal the state policy to promote marriage. There is no way around this. (See attached, one-page of excerpts from the Brief of James Q. Wilson, et al.)

    It may be tempting to approach this from the point of view of a particular child or children. Under this approach, if the Legislature were to say: We will bestow on whatever partners who have children the same benefits of a married couple, this would eliminate any incentive to be married before having children. At first glance, this approach would appear to give the same legal benefits to every child. But that is not what will happen. This approach would discourage marriage and would discourage advance planning for children; it would promote after-the-fact, after-birth planning for children, and would not encourage any type of parental relationship as the more desirable one for children. The predictable effect would be that there would be more and more children that would be raised in relationships that are shown to be less advantageous for children than that of a married husband and wife.

Thus, if the Legislature, out of a desire to help the few children being raised by gay parents, passes a law that recognizes gay marriages, then the Legislature will put in motion the measures that will cause many times more children to be adversely affected because they are denied the opportunity to be raised by their own mothers and fathers.

Even if the State were to somehow confer on gay partnerships all the legal benefits of a marriage, this will not guarantee that it would eliminate the ostracism of children. Even if a gay partnership were given the title "marriage," it would still, obviously be a "gay marriage." There will be no hiding of the fact that John has two "moms" or two "dads." Much of society still regard gay relationships as morally wrong. This societal attitude will not be changed by legislative fiat. The Legislature cannot pass a law that will make people think that gay relationships are either right or wrong. Thus, if the Legislature were to confer the benefits of "marriage" on gay partnerships, then these results would follow: (1) the partners would get additional rights and benefits; but (2) the children of such partnerships would continue to get the adverse fallout from the partners' relationship.

Studies show that children raised by gay partners have significantly higher risks of problems—including physical health, emotional and mental problems, and substance abuse. (The summary I previously submitted gives the reference to such studies.) Conversely, children raised by a father and a mother tend to be healthier, wealthier and happier. It's not enough to raise a child to read well, to do mathematics well, and to perform well academically. Children also need to learn how to live as heterosexuals; they need to learn how to relate to men and to women; they need to learn how to be a good father or a good mother; they need to learn the differences and complementary qualities of the two sexes.

One of the arguments made for the recognition of gay marriage is the request of the gay couples to obtain for themselves the same rights as married couples. This argument is typically couched in terms of correcting their denial of Equal Rights. This argument was one of the principal arguments addressed by the Court of Appeals recently in *Conaway v. Deane*. The Court dismissed this argument as a misinterpretation of the application and meaning of Equal Rights under the Constitution. Nevertheless, the State **can** bestow such rights if it so chooses. But for those who urge the passage of laws to recognize gay marriage in order to secure for themselves legal benefits for their intimate relationships—I suggest that this should not be the focal point of concern. The most important issue is "What is best for the children?" That is the issue that should be controlling, not the question of what special rights to bestow on partners. The best interests of children and society were the bases for establishing state control of marriage in the first place. And that should continue to be the point of focus.

The increases in divorces, out-of-wedlock births, and single-parent households during the last 40 years certainly indicate that marriage and the family are being marginalized in our society. But it does not follow that the State should therefore abandon and scrap marriage. On the contrary, these increased problems have been caused by a departure from mother **and** father parenting; and the negative trend could be reversed by a return to traditional mother **and** father parenting. It would not be best for children to abandon the state policy to encourage traditional marriage; it would be better for the state to reaffirm its commitment to traditional marriage as best for the children and for the State.

Sweden, Norway and Denmark have had something close to same-sex marriage for over ten years, and according to one analyst, this has undermined the institution of marriage. (See, Stanley

Kurtz, "The End of Marriage in Scandinavia; the conservative case for same-sex marriage collapses." *The Weekly Standard.* Feb. 2, 2004, Vol. 9, Issue 20.) Kurtz reported that the out-of-wedlock birth rates have jumped from 39% to 50% in Norway and from 47% to 55% in Sweden. In Denmark the rate dropped slightly, from 46% to 45%, but "about 60% of first born children in Denmark now have unmarried parents (Kurtz, p. 2). (I am sending a copy of this article to Chairman Vallario.)

Those gay couples who seek to legalize same-sex marriage have often sought to use the children to make the case that the State should recognize same-sex marriage. The sympathetic appeal of this argument cannot be denied. Especially, when the gay couples send the children over whom they have guardianship before this Committee to tell of the ostracism they feel because their "parents" aren't married. The plight of these children is indeed heart-wrenching. But their "parents" knowingly and with planning and calculation brought the children into their gay relationships. I have great concerns for these children. But to pass laws that will encourage more children to be raised by gay parents will not help the situation; rather it will most likely cause more children to have problems.

Without fail, the gay couples take the implicit (and sometimes explicit) position that they were born that way or that they cannot change. It seems to be politically correct to embrace this point of view, but the science does not support this position. There is no scientific evidence that homosexuality is innate; there is abundant evidence that homosexuality is affected by environment, conduct and choices; and there is undeniable evidence that some homosexuals have changed. I recognize that what I said irritates and angers many gays. But I would suggest that it would be best for the Legislature to pay closer attention to the legitimate scientific studies on the issue, rather than to be manipulated by the anecdotal testimony that is given and repeated almost every time these issues come before the Legislature.

If the Legislature heeds the siren cries of those who approach this marriage debate as an Equal Rights issue, then the Legislature is likely to make the serious mistake of undermining and destroying marriage. Maryland public policy has promoted and preferred marriage for over two hundred years.

In conclusion, if the State were to recognize gay partnerships as either "civil unions," "domestic partnerships," or "marriages," then the State would be repudiating the policy and preference it has embraced for over two hundred years that it is best for children to be raised by their two parents—the mother and the father. The State cannot both give gay partnerships the benefits of marriage and at the same time continue to promote traditional marriage as the best social unit for the rearing of children. For the reasons stated above, it would be best for the State to strengthen its endorsement of traditional marriage by amending the State Constitution to provide that marriage in this state is only between a man and a woman.

Respectfully submitted,

C. Paul Smith

Encl.

This letter was reformatted to be three pages in length, instead of the four-page letter sent to Chairman Vallario.

Excerpts from Brief of James Q. Wilson, et al., on the value of traditional marriage for society—

The philosophical and legal bases for a state to pass laws to promote traditional marriage (between a man and a woman) as the preferred social unit for the bearing and rearing of children are stated succinctly in one of the *Amici Curiae* briefs that was filed in the case of *Conaway v. Deane*:

> Marriage has a unique and indispensable social purpose: creating families in which children will be known and loved by their own mother and father. . . .
> Virtually every know human society has recognized the need for a public institution to regulate the procreative consequences of sexual attraction between men and women, both because reproduction is a necessary task, and because the alternative to some form of successful social regulation is fatherless children who suffer serious harms themselves and pose substantial burdens and dangers to society.
> The scientific evidence strongly suggests the prime way marriage benefits children is not by bestowing a set of legal benefits (transferable to other family forms) but by increasing the likelihood that children will be born to and raised by their own mother and father. The vast majority of children born to a married couple begin life with their own mother and father committed to jointly caring for them. Only a minority of children in other kinds of sexual unions do so. Marriage serves many individual needs, but this is its most unique and irreplaceable *social* function: encouraging men and women to procreate responsibly. As a matter of historical record, marriage is not rooted in animus towards gay[s] and lesbians, but is a classification that responds to real and enduring human realities: only opposite-sex unions can both create the next generation and connect those children to the mother and father who made them.
> [W]hen the connection between marriage and procreation weakens, many children suffer, and so do the communities faced with **higher rates of poverty, crime, juvenile delinquency, welfare dependency, child abuse, unwed teen motherhood, infant mortality, mental illness, high school dropouts and other education failures.** [Emphasis added.]
> Same-sex marriage would strip from the law of Maryland the one feature of marriage that has been virtually universal throughout human history. It [would] put[] law and government in the position of educating the next generation that: (1) Any two committed adults are just as good as a mother and father, when it comes to raising kids; and/or (2) Marriage has little or nothing to do with children; it is primarily about adult needs for intimacy. Such a dramatic shift in the legal meaning of marriage is likely to have real social consequences.

(Brief Amici Curiae of James Q. Wilson, et al., Legal and Family Scholars, in Support of Defendants-Appellants, pp. 2-3. *Frank Conaway, et al., v. Gitanjali Deane*, et al, in the Court of Appeals of Maryland, September Term, 2006, Case No. 44.) The studies that provide the support for these conclusions in contained in the 50-page brief, a copy of which is being furnished to Chairman Vallario.

234

3.1

CONSTITUTIONAL LAW UPDATES

| VII:iii | September 2008 | No. 14 |

2008 Presidential Campaign Heats Up
John McCain (R) vs. Barack Obama (D)

by C. Paul Smith

The 2008 presidential campaign is already a year old, and we are less than 90 days from Election Day (November 4, 2008). Regardless of the outcome, this election has already proved itself to be one of the most interesting and intense of any in recent history. A year ago, we were already anticipating the election of **the first woman president**; the big issues seemed to be who would Hillary select as her VP, and what would Bill be doing in the White House. But, a year later, the Democrat Party has rejected Hillary and embraced Barack Obama, who may become **the first black president**. And things were just as tumultuous on the Republican side, where a year ago former New York Mayor Rudy Giuliani was the front runner to obtain the nomination. John McCain had dropped out of sight in the polls, and former Massachusetts Governor Mitt Romney (who hoped to become **the first Mormon president**) was emerging from the crowd of candidates, making a concerted effort to apply his business skills to win the nomination. But in a matter of months, Giuliani faded into oblivion; Romney quickly took a lead in the early primaries; former Arkansas Governor Huckabee came from nowhere to play a prominent role in the primaries; but John McCain raised himself from the dead, won a couple of primaries, and then in February, he staged impressive wins in several states that catapulted him to a lead that he never relinquished.

The one "first" that is still up for grabs is whether Obama will be the first black president. This certainly looks possible. However, for my part, electing Obama would be a mistake. Race and color and religion have nothing to do with my views—my positions are issue-oriented, and here they are:

FOREIGN AFFAIRS—McCain, who proudly proclaims himself to be a foot soldier under President Reagan, will employ an approach to foreign relations that will mirror that of President Reagan—Peace through Strength. McCain's personal courage and bravery is legendary. The Democrat Party's nominee doesn't bring either the personal resume nor the principled philosophy to qualify him to lead the nation in international dealings. Merely proclaiming peace and decrying war is not an adequate foreign policy, and it does not appear that Senator Obama has learned the lessons from world history, that evil will not just magically disappear through the appeasement approach. Those who understand world history recognize that during World War II millions of people were innocently killed by the Nazis and the Communists, and that America played a key role in liberating the world from those evil powers. Over 400,000 Americans gave their lives in World War II to suppress the evil powers and to liberate millions of people. Failing to appreciate this, the Democrat candidate echoes the naïve pacifist approach of Neville Chamberlain in the late 1930's, who sought to avoid confrontation in the guise of championing peace. That flawed approach was a failure then, just as it would be today in dealing with terrorists and insurgents. He will return the nation to the touchy-feely international relations policies of Clinton, thinking that talks and negotiations can solve any and every international crisis, all the while alerting terrorists that open season is here again.

The **WAR** in Iraq and Afghanistan—McCain insists that we must not leave Iraq prematurely, for this would invite a blood-bath of thousands of innocent people who had been friendly to us, but who would be left to suffer abuse, torture and death at the hands of evil terrorists. The "surge" has worked, and is enabling us to withdraw from Iraq successfully, leaving a new government that appears capable of maintaining an acceptable level of peace and stability in Iraq. This is a tremendous accomplishment! It could be a tremendous benefit to that region and to the entire world. Now that the surge has proved successful, most Democrats (including Senator Obama) have become resigned to victory in Iraq. But "during the times that tr[ied] men's souls," Obama showed himself to be a "sunshine soldier" whose resolve wilted under pressure.[1] Obama's position on the War has mirrored the changing popularity of the conflict. When the war was unpopular, Obama insisted that we set immediate time-tables and get out immediately. When the going got tough in Iraq, Obama led the call for retreat.

The contrast between McCain and Obama could not be more stark. McCain refused to give in to the demands of Obama and his followers, who urged precipitous retreat when we were on the verge of securing victory. McCain called for the surge, because he saw that it could obtain victory for us and stability and peace for the Iraqis. The U.S. did not go to Iraq for oil or to nation-build; we went there with 70 % national approval to eradicate an evil dictator who fomented and sponsored terrorism in Iraq and abroad; Hussein offered monetary awards to families who would sponsor suicide bombers to kill Israelis. He harbored those who sought to destroy America. And once Sadaam Hussein was taken out, we owed a moral duty to help the Iraqis form an operable government that could protect its people. In retrospect, it appears that many Americans now regret our intervention in Iraq, but a majority continue to recognize our moral responsibility to leave Iraq better than we found it. That is why the premature withdrawal option would have been a mistake.

Senator Obama has begun to flip-flop on multiple issues recently, now that he sees the need to move from the left to the center. Now he's trying to distance himself from himself when he was the spokesman for withdrawal and defeat in Iraq. Obama does not possess the courage and resolve of McCain, who has and will steadfastly stand up against the evil terrorists, regardless of the fickle and politically correct cat calls of those who can't stomach the cost of liberty and who lack the backbone to take a brave stand for the defense of our own nation and for the liberty and freedom of our brothers and sisters around the world. McCain has the backbone to do this, whereas Obama repeatedly shows that he does not.

The **ECONOMY**—McCain seeks to cut taxes and to cut government spending. Obama promises to raise taxes and to add multiple new government programs at a cost of billions.

---

[1] These phrases are taken from Thomas Paine's pamphlet *Common Sense*, that encouraged the patriots during the Revolutionary War.

2

Apparently there is no limit to the size of government that Obama seeks to build. Obama has the most liberal voting record of any U. S. Senator.

It's not that Senator Obama opposes having a strong economy—it's just that his commitment to left-wing special interests put him on a course that would severely damage the economy. Specifically, he wants universal health care, he wants to stop global warming, and he wants to stop drilling for new oil in America. His radical loyalty to the left-wing fanatics on these issues would lead the nation into full blown socialism and would hamper and destroy the businesses that have been the foundation of our economy—the strongest economy in the world. Senator Obama does not recognize how the environmental special interest groups have already weakened our economy based upon biased science and hysterical threats that the sky is falling. For example, the cost to build roads has skyrocketed because of the environmental impact studies and ever-expanding procedures that have multiplied since the Interstate Highway System was initiated in the 1950's. This lunacy has got to stop, and adjustments must be made in our laws—some must be repealed. But Barack Obama will not be the one to do this—he supports increased environmental laws, increased bureaucracy, increased red-tape, and of course, increased taxes to pay for the bigger bureaucracy.

The increased governmental programs Obama is calling for amount to socialism. Obama feels everyone's pains, and he intends to expand government to solve all problems. But this undisciplined approach to government leads to excessive government, which can survive only by increasing taxes. This approach must stop! We cannot continue to act like government has to solve all our problems. Obama does not recognize this, whereas McCain does. McCain is clearly the better choice on economic issues.

SOCIAL ISSUES—Senator McCain supports traditional marriage as the preferred unit in society for the rearing of children, and he is pro life. But Senator Obama does not stand up for traditional marriage, and he champions a woman's right to choose death for her unborn child. It is critical that the presidential candidates take a stand on these most important social issue—Will you support the continuation of the traditional family as the bedrock of our society, OR will you support the causes of those who will destroy marriage by redefining it to be available to any and every adult relationship that one can conceive (pardon the double entendre). And as for abortion—anyone who supports partial birth abortion is either ignorant of what it is or else his judgment is so fundamentally impaired that he must not be elected to lead a civilized nation. Partial-birth abortion kills the unborn baby in a painful, gruesome manner for no valid purpose. The theory that such a procedure is justified to preserve the life and health of the woman is a fiction. And it was Barack Obama who, in the Illinois State Senate, blocked legislation that would require the participating parties to attempt to save the lives of children who were born alive after abortions. This was a barbaric and disgraceful position—and demonstrates a total disregard for those humans who are least capable of defending themselves.

PERSONAL LIBERTIES—John McCain fights to preserve the right to bear arms. Obama sided with the minority in *D. C. v. Heller*. Obama does not believe that the right to bear arms is an individual right. McCain believes it is.

McCain fights to preserve the nation's heritage of being a God-fearing nation. And while the Democrat Party gives lip service to love of God, they are the party that interprets the First Amendment to require "freedom from religion," as they regularly champion the causes of those groups whose stated goal is to eliminate God from government. Conversely, the Republican Party recognizes that government can and should accommodate God and religion because they are vital components of a good society. The First Amendment's prohibition from the establishment of any one religion does not mean that all references to God must be excised from government.

Except for his lapse in judgment in sponsoring the Bipartisan Campaign Finance Reform Act, McCain is an advocate for freedom of speech.[2] But while McCain has been shaky on this issue, Obama's position is no better.

THE SUPREME COURT. Finally, one of the most important issues in this presidential campaign is what direction each candidate would take the Supreme Court. We must expect there to be 1 – 3 vacancies in the Supreme Court in the next four years. Right now the Court is pretty much evenly divided between four strong conservatives Justices (Scalia, Thomas, Roberts (Chief Justice) and Alito), and four strong liberal Justices (Stevens, Souter, Ginsburg and Breyer). The ninth Justice, Kennedy, is mostly conservative, but he is clearly the swing vote in many close cases. As this issue of *Constitutional Law Updates* will demonstrate, the next appointments will indicate whether the Court turns either to the left or to the right. John McCain and Barack Obama are clearly on opposite sides of this issue. Obama will take us to the left—towards bigger government and more socialism and fewer individual rights; and McCain will take us more to the right—limiting the size of government, cutting government expenses, and standing up against those who seek to expand the right to abort the unborn. I have hope that McCain will stand firm for traditional family values, that he will recognize the need to protect our borders, and that he will back off from his mistake in championing campaign finance reform (at the expense of jeopardizing free speech rights). But I have no hope with Obama on these issues; so once again, McCain is clearly the better choice.

CAN OBAMA PULL IT OFF?. Up to this point, Obama has been the Houdini of politics. He has magically, masterfully proclaimed that we need to change Washington, and that he's the man to do it. His followers have hypnotically nodded and given their support—although he has escaped being pinned down to state exactly what it is that he intends to change. Now that he has won the Democrat nomination, he has had some time to figure out some specific changes that will go into his platform. Until now, most of his supporters have not really cared much about most of his positions—he won the nomination based upon his charisma and his style, not based upon the substance of his positions. Whether Obama can continue to pull-off this political magic show through November 4th, remains to be seen. As for me, I see his recent move toward the center to be merely a political expediency, which I suspect he will abandon upon election. In predicting what Obama really stands for, one must go on his previous voting record (albeit a short record). Obama will increase the size of government, raise taxes, encourage abortion and same-sex marriage. He will heap increased burdens on our economy in a mindless fanaticism to stop global warming.

I do not know whether this nation will awaken from the hypnotic sleep that has hoisted Obama to front-runner status in the presidential race. And while I differ deeply with John McCain on several issues, there are more than enough issues on which McCain is in the right, and on which Obama is wrong. Therefore my support is unequivocally for McCain.

---

[2] Perhaps Senator McCain sees the light now, since *The New York Times* refused a few weeks ago to print his response to an editorial by Senator Obama. McCain must recognize that the mainstream news media, especially The New York Times, has a blatant liberal bias. And as liberal as he may be at times, Senator McCain is far right of where Senator Obama is. This is why the Campaign Finance Reform law was so bad—it empowered the liberal media to have increased power and influence in the days just prior to elections, at the same time it blocked others from speaking up on current issues.

Supreme Court Holds the Right to Bear Arms Is an Individual Right

District of Columbia v. Heller, 554 U.S. _____ (2008)

by C. Paul Smith

On June 26, 2008, the Supreme Court issued its ruling in the case of *District of Columbia v. Heller*, 554 U. S. _____ (2008), holding unconstitutional the District of Columbia law which prohibited the possession of usable handguns in the home. In this 5-4 ruling, the Court held that the right to bear arms in the Second Amendment was an individual right, and not merely the right of a governmental militia.

The question of whether the right to bear arms belonged *to the individual* or *to the militia* has been a subject of debate for decades. The only question was which side the Supreme Court would take on the issue. In my opinion, the Supreme Court got it right. But I am concerned and disturbed that vote was so close (5-4). With the Supreme Court's recent penchant to ignore the principles of *stare decisis*. I personally have concerns about the permanency of this ruling. Nevertheless, as it now stands, this is a good and important ruling.

D.C. law made it a crime to carry an unregistered firearm, and the registration of handguns was prohibited.[1] Dick Heller sued to enjoin the District of Columbia from enforcing this law, contending that the law violated the Second Amendment of the Constitution. That amendment reads: "A well regulated Militia, being necessary to the security of a free State, the right of the people to keep and bear Arms, shall not be infringed."

[1] See D. C. Code Sec. 7-2501.01(12), 7-2502.01(a), and 7-2502.02(a)(4) (2001). Another section of the D.C. Code provides that no person may carry a handgun without a license, and that the chief of police may issue licenses for one-year periods. D. C. Code Sec. 22-4504(a) and 22-4506. Finally, the D. C. Code requires that any firearms located in a home be "unloaded and disassembled or bound by a trigger lock or similar device. D. C. Code Sec. 7-2507.02. (These references are taken from page 1 of the Court's majority opinion.)

If the Amendment means what it says, then there should be no question that the right spoken of, the right to bear arms, belongs to the "people," and not to the "militia." However, this plain reading of the Amendment was challenged by the District of Columbia and by four of the Justices (Stevens, Souter, Ginsberg and Breyer). They argued (1) that the prefatory clause changed the meaning of the operative clause in the Amendment, and (2) that the handgun ban was a reasonable limitation on the right to bear arms that did not violate the general spirit of the Amendment. But the majority rejected both of these assertions.

I. The Majority Opinion

Justice Scalia, who wrote for the majority, pointed out that a prefatory clause (such as "A well regulated Militia, being necessary to the security of a free State") does not normally modify the operative clause that follows ("the right of the people to keep and bear Arms, shall not be infringed")—but rather gives **one** reason as to why the operative clause may be necessary. Justice Scalia said that the normal reading of the two clauses was appropriate here. In fact, he pointed out, the operative clause specifically states that the right belongs to the "people." The right, therefore, is an individual right of the people.

Justice Scalia further pointed out that the very nature of the militia in the early days of our nation, was that it was comprised of individuals in the community who bore arms. It would have been illogical and contradictory for the Amendment to state that the people did not individually possess the right to bear arms. Additionally, he pointed out that if the intent of the amendment was to limit its meaning to only be a right if the militia should need a person's participation, then there would have been no purpose for the operative clause. Justice Scalia points out that historically the amendment was widely understood to recognize an "individual" right, and he found no evidence to the contrary. Finally, Justice Scalia pointed out that the Second Amendment did not create a right, but rather only recognized a right that already existed, and prohibited the government from infringing upon it.[2]

In concluding his opinion, Justice Scalia wrote these words: "[W]e hold that the District's ban on handgun possession in the home violates the Second Amendment, as does its prohibition against rendering any lawful firearm in the home operable for the purpose of immediate self-defense" (p. 64).

Reading Justice Scalia's majority opinion was somewhat fascinating, because he painstakingly dissected every word and phrase in the short, Second Amendment to show that his interpretation was correct. It is interesting to see how the Court's three opinions took 154 pages to dissect and analyze the 27-word, one-sentence amendment. And it is disconcerting to see how so many points in Justice Scalia's opinion were disputed and contested by the two dissenting opinions. The dissenters impressed me as being strained and illogical and as denying important historical facts pertaining to the original purpose and meaning of the right to bear arms, as memorialized in the Second Amendment.

It is my judgment that the *Heller* case will be one of the most important cases in this nation for the next twenty years. I think it will be important to have some in-depth understanding of the case. I will now provide some analysis of and commentary on the dissenting opinions.

II. The Dissenting Opinions

A. Justice Stevens' Dissent. To start with, consider what the four Liberal Justices stated as their fundamental opinion. They said this: "Specifically, there is no indication that the Framers of the Amendment intended to enshrine the common-law right of self-defense in the Constitution" (p. 2). It is chilling to me to think that four of the current Justices of the Supreme Court hold this opinion.

The heart of *Heller* is *whether the right to bear arms is an individual right OR whether it is merely a privilege to participate in a militia at*

the pleasure of the state. The Court (the majority) held it to be an individual right. After all, the Second Amendment says it is a "right." But the dissenters said that the Amendment does not mean that. The two dissents (by Justices Stevens and Breyer) go on to employ their considerable intellectual and legal skills to argue that the Second Amendment does not mean what it says. They say that because the "right to bear arms" is connected to the need for a militia, that therefore this cannot be an individual right. (Justice Stevens says it is a "right" and a "duty" [p. 16].) But the end result of Justice Stevens' opinion is that absent a militia there really is no "right." This leaves nothing but an obsolete "duty" in the Second Amendment. The dissenting Justices never do answer the question of why our Founders called it a "right" if it really isn't a "right." Somehow they confuse "duty" with "right"—that is they say that the Second Amendment says that because militias are so important, therefore citizens can have certain arms, but *only for use in the militia.* This is a ridiculous interpretation. That's not what the Founders meant, and that is not what the Founders wrote. Even if militias are obsolete, the Amendment continues to have a meaning in that if individuals should not have operable arms for their self defense, then it would be impossible to have militias.

Justice Stevens at one point did acknowledge the point that the Second Amendment did not create the right to bear arms (Stevens, J., Dissent, pp. 17 & 38), but he did not seem to appreciate what he acknowledged. Let me briefly explain what Justice Stevens seemed to miss: The technical wording of the Second Amendment does not create any right, but rather it states that the government shall not "infringe" on "the right of the people to keep and bear arms."

If you know much about James Madison (who drafted the Second Amendment), you know that he felt there was no need for a bill of rights because these rights already existed, and that there was no need to make a partial list of existing rights. In fact, he felt this could have undesirable consequences, if the partial listing of rights were used to later deny that some rights did not exist because they were not enumerated. (The Ninth Amendment was included to avoid this problem.) But, returning to the Second Amendment, Madison's language again does not create any

---

[2] It should be noted that in 1791 handguns were rare, and that the guns that were prevalent required a timely insertion of gun powder before they could be fired. Today's handgun was not common place in that era.

new right, but rather only restricts the government from infringing upon an existing right.

Well, having said this, what if the minority was right, and the Second Amendment only pertains to bearing arms as may be needed in the militia. If so, then, there is yet an individual right to bear arms that is not referenced in the Second Amendment. The Court never really discusses this issue because (a) the Liberal Justices don't want to consider those implications; and (b) the majority interpret the Second Amendment to cover the right of individuals to defend themselves with guns, and therefore there was no need to go there.

1. "A Well Regulated Militia . . . ." Justice Stevens spends virtually all of his dissenting opinion to attempt to prove that whatever "right" is mentioned in the Second Amendment is entirely contingent upon and subject to the government's use of militias. Justice Stevens made numerous strained arguments in his effort. Here are a few of them.

a. He argues that "bear arms" has reference only to using arms in the military (pp. 11 & 14). However, even some of the citations he includes in his opinion refute this unreasonable interpretation.

b. He says that because the Amendment did not include the words "a personal right to use arms in self defense" that therefore the Amendment could not have included such a meaning. This is a ridiculous argument. This is precisely the type of reasoning that James Madison was concerned about—that some would deny the existence of rights because a right may not have been specifically articulated. And while we're on the issue—the failure to mention something does not mean that that thing does not exist. Yet that is the very argument that Justice Stevens makes. To have added the words "for self defense" would have been superfluous. The wording that was used plainly implies the use of arms for self-defense—otherwise the references to participation in militia actions would have made no sense.

c. Justice Stevens argues that the words "the people" could not possibly mean in the Second Amendment what it means in First and Fourth Amendments. He asserts that in the First and Fourth Amendments the people means all people, but that "the people" referenced in the Second Amendment is subject to considerable

limitation. (For example felons and insane people can be barred from possessing arms.) Therefore, Justice Stevens makes the argument that the Second Amendment could not possibly confer a right on all "the people." Frankly, this is pathetic reasoning.

2. Does the prefatory clause restrict the meaning of the operative clause? We now get to the main argument—does the prefatory clause (or preamble) restrict the meaning of the operative clause that follows? The obvious answer is "not necessarily." Yet the four Liberal Justices insisted that the prefatory clause limits the operative clause (p. 8). This is blatantly false. Yet, not only do they refuse to acknowledge the error of their thinking, but they accuse the majority of being illogical.

3. The Miller case. Finally, let's look at the case of United States v. Miller, 307 U.S. 174 (1939), where the Supreme Court addressed the issue of whether a person had a Second Amendment right to possess a sawed-off shotgun. In this cased the Supreme Court upheld a statute that outlawed the possession of a sawed-off shotgun (less than 18" in length). This case established that the right to bear arms is not absolute, and that some weapons can be prohibited. The Supreme Court in Miller stated that there was no evidence that a sawed-off shotgun would have any use in a militia, and therefore the law banning them was upheld.

The dissenting Justices in Heller argue that the Miller case establishes that the prefatory clause does indeed control all the rest of the Amendment, and that whatever "right" does exist is subject to the government's power to regulate a militia. The majority, however, did not read Miller that way; they acknowledge that not all "arms" are covered by the amendment (machine guns, bazookas and hand grenades could also be prohibited), but the majority did not find anything in Miller that infringed upon the fundamental meaning of the Second Amendment to include an individual's right to bear arms to protect one's hearth and home.

B. Justice Breyer's Dissent. Justice Breyer also wrote a dissent, but his dissent is of lesser importance in my view. He argues that even if the Second Amendment included a personal right to use arms in self-defense, that the government could still impose reasonable limitations and regulations for the safety of

3

society. He then concluded, that the District of Columbia did in fact have a reasonable basis to prohibit the use of handguns. (All four Liberal Justices joined in Justice Breyer's dissent as well as in that of Justice Stevens.)

C. Stare Decisis. Although the liberal Justices all but abandoned *stare decisis* in reaching their opinion in 2003 in *Lawrence v. Texas*,[3] they nevertheless accuse the majority in *Heller* of doing just what they have been doing—lightly throwing aside Court precedents without adequate justification. This accusation by senior Liberal Justice Stevens (p. 4 of his Dissent), would be valid only if the majority interpreted the Second Amendment as he does. But they do not, and his criticism that the majority has not been faithful to *stare decisis* is without merit. But what makes this accusation by Stevens infuriating is that fact that Stevens and the other three liberals are the ones who have blatantly discarded *stare decisis* in *Lawrence v. Texas* and in *McConnell v. FEC* (campaign finance reform case).[4]

D. Judicial Activism. The same can be said for judicial activism. Justice Stevens concludes his 46-page dissent by accusing the majority of failing to exercise "judicial restraint." This criticism is baseless—it is the liberal four who are attempting to legislate from the bench in *Heller,* just as they did in *Boumediene, Lawrence* and *McConnell.* And it is irritating to see them give lip service to the principal of judicial restraint all the while they themselves routinely ignore the principle because it regularly gets in the way of their philosophical agendas.

III. Summary

The *Heller* case is a critical case for Americans to understand because it high-lights the internal philosophical battle that is going on both in the Supreme Court and throughout the nation. On the most obvious level, this case is about whether individual Americans have the right to possess arms to defend themselves in their homes. But on a deeper level, it is also about whether individual rights are to be superseded by

governmental control. And on this deeper level, the issue is whether we the people will turn our individual rights over to the government, and whether it is us or the government who know and decide what is best for us. As for me, I neither want nor need the government to take over my life.

This is part of the battle between socialism and free enterprise. Free enterprise entails risks and it rewards hard work and initiative, while it leaves unrewarded the passive, the indolent and the slothful. Socialism fails because its fail-safe approach guarantees everybody a certain quality of life without exacting a corresponding requirement to work—which system effectively stifles initiative and hard work. The free enterprise system (including capitalism) succeeds because it rewards initiative and hard work—which in turn promotes these same qualities in others.

The *Heller* decision is a part of this important societal debate—Who is to be empowered, the individual or the government? The answer is, in the words of Laura Ingram—*Power to the People!* And this means that it is best for the people to continue to have the right to bear arms. The Supreme Court got it right in *Heller,* despite the strong protestation from the liberals on the Court.

The Court's ruling in *D. C. v. Heller* should have been a no-brainer for all nine Justices. It is disconcerting and worrisome that four of the Justices could dispense with logic and history in order to promote a reading of the Constitution that comports only with their political agenda. With regard to this, Justice Scalia concludes his opinion by stating: "Undoubtedly some think that the Second Amendment is outmoded in a society where our standing army is the pride of our Nation, where well-trained police forces provide personal security, and where gun violence is a serious problem. That is perhaps debatable, but what is not debatable is that it is not the role of this Court to pronounce the Second Amendment extinct" (p. 64).

In this era, where militias are obsolete, does that mean that the Second Amendment is also obsolete. According to the liberal Justices—Yes. But they will not overtly state this; rather they attempt to void the Amendment of any meaning and leave it a meaningless collection of words.

---

[3] 539 U.S. 558 (2003). In this case the Supreme Court overturned the case of *Bowers v. Hardwick*, 478 U.S. 186 (1986) (which it had only decided 17 years earlier), and for the first time recognized a Fifth Amendment "liberty" to engage in private, consensual homosexual conduct.

[4] 540 U.S. 93 (2003).

Supreme Court Confers Habeas Corpus Rights on Alien Enemy Combatants

Boumediene v. Bush, 553 U.S. __ (2008)

by C. Paul Smith

On June 12, 2008, the Supreme Court ruled that alien enemy combatants[1] detained abroad by our military forces in the course of an on-going war have a constitutional right to habeas corpus relief. Never before has the Constitution given this right to aliens abroad.

This (5-4) ruling is very important and will have far-reaching impact for years to come. Democrat Presidential candidate Barack Obama praised the ruling, while Republican Presidential candidate John McCain sharply criticized it.

On some levels, the ruling was relatively simple—the Court wanted to extend additional rights to foreign enemy combatant detainees. But on close examination, there were several complex issues involved. While few people will read the decision, this will not deter them from offering their opinions on the merits or flaws of the ruling. I encourage all citizens to read it and to get a thorough understanding of what the Court did in this case. This case is one of the most egregious examples you will find of judicial activism, lack of judicial restraint, and judicial pre-emption of foreign policy power and national defense power from the Executive and Legislative branches of the government. The implications of this decision are extensive and profound.

It is difficult to distill in a few words a concise summary of what happened in this case. The Majority opinion (authored by Justice Anthony Kennedy) took 70 pages. The dissent of Chief Justice John Roberts took 28 pages, and the dissent of Justice Antonin Scalia took 25. When you add in Justice Souter's 3-page concurring opinion— the total pages reach 126. But the reading of this opinion is a must for all patriots.

By the time you get to page 70 in Justice Kennedy's majority opinion, you may be mesmerized or persuaded by his reasoning. The majority feels the pain of the enemy combatants at Guantanamo Bay, who for six years (some of them) have remained detained after they were captured in foreign lands fighting against our troops. To some, the length of this detention is intolerable. To some, the criticism that some international peoples level at the U.S. for maintaining the Guantanamo detention facility is more than they can stand. Five of the Supreme Court Justices appear to be in this group. Their impatience and disapproval of the nation's operations in Guantanamo Bay has led them to hastily and abruptly take actions that have undermined over 200 years of constitutional precedence to attempt to appease enemies of America who will never be appeased because their hatred for America is unreasonable and intractable.

---

[1] It is important to understand the definition of an "enemy combatant." This is to be distinguished from a prisoner of war, in the uniform of its country. An enemy combatant is one who is not dressed in the military uniform of its country, but who for all appearances is a civilian, and who nevertheless fights against our troops. In other words, an enemy combatant is like a spy or a terrorist who may by subterfuge and stealth infiltrate our ranks to wreck havoc through covert means.

I.   Background

Previous to the *Boumediene* ruling, alien enemy combatants had no rights to habeas corpus protection in U.S. courts if they were confined abroad in places where the U. S. was not sovereign. The case of *Johnson v. Eisentrager*, 339 U.S. 763, (1950) specifically held this. (See, e.g., Scalia, J., dissenting, p. 10.) The Bush administration properly relied on this precedent, as it detained captive, alien enemy combatants at Guantanamo Bay. But this year's ruling in *Boumediene* abandoned *stare decisis* and overturned *Eisentrager* (1950) and effectively overturned *Hamdi v. Rumsfeld*, 542 U.S. 507 (2004) for no compelling reasons. A close examination of the *Boumediene* ruling will show that it will not give these enemy combatants any significant additional rights, and that the *Boumediene* holding will serve only as a rebuke of the Bush administration by the Court, when the Bush administration had in good faith relied on Supreme Court precedents. Consequently, all that this case accomplished is to diminish the power of the Executive Branch and to enlarge the power of the Judicial Branch.

II.   Problems with *Boumediene*

Here is a list of some of the major problems in *Boumediene v. Bush*:

1. The Supreme Court, for the first time, confers on non-citizen, alien enemy combatants the right to seek and obtain the protections of a writ of habeas corpus in U. S. Courts.

2. This ruling by the Supreme Court effectively overturns the 1950 case of *Johnson v. Eisentrager*, 339 U.S. 763. Until now, there was no question but that alien enemy combatants at the Guantanamo Bay facility would not have the right to access to

U. S. courts through the filing of writs of habeas corpus. But the majority decided to interpret *Eisentrager* differently—they said that since the U.S. has effective control over Guantanamo Bay, that therefore the habeas writ should be made available. The Majority denies that they overturned *Eisentrager*, but they offered only obfuscation and linguistic contortions rather than sound reasoning in support of their conclusion. The majority's effort to reconcile its ruling in *Boumediene* with its ruling in *Eisentrager* is a total failure—and will convince only those whose analysis processes do not insist upon facts and sound reasoning.

3. This ruling by the Supreme Court also effectively overturns major parts of the recent, 2004, case of *Hamdi v. Rumsfeld*, in which case the Supreme Court recommended the precise procedures and practices that Congress and the President then enacted to ensure that the detention of alien enemy combatants satisfies all constitutional requirements. In that regard, Chief Justice Roberts wrote this:

The plurality in *Hamdi v. Rumsfeld*, 542 U.S. 507, 533 (2004), explained that the Constitution guaranteed an American citizen challenging his detention as an enemy combatant the right to "notice of the factual basis for his classification, and a fair opportunity to rebut the Government's factual assertions before a neutral decisionmaker.

The plurality specifically stated that constitutionally adequate collateral process could be provided "by an appropriately authorized and properly constituted military tribunal," given the "uncommon potential to burden the Executive at a time of ongoing military conflict." *Id.*, at 533, 538. This point is directly pertinent here, for surely the Due Process Clause does

not afford non-citizens in such circumstances greater protection than citizens are
due.

If the CSRT [2] procedures meet the
minimal due process requirements outlined in *Hamdi*, and if an Article III court
is available to ensure that these procedures
are followed in future cases, . . . there is no
need to reach the Suspension Clause
question. Detainees will have received all
the process the constitution could possibly
require, whether that process is called
"habeas" or something else. The question
of the writ's reach need not be addressed.
(Roberts, C. J., dissenting, pp. 4-5.)

4. In this case the Supreme Court
specifically holds unconstitutional portions of
the Detainee Treatment Act of 2005 (DTA)
and the Military Commissions Act of 2006
(MCA), which acts were specifically passed
by Congress and signed by the President to
comply with the requirements that the
Supreme Court articulated in *Hamdi*.

5. The Majority in *Boumediene*
erroneously concluded that Combatant Status
Review Tribunals (CSRTs) do not have the
authority to release detainees if their detention is not warranted. The majority's view on
this issue is patently absurd. The authority to
release one who is not properly detained is
clearly implicit in the law's language, and
some detainees had been released. The
majority's reasoning here is pathetic. [3]

6. The action by the majority in
Boumediene is wholly inconsistent with the
Court's precedents, and amounts to a
repudiation of the Court's doctrine of *stare
decisis*, which the Court used to honor in

attempting to be consistent with its prior
rulings.

7. The Court in *Boumediene* ruled that
because the CSRT procedures provide that
"newly discovered evidence" may be
presented only by a new proceeding, and not
during an appeal, that therefore such CSRT
procedures violate the constitutional rights of
the alien enemy combatants. This is a
distinction without a difference—it is an
inconsequential matter that does not affect
any substantive right. The majority was
straining to find fault with this technicality.

III.   Justice Scalia's Comment

Here is what Justice Scalia said about
the *Boumediene* ruling:

> Today the Court warps our
> Constitution in a way that goes beyond the
> narrow issue of the reach of the
> Suspension Clause, invoking judicially
> brainstormed separation-of-powers
> principles to establish a manipulable
> "functional" test for the extraterritorial
> reach of habeas corpus .... It blatantly
> misdescribes important precedents, most
> conspicuously Justice Jackson's opinion
> for the Court in *Johnson v. Eisentrager*. It
> breaks a chain of precedent as old as the
> common law that prohibits judicial inquiry
> into detentions of aliens abroad absent
> statutory authorization. And most
> tragically, it sets our military commanders
> the impossible task of proving to a civilian
> court, under whatever standards this Court
> devises in the future, that evidence
> supports the confinement of each and
> every enemy prisoner.
>
> The Nation will live to regret what the
> Court has done today. [Scalia, J., at 25.]

---

[2] Combatant Status Review Tribunals
[3] It should be pointed out that some of the
detainees that were released later returned to the battle
field to kill American troops.

IV. Chief Justice Roberts' Conclusion

Chief Justice Roberts concluded this about *Boumediene*:

> For all its eloquence about the detainees' right to the writ, the Court makes no effort to elaborate how exactly the remedy it prescribes will differ from the procedural protections detainees enjoy under the DTA. [Roberts, CJ, at 25.]

The majority instead compares the undefined DTA process to an equally undefined habeas right—one that is to be given shape only in the future by district courts on a case-by-case basis. This whole approach is misguided .... All that today's opinion has done is shift responsibility for those sensitive foreign policy and national security decisions from the elected branches to the Federal Judiciary.

[Roberts, CJ , at 2-3.]

Today the Court strikes down as inadequate the most generous set of procedural protections ever afforded aliens detained by this country as enemy combatants. The political branches crafted these procedures amidst an ongoing military conflict, after much careful investigation and thorough debate. The Court rejects them today out of hand, without bothering to say what due process rights the detainees possess, without explaining how the statute fails to vindicate those rights, and before a single petitioner has even attempted to avail himself of the law's operation. And to what effect? The majority merely replaces a review system designed by the people's representatives with a set of shapeless procedures to be defined by federal courts at some future date. One cannot help but think, after surveying the modest practical results of the majority's ambitious opinion, that this decision is not really about the detainees at all, but about control of federal policy regarding enemy combatants?

[Roberts, CJ, at 1-2.]

American Citizens Have Right to Habeas Corpus Relief When Detained Abroad

On June 12, 2008, a unanimous Supreme Court ruled in *Munaf v. Geren*, 554 U.S. ___ (2008) that American citizens detained outside the United States and charged with war offenses against the U.S. have the right to seek and obtain habeas corpus review of their detention.

Although the Court was sharply divided (5-4) in its ruling in *Boudiemene* that alien enemy combatants had a right to habeas corpus review of their detention, in *Munaf* the Court was unanimous in holding that American citizens have the right to habeas corpus review no matter where they may be detained.

4

The *Roe v. Wade* Scare Ad Tactic

by C. Paul Smith

The selection of Sarah Palin as the Republican Vice Presidential nominee has been a home run for Senator McCain and the Republicans. She is a true conservative. She wants to drill for oil in Alaska, where she is governor. Not only does she say she is pro-family, but she has a large family to prove it. Not only does she say she is pro-life, but she loves the Down syndrome baby that she bore at age 44, five months ago. She is attractive and articulate. She is proud of her small-town roots. She challenges the man-made global warming alarmists. She despises the politically correct, left wing mantras. She is one of us! She has done for the Republican Party what John McCain could not do—energized the conservative base. Both Senator McCain and Governor Sarah Palin are solidly for the Right to Life—and starkly opposed to the Democratic ticket's pro-abortion stance. Sarah Palin's nomination has catapulted the McCain/Palin ticket ahead of Obama/Biden in the polls.

This is not good for Senators Obama and Biden. In fact it is bad for them. In fact they are desperate to stop the McCain/Palin Express before they get run over. This calls for an early deployment of the Democrats' Ace Card—the *Roe v. Wade* Scare Ad Tactic! The Democrats had hoped to wait until later in the campaign to play this card, but the explosive success of Sarah Palin has precipitated the Democrats' plunge in the polls, and has put them in panic mode. Tonight (September 5, 2008) on the way home from work, I heard on the radio three times a new ad from Senator Obama—an ad that attempts to counteract the Palin bounce; the ad warns the women of America that McCain will overturn *Roe v. Wade*, and that this will endanger the health of American women and deprive them of their cherished right to an abortion.

During the last 35 years no Supreme Court case has been more of a lightning rod for polarizing political debate than the *Roe v. Wade* decision of 1973. That case was controversial from the moment it was announced, and it has remained controversial ever since. Every time a president nominates a new Justice for the Supreme Court, the most important question for interrogation is whether or not that nominee would overturn *Roe v. Wade*. But, other than addressing the *Roe v. Wade* issue superficially, with 3-second, sound-bite answers,

there has been very little in-depth discussion of this issue. Perhaps in this year's campaign there will be an opportunity for a more meaningful discussion of *Roe v. Wade* than normally occurs. This discussion would be very good.

As one who has been a student of the *Roe v. Wade* ruling for over 30 years (including having written a book on the issue in 1977 [*The Fetal Right to Life Argument*]), let me share some important insights on this important issue.

1. Overturning *Roe* would not have to eliminate a woman's right to privacy. If *Roe v. Wade* ever were overturned, there are several ways in which it could happen—none of which would require eliminating a woman's right to privacy and of control over her own body. These alternatives would limit a woman's right, but not extinguish it. To understand the ways *Roe v. Wade* could be overturned, you must first understand the three legal problems that were part of this ruling. Correcting any one of these problem areas could be overturning a part of *Roe v. Wade*.

2. There are three major flaws in the *Roe v. Wade* ruling. The *Roe v. Wade* opinion is rather complex. That ruling was one of the worst decisions of all time. It ranks right up there with *Dred Scott v. Sandford*. There are at least three distinct, serious flaws in *Roe v. Wade*.

First, the Supreme Court should have exercised *judicial restraint* and left the Texas legal matter in the hands of the Texas Supreme Court. The U. S. Supreme Court should not have taken the case; the regulation of abortion had been and should have continued to be a matter of state regulation and concern. But even after taking the case, the Court could have recognized a woman's right to privacy without extinguishing the fetal right to life. But the Court's over-reaching was uncalled for and grossly excessive.

Second, the Supreme Court went out of its way to state that a fetus is NOT a "person" within the meaning of the Due Process Clause of the Fifth and Fourteenth Amendments. This gratuitous swipe at unborn children was totally uncalled for, unprovoked, illogical, barbaric and a repudiation of two hundred years of legal precedent in America. The eliminating of a fetal right to life was an act of outrageous over-reaching by the Judicial Branch of

CLU 09/08

the government that encroached upon the Legislative Branch of the federal government (by usurping a power that should be only legislative and not judicial.) By what authority did the Supreme Court eliminate the fetal right to life in order to bestow on women a right to kill their unborn children without any consideration of the life of the unborn? The Court had no right. The Court usurped the authority of the states, the legislature and the people when it did this.

Third, the Supreme Court should not have legislated a resolution to the abortion debate. But they did. They constructed a complicated and contradictory legislative scheme to regulate abortions throughout the states: They came up with the trimester scheme where in the first trimester states could not prohibit abortions; in the second trimester states could regulate abortions, taking into consideration the health of the pregnant women; and in the last trimester states could protect potential human life. But the Court also stated that states could protect potential human life when the fetus becomes "viable." As science and technology have advanced, this standard conflicts with the trimester scheme.

3. *Roe v. Wade* allowed States to prohibit partial-birth abortion. As terrible as was *Roe v. Wade* in 1973, today many interpret *Roe* to extend a woman's right to an abortion to encompass the right to partial birth abortions. Partial birth abortion literally kills a viable fetus by crushing its skull and sucking its brains out. In 1973, *Roe v. Wade* specifically provided that states could outlaw this barbaric procedure. But since then, many have interpreted the right to an abortion to supersede the right of a state to prohibit abortions in the last trimester. This broadened interpretation of *Roe* is reprehensible and should be challenged.

4. A President can neither overturn a case nor amend the Constitution. Contrary to the assertion in the Obama ad, the President of the United States cannot overturn *Roe v. Wade*. That can happen only by the Supreme Court reversing itself or by passage of a constitutional amendment, the latter of which can only be done by the consensus of a supermajority, i.e., the approval of three-quarters of the states.

5. Part of Roe v. Wade is good—recognizing a woman's right to privacy. The idea that every part of *Roe v. Wade* could be or would be overturned is ridiculous. Remember, *Roe v. Wade* is a very complex case. Up to this point, I don't ever recall a serious political discussion about what part of *Roe v. Wade* one would or would not want to overturn. The woman's right to privacy—the right

to control her own body—that will never be overturned. That part of *Roe v. Wade* is laudable. But it would be good for the law to acknowledge the existence of a fetal right to continue living that would have to be weighed against a woman's right to control her body. Extinguishing the fetal right to life was the most opprobrious part of *Roe v. Wade*. It should be restored, and such a restoration would mean that the right to an abortion would not be an absolute—it would have to be weighed against the fetal right to life. In summary, if *Roe v. Wade* ever were to be "over-turned," it would only be one or two aspects of that ruling that would be changed. Possible changes could include: (a) returning the abortion issue to the states; (b) restoring the fetal right to life; and (c) correcting the ruling that a fetus is not a "person."

The discussion about what parts of *Roe v. Wade* should be overturned and which should remain would be an important discussion. I welcome it. Parts of *Roe v. Wade* should be overturned. But those who cling to abortion as the sacrament of their political religion—they don't want the discussion. They do want to turn the debate into a health issue—but it is not.

There are multiple types of support for the "right to life." But not all "right to lifers" have the same beliefs and principles about whether abortions are ever justified, and about what conditions might justify an abortion. In the rare instances where abortion would preserve a mother's life, it would be acceptable. It may be proper in the case of certain severely deformed babies. And it may be allowable in cases of rape or incest—because in those cases a pregnancy was forced upon a woman against her will. Recognizing and addressing these various competing rights would not be easy or convenient. Extinguishing a fetal right to life does simplify the administration of the law—but that law is cruel, oppressive and barbaric. Correcting this serious flaw would require overturning part of *Roe v. Wade*. But that's okay—it would be an improvement.

It appears that the McCain/Palin ticket supports changing our law to give the unborn greater protection than is currently afforded under *Roe v. Wade*. This would be good. But it need not prohibit ALL abortions. I heard that McCain was once quoted as having stated such a position, but I do not support that absolutist position, and I do not believe it would ever become law.

The taking of human life is a serious matter. Protecting those who are most helpless and vulnerable is critically important. If the Democrats want to debate whether or not *Roe v. Wade* should be overturned—I welcome the debate.

There Is No "Class of One" Under the Equal Protection Clause

On June 9, 2008, the Supreme Court ruled (6-3) that the claim of a "class of one" is not recognizable as an illegal discrimination under the Equal Protection Clause. *Engquist v. Oregon Department of Agriculture*, 554 U.S. ___ (2008).

Anup Engquist gets a star for her creativity in asserting that the State of Oregon discriminated against her as a "class of one" individual when the State fired her.[1] But neither creativity nor determination were enough to tempt a majority of the Supreme Court to totally undermine the meaning of equal protection under the Constitution by adopting a rule that one person can constitute a class of persons under the Equal Protection Clause of the Fourteenth Amendment.

To grasp what this issue is one must first recognize that all our laws against discrimination are based upon the Equal Protection Clause of the 14th Amendment. Second, that law does not prohibit all discrimination—it only prohibits discrimination against certain classes of people. For example, if the State of Oregon decided to pass a law precluding all felons from becoming lawyers, this would clearly be discrimination, but it would be permissible discrimination. Our laws routinely discriminate—we give speeding tickets to speeders, but not to those driving within the speed limit.

The 14th Amendment originally prohibited discrimination by the government against people based upon their race, color or national origin. But in the last 50 years Congress has passed multiple laws to expand the number of classes that are "protected" under the 14th Amendment. Two of these laws are the Americans with Disability Act and the Age Discrimination Act.

However, Congress has yet to pass a law making one person a class by himself/herself. If Congress were to do that it would open the flood gates of litigation to virtually every conceivable disparate treatment that a person might receive. This would be a cataclysmic disaster for the Constitution; it would be tantamount to expanding the scope of the Equal Protection Clause so broadly that everything and anything could be a violation. Such an overly broad interpretation would shut down governments and any businesses that might be subject to such a standard. The theoretical foundation for a "class-of-one" is plainly ludicrous.

Enter three bold Justices, Stevens, Souter and Ginsburg. Failing to grasp the dire repercussions of such an ill-conceived proposal, these Justices were not deterred from championing the poor Ms. Engquist. The three of them filed their heroic defense for the downtrodden woman.

Fortunately, six Justices saw through this ruse.

---

[1] In fairness to Ms. Engquist, her law suit also alleged that she was discriminated against on the basis of her race, sex and national origin. The jury rejected these traditional discrimination claims, but they found in her favor on the "class of one" theory.

Not All Supreme Court Opinions
Have a Liberal-Conservative Split

Many Supreme Court decisions break down into 4-4 splits that reflect the political philosophies of the Justices (Justice Kennedy frequently being the swing vote). But there are some cases that result in opinion alignments that are totally different. Here are a few cases that illustrate this. This certainly demonstrates that the Justices are all independent thinkers.

Appeals Court Cannot, on Its Own Initiative, Increase a Defendant's Sentence

Defendant Michael Greenlaw was convicted in U. S. District Court in Minnesota on several drug and firearms charges that led to his being sentenced to prison for 442 months. Greenlaw appealed to the Eighth Circuit Court of Appeals, arguing that his sentence (almost 37 years) was too long. On review, not only did the Eighth Circuit disagree with Greenlaw, but they felt that there was a "plain error" at the trial, and that the sentence should have been for an additional 15 years—bringing the prison term to 52 years. However, no party has asked the court to lengthen Greenlaw's sentence—the Eighth Circuit just took it upon themselves to correct the "plain error."

On June 23, 2008, the Supreme Court reversed the Eighth Circuit, holding that the appeals court did not have authority *sua sponte* (of its own initiative) to increase the length of a defendant's sentence. The majority opinion was authored by Justice Ginsburg, and was joined by Chief Justice Roberts, and by Justices Scalia, Kennedy, Souter and Thomas. Justice Breyer joined in the conclusion, but filed a concurring opinion. Justice Alito filed a dissenting opinion that was joined by Justice Stevens, and in which Justice Breyer joined as to Parts I, II and III.

I find the alignment of Justices in this case to be quite interesting.

Is There a Right Not to Be Represented by Counsel? Apparently Not!

Ahmad Edwards, a schizophrenic, was convicted of attempted murder and other crimes for a shooting during his attempt to steal a pair of shoes. Edward demanded the right to defend himself, without counsel at trial. Prior to the trial Edwards was examined and found competent to stand trial but not competent to defend himself at trial. As a result, the State of Indiana appointed counsel to represent Edwards, and Edwards was then convicted on two counts. Edwards appealed, arguing that the trial violated a constitutional right to represent himself, without aid of counsel. The Indiana Supreme Court agreed with Edwards. The State of Indiana requested the U. S. Supreme Court to review the case. Upon review, on June 19, 2008, the Supreme Court by a 7-2 vote reversed the Indiana Supreme Court, and ruled that the state power to determine whether a defendant must have the assistance of counsel supersedes an individual's right to represent one's self without counsel. *Indiana v. Edwards*, 554 U.S. ____ (2008).

The majority opinion in this case was authored by Justice Breyer and was joined by Chief Justice Roberts and by Justices Stevens, Kennedy, Souter, Ginsburg and Alito. Justices Scalia and Thomas dissented.

Supreme Court Upholds Limitation in Permissible Age Discrimination

On June 19, 2008, the Supreme Court upheld (5-4) a Kentucky disability plan that gave a different benefit to workers based on age. *Kentucky Retirement Systems v. Equal Employment Opportunity Commission*, 554 U.S. ____ (2008). The federal government's Equal Employment Opportunity Commission (EEOC) had sued the State of Kentucky for having a retirement plan that discriminated against Charles Lickteig (who retired at age 61), in violation of the Age Discrimination in Employment Act of 1967 (ADEA). The Supreme Court ruled that the mere inclusion of age as a factor in determining retirement benefits does not mean that the plan violates the ADEA. The Supreme Court stated that it must be proved that age "actually motivated the employer's decision," and the Court ruled that this improper motivation did not occur under the Kentucky plan with Mr. Lickteig.

For those interested in grasping the technical distinction that the Court recognized in this case, you will want to read the opinion in its entirety. However, what interests me in this case is the composition of the majority and dissenting Justices. The majority opinion was authored by Justice Breyer, and was joined by Chief Justice Roberts and by Justices Stevens, Souter and Thomas. The dissent was written by Justice Kennedy, and was joined by Justices Scalia, Ginsburg and Alito. I find this a strange alignment. In a rather simplistic analysis of this case, the Court ruled for the State over the federal government.

Court Limits Reach of Federal Money-Laundering Statute

One of the most unusual alignments of the nine Justices is found in the Court's ruling in United States v. Santos, 554 U.S. ___ (2008).

Efrain Santos and Benedicto Diaz were convicted of violating the federal money-laundering statute (18 U.S.C. Sec 1956), which prohibits the use of "proceeds" of criminal

activities to promote unlawful purposes. Later, the Seventh Circuit defined "proceeds" to mean "criminal profits" and not "criminal receipts." This led the district court to vacate those convictions. The government appealed, but the Seventh Circuit affirmed the district court ruling. The Supreme Court also affirmed the outcome.

The judgment of the Supreme Court was announced by Justice Scalia, in an opinion joined by Justices Souter, Thomas[1] and Ginsburg. Justice Stevens concurred in the result, but based upon different reasons, therefore he filed a concurring opinion. This creates what is called a "plurality" opinion, where there is no majority rationale for the result reached by the Court. Justice Breyer filed a dissent. Justice Alito also filed a dissent, which was joined by Chief Justice Roberts and Justices Kennedy and Breyer.

Supreme Court Strikes California Law Regulating the Use of Employers' Funds to Assist or Deter Union Organizing

On June 19, 2008, the Supreme Court, in a 7-2 vote, ruled that the National Labor Relations Act (NLRA) pre-empts California from regulating employers in using funds "to assist, promote, or deter union organizing." This case concerned the question of whether the State of California, in addition to the federal government, could impose a regulation upon employers with respect to assisting or deterring union organizing. The Supreme Court ruled (by a 7-2 vote) that federal regulation had pre-empted the field, such that California could not have additional or different regulations.

In this case the five conservative Justices were joined by Justices Stevens and Souter. Justices Breyer and Ginsburg dissented.

To me it is of interest to note that all five conservative Justices sided with the federal government and not the state. I also find it interesting that two of the liberal Justices, Breyer and Ginsburg, sided with the State of California over the federal government.

---

[1] Justice Thomas joined in all but Part IV of the Opinion.

Supreme Court Limits Punitive Damages to Value of Compensatory Damages

In case you haven't noticed—it's been 19 years since Exxon oil tanker *Valdez* spilled millions of gallons of oil into the Prince William Sound in Alaska. In the intervening years, Exxon has paid over $3 billion in clean-up efforts and in fines and compensatory damages to parties injured by the oil spill. The latest episode in this saga resulted in a ruling by the Supreme Court on June 25, 2008, where the Court ruled that punitive damages against Exxon cannot exceed the compensatory damages against Exxon. *Exxon Shipping Company v. Baker*, 554 U.S. ____ (2008).

Exxon had already paid $2.1 billion in cleanup efforts; over $900 million to the United States and Alaska; and over $300 million in payments to private parties. But in addition to this, in 2006(?) a jury awarded $287 million to several additional plaintiffs for damages that Exxon caused **plus $5 billion in punitive damages!** Exxon appealed. The Ninth Circuit Court of Appeals reduced the punitive damages to $2.5 billion in 2007. Exxon requested the Supreme Court to reduce the punitive damages even more. On June 25th, the Court complied, and ruled that punitive damages cannot exceed the compensatory damages ($287 million).

The result of this ruling is that Exxon's losses from the oil spill will stop at approximately $3.6 billion rather than running up to $8.3 billion.

Death Penalty Unconstitutional for Rapist of 8-Year-Old Child

On June 25, 2008, the Supreme Court ruled (5-4) in Kennedy v. Louisiana, 554 U.S. ____ (2008) that the Eighth Amendment prohibition against cruel and unusual punishment bars imposing the death sentence upon the perpetrator of the rape of an 8-year-old child. (The Court left open the possibility that capital punishment could be imposed if the perpetrator had intended to kill the child.)

Justice Anthony Kennedy delivered the majority opinion that was joined by Justices Stevens, Souter, Ginsberg and Breyer. Justice Samuel Alito filed a dissenting opinion that was joined by Chief Justice Roberts and Justices Scalia and Thomas.

Supreme Court Carves Out New Right For Aliens Seeking to Pro-long Their Stay in America

One of the well-known abuses of immigration law occurs in connection with sham marriages that are entered into with the sole purpose of helping an alien to become a U. S. citizen. Where an Immigration Court finds that a person's application to remain in America is based upon a sham marriage, then the alien is ordered to leave. Such was the situation of Nigerian Samson Taiwo Dada in 2003, whose marriage to an American citizen in 1999 was found not to be bona fide. Faced with removal, Mr. Dada requested and was granted a "voluntary departure" dispensation (under 8 U.S.C. Sec. 1229c(b)), whereby Dada was given 30 days to leave. Two days before his departure deadline, Dada withdrew his voluntary departure request and filed a motion to reopen the removal proceedings against him. The Board of Immigration Appeals denied Dada's motion, ruling that a voluntary departure request cannot be withdrawn. The Fifth Circuit Court of Appeals affirmed. But the Supreme Court reversed (5-4). *Dada v. Mukasey*, 554 U.S. ___ (2008). (Michael B. Mukasey is the Attorney General of the United States.)

One way to look at this case is that the liberal Justices sided with the alien, while the conservative Justices sided with the Department of Homeland Security (which now supervises the Immigration and Naturalization Service).

Federalism   Environment

National Association of Home Builders v. Defenders of Wildlife

On June 25, 2007, the Supreme Court, in a 5-4 decision, resolved a procedural conflict between two federal agencies pertaining to the protection of endangered species, the result of which is to lessen the protection given to endangered species. *National Association of Home Builders v. Defenders of Wildlife,* 551 U. S. ___ (2007).

The legal question around which this case centered is whether the Environmental Protection Agency (EPA) is required to consider whether a construction project would jeopardize an endangered species before transferring permitting authority to a state (Arizona). The Supreme Court answered this in the negative; they said that the Clean Water Act of 1972 requires that the EPA transfer permitting responsibility for a project to the applicable state once nine criteria are satisfied. And that is what the EPA did. Thereupon, Defenders of Wildlife filed suit directly in U. S. Court of Appeals for the Ninth Circuit, requesting the court to order the EPA to first insure that a water project would not endanger the cactus ferruginous pygmy-owl and the Pima pineapple cactus. The Ninth Circuit ruled in favor of the petitioners (Defenders of Wildlife). However, the Supreme Court reversed, ruling that the EPA had correctly transferred permitting authority.

Having given this brief description of the case, you might ask, "So what?" What makes this case important? The answer is that this ruling is a setback to those who have sought to place protection of endangered species as a higher priority than the primary purposes of other federal agencies and programs. The four dissenting Justices (Stevens, Souter, Ginsberg and Breyer) argued that the majority's interpretation of the Clean

Water Act reverses a long-standing mandate that Congress must make protection of endangered species a priority over the "primary missions" of other federal agencies (J. Stevens, dissent, p. 2). But the opinion of Justice Alito (joined by Chief Justice Roberts and Justices Scalia, Kennedy and Thomas) disagrees.

This case was necessary because of a difference in the Circuit Courts in addressing this procedural issue. It is not clear to me that the decision will necessarily be more or less protective of endangered species. I believe it will relegate to states more of the enforcement of endangered species protection; perhaps this will yield some inconsistent interpretations of law. But I favor this deference to the States; it should mean that decisions regarding the protection of endangered species will be made by the people closest to the situation, and therefore perhaps more sensitive to the affects and influences of such issues. It certainly divests the federal government of some control over protection of endangered species.

254

2.7, 6.2
13.4 – 13.5

CONSTITUTIONAL

LAW

UPDATES

VIII:i   March 2010   No. 15

Congress and President Obama Make It Official: We Are Now a Socialist Nation!

—with passage of massive health care reform law—

by C. Paul Smith

At noon today (March 23, 2010), President Barack Obama proudly signed into law the massive health reform bill, which is opposed by all Republican Congressmen and a few Democrat Congressmen.

Since President Obama wants all the credit for cramming this law through, it is only right that this brand of health care be dubbed, "Obamacare." And, just to be clear—to make sure you understand what this new law will do—here is a brief summary.

> It will provide health care for all Americans, giving coverage to the 38 million uninsured and all others who are able to sneak inside our borders. Health insurance premiums will go down, and those who don't have health insurance and who can afford it will be required to purchase health insurance or pay a federal tax to get the government-provided health care. It will save the nation a trillion dollars in twenty years. Everyone will get the best health care. No one will be denied health care because of pre-existing conditions. Insurance companies will be prevented from making obscene profits.

Wow! How could anyone oppose this?

The problem is that this "too good to be true" proposal is just that—it **is too good to be true**. Do you really believe that this Obamacare will cure all these ills? It is amazing that half of the nation cannot see the economic flaws in Obamacare. But because, in fact, about half the people cannot see clearly, let me take a few minutes to point out what should be obvious to all of us. Obamacare is nothing less than pure socialism—an economic system that is not economically sustainable; therefore it will fail. Here is why this health care reform law, if allowed to go forward, will fail.

CONSTITUTIONAL LAW UPDATES is a newsletter edited and published by C. Paul Smith, J.D. To order copies ($5.00 per issue), write *CLU*, P. O. Box 1204, Frederick, MD 21702-0204. For further information visit www.cpaulsmith.com. Copyright C. Paul Smith 2010.

Continued, from Page 1—

Can a nation deliver quality health care to 38 million more people than are presently being served, and save $50 Billion a year in doing so? Does anyone really believe this? But that is exactly what Obama/Pelosi/Reid are promising.

What will happen to the insurance industry if you require them to insure all pre-existing conditions? Have you really thought this through? It will kill the insurance Industry, which is based upon contracts and probabilities and cost projections. What's left will not be insurance—it will be socialism.

How can health insurance premiums go down if insurance companies are required to cover pre-existing conditions? The answer is they can't; they can only go up—unless the law requires it. And if the law requires it, then either the insurance companies will go out of business or taxes will be raised to pay for the increased coverage. In fact, both will happen. And just to make sure we kill the insurance companies, the Obamacare law prevents them from making excess profits; you know, corporate greed must be punished in order to re-distribute the wealth to those in need. Socialists do not understand that profit incentive and competition is what has made America great; and they certainly don't see that by eliminating profit from business they kill the incentive for excellence, achievement and hard work. Obamacare will replace an incentive-driven economy with one of entitlements and sloth. Socialism will work only until the receivers take everything away from those who have. Then socialism dies, too. And that is exactly what will happen. The insurance industry will be killed, and/or

transformed into socialism, which will lead to economic ruin.

If everyone is being guaranteed health care—at least 38 million more—and if we are going to save $50 Billion a year in the process, will we continue to attract the brightest and best people to be doctors and nurses. No, there will be a marked decline in the number of the best people who elect to be doctors. Many of the best will choose another field to apply their superior skills and intellect. But don't worry, there will be more than enough lesser qualified people to take up the slack and become our doctors of the future. The result will be a decline in the quality of health care that is offered in America.

The problems wrought by Obamacare are even worse than what I have just described. It takes a little bit of analysis and education to understand, but not much. The passage of Obamacare stands as a condemnation of our entire national education system, because the liberal teachers who run our education system have finally succeeded in passage of this self-destructive law. The liberals are celebrating this political success, even though it is sowing the seeds of economic destruction. The liberals are oblivious to the serious blow Obamacare has dealt to the economic foundation of America. Today America has embraced Marx and Lenin and has rejected Adam Smith.

Educating America is the only way to cure the economic poison that America has swallowed today. But this will be a difficult task; we have a nation that is pre-occupied with getting their entitlements from the rich in order to level the playing field. Hopefully this poison can be eradicated before it irreversibly cripples America.

More on the Health Care Reform Law

President Obama has applied his rhetorical skills to support the health care reform law, and in so doing he criticizes the free enterprise system. He chastises businesses for making money. He blames greedy American capitalists for the recession. He refuses to acknowledge that bad laws and excessive regulation are primary causes of the credit collapse. Neither does he acknowledge that the trillions of dollars of new national debt will exacerbate the economic crisis more than help it. Perhaps the theme of President Obama's administration is best typified by his adeptness in speaking out of both sides of his mouth. The very day when he announced his proposed budget—which would increase the national debt ceiling to $14 Trillion—he also called for the government to live within its means, beginning late next year. Even a fifth grader can see through this.

But the new law is 2,000 pages long—that's a lot of pages—that's five, 400-page books. Who can possibly speak authoritatively on the 2,000-page health care reform law? Even if someone read it once, he or she would have difficulty mastering what was contained in all those pages. There can be no doubt that most of the Senators and Congressmen do not comprehend the law that they just passed; even if they were to trim it down to 1,000 pages, or to even 500 pages. Does this legislative process bother anyone besides me?

When I represent someone in a trial, I try to limit what my client says, because whatever the client says can come back to haunt him or her. The more words there are, the more likely it is that there will be contradictions, confusion and ambiguity. Legislation is no different: The more lengthy the law, the more likely it is to have problems.

Conversely, a short and concise law is less prone to have problems.

With this backdrop, I fully expect the new health care reform law to have multiple problems.

Based upon my observation, here are some of the troubling aspects of the health reform law (HB3200) that have been brought to my attention[1]:

1. The law will provide insurance to all non-U.S. residents, whether or not they are here legally. (See Page 50 – section 152)
2. The government will have access to our bank accounts, with authority to make electronic fund transfers from those accounts. (See Pages 58-59.)
3. The federal government will hire150,000 new employees to administer the new health care law. (I understand most of these will be with the IRS, who will be using the tax enforcement laws to collect from the taxpayers the funds required to provide universal health care.)
4. The government will set doctor fees, and doctors will be paid the same, regardless of any specialty. (See pages 241 and 253.)
5. Cancer hospitals will ration care according to the patient's age. (See page 272 – section 1145.)
6. The law does not apply to members of Congress, who can have different coverage.

I have heard of so many problems with this law, and the law is so long, that it is almost impossible to discuss it properly. I heard Senator Harry Reid today proudly claim that the law not only provides health care, but that it will also help the economy and reduce the national debt. Everything I have learned

---

[1] The following comments are taken from the comments of Judge Kithil, from Marble Falls, Texas.

about the law contradicts this, and I'm not prepared to suspend my common sense and drink the Obama/Reid/Pelosi cool aid.

I take seriously the need to understand both history and economics. And my study of them causes me to have grave concerns about the health care reform law. It has too many bad parts; it repudiates and attacks the free enterprise system; it attacks capitalism; it embraces socialism.

And now that President Obama has signed the law, he needs desperately to move on to other issues—hoping that the nation will forget about the health care reform law fiasco. Desperate for diversion, on March 26th, President Obama announced that he has reached a nuclear arms reduction agreement with Russia. There is no urgency for this—except for the diversion it might supply.

But we cannot forget the health care reform law CATASTROPHY. Because of the grievousness of the flaws in the health care reform law, it must be challenged, exposed, contested, defeated and repealed. It under-mines the last vestiges of a free enterprise system in America. It is currently the crowning jewel of the socialists, who in the last 14 months have taken over the automo-bile, banking, insurance and health care industries in America. This is one law that must not be allowed to stand.

Constitutional Challenges to Obamacare

Within hours after President Obama signed the health care reform law, fourteen states filed law suits seeking to stop the law.[2] Wholly apart from the socialism aspect of the new, health care reform law, the law may be

unconstitutional for three reasons: **First**, the procedure that Congress employed to pass the law ("deeming" the bill passed), may violate Article I, Section 7 of the Constitution. **Second**, the substance of the law may exceed the powers of Congress, as set forth in the "Commerce" Clause (Article I, Section 8) of the Constitution. Because the health care reform law takes over the insurance industry—which has historically been a matter of private contracts and state domain—the law may be an improper regulation of state commerce. Congress may only regulate "interstate" commerce. The new law proposes to transform state-regulated health care and insurance into federally-regulated health care and insurance. **Third**, because this law impairs private contracts and takes private property without due process (a violation of the Fifth Amendment of the Constitution), the law may be fatally flawed.[3]

The Supreme Court has previously upheld both Social Security, Medicaid and Medicare, but those laws were not nearly so far-reaching in attempting to interfere with private industry and private contracts. It is true that the Supremacy Clause (Article VI) makes the Constitution controlling in areas where both the federal government and the States have concurrent jurisdiction. But the Commerce Clause and the Tenth Amendment limit the scope of federal legislation, and the current Supreme Court has previously shown its recognition and support of this restrictive interpretation of Congressional power. Accordingly, in my judgment, at this point there is a good chance that the Supreme Court could invalidate some or all of the new health care reform law.

Stay tuned for the development of these cases that are being filed, some of which will eventually make their way to the Supreme Court.

---

[2] States suing the federal government to stop the health care reform law include: Alabama, Colorado, Idaho, Florida, Louisiana, Michigan, Nebraska, Pennsylvania, South Carolina, South Dakota, Texas, Utah, Virginia and Washington.

---

[3] Virginia has an additional basis for challenging the new health care reform law; Virginia has a state law that prohibits federal, unfunded mandates.

2.7, 6.2
& 13.4

The True State of the Union

Commentary on President Barack Obama's January 28, 2010 State of the Union Address

by C. Paul Smith

In January we heard President Obama's State of the Union message to the American people. One interesting aspect of the speech is that is was defensive and complaining. These are not characteristics of power, but rather of frustration and defeat. And indeed, the election of the new Republican Senator Brown (from Massachusetts), to fill the seat left vacant by the death of ultra liberal Ted Kennedy, was a clear repudiation of the Democrat-sponsored health care reform bill. Let me be "clear" about that—it is a repudiation of the Democrat-sponsored health care reform bill.

When President Clinton suffered a similar repudiation in 1995, he had the good sense to abandon the project and move on. President Obama, however, announced that he will not give up—"I will not quit," he said. With religious fervor, he continues to insist that Congress must reform our health care system because it is a national sin for us to not provide affordable health care for every American and everybody else who finds a way to get within our borders.

We need to analyze this position and purpose; it typifies President Obama's philosophy of government, his superficial and flawed understanding of economics, and his view of the Constitution. When you analyze and understand President Obama's fundamental views on these important matters, you cannot help but have grave concerns for the state of America under his leadership. The only hope is for We The People to make our voices of reason heard by our elected leaders so that We can withstand the remaining onslaught that he will wage against America as he presses forward with his dangerous agenda.

President Obama's Philosophy of Government—ENTITLEMENTS.
President Obama rejects the philosophy of our founders that the federal government is one of specified, limited purposes. He feels he knows better; he thinks he's smarter than the founders. So, with religious fervor, he preaches that the American government is responsible to provide food, shelter and health care for all within our borders.

We don't quarrel with those who desire to help others. We encourage churches, charities and private individuals to help those in need. The problem is that the role of PROVIDER was never intended for the federal government. By transforming the federal government from a defender of freedom and opportunity TO A GUARANTOR OF BENEFITS FOR ALL will multiply the size and cost and inefficiencies of government to gargantuan proportions, and will eventually ruin America.

Up to this point, I've avoided using the word, SOCIALISM, but that is exactly what President Obama seeks to make America—a socialist nation. President Obama gives lip service to principles of economic soundness, but he frankly chooses to deny the economic dangers that inevitably come from socialism. Again, if you listen to his words—his philosophy of government is a religious fanaticism towards socialism. He insists that the federal government must provide for the needs of the people. He claims a moral mandate to advance this agenda, regardless of the terrible side effects that his socialism will cause.

Within the last year Congress has already taken over the automobile industry and much of the financial industry. And before that, it was the government control of the housing industry, including forcing banks to lend to unqualified buyers, that was a contributing factor to the real estate and financial crash of 2008. Despite this, Mr. Obama does not understand that government has been a major cause of our problems; and his cure is to make government bigger to solve the problems government created.

Our founding fathers wisely set up a federal government with only specific, limited powers. The role of the federal government was only to do what the individual states could not do—such as provide for national defense, a national monetary system, national roads, and other national concerns. But President Obama sees no limits to the role of the federal government; he clearly rejects the limitation of Congressional power stated in Article I, Section 8 and in the Tenth Amendment. President Obama rejects the notion that the role of the Constitution is limited to providing OPPORTUNITY—that approach of restraint is a sin to him—he insists that the role of the federal government is to PROVIDE BENEFITS. He seeks to make America the land of ENTITLEMENTS.

President Obama's Flawed Understanding of Economics—IGNORANCE IS BLISS! For the most part, President Obama either denies or ignores the economic principles of national prosperity. We all know he's smart; and we know he's a smooth speaker (as long as he sticks to the words on the teleprompter). Because of this, some conclude that President Obama is intentionally trying to hurt the country. While I believe his policies will hurt America, I don't think President Obama believes they will. He's not trying to hurt America; he just doesn't know what he is doing. I believe he has several major blind spots in his thinking. He may have a high IQ, but he denies the economic principles of prosperity; I believe he is blinded by his religious fervor, the inflated views of his own wisdom and intelligence, and the socialist indoctrination that molds his views.

At his January 28th State of the Union Address, President Obama proclaimed that he is not an ideologue—he claims to be a practical leader. This denial is false, but President Obama thinks it's true; he really doesn't think he's an ideologue. He doesn't recognize that he was the most liberal of all 100 Senators—he just doesn't see himself for what he really is. He has been so indoctrinated by socialists and liberals that he cannot understand the point of view of either conservatives, capitalists or proponents of the free enterprise system. Again, from his religious point of view, capitalists are greedy, evil people who horde all the wealth. President Obama's disdain of capitalists prevents him from understanding the fundamental role of capital and capitalists in a thriving free enterprise/free market economic system. President Obama doesn't see the difference between creating government jobs (funded by taxes) and creating private market jobs (funded by a free market). You have not yet heard President Obama explain how a thriving free market economy lifts everyone. If he happens to say something about the importance of a free market economy it is not because he understands it—it is only because he senses he needs to say it. President Obama's actions clearly indicate—let me make that perfectly clear—that he does not understand what makes a prosperous economy. Here are some notable examples.

In case you missed it, during his first year in office, the Democrat Congress passed, and he signed into law a substantial increase in the minimum wage (from $6.55/hr. to $7.25/hr.). He should have vetoed the bill if he knew what he was doing. During the first year, unemployment in America rose from 7.7% to 9.7%. The increased minimum wage law discourages employers from hiring. In fact, employers have been cutting the size of their work forces. President Obama denies that this law is contributing to unemployment. Regardless of his excuses and his faulty reasons, his actions show his ignorance of economics. The nation has lost about 8 million jobs during the last year. President

CLU 03/10

Obama seeks to deflect this result by claiming that the nation would have lost 2 million more jobs had it not been for the stimulus package; he claims to have created 2 million jobs. First of all, let's point out the obvious—than when the best argument he can make is that it would have been worse without his stimulus package, then his knees are buckling, and he is already reeling. I do not believe what President Obama says unless I can verify or confirm it, but whatever jobs were created were predominantly government jobs; and government jobs never stimulate economic growth. Government jobs just moves money around without creating goods and services. All those new jobs do is move the nation that much closer to socialism. It is true that some government jobs can contribute to the economic well-being of the nation. But there is no substitute for job creation in the private sector—and this is what has been stifled and stopped. Mr. Obama does not have a clue how to stimulate the private sector—let me be perfectly clear about this—President Obama does not have a clue how to stimulate the private sector; and he does not intend to promote the prosperity of private business; he condemns profitable private businesses, and he seeks to take their wealth from them through taxes; his goal is to redistribute the wealth—and stimulating private enterprises is not a part of his plans for us.

The biggest mistake of President Obama is one that is shared by most of his Democrat friends—that is he insists that America must continue to borrow money or print new money, but continue to spend without constraint. His rationale for this approach is that the "spending" will prime the pump, so to speak; that the "spending" will quick-start the economy. This is the Keynesian approach to economics. Sometimes this approach has been helpful. But in our current economic recession, the deficit spending is only hurting—it is lengthening the recession, and it is multiplying the size of our national debt so that we and our children and our grandchildren will be paying off this enormous debt for the next fifty years.

President Obama boldly states that he "won't do nothing." He is determined to do something. Like FDR before him, Obama insists on trying things. But the wisdom and insight on which his determination is based is no more insightful than merely hoping something works. Basically, he is just throwing stuff against the wall, hoping that something sticks. President Obama refuses to accept that doing nothing could be better than doing some things. In the fall of 2008 when the economy had fallen and Congress was considering the $900 Billion Stimulus bill, Congressman Roscoe Bartlett (R –MD) warned that doing nothing would be better than passing that flawed stimulus bill; Congressman Bartlett advised to merely ride out the problem—that we were living through a major market correction—correcting the inflated property values that had been jacked up through easy and excessive credit. When the house of credit cards collapsed, the values of stocks and properties dropped as a part of the economic correction. You will recall that neither presidential candidate took the lead in addressing the economic meltdown. Senators Obama and McCain joined with President Bush in passing that economic mistake—called the Stimulus Package. Senator Obama is just as responsible for that trillion dollars of debt as is President Bush—even though President Obama repeatedly blames Bush for that portion of the debt; President Obama falsely asserts that he inherited that debt from President Bush. And now in the fourteen months since he has been in office, President Obama has more than doubled the stimulus money that Congress has thrown at the market correction (which we call a recession). President Obama continues to insist that the stimulus monies are needed and that they are helping. President Obama asserts that things would have been worse if we had not added Two Trillion Dollars of additional debt. But his assertions are not supported by reasoned analysis of facts. One thing is indisputable—the debt burden that came from the three

261

million dollars of stimulus will cause us serious financial burdens for decades.

The most obvious showcase for President Obama's economic ignorance is his fanatical zeal for passing some national health care reform law. President Obama either denies or ignores the simple fact that if the government is going to provide health care for 40 million more people (people who can't afford it), then the tax burden of the American people must be increased to pay for it. This really is a simple concept to understand, yet President Obama—with all of his religious fervor—denies this reality. In fact, he insists that the Democrat health care reform bill will actually save taxpayers money. That's false, and he knows it! And the American people are not buying this one. President Obama has the audacity to declare that the bill will lower the national debt because we will pay for it for 10 years, and only get benefits from it for 6 years. But even a Fifth Grader understands that on a yearly basis it is going to cost more.

America also took note of how the Nebraska Senator had to be bribed with pork before he would support the bill. Again, American Fifth Graders are not fooled by this trick. And as for "transparency" the mantra of the Obama Administration—their version of transparency is pure hypocrisy. The health care reform bill (2,000 pages) hasn't been read by most of those who voted for it, and its passage in Congress was orchestrated behind closed doors—attempting to package it in a way to make it acceptable to the public, but trying to hide from the public its many damaging terms. Private businesses were attacked in the bill; health insurance premiums would be raised by the bill; and the insurance and health care industries would be socialized through the bill. Eventually people will drop their private plans to get the cheaper governmental benefits. Employers, too, will eventually stop providing health insurance for their employees when the government plan becomes cheaper. This will eventually drive private insurance companies out of business—and we will be left with

government-only health care. President Obama and his faithful ignore or deny all of this. Why? I think a main reason is that they are so intoxicated with their goal to make the American government provide benefits for everyone, that they are denying or ignoring the economic principles of a prosperous national economy.

President Obama's Views on the Constitution—Lip Service Only! Long before he was elected President, Barack Hussein Obama openly stated his dissatisfaction with the concept that the federal government was one of specific, limited powers. President Obama denies that the Constitution limits him from turning the nation into one of socialism. He ignores or denies the requirement to pass an amendment if he wants to expand the federal government beyond the limits of Article I, Section 8 and the Tenth Amendment.

CONCLUSION: This nation got exactly what Barack Hussein Obama promised us—a liberal, socialist ideologue who doesn't have a clue about the economic principles that have made American strong and prosperous. He is determined to destroy the wealthy, thinking that by bringing down the rich, he will bless the poor. He denies the principle that made America great—that economic freedom and private initiative and capital—unimpaired and unhindered by excessive government taxes—will benefit rich, middle class and poor. President Obama chooses to follow the proven failed policies of his role model, Franklin Delano Roosevelt—to demonize and attack the rich; raise taxes; and increase government programs and control—all of which will delay economic recovery and burden the nation with more debt.

Today, two months after President Obama's State of the Union Address, his message is endorsed by a slim majority in Congress—and that majority, as it forges ahead, has passed a health care reform law that will greatly damage this nation if not corrected. The state of the Union is not good.

Supreme Court "Global Warming" Ruling—
A Monument to Bad Science and Judicial Activism
Massachusetts v. Environmental Protection Agency, 549 U.S. ___ (2007)

by C. Paul Smith

It has been three years since the Supreme Court handed down its decision in *Massachusetts v. Environmental Protection Agency*, 549 U.S. ___ (2007). But the significance of this case requires that it be exposed and discussed. The Supreme Court ruled 5-4 in this case that the EPA "abdicated its responsibility under the Clean Air Act to regulate the emissions of four greenhouse gases, including carbon dioxide." In this case the Supreme Court sided with speculation over scientific evidence, as it endorsed the man-made global warming fanatics, whose purposes attack America's economic strength based upon unsupported speculation.

This is a ruling of profound significance for America. The Supreme Court (by a slim majority [5-4] leaped forward to conclude that man-made C02 emissions (a) cause global warming, (b) are increasing too rapidly, and (c) that America will suffer catastrophic damages if the EPA does not do something to stop these increases. The problems with the *Massachusetts v. EPA* opinion are fundamental and far-reaching. This opinion stands with *Lawrence v. Texas* and *Boumediene v. Bush* as examples of a slim majority of five Justices who abandoned established constitutional principles and echoed politically popular themes to reach a pre-determined result. The legal processes and analysis of the majority represents a departure from intellectual honesty and disciplined analysis, and stands as a blatant example of judicial activism.

1. The Standing Problem. The Supreme Court never should have heard this case because Massachusetts did not have standing to bring this case. It lacked standing because it never articulated any "particularized injury." Rather Massachusetts only asserted that global warming was

"harmful to humanity at large" (Robert, C.J., dissenting, p. 7). The injuries that Massachusetts alleged were all non-specific and speculative (*Ibid.* 8). In addition, some of the asserted injuries were specifically admitted to be caused by other factors. For example, it was admitted that a "significan[t]" cause of the projected loss of Massachusetts' shore line was due to the land's sinking (*Ibid.* p. 8). Previously the Court has held that "[a]llegations of possible future injury do not satisfy the requirements of Art. III" [the injury requirement] (*Ibid.* p. 9). But the majority disregarded this, and treated speculation to be specific, proven facts. As the Chief Justice stated:

The Court ignores the complexities of global warming, and does so by now disregarding the "particularized" injury it relied on in step one, and using the dire nature of global warming itself as a bootstrap for finding causation and redressability. *Ibid.*p.10.

Although the EPA set forth the complex reasons[1] that prevented it from

---

[1] The EPA stated the following as a basis for not linking green house gases to global warming:

"Predicting future climate change necessarily involves a complex web of economic and physical factors including: our ability to predict future global anthropogenic emissions of [greenhouse gases] and aerosols; the fate of these emissions once they enter the atmosphere (e.g., what percentage are absorbed by vegetation or are taken up by the oceans); the impact of those emissions that remain in the atmosphere on the radiative properties of the atmosphere; changes in critically important climate feedbacks (e.g., changes in cloud cover and ocean circulation); changes in temperature characteristics (e.g., average temperatures, shifts in daytime and evening temperatures); changes in other climatic parameters (e.g., shifts in precipitation, storms); and ultimately the impact of such changes on human health and welfare (e.g., increases or decreases in agricultural productivity, human health impacts)." App. To Pet. For Cert. A-83 through A-84.

ruling that green house gases caused global warming, the Court either disregarded or rejected those reasons, and went on to require the EPA to rule that green house gases cause global warming. The Supreme Court ruled that CO_2 is a pollutant that causes global warming; the Supreme Court said that the EPA was wrong for not concluding this. The Chief Justice concluded that it is "pure conjecture to suppose that EPA regulation of new automobile emissions will likely prevent the loss of Massachusetts coastal land" (*Ibid.* p.13).

2. The statute interpretation problem. Not only did the majority botch the standing issue in its haste to solve the global warming debate, but the majority also botched its fundament task of strictly interpreting a statute. The majority made two distinct misinterpretations in order to reach its desired result.

First, under Section 202(a)(1) of the Clean Air Act (CAA), there is no authority granted to challenge an action of the EPA until the EPA Administrator makes a "judgment" (Scalia, J., dissenting, p. 1). The majority simply ignored this requirement, and held that the EPA should have adjudged that CO_2 causes global warming. There is no justification for imposing this mandate. The majority holding is blatant judicial activism to achieve a predetermined result.

Second, the majority concluded that CO_2 was a pollutant by ignoring the first part of the statutory definition that had to be met in order to regulate CO_2. An "air pollutant"

is defined as "any air pollution agent or combination of such agents, including any physical, chemical, . . . substance or matter which is emitted into or otherwise enters the ambient air." 42 U.S.C. Sec.7602(g). The majority focused on the latter part of this definition, and reasoned that since CO_2 is emitted into the air, therefore it is a pollutant. But the problem with this is it totally ignores the first part of the definition which states that only "air pollution agent[s]" which are emitted into the air constitute "air pollutants." As Justice Scalia pointed out, "[t]he Court simply pretends this half of the definition does not exist" (*Ibid.* p. 9). Either the Court ignored the first half, or it used circular reasoning to conclude that CO_2 is an air pollutant. Either way, the reasoning of the majority is flawed.

Conclusion. In conclusion, what do we get—we get a Supreme Court ruling that is scientifically flawed, which was arrived at by ignoring logic and legal precedent, in order to reach a result that would please the global warming fanatics.

99% of Americans will never know about the legal errors that led to this ruling. Eventually the scientific community will come to acknowledge that the Massachusetts v. EPA case was politically based and scientifically flawed. But for now, the case represents a theory that is falsely held to be a fact, which has risen to the top by popular demand, regardless of true science.

2.2.2
9.1.4

Supreme Court Delivers a Major Victory for Freedom of Speech—
Court Invalidates Prohibition Against
Corporate Expenditures for Political Purposes
Citizens United v. Federal Election Commission, 558 U.S. ___ (2010)

by C. Paul Smith

On January 21, 2010, the Supreme Court ruled (5-4) in *Citizens United v. Federal Election Commission*, 558 U.S. ___ (2010) that the federal law prohibiting corporations from making independent expenditures for "electioneering communications" is unconstitutional. This ruling invalidated an important provision in the Bipartisan Campaign Reform Act of 2002 (BRAC). President Barack Obama announced his disagreement with this decision a few days later in his State of the Union Address, when he incorrectly chastised the Supreme Court for wrongly overturning a century of settled law on this important issue.

I don't ever recall seeing the President openly attacking the Supreme Court in a State of the Union Address. The impropriety of this was apparently lost on President Obama—who committed three distinct errors: (1) The State of the Union Address, an event at which all three branches of the government convene, is not the proper forum for the President (one Branch) to chastise another Branch (the Judiciary); (2) The President's statement that the Supreme Court had "reversed a century of law" was incorrect and misleading; and (3) President Obama failed to appreciate that this Supreme Court ruling and opinion was a good and important decision to strengthen the freedoms of speech and press in America.

The *Citizens United* decision can be summarized as follows: It struck down the BCRA provision (2 U.S.C. Sec. 441b) that prohibits corporations from making political communications within 30 days of a primary and within 60 days of a general election. There are two principal reasons why the Court struck down this provision: First, there is no

valid constitutional reason to discriminate against corporate speech versus the speech of any other entity. Second, Section 441b exempted public media corporations from the prohibition—and there is no logical or legal basis for treating public media corporations differently. There exists no justifiable reason for this disparate treatment of corporations in their exercise of political speech. There is no constitutional basis for penalizing certain corporate speech based upon who the speaker is.

Once the Court determined that the corporate prohibition was wrong, they next had to address the 1990 case of *Austin v. Michigan Chamber of Commerce*, 494 U.S. 652, where the Supreme Court held for the first time that the political speech of corporations may be banned. As Justice Kennedy explained, the principal of *stare decisis* prevents the Supreme Court from overturning prior decisions "unless the most convincing of reasons demonstrates that adherence to it puts us on a course that is sure error." The Court found such to exist (J. Kennedy, Slip Opinion, p. 47); the Court found that "*Austin* abandoned First Amendment principles" (J. Kennedy, Slip Opinion, p. 48) and therefore the Court overturned *Austin*. The Court stated that *Austin* was actually the aberration—that *Austin* "itself contravened this Court's earlier precedents in *Buckley* [1976] and *Bellotti* [1978]. *Ibid*. The Court pointed out that when the Supreme Court first considered the constitutionality of the BCRA in *McConnell v. Federal Election Commission*, 540 U.S. 93 (2003), that no one argued in that case that the *Austin* case was wrong and should be reversed. So the McConnell ruling did not address the fundamental issue that now requires the Court to invalidate this important part of the BCRA.[1]

Thus, the *Citizens United* decision overturned a 20-year-old case, that was manifestly incorrect; there was no 100-year-old precedent that was overturned in *Citizens United.*

The Dissenting Justices argued that *stare decisis* should uphold the corporate prohibitions of the BCRA, and prevents the Court from revisiting the *Austin* case. The Majority disagreed.

The Dissenting Justices also argued that the corporate prohibition helps to prevent corruption of elections by preventing corporations from buying elections with infusions of their monies. But the Majority found that the prohibition against indirect corporate speech was without constitutional merit; that the alleged corrupting influence cannot be shown; and that the disparate treatment of media corporations from other corporations is a blatant violation of First Amendment principles.

On another provision of the BCRA, the Court upheld the BCRA requirement (Sections 201 and 311) that the identity of the speaker of electioneering speech must be disclosed and reported. Justice Thomas was the lone dissenter to this ruling. The Court acknowledged that this imposed a minimal restriction on speech, but that the requirement enabled voters to be fully informed of who is speaking, and thus better enabled to give proper weight to the messages. (J. Kennedy, Slip Opinion, pp. 52-55.)

---

[1] *Constitutional Law Updates* has followed this important issue for almost a decade. We addressed the BCRA upon its passage in July 2002; in May 2004 we criticized the *McConnell* decision; and in October of 2007 we wrote about *FEC v. Wisconsin Right to Life*, 551 U.S. ___ (2007), which overturned an important part of the BCRA.

CONSTITUTIONAL LAW UPDATES

IX:1   September 2012   No. 16

Romney for President--a clear choice

by C. Paul Smith

America needs Mitt Romney now. Romney has the experience and leadership qualities that will bring America out of the current recession and re-establish the nation on principles of economic soundness and individual liberty.

But, some say, Romney's too stiff; he's just not a great speaker; Obama's more likeable. But if this is the best argument for Obama, then he's in deep trouble. He certainly does not have a good record to run on. And when confronted with his failures, Obama's best line is: "It's Bush's fault." Recently, even Obama himself has acknowledged the he should only get an "incomplete" grade for the work he's done. But after three and a half years of excuses and apologies, this just doesn't cut it. This year the nation's voters won't pick fluff over substance. On the substantive issues, Romney beats Obama in virtually every area.

Democrat loyalists insist that President Obama has done a great job in turning around the economy. They can even say this with a straight face. They make no apologies for the exploding national debt (now more than $16 Trillion—or approximately $48,500/person). They insist that an unemployment rate of over 8% for 43 straight months is good,

insisting that it would be worse were it not for Obama's great work. They don't like being reminded that four years ago Obama said that if he were not able to fix unemployment by now, he'd be a one term president. Obama promised to bring the rate to 5% after four years—but he hasn't come close. Those who are in the tank for Obama see the world through happy, distorting lenses. They ignore the 47 million Americans on food stamps. America is still in the same economic slump it was in four years ago—plus Obama has given us $5 Trillion more debt—this is not good! Obama brags that his administration has helped millions of people (citizens and aliens)—but he has only done this through reckless borrowing that has impaired the nation's credit and has burdened future generations with an enormous debt. Obama's (and the Democrats') vision for America is to continue doling out entitlements—government loans, government grants, government food stamps, government supported housing, government health care and government jobs— But they will not and cannot explain how this approach is economically sustainable; they don't understand that neither an individual nor a nation can long survive if it refuses to live within its means.

CONSTITUTIONAL LAW UPDATES is a newsletter edited and published by C. Paul Smith, J.D.
To order copies ($5.00 per issue), write CLU, P. O. Box 1204, Frederick, MD 21702-0204.
For further information visit www.cpaulsmith.com. Copyright C. Paul Smith 2012.

Democrats are desperate to find fault with Romney, but they are having trouble doing it; so they regularly resort to out-and-out lies. Uninformed voters will have a hard time figuring out what to believe. But those who will check the facts and examine the issues in depth will discern Obama's lies and will expose his fatal flaws.

Nevertheless, there are some differences between Obama and Romney that are not in dispute, and for which analysis can be made and conclusions reached. One of the most important ones is that Obama continues to promise a broad and increasing role for the federal government in helping people—even though his policies are too costly and are being financed by increasing our debt. Democrats do not acknowledge that their approach is reckless and unsustainable. Romney, on the other hand, advocates stopping the expansion of entitlements, and returning to the people the primary responsibility to provide for themselves.

President Barack Obama has not only failed to direct an economic recovery on sound fiscal policies—but he has made things worse. All Obama has done is to attempt to borrow our way out of an economic crash that was caused by excessive and unwise borrowing. And Obama has weakened America around the globe with his effusive apologies for America. Obama can't figure out if he's on Iran's side or on Israel's side in the Middle East. President Obama's policies have a proven track record of prolonging the recession. Obama's rejection of the free enterprise system (i.e., he advocates for socialism) would spell an end to America's being the land of opportunity.

A comprehensive comparison of the positions of Mitt Romney and Barack Obama on the major issues shows that Mitt Romney is clearly a better choice than Barack Obama on virtually every issue, and certainly on all of the issues as a whole. This article will examine both candidates' economic policies, their foreign policies, their social policies and their respective executive abilities.

I. ECONOMIC POLICY

Never before in any presidential race has the economic philosophy of the two contenders been as different as it is in 2012. President Obama is campaigning for pure socialism, and he openly criticizes the free enterprise system for causing the current recession. Conversely, Governor Romney argues that it is a return to the principles of the free enterprise/capitalism system that will restore economic vitality to America. President Obama would deny that the free enterprise system brought America its economic greatness, but he is wrong. Personal initiative, creativity and hard work is what made America great; and returning to these principles will help the poor, the middle class and the wealthy—pulling all of us out of the current recession.

A. "You didn't build that." You don't have to guess what economic philosophy guides Obama—it's called socialism. All business owners in America will never forget Obama's statement discounting the work it takes to make a successful business: "You didn't build that!" We all know what he meant--he believes that government gave us our prosperity; he disdains successful businesses. Obama says he is pro business, and that he wants to help the middle class--but his actions and his policies show that he is intent on raising taxes on big and small businesses and giving their wealth to others.

Obama doesn't have a clue what it takes to run a small business. Obama's sole tool for creating jobs is to raise taxes to hire people for government jobs. As Niall Ferguson wrote in *Newsweek*: "If only Obama had worked at Bain Capital for a few years instead of as a community organizer in Chicago, he might understand why the private sector is not "doing fine" right now." (Niall Ferguson, "Why Obama Must Go," *Newsweek*, Aug. 27, 2012, p.25.)

B. Free Enterprise vs. Socialism. Socialism is great at spreading wealth around, but not at creating it. The free enterprise system is best at creating wealth and economic growth because it fosters creativity, initiative, hard work, limited government and fiscal restraint.

Obama says we tried Romney's plan, and that it didn't work; Obama said that Romney's plan is what got us into the mess we're in. No so fast, Barack Hussein! Your glib conclusions cannot withstand either logical scrutiny nor the smarter-than-a-fifth-grader test. Free enterprise, capitalism, limited government, initiative, hard word and discipline are what made America, the land of opportunity, the most prosperous nation on the face of the earth. It was not socialism that made America prosperous. Socialism may be good at spreading the wealth around (until we run out of wealth), but it's not good at creating wealth. After socialism extracts all it can with taxes, next it will take control of all our property—real and personal. At that point we will have lost our liberty. Not only does socialism stifle economic growth, but it also smothers, then kills liberty. The cure for the current recession is a return to free enterprise and liberation from excessive government regulation and taxes.

C. Class Warfare--the Haves and the Have-nots. President Obama blames our current recession on the rich, for not paying their fair share of taxes; he says the rich are hording the wealth and not spreading it around enough. This is the classic, Marxist philosophy of socialism—the focus is on spreading around the wealth, rather than creating an economic system that both creates wealth and rewards those who work hard and take initiative. Once again, the Obama approach neglects the very foundation of economic strength—fostering and creating an economic system that creates wealth in the private sector. Obama's approach focuses almost exclusively on spreading wealth around, oblivious to the effect his approach is having on those who are the catalysts of real economic growth, which is mostly the more wealthy.

Obama combines his class warfare approach with the political tactic of making more and more voters dependent upon the government's largess—the result is that the "have-not" voters may now out-number the "have" voters. And this situation puts at risk the entire American economy. For if the recipients exercise the power to tell the providers what to do, then it will not be long before a majority of voters will succeed at taking the wealth from the rich—leaving the wealthy without capital to create jobs. Then the poorer people will spend or lose the money— but without creating jobs. This will lead to more unemployment and no job growth. Other nations will then supplant America as the world's leading economic strength. This will

compromise our military strength. Loss of liberty and national financial ruin will be next. All of these disastrous consequences flow from destroying the job-making foundation of the economy. And that is exactly what Obama's plan would do. The nation must adopt the approach that acknowledges and encourages wise, private enterprise; we must eliminate oppressive taxes. The nation must honor sound capital investments and the men and women who do it. Obama's policies, which deal with higher taxes and more regulations, are nothing more than a quick "fix" for drug addicts; those policies have an immediate, short-term effect, but they ultimately make things worse.

D. Who's plan is best for the middle class? President Obama attempts to appeal to the middle class by attacking Romney's policies as being harmful to the middle class. For the reasons stated above, Obama is exactly wrong; just the opposite is true. Romney's approach will help restore economic strength to all classes in our economy. Notice again, that Obama's primary approach is to insist that the rich pay more taxes. Obama's approach doesn't begin to address whether or not his approach would create new jobs. Obama's new jobs are almost all government jobs, paid for by increased taxes. Obama has no plan for how to strengthen the private businesses. Let me repeat that, Obama has no plan to build private business strength; his only plan is to redistribute wealth in order to help the middle class and the poor.

E. If the rich are not paying their fair share – What is their fair share? The fact is that 20% of taxpayers get back more than they pay in taxes, 80% of the people in the United States pay only 11% of the total taxes; and 20% of the people (the most wealthy) pay 89% of the total taxes. In light of these percentages, it sure sounds like the rich pay their fair share. What percentages do the Democrats think would be better? Make them say what their answer is. And if a Democrat thinks that some tax should be raised, make them identify the tax and the rate to which that tax should be raised.

On August 20th I saw an Obama ad that attacked Mitt Romney because he was rich and because he only paid 14% of his income as taxes. This ad may play well with the poor people who believe that it is the role of government to spread the wealth around—so that the poor have more and the rich have less. This is raw socialism, and Obama knows it, and he is banking on persuading the nation to abandon the free market system and embrace socialism. But, focus a minute on the two criticisms that Obama is making on Romney: that he is rich and that he doesn't pay enough taxes—neither is a legitimate reason to vote for Obama; on the contrary, Romney's wealth is a reason to vote for him, as is the fact that he pays the lawful amount of taxes that the law requires.

Most of the men who have become President of the United States have been wealthy—beginning with George Washington, John Adams and Thomas Jefferson. Those presidents who were not wealthy are relatively few. Who does this nation need to guide us to prosperity in difficult economic times? Someone like Obama, whose expertise is in taking government money to advance his political agenda? Or someone like Romney, who is a self-made millionaire, who understands national and international economic forces and who has the knowledge and experience to turn troubled businesses into profitable ones? Obama doesn't know how to make businesses successful: The policies of his presidency prove it; and the messages of his political campaign prove it. President Obama attacks and vilifies the rich, and he either ignores or denies the need for policies that will encourage the wealthy to invest in American jobs. Obama's class warfare continually blames the rich and attempts to tax them until they are brought down to the "middle class." If the "class warfare" theme prevails, then Obama will win, and the nation must brace for a protracted depression that could lead to national bankruptcy. If Obama drives away the rich people with capital, this will prolong and increase unemployment. It's not the poor who have the ability to create the jobs we need; rather it is the more wealthy.

This nation has fared well under the leadership of wise, wealthy men, whose understanding of the principles of economic strength brought them personal wealth and prepared them to establish policies that fostered national wealth.

If the USA were a business, looking for a leader to guide it to economic success, and if the executive search committee had before it the resumes of Barack Obama and Mitt Romney, the selection of Mitt Romney for CEO would be a no brainer. Obama would never get past the initial cursory review; he would never get invited for an interview. Obama has no business successes, let alone any business experience. He does have some good sales experience—he might be a good member of the sales force. But he has no qualifications to lead a business to success. And then, on top of that, he advocates policies that would kill businesses. Obama's constantly repeated antidote for sluggish business is that businesses need to pay more taxes and pay the workers more money. Any good union boss would say this. But not the company executive; a successful business model is more complex. I think we have just identified where Obama's next job should be— after he loses in November, he could apply to be a union rep—and he'd be a good one. But if you're looking for someone to direct the American economy to prosperity, Romney is the obvious, best choice.

And what about Obama's allegation that Romney doesn't pay enough taxes. This attack may also play well in Obama's class warfare campaign, but it doesn't withstand any logical scrutiny. The reason Romney currently pays only 14% in taxes (assuming Obama's ad is correct) is because most of Romney's income is "passive" and "long term capital gain" income. Romney's "earned" income would be taxed at the highest rate—35%. But passive income is taxed at a lower rate (e.g., 15% federal tax on long term capital gain). Passive income comes from "capital"—assets that can be used for investment purposes. The lower rate on this type of income was established by Congress to promote investment and jobs. Therefore, if Obama thinks that the 14% tax rate is too low, he should be consistent with himself and call for an increase in the capital gains tax rates. But Obama doesn't do this. He is content to play his class warfare game—attack the rich, and hope that this will work with the voters. Obama is slick and smart. But his philosophy is more designed to convince superficial thinkers than to convince sound thinkers.

President Obama is so fixated on his commitment to help the poor and increase taxes on the rich, that he cannot bear to cut any entitlements for the poor. In fact, it does appear, now that we have more and more people who get government benefits but pay no taxes— it appears that he is committed to pit the poor against the rich in order to get enough votes to win election and continue his self-destructive financial philosophy of demonizing the rich to get the votes of the poor. America may have reached the state where those voters who receive government benefits outnumber those who pay in to the government. This presents a crisis of unprecedented gravity. Many wise leaders have cautioned against this situation in the past. If you get to the point where those who receive benefits control how much the more wealthy citizens must give to the government, this can benefit the poorer citizens for a time, but it will eventually lead to the economic ruin of the nation. It appears that America has gotten to that point, where the poor and the less affluent must be urged to resist the Siren call of President Obama to support his philosophy of increased entitlements through loans from China and others.

It would be appropriate now to point out what will happen if Congress and the President raise the taxes too high on the rich. The rich will move to locations where the taxes are less repressive. (This includes moving away from states and nations whose taxes are too high.) The rich will divest themselves of assets and businesses that are subject to repressive taxes, and they will invest in things and in places that are more favorable. If employment taxes and wages become too high, businesses will hire less people, and they will outsource services when it is economically feasible to do so. (President Obama decries outsourcing, and yet he promotes policies that encourage it.) When income taxes on services and production get too high, wealthy people put more of their capital in passive income projects (investments, for which the tax rates are lower). Rich people put large amounts of money into investments for which capital gains and interest taxes are less.

Investors with a lot of money shop around the world for the best investments—and the United States will lose some of these investors when our tax policies are too steep.

America became great because hard-working, disciplined people came here from all nations around the world. These people came here for the opportunity to achieve financial success through hard work. President Obama's campaign promises of increased entitlements for all, whether or not one can afford it—all of this to be achieved by making the rich pay more—this is a flawed economic policy that may provide short-term benefits to President Obama (through re-election) and to his eager supporters who are ready to stand in line for handouts, but it will ultimately bring financial ruin to the U.S.

F. Obama's philosophy of excessive borrowing, higher taxes and more government was a major cause of the recession. President Obama blames Bush for the recession. But President Obama's version of what caused the recession is seriously flawed. The recession was caused by a collapse of property values that had been artificially inflated by government loan policies that were too generous in extending loans to those who could not afford them. In 2008 the bottom fell out of the real estate market, after several years of property values escalating to "appraised" values that exceeded their real values. The real value of thousands of properties was actually less than the loans that were made to acquire them—this was a recipe for disaster. The market correction in 2008 brought values crashing down to reality. Of course stock values also plummeted at this same time. There were other causes of this recession as well. But it should be viewed as a major market correction—which events have happened from time to time throughout our history. While those in power will always be tempted to borrow money to jump start a faltering economy, the best approach is to incur as little debt as possible in getting through the recession. Allow the economy to rebuild without increasing debt—as much as this is possible, this is the best economic approach because it was excessive debt that caused the crash; it is folly to think that increasing the debt will cure the crash that was caused by debt.

I do agree that some of President Bush's actions contributed to the crash of 2008—the wars in Iraq and Afghanistan added to the financial pressure on the U.S.; and President Bush supported the first bailout of almost $1 trillion. (Of course, Senator Obama also voted for this, so he can't blame Bush for this.) But President Obama added other bailouts as soon as he took office. And Obama can't really blame Bush for the war debt either—no sooner than he took office in 2009, President Obama dramatically increased the U.S. involvement in Afghanistan; he now owns the Afghanistan war effort. Nevertheless, President Obama attempts to blame the nation's financial problems on the Bush tax cuts at the same time he continues to increase the role and size of government. But he's just wrong on this matter. He can't continue to increase the cost of government when we have to borrow money to do it—it's a matter of basic arithmetic. The minor Bush tax cuts actually help our economy. Where does this leave President Obama? He is wrong in blaming Bush for the recession. But let me mention another thing that President Bush and the Democrat controlled Congress did that contributed to the recession, but which President Obama will not criticize—passage of the No Child Left Behind (education) Act. This act increased the involvement of the federal government in state education. This has driven education costs higher by requiring the states to spend more time and money to ensure that every child gets an education—whether or not they have the ability to learn, whether or not the child is determined to be disruptive, and whether or not the education program is even effective. The Constitution does not give the federal government the authority to control public education—Both Bush and Obama and Congress can take the blame for this usurpation that is contributing to excessive national debt.

G. Unemployment. Unemployment has remained at over 8% for all of Obama's term. He has not increased jobs. Obama claims that his plan is working, and that were it not for his plan the unemployment would be even higher. But this is hardly the type of job

growth that will pull the nation out of the recession. On the contrary, federal jobs that are funded by increased taxes will further burden the nation and prolong the economic recovery, and will burden future generations with debt. Obama doesn't seem to understand that not all jobs are equal: Government jobs that are funded by taxes are not as good as private sector jobs. And it is the private sector jobs that are needed to pull the nation out of the recession and bring jobs and prosperity to the nation.

Obama promised that his policies would reduce national unemployment--reducing it from over 9% in 2009 to 8% in 2010, 7% in 2011, 6% in 2012, and to 5.6% in 2013. To those of us who analyzed the policies he enacted to obtain these results, we knew that this made no sense. If Obama were to achieve these goals it would be in spite of, not because of his policies. Predictably, his policies were the failure we knew they would be: Actual unemployment got higher in 2010 (9.6%), was 9.0% in 2011, and has been 8.5% in 2012. Obama and his policies have been an abysmal failure in addressing unemployment! And the results would be even worse if the unemployment rates included those out of work who stopped looking for work. If it weren't for the government jobs that Obama has created, the jobless rate would be even worse.

Romney, on the other hand, believes that the growth of federal government is harmful to the economy; he proposes to shrink the federal government through attrition. This will gradually ease the burden of taxpayers, which will strengthen businesses and individuals.

H. National Debt. And speaking of debt—President Obama has increased the national debt by over $5 trillion dollars in 3 ½ years. He has accumulated more debt for the nation than any other president ever. Pres. Obama will not acknowledge that this debt burden comes with a steep price—it will prolong the recession and weaken us with respect to other nations.

Long-term national recovery from a severe recession/depression must be made by following sound economic principles. When a nation has become "hooked" on debt (much like a drug addict can be "hooked" on drugs), long-term recovery only comes when the addict gets off the drug—i.e., when the addict totally stops depending upon the drug. Similarly, America must free itself from dependency on debt—we must get out of debt. Only when America stops piling up debt will there be a recovery.

Admittedly, some debt is legitimate—reasonable home mortgage debt and sound business debt can always be appropriate. But going into debt to buy food, clothing, a second car, electronic gadgets, vacations, toys, etc. must stop, or else the consumer will face bankruptcy. The same is true for nations. Excessive debt will sink nations, just as it will ruin individuals. And America has a serious debt crisis. One of President Obama's biggest flaws is his failure to acknowledge and address the debt crisis. Although Barack Obama complained in his 2008 campaign that Bush had given the nation too much debt, nevertheless, once elected, President Obama proceeded to increase the nation's debt more in 3 ½ years than Bush did in 8 years. President Obama's approach was to promote and pass stimulus legislation that increased our national debt by several trillion dollars, and then to promptly say that he would now work to balance our budget. President Obama's loyal followers don't mind this double-talk, but rational people who haven't drunk the Obama cool-aid see this for what it is: Foolish hypocrisy that will provide the nation a quick fix, but which will prolong recovery and increase the negative impact of debt addiction.

The cure from debt addiction is a long-term regimen of sacrifice and work. Governments and individuals must make budget cuts; some government services must be trimmed and others eliminated. Work must be re-enthroned as a part of every citizen's constitution. Sloth and voluntary dependence must become disgraceful in the eyes of all society. The nation must brace for a lengthy period of time where all citizens commit to work hard and sacrifice until economic strength is restored. All unnecessary government debt must stop. This will mean that some government jobs will be lost—because unnecessary government programs are administered through government jobs. This will add to national unemployment. But nevertheless this must happen—it is the

retrenchment process that must occur in order for there to be a sound recovery.

President Obama has not had the courage or the wisdom to implement this retrenchment approach. On the contrary, he has kept the size of government the same (with some job cuts and with some new jobs), and he has borrowed like a drunken sailor to keep the U. S. government the same size it has been. In addition, President Obama continues to extend unemployment benefits, and he recently dropped the work requirement for some of those benefits. Again, comparing President Obama's approach to the rehabilitation of a drug addict—President Obama continues to give the addict the drug to prevent the addict from crashing. President Obama will not cut the funds; he will only continue to pile up the debt—hoping that the economy will recover in spite of his actions to prolong that recovery.

1. Bailouts and Stimulus Funds.
President Obama's bailout of GM is another example of his lack of business acumen. President Obama brags about how, with a federal loan to GM of $49.5 Billion of federal money, he was able to save GM. But as one who practices bankruptcy law, I have to ask the question: "What difference does it make?" The bankruptcy option would serve to relieve GM of a certain amount of liabilities, just like a government loan (other people's money) enabled GM to pay a certain amount of liabilities. In connection with the government bailout, the federal government actually became the owner of GM—General Motors became Government Motors. President Obama touts the GM Bailout as an example of what he would like to do to other ailing industries; he thinks the bailout has worked out well. But the government still owns 26% of GM, and GM stock prices are so low that current projections are that the government will lose $25 Billion when all is said and done. Hardly a success story to brag about. The main thing that saved GM, assuming it has been salvaged, is the restructuring of its debts, its benefits and its business model. Either bankruptcy or the bailout would have enabled GM to do this. The disadvantage of the government bailout is that it took scarce federal, taxpayer dollars; it offered

GM a benefit that the government cannot afford to equally offer to other businesses; and it put the federal government in control in making the decisions that will guide GM in the future. That last effect is really scary! With all things considered, Romney's solution would have been better—let GM use the bankruptcy laws to solve its problems, just like every other business would have to do.

J. **Deregulation.** Obama argues that Romney will bring back deregulation, which caused the recession. This is a baseless argument. Conservatives favor eliminating and/or reducing regulations that are burdensome, ineffective and expensive. *FactCheck* reported (on June 15, 2012) that the cost of the new regulations under Obama in 3 ½ years is $18.8 billion, compared to a $4.3 billion cost for regulations under Bush in 8 years. Excessive and burdensome regulations hurt private industry, and only grow government jobs. Eliminating these types of regulations will be a benefit to the economy. There will be some short-term job losses that result from terminating the employees that administer the deleterious regulations. But the long-term effect on the economy will be better. Excessive taxes contribute to excessive and repressive regulations—both need to be reduced. Thus some deregulation is a very good thing, and Romney favors this.

But what about Obama's argument that deregulation caused the recession? I don't buy it. My recollection is that one of the principal reasons for the collapse of the housing market was the flawed mortgage lending regulations that led to unqualified buyers getting loans that were not secured by equity. The Bush administration had urged Barney Frank and Chris Dodd to revise these flawed regulations, but to no avail. Ultimately the bad regulations were a major contributor to the mortgage crisis and housing collapse.

In fact, the eliminating of bad regulations and the streamlining of good regulations will help to establish a sound fiscal foundation for a growing, prosperous economy. This process is "deregulation." It is a good thing. Such deregulation did not cause the recession, and it will actually help rebuild the economy.

Perhaps the worst new regulation enacted by Obama is the Affordable Care Act (ACA or "Obamacare"), which will be discussed below. The bad economic consequences of this are enormous.

Another terrible piece of legislation that Obama takes credit for is the Dodd-Frank Law, also called the "Wall Street Reform and Consumer Protection Act." This law represents an effort by the Democrats to blame the 2008 stock market crash on rich Wall Street investors. I don't deny that some blame is due here, but the Dodd-Frank Law has primarily been used to feed the Democrat mantra that it is the greedy rich that caused the 2008 recession--this, of course, plays into Obama's class warfare campaign. But the reality is that Dodd-Frank is a terrible piece of legislation. At 2,318 pages, it's almost as long as the Affordable Care Act; it creates 247 new rules, calls for 67 new studies, and requires 22 new, periodic reports. Not only do new regulations increase the number of regulators (and the cost of government), but some regulations stifle economic growth. Obama doesn't seem to understand this.

K. **Energy and Environmental Issues.** President Obama's fanatical support of environmentalist and green energy is showcased by the $528 Million bailout loan that he directed the government to give Solyndra, a solar energy company. That money was quickly lost, as Solyndra folded within months of receiving the money; it filed for bankruptcy in 2011. This incident showcases Obama's inability to make wise business investments; the rapidity with which Solyndra failed after getting the federal dollars makes it clear that Obama did not give due diligence in checking out the wisdom of a grant to Solyndra in the first place. It was a dumb investment, even if some green investments could be wise. The Solyndra fiasco is strong evidence that Obama has poor business judgment.

Not only does the Solyndra example showcase Obama's lack of good business judgment, it also shows that he is too easily influenced to support environmentalist proposals without ascertaining their soundness—either their fiscal soundness or the viability of their alleged environmental benefits.

This combination spells economic disaster for the nation—when we have a radical environmentalist running the national economy, we are going to see both bad business decisions and failed environmental policies. That's exactly what we've got under Obama's leadership. The solution is really quite simple: Both economical and environmental consequences must be examined and analyzed before implementing policies. And this analysis needs to be done by intelligent, experienced, courageous people. We need to make sure of facts and projections before implementing policies that would wreck the economy—but Obama has not done this. New leadership is required; the nation must clean house in the EPA.

Another example of Obama's failed energy leadership is his opposition to the Yucca Mountain nuclear waste storage project (in Harry Reid's Nevada). Although the scientists have thoroughly studied the safety and environmental acceptability of the Yucca Mountain project, President Obama catered to an anti-nuclear energy contingency (led by Sen. Harry Reid), and halted this project--and thereby made it more difficult for nuclear power plants to be built. Twenty percent (20%) of the electricity produced in America comes from nuclear facilities. This energy is safe, and it produces no green house gases. Many nations in Europe are availing themselves of this technology, but in American the fanatical environmentalists block the development of this efficient energy source because of unreasonable fears.

Following the BP oil spill in the Gulf of Mexico, BP spent $23 Billion to clean up the Gulf--and they succeeded. So how did Obama lead in this matter? He heeded the cries of his environmentalist friends, and he shut down drilling in the Gulf. This was reactionary--not strong leadership. President Obama has encouraged investment in drilling for oil off of shores in South America, but not on American shores. This is hypocritical as well as short-sighted. The nation who controls the most energy sources will control the world. Thus for national defense reasons as well as for economic reasons President Obama should have done more to advance oil production at home. Obama's energy policy is to stop the production

of oil, and attempt to meet America's energy needs with wind power and solar energy. This type of extreme environmentalism has hurt America. Environmental policies must be founded in facts and soundness—not founded on "Chicken Little" fanaticism.

L. Health Care—The Affordable Care Act. The signature legislation for which Obama will be remembered is his enacting of the Affordable Care Act of 2012 (ACA), or "Obamacare," as we call it. As I listened to the Senate debate before it passed this legislation, the proponents for Obamacare sounded like preachers at a religious revival, as they preached about how Obamacare was a panacea for the ills of Americans: Obamacare would provide "affordable" health care for all. Everybody would get the health care they need; taxes would be lowered—we would have Nirvana. But the devil was in the details of the 2,000 + page legislation that virtually no Senator nor Representative had read. Obama and his supporters insisted that the law would lower, rather than raise taxes. And, of course, they insisted that the increased payments that it called for were not actually "taxes." The opponents of ACA pointed out that it would raise taxes; that it would jeopardize the quality of health care; that it would put excessive strain on the economy; and that it would put the government in charge of an additional 1/6 of the economy, which would lead to a demise of our economy. The Democrat-controlled Congress prevailed, and Obamacare became law.

As we all know, the Supreme Court recently ruled that Obamacare was indeed a "tax," regardless of how the Democrats choose to label it. The Supreme Court struck down the expanded Medicare part of Obamacare—Thank goodness! That would have put excessive financial burdens on the state and local governments that are already struggling. But the Supreme Court did uphold the "individual mandate" part of Obamacare, which will require the younger, healthy, uninsured citizens to either buy health insurance or to pay a "tax" to fund health care for the rest of the nation. Romney and the Republicans vow to overturn Obamacare, and it will be good if they do.

The dire economic consequences of Obamacare require its repeal. In Section III, A, below, I explain how Obamacare will impair the quality of health care for America in the future.

M. Immigration. Immigration policies impact America on multiple levels—the economy, national defense and social policies. See Section II, C, below.

N. Conclusion. The most important thing that Romney will do to strengthen our economy is to reverse the several repressive policies of Obama, so that the private sector will be freed from the bondage of excessive regulations and taxes, so that the private sector will be empowered to create more jobs. This will increase jobs and incomes for poor, middle class and rich alike.

II. FOREIGN POLICY
A. The Military and the War on Terror.
On the surface, both Romney and Obama have taken similar positions on the importance of the U. S. military. But now that we are in the middle of a campaign, Obama is silent on the cuts he recommended in Defense spending. And Obama is also hoping the voters will forget his dismantling of our missile defense system in eastern Europe (particularly Poland). President Obama did not do this at the request of our European neighbors; he did it because of his own desire to dismantle our defense system, and because he doesn't believe American will never face another threat from either Russia or China. It was in this context that he was overheard telling Russian President Putin, that after the election he (Obama) would have more flexibility. Governor Romney wisely took the President to task for this policy; Romney said that if he is elected Putin would find that America has "less flexibility and more backbone." Romney believes that America and all the world is safer when America remains so strong that our enemies are afraid to confront us. Romney supports peace through strength; Obama's goal is to reduce nuclear weapons and to hope that Russia and China will never become our enemies.

To this point, the war on terror has not been a campaign issue because the Democrats aren't complaining about it, since their guy is in office. But the situation has not improved. While USA

extricated itself from Iraq, Obama has the nation mired in Afghanistan. In August, Afghan forces that we thought we were helping, turned on American soldiers and shot and killed two of them. A few days later, six other Americans were killed the same way.

The headline of an August 22nd AP article states this: "Americans tune out Afghan war as fighting rages on." This is telling commentary on this nation's support of President Obama's leadership in the war on terror. The significant part of this story lies in what is not stated: While the death toll from this campaign continues, the war effort does not appear to be a major presidential campaign issue. Actually, I submit it is an important campaign issue this year. But the reason it is receiving little media attention is because the Democrats are in charge, rather than the Republicans. The Republicans are not going to undermine the nation's war efforts abroad by constantly working to undermine the effort at home. The Democrats' handling of this was totally different when a Republican was in office—Democrat criticism of Republican-led war efforts were sharp and incessant; and the Democrats didn't care whether their criticism undermined the war effort or not. But the Republicans know that too much criticism at home serves to embolden our enemies abroad, and they will not be a part of such criticism. However, the time is right now, on the eve of the presidential election, to insert an appropriate amount of criticism and comment about our campaign in Afghanistan—and here it is.

First of all, Obama has total ownership of the Afghanistan campaign. After his election, he directed a major step up in military action there. Rather than attempting to get out of the region, as is occurring in Iraq, President Obama increased and accelerated our involvement in Afghanistan. But the wisdom of this exercise is not apparent. As one retired military officer said in August, Afghanistan is a "worthless piece of dirt." There were 630 American Fatalities in Afghanistan from 2001 to 2008. But under Obama's leadership (2009-2012) there have been 1,484 casualties—more than twice as many in half the time.

In August the Afghan soldiers that we had been training turned their weapons on American soldiers who were training—killing eight Americans in two separate attacks. So far in 2012, 39 Americans have died from such attacks; 35 died from such attacks in 2011. The Taliban leader, Mullah Muhammad Omar, takes great pride in infiltrating and killing Americans. And after a recent fast, he called for more security forces to do this. Why are we helping to train such crazy people who hate us?

Although 70 percent of Americans favored our entry into Iraq to take out Saddam Hussein in 2002, the national consensus has changed in the intervening ten years. It is not worth the many American lives that are being sacrificed to attempt to build a democratic government among ruthless people who are anxious to kill us. The better approach from this point forward is to limit our involvement to short-term campaigns to take out evil, oppressive regimes that threaten our national interests, but limit our long-term involvement where it presents excessive risks to American lives. Applying this approach to Afghanistan—let's get out of there.

B. Fast and Furious. The Obama Administration's support of gun sales to criminals and drug dealers in Mexico is terrible. I am not aware of evidence that President Obama actually had knowledge of this terrible program (called "Fast and Furious") until it was discovered. But there is some linkage to Attorney General Holder. Congress has subpoenaed hundreds of documents pertaining to what Holder knew and when he knew it. And Attorney General Holder is refusing to produce many of them. The problem is that the guns that the federal government sold to the foreign criminals have been used to kill people, including at least one American Border Patrol Officer, Brian Terry. Obama's Administration can articulate some rationale for this program; and then they also will blame Bush for it. But this Administration owns the program. It is a bad one. And unless Holder can produce all requested documents, then he must be fired. And since President Obama won't take this action—the responsibility for this terrible

program must rest squarely on his shoulders—the buck stops at Barack.

C. Egypt. In early 2012, President Obama (without Congressional approval) went out of his way to support a political coup in Egypt that eventually toppled Egyptian President Hosni Mubarack. President Obama was proud of his role in toppling a government that had some flaws. But then, the government that emerged in Egypt has become a communist/socialist government that is adversarial to the US. The feather that Obama put in his hat last spring now needs to be pulled out. The "Arab Spring" that Obama thought was good, is not. The President was overanxious to involve himself in overthrowing Egypt's government; Congress did not support the action. President Obama's actions have not been helpful.

D. Israel. And what about Israel? President Obama is so intent on lending support to his Muslim brothers that his support of Israel is tepid at best, and probably lacking. It is hard to support the hate-filled Iran dictator Mahmoud Ahmadinejad, and at the same time to be supportive of Israel. Obama tries to do both. Obama should ponder the verses in Matthew that caution that you "cannot serve two masters." You cannot support Israel, and at the same time support Iran, whose leader declares that Israel must be destroyed. Obama seems to think that he can reconcile the two without making enemies with either. But Obama has not learned the simple lesson that you cannot be all things to all people. And there are some issues where he must take a side. The Israel-Iran relationship is one of them. Most nations in the world do not want Iran to get the nuclear bomb because Iran's leadership is so volatile, hate-filled and radical that it would threaten the world. At a time when strong leadership is critical in bringing Iran under control—the vacillating leadership of Obama is harmful to the United States. Since Obama can't figure out whose side he's on, it's time for America to turn to Governor Romney who already has this one figured out.

E. Immigration. President Obama has no interest in stopping illegal immigration into the United States. Governor Romney wants to stop illegal immigration. Just stop for a second, and consider these two statements. President Obama's policies are terrible—he won't enforce the immigration laws; he actually encourages illegal immigration through his words and actions. And in so doing President Obama threatens national security and he puts excessive strain on the federal, state and local governments—as he demands that they provide free education for and give welfare benefits and other entitlements to the illegals. And Obama encourages illegals to come here, when we already have too much unemployment—this puts a terrible strain on our suffering economy. Put it all together, and Obama's policy is stupid.

Let me remind the reader of some of the mistakes Obama has made and is making in his immigration policies. First of all, Obama will not enforce some of the existing federal immigration laws—Obama has withdrawn his full support from the ICE (287g) program that allows local law enforcement to identify and expel illegal immigrants who are arrested for violating other laws. When the Supreme Court upheld Arizona's law to authorize that State to take action to work with the federal government in enforcing immigration laws (*Arizona v. United States*, 567 U.S. ___ (2012)), President Obama announced that the federal government would no longer enforce those federal laws—President stuck out his lower lip and announced that the federal government was withdrawing from doing its federal immigration duty in Arizona. This was a juvenile and pathetic act.

III. SOCIAL POLICY
A. Health Care – The Affordable Care Act.
Not only is the "Affordable Care Act" (ACA) a financial and economic disaster, but it would also undermine and impair America's once great health care system.

Here are three reasons why Obamacare would harm America. First, the ACA will increase taxes and the costs of medical care. It is impossible to expand medical coverage to more individuals without either cutting the costs of medical coverage or increasing taxes. President Obama denies this simple truth. Frankly, taxes will be increased and doctor's pay will be cut. The cut in doctor's pay will de-incentivize the medical profession. The brightest and best will begin to choose other

careers; then the quality of health care will decline; this will only increase the problems and the costs of medical care. Second, the ACA will destroy the health insurance industry. If all insurance carriers are required to cover "pre-existing conditions," then this will undermine their ability to make contracts to provide coverage, and it will undermine their very ability to stay in business. The insurance industry will be destroyed. Now, a lot of us have gripes with insurance companies—but the undermining of insurance will have a far-reaching effect on the American economy. Third, the ACA will greatly expand the role and size of the federal government. The number of health care providers, regulators and tax collectors will multiply, with all the inherent inefficiencies of government control; this will eliminate the efficiency incentives that attend private-run health care. The result of this will be to increase waste, to impair service, and to continually increase taxes to support a system that is inherently inefficient and plagued with poor service. Fourth, the ACA creates a new, "right to healthcare." Never before has such a right existed—and the ACA does not identify the level of care to which one will have a right. This is a serious problem, because it appears that the ACA bestows a right to the highest available quality of healthcare. Sure, the highest quality health care is desirable. But never before has it been guaranteed as a right to everyone. This would mean that every time there is an innovative machine or medicine that would be a little bit better, then every citizen has a right to it regardless of the cost to taxpayers. As wonderful as this would be for the individual receiving the care, it is not economically sustainable. Such a policy would ultimately wreck the economy. Obamacare is fatally flawed with idealistic dreams that are totally divorced from economic reality. The Affordable Care Act is a train wreck waiting to happen. If not repealed, it will cause an economic disaster for America that will be extremely difficult to repair, and it will also undermine and sabotage America's quality health care system.

B. Environment.
At this point in the presidential campaign, very little has been said

about the environment. The silence on this issue is telling; it indicates that both candidates know that the economy is the number one issue, and advancing environmental issues typically hurts or stops economic growth in the short run. If the nation's economy were not in such a serious condition, you would expect to hear President Obama speaking up more about clean air, clean water and green energy. But again, with the economy suffering, the Obama campaign rarely, if ever, brings up these concerns. However, at some point the candidates will have to address environmental issues before November.

Both candidates are for clean air, clean water and for a sustained, healthy environment. But President Obama has consistently sided with environmental extremists, to the detriment of the economy and of good energy policies. President Obama opposes the Keystone Pipeline project, which is costing the nation a valuable source of energy and good jobs. President Obama has shut down drilling for oil off of America's shores and in the Gulf of Mexico because of the BP oil spill, even though BP has cleaned the Gulf after spending $23 Billion of its own, private money to do it. The EPA has become one of the most powerful agencies in the federal government, and it continues to exert that power to enforce some excessive, repressive and expensive regulations that have only minimal impact on helping the environment, but which hurt the economy by mandating expensive regulations. Bolstered by the terrible ruling of the Supreme Court in *Massachusetts v. EPA*, 549 U.S. 497 (2007), where the Court ordered the EPA to identify CO2 as a "pollutant," this has empowered fanatical environmentalists with unprecedented power to wreck the economy. Obama and the EPA are ruining our economy.

No state can appreciate this repressive situation more than Maryland, where "Clean the [Chesapeake] Bay" controls the Governor's administrative agenda. Cleaning the Bay is important; the problem is that the State and federal regulations being promulgated to do it are shackling business with expensive measures that have only a negligible, positive affect on the Bay. It is the extremist, fanatical regulating that is the problem. We need to enforce sound

environmental regulations; but neither Obama nor O'Malley can tell the difference between a good regulation and bad one.

Part of the problem that has led Obama astray is the global warming crowd. While the year 2012 has been warmer than other years, the fact is that there has been only minimal global warming in the last decade. Frankly, until 2012, over the prior ten years, the temperatures had been flat. But, acknowledging a minor increase in global temperatures over the last one hundred years (approximately 1 degree F), the next question is: "To what extent is this increase caused by humans?" Human life, including its industries, cars and power plants, clearly produces green house gases (CO2), too much of which has a warming effect in the atmosphere around these things. But whether these effects are causing the entire planet to overheat is another question; and the experts are divided on this question. Some scientists argue that man's activities are the cause of the slight, global warming over the last century. But just as many other scientists disagree; many of these scientists identify the sun, and sun spots, as being primarily responsible for most variations in global temperatures.

To summarize the global warming matter:
* **Over the last century there has been slight global warming.**
* **Sun Spot activity is one of the primary causes of global warming.**
* **The causative impact of humans on global warming is not certain, and to the extent it exists the impact is slight.**
* **Most measures to combat global warming are expensive and have negligible benefit.**

Based upon these conclusions, what does one do? Well, the global warming fanatics have shifted their concern now to "climate change"; since they can't prove that humans are causing global warming, they now argue without proof that humans cause all changes in weather patterns and in the environment. They blame humans for every unusual weather occurrence. They blame the back-to-back blizzards of 2010 on human life; they blame the tornadoes, the hurricanes, the tsunamis, the droughts, and of course the hot summer of 2012—they blame all of this on human life. Never mind the fact that they can't prove any one event in particular— nevertheless they confidently conclude that the sum of these occurrences proves that human life causes "climate change." Pardon me, but merely switching mantras from "global warming" to "global climate change" does not obviate the need to prove causation. And, before "climate change" can be used to justify punitive environmental regulations, some of us require some level of proof—some level above pure speculation.

Attention: "The Sea is rising!" Environmental alarmists predict that the ocean level will rise by two to four feet in the next one hundred years. If so, this would cause serious problems in seaboard states, and Maryland is one of these—with the Chesapeake Bay (the largest bay in the United States), Maryland has the sixth most shoreline of all the states. The so-called experts contend that melting global ice will cause this incredible rise in ocean levels. But the more you listen to them, the less intelligent their arguments sound. A June 29, 2012, an Associated Press article reported that the ocean levels had risen 2.8 inches in New York City; 3.7 inches in Philadelphia, Pennsylvania; and 4.8 inches in Norfolk, Virginia. But these variations cannot be accurate because the true sea rise in New York would be identical to that in Norfolk—because a body of water, including the ocean, always reaches the same level everywhere. The writers of this article didn't seem to acknowledge this law of physics, but rather gullibly accepted someone's reports without even addressing the question of how these varying results could be accurate if water levels must be consistent for the entire body of water.

No state is facing more stringent, expensive water clean-up expenses than Maryland. The EPA is partly responsible, and Governor Martin O'Malley is making it much worse. In Maryland, we know that Governor O'Malley is already running for President in 2016. So those of you in other states need to be warned. His water clean-up policies are fanatical, unsupported by scientific proof, and they are exorbitant in cost—they are driving jobs and people out of the State. Despite some

businesses leaving the state, Maryland's economy continues to be relatively strong because of the presence of so many government jobs here. But, if not corrected, O'Malley's environmental policies will seriously harm Maryland's economy. If applied nationally, O'Malley's policies will ruin America. So be warned. Watch out for O'Malley.

C. Abortion – Women's rights and Rights of the Unborn. President Obama supports a woman's right to an abortion as an absolute, with no recognition or belief that the human life within a pregnant woman is entitled to any right to remain alive. Some Republicans contend that in cases of rape or incest a woman's right to choose can prevail over any right of the unborn to continue living. But Obama does not recognize the sanctity of unborn human life. The Republican position on this important issue is much better.

In mid-August, the nation focused on Rep. Aiken's gaff, when he said that in cases of "legitimate" rape, the woman's body has a way to take care of itself. Democrats have triumphantly broadcast Aiken's gaff for a week, and they salivate at the opportunity to cast all Republicans as being ignorant and anti-women. But no president or presidential candidate has ever had a more radical, offensive stance on abortion than Barack Obama. His support of abortion was so extreme that as an Illinois State Senator he blocked legislation that would require the participating parties to attempt to save the lives of children who were born alive after failed abortions. This barbaric, reprehensible position is disgusting. Obama's support of this position should disqualify him from ever being president. Somehow he overcame this four years ago, but this serious flaw should be pointed out again.

The right answer to the abortion issue is that women have a right to control their own bodies, but it is not an absolute right. The right of a human fetus to continue living outside the mother's womb should also be recognized; and human fetuses should be protected—but, in my opinion, their right to life is not absolute either. In my opinion, if a woman voluntarily becomes pregnant, then her right to an abortion should be limited to those situations where her life would be jeopardized. Abortions for convenience should not be encouraged.

The *Roe v. Wade* case (1973), extinguished any fetal right to life. In my opinion, this part of *Roe v. Wade* was a gross error; this was judicial legislation at its worst. *Roe v. Wade* gave the States the right to prohibit abortions in the second trimester for the health of the mother-to-be; and it gave the States the right to protect the potential human life in the last trimester of the pregnancy. *Roe v. Wade* would allow States to outlaw partial birth abortion since this by definition is a last trimester abortion procedure. Abortion should be outlawed by the States in the last trimester because at that point human fetuses are capable of surviving outside the mother's womb. However, even then, it is my opinion that IF a woman's life would be endangered more by carrying the baby full term than by aborting the baby, then this would be a legitimate legal basis for an abortion.

Drawing the fine lines as to when an abortion might be legal and when it could be prohibited will never satisfy everyone. There must be an acknowledgement that there are some instances, even though they may be only a few, when the health of the mother can justify an abortion. But the total disregard for the sanctity and preciousness of developing human life in the mother is a grievous moral deficiency. The value of each and every independent human life is unsurpassed. Our laws should protect life as much as possible. The Republican platform does this, whereas President Obama's disregard for human pre-natal life is disgraceful.

D. Gay Rights. During his term in office, President Obama has changed his political position from one of tolerance of gays, to full support of the militant gay, bi-sexual and transgender agendas. The primary mistake in Obama's current position is that he promotes same-sex marriage. The problem with this is that it is not the best policy for the children. When one focuses on the rights of two individuals to have same-sex relations, a lot of people are willing to look the other way, saying that as long as it doesn't hurt someone else, then no one should care. But, where the studies show that traditional marriage is best for the

rearing of children, and that same-sex marriages cannot provide for children the same quality of rearing that a traditional heterosexual couple can—then it is good and proper for our state and national laws to promote and prefer traditional marriage over same-sex marriage.

Those who wish to promote gay sexual conduct and the rearing of children in gay families are promoting practices and situations that will harm children. Studies show that children reared in traditional marriages have better health, fewer mental and emotional problems, less incidences of crime and juvenile delinquency, better incomes, and happier lives than the children in same-sex marriages.

Despite this evidence, self-centered gay activists insist that they have a right to marry someone of the same sex; they deny that heterosexual parents are better for the children. But this denial does not change the fact that heterosexual marriage is the best policy.

And while we're on this issue, I would remind the reader that there is no scientific support for the theory that people are born that way. There is no gay gene. Scientific studies for twenty years have confirmed that it is experience and circumstances that cause same-sex attractions. Studies also confirm that people can change—to change from straight to gay; and to change from gay to straight. Thus, sexual orientation is not immutable, like race and color.

Once again—President Obama is on the wrong side of this issue. He does people a disservice by morphing a stance of tolerance into support for a lifestyle of choice that brings with it bad and predictable negative consequences.

Romney's approach to the gay issue is the better one: He champions traditional marriage. He does not attack gays, but he does draw a line. Whatever opportunities and rights society may give to gays stop at the altar. Marriage is between a man and a woman—to promote the only relationship that can bring children into the world, and the best unit of society to raise children.

IV. EXECUTIVE ABILITY
A. Vice President Selections. As a Republican I am very pleased the Romney has

selected Paul Ryan to be the Vice Presidential candidate. Ryan is the most knowledgeable person in Congress on budget issues. His experience in this area is crucial to repairing the economy. Vice President Biden has put together such an impressive string of gaffs that I am glad he's connected to President Obama. Biden can help bring about the defeat of Obama, so I'm glad President Obama is leaving him on the ticket. Conversely, Congressman Ryan's expertise on the budget will help Mitt Romney.

B. Uniformed voters. In America the right to vote is extended to almost every adult citizen that will register. There is no IQ test; no requirement to know basic facts about our nation and our government. In fact, stupid people have just as much right to vote as intelligent and informed people. This presents a rather scary situation, doesn't it. And in a close election, the stupidity factor could be fatal to one side or the other. The fact is that candidates know this, and they make intentional efforts to appeal to all voters, including the uninformed and the stupid ones.

We can't totally correct this inherent flaw in our system, but it is still important to educate voters the best we can. This article is intended to help those who are willing to become better informed about the issues.

C. The intangibles. As I pointed out at the top, Obama's hopes for re-election are hinged on his desperate hope that he will win the "likability" contest. Admittedly, Barack Obama is a smooth talker—he is the epitome of a snake oil salesman. Interestingly, a recent line from Obama accused Republicans of attempting to sell "snake oil." Well, if the Republicans were to pick a "snake oil salesman," or any old salesman, it would not be Mitt Romney. Romney is a roll-up-your-sleeves, pitch in and help, hard worker. He personifies integrity and competence and goodness; but he is admittedly less charismatic than Obama. We've tried the glib, movie star type; American needs someone who knows how to run a business and a state and a nation. We tried the community organizer who apologizes to other nations for America's greatness. We tried the class warfare cheerleader who makes no secret about his hostility towards business. If the best argument

against Romney is that he's too stiff—so be it. We need a president who can lead a nation to business success; our experience with a slick leader who is a smooth talker has only made things worse for America.

Also, I do not concede that Romney is less likable than Obama. Romney is extremely well liked by most people who have worked with him. Perhaps he is less flamboyant than Obama—but flamboyance and likableness are not the same thing. Romney is courteous, charitable, kind, honest, diligent, trustworthy, helpful and competent. When you break Romney's character down into the individual traits he possesses you realize that you have described a wonderful person and a highly effective leader. To those who contend that Obama is more likable, I respond "No!" Romney is much more likable. The real difference they have identified is a superficial charisma about Obama—not a person who is more likable. And frankly, a better question than who do you like best at first glance is WHO HAS THE BEST CHARACTER TO PROVIDE THE LEADERSHIP FOR AMERICA? Mitt Romney is the clear answer to this question.

V. CONCLUSION

Romney is clearly a better choice for president than Obama in every area of national interest. The contrast is stark and deep. The consequences of this election will be drastic and long-lasting: Will we continue down the path of socialism--a path that will end in economic ruin? Or will be cut our losses, stop the bleeding, and restore the values and principles of liberty and free enterprise and individual responsibility that made America great in the first place?

Obama insists that socialism would be better than capitalism. Obama's recipe for prosperity is to increase taxes on the rich and spread the wealth around. But this socialist solution has never worked before; it always leads to economic disaster. Romney knows how the free enterprise system can work to raise the prosperity of the entire nation. A vote for Romney is a vote to restore America to the principles and values of liberty and prosperity.

CONSTITUTIONAL LAW UPDATES

| IX:ii | December 2012 | No. 17 |

Obama, the Man, Won the 2012 Election, But Not the Obama Policies

by C. Paul Smith

Interpreting the meaning of the recent Presidential Election is somewhat complicated. The election was close. While the Electoral College vote gave President Obama a substantial margin of victory (332-206), the national popular vote was fairly close (51.0 % - 47.3% [65.5 million – 60.8 million]). Obama won the presidency, but polls show that the GOP position on major issues continues to be more popular. For example, a majority of citizens disapprove of Obamacare, and a majority agree that federal government spending cuts are needed. The GOP continues to control the House of Representatives, which means Obama will not be able to pass new legislation without the concurrence of the Republican-held House. Stated conversely, Romney lost the election, but his economic policies won.

The Smear Campaign Worked! Obama won the election, but he has no clear mandate to advance his economic policies. Although the pundits predicted that this election would be about the economy—as it turned out it was not the economic issues that decided the election—rather it was the smear on Romney. Unlike Obama's campaign of hope and inspiration that brought him the election victory in 2008, in 2012, it was his relentless campaign to smear and misrepresent Romney that prevailed. We saw a drastically different Obama campaigning in 2012; he was constantly sarcastic, cutting and misleading in marshalling opposition to Romney. Obama's negative, divisive, class warfare campaign worked.

A Coalition of highly motivated groups that hated Romney and Republicans. Obama's victory was not one of a platform or philosophy that carried the day; rather he developed a coalition of highly motivated groups that hated Romney and Republicans. Here's the coalition: The Gay vote, the anti-rich vote, the Women's Lib vote, the "have nots" vote, the Black vote, the younger people vote, the Hispanic vote, the anti-Republican vote, and the uninformed vote.

The latter group is actually quite extensive, and Obama did well in capitalizing on this group. It is interesting to note the important issues that the voters relegated to be unimportant in this election:

Business and economic issues;
The exploding national debt (Obama made this a major issue 4 years ago);
The war on terror (Obama's criticism of the war was a major issue in 2008)[1];
Obamacare (the nation disapproves of it by a few percentage points); and
Foreign policy (despite Obama's weak and embarrassing record).

Obama's Blunders Are Overlooked.
In any election prior to 2012, if an incumbent president had made the major blunders that Pres. Obama made, he would have been handily defeated by even a weak opponent. But there were significant changes in American voters in 2012, such that a very flawed President (Obama) was able to win re-election.

Two, major specific blunders that Obama made in the presidential campaign were (1) He severely criticized the free enterprise system that has made America economically strong and free; and (2) He committed acts of negligence and ineptness that cost the lives of the U. S. Ambassador to Libya and three other Americans. Not only did most of America give Obama a pass on these blunders, but the American media defended Obama in these gaffs, and the media combined to blame Republicans for attempting to politicize these events. President Obama's re-election is a big win for the liberal, main stream media. But it is a sad and foreboding defeat for America and the principles of freedom and prosperity. If America does not change—if America does not return to the principles of personal responsibility and fiscal responsibility (meaning living within the nation's means), then America will continue down the road of irresponsibility, which will ultimately undermine our economy and our liberties.

"You didn't build that!" This signature quote by President Obama is a repudiation of America's free enterprise, capitalism economic system. This is not an isolated quote. Obama's campaign theme was to spread the wealth; make the rich pay a little bit more; and whatever you do—don't cut back on any government handouts, even if the federal government has to borrow from future citizens and the Chinese in order to pay for it. Obama is determined to maintain the level of entitlement payments that cost America $1 Trillion per year more than our revenues. (America brings in $3 Trillion a year in revenues, but it pays out $4 Trillion a year.) America's ignoring this fiscally irresponsible leadership will eventually cripple us.[2]

One month after the election, the biggest national issue is whether the nation will go over the fiscal cliff, and whether "sequestration" will take effect, which will trigger substantial cuts in federal expenditures. The Democrat line on this problem is that is an "artificial," "manufactured" crisis, and that it can be easily resolved by merely increasing the debt ceiling. But that is the very problem, the Democrats don't think there's a problem, and they have no qualms about continuing to operate government by going in debt $1 Trillion per year. The Democrat line is that the government has already made cuts, and that no more cuts are needed. Republicans

---

[1] President Obama's unrestrained spending (that increased the national debt by $5 Trillion in one term—more than any other president ever) was a non-factor in 2012 even though Obama quickly assumed total ownership of the expensive war in Afghanistan, and even though the casualties were higher under his administration than they were under Bush, and even though the cost has continued to run higher than what he said was acceptable in 2008.

[2] Many Americans are very concerned to advance environmentally sustainable policies, but many of them are oblivious to whether or not our fiscal policies are economically sustainable. This is a disaster waiting to happen.

have to continue to take a stand against such a reckless and destructive course of action. No business could survive by such a policy, and neither can the government if the policy is not changed.

Obama's Victory Was Not a Policy Victory. The point is that Obama's election victory in 2012 was not a policy victory. Again, it was a coalition of groups that hated Romney and Republicans. When you understand the nature of Obama's victory, this can help one handle the issues that will come before the nation. We are winning the national debate on the main issues, so we should continue to make the case for wise government and for sound fiscal policies.

Romney's Platform Is the Right Plan for America. Just because the Republican presidential candidate lost does not mean that Republicans should embrace the ill-conceived, counter-productive philosophies of President Obama. We cannot deny the fiscal truth spending beyond one's means leads to crippling debt and eventually to loss of liberty. The GOP should continue to urge our elected leaders to enact wise policies and programs that will strengthen America economically and keep us strong and free. If Obama is smart he will change his policies and programs. If he does not, he will continue to weaken the nation, and he could leave the nations in ruin by 2017.

In retrospect, Mitt Romney's platform is indeed the best agenda for the President and Congress. All the reasons why Romney's positions were better than those of Obama continue to be true and continue to provide the best direction for the President and Congress. To the extent Obama adopts them, this will help America. To the extent Obama ignores or discards them, it will hurt America.

2012 Presidential Election Summary. We are stunned at the results of the 2012 Presidential Election, in which a majority of Americans rejected Mitt Romney and his plan for the nation. This result gives me grave concern for America. In every major respect, Romney's platform was exactly right for the nation. But President Obama's smear campaign was successful. The electorate has become mostly a nation of takers, who lined up in support of the reckless campaign promises of a leader who continues to promise that the government will give the poor and the middle class more and more benefits regardless of the fact that the government has to borrow 25% of the annual budget ($1 Trillion of $4 Trillion) to do it. This is a recipe for economic disaster. President Obama's war against the private job creators will seriously damage this nation if not corrected. President Obama's foreign leadership has been an embarrassment to America, and his failure to protect our Ambassador and other Americans in Libya was neglect. This Administration's calculated lies to deceive Americans about what happened in Libya should have ruined his re-election chances. But a compliant national press helped the President to spread the message to the nation that he handled this just right, and that Mitt Romney was as fault for attempting to politicize the event.

That President Obama was able to win re-election despite his many, serious flaws is baffling. The election signals a shift in the majority of American voters to support an approach to government that will seriously hurt America, if not corrected. Some may label my commentary as the whining of a sour loser, but that's not what it is at all. The spiritual core of America has changed from that of shared sacrifice, which helped this nation to prevail in World War II; and this has been replaced with an attitude of entitlement, where a majority of Americans ask what their country can do for them, and not what they can do for their country. This change in the national attitude will be ruinous, if not corrected.

| X:i | January 2017 | No. 17 |

Razor-thin Trump victory—
serious harm to the Constitution is averted

by C. Paul Smith

At about 3:00 a.m. on the morning of November 9, 2016, after the State of Pennsylvania was projected to be a win for Donald Trump, Hillary Clinton called Trump, conceded that he had won, and congratulated him. Donald J. Trump was elected to be the 45th President of the United States. Hillary Clinton won the popular vote. But the Electoral College gives a slight advantage to the smaller rural and farming states; and when those states are predominantly Republican this makes it possible for the winner of those states to prevail. That is what happened on November 8th. The final tally of Electoral votes was 304 for Trump and 227 for Clinton.

Trump's election victory was very close, and the nation is sharply divided on many issues. But the consequences of this victory could be enormous, especially when the results of the national elections continue to give Republicans control of both the Senate and the House of Representatives. This represents the biggest win for Republicans since Ronald Reagan's victories in the 1980s. In the "Post-Election Analysis," which begins on the next page, we will discuss a number of expected changes which could be a great benefit to America.

This issue of *CLU* will discuss ramifications of the 2016 Presidential Election, including the enormous effect it will have on the Constitution. This issue also includes articles on the following: Fake News, the Electoral College, the Evan McMullin Factor, and Supreme Court cases on the Affordable Care Act, same-sex marriage, Presidential powers and prayer.

--our Post-Election Analysis begins on the next page

CONSTITUTIONAL LAW UPDATES is edited and published by C. Paul Smith. To order copies ($10.00 per issue), write CLU, P. O. Box 1204, Frederick, MD 21702-0204. Visit www.cpaulsmith.com. Copyright C. Paul Smith 2017.

Post-Election Analysis:
The Election of Donald J. Trump—
Will he make America great again?

The election of Donald J. Trump to be the 45th President of the United States could provide some great help for America—its economy, its Constitution, its peace, its prosperity and its strength. But about half the nation is upset and worried and offended—offended at Trump's campaign slogan, "Make America Great Again"—especially the implications of the word "again." Although many people are offended, they should not be.

One of the great ironies that has unfolded in this election is how the liberals ridiculed Trump after one of the last debates because he would not promise to accept the results of the election. But many of those same people who ridiculed Trump were the very ones leading the charge to question and challenge and **not** accept the election results that put Donald Trump in the White House. As the Inauguration approaches, a major news item has been the many liberals who are announcing that they will boycott the Inauguration, and some are planning to participate in protest marches instead. America is indeed divided. Donald Trump will have consistent resistance as he seeks to repair the damage done to America by Barack Obama.

I. Trump Victory Is a Rejection of the Obama Agenda.

In many respects the Trump victory is not a typical Republican victory—with some of the prominent Republicans supporting Hillary (directly or indirectly--including John Kasich and the Bushes), nevertheless it is clearly a Republican victory that can help

correct serious flaws in America that were created and/or made worse by President Barack Obama and his supporters.

II. The Result of Obama's Campaigning for Hillary Clinton.

In the last two weeks of the recent campaign, President Obama did a lot of campaigning for Hillary Clinton. Obama repeatedly warned his crowds that they needed to elect Hillary in order to preserve the many advances that he had brought to America. Never before have I seen an out-going president campaign so hard for the one he wanted to succeed him. And the result of this was a sound rejection of Obama's agenda, a rejection of Obama's policies and achievements, and a rejection of Hillary Clinton's quest to continue what Obama started. Thus, Obama's unusual insertion into the Clinton campaign, which failed to bring success, has actually created a national mandate to reject Obama's agenda, and to enact Trump's agenda.[1]

---

[1] What about Obama—when his term ends on January 20th, will he restrain himself from criticizing Trump for a period of time? Or will he actually take the lead in opposing Trump and his policies? I predict that he will fight against Trump like no past president has ever fought against his successor. This is clear from what Obama has said about Trump following the election. Obama is not about to ride off into the sunset. He proudly announced that he will be staying around in Washington, D. C., and that he will speak up when he feels it appropriate. But that, of course, is a big part of the problem—he has been way out of line in advancing what he believes to be "appropriate."

President Obama's agenda was to "transform" or "remake" America. He sought to turn America into a socialist nation, which he felt would be a fairer nation. He sought to punish the free enterprise system (which is part of the foundation of America's greatness). He sought to replace the Constitutional government with unlawful Executive Orders that he said were "best" for America. He sought to build world peace through appeasement and ineptness and dismantling of our military. He increased racial tensions by consistently supporting the claims of black criminals that they were being arrested only because they were black. He consistently and falsely characterized Republicans as evil and ignorant—which only increased the national divisiveness. He doubled the national debt in 8 years—creating a bondage to and dependency on debt that will cripple our economy and our freedom for decades. And he pursued fanatical and economically debilitating climate change policies without presenting credible evidence that such policies will have any discernible effect on the climate. The cost of those policies are causing serious economic harm to America and puts America at a great disadvantage in trading with the rest of the world (that is not subject to the same restrictions).

The Democrat Party and Hillary's supporters do not acknowledge or agree with the serious problems that I described in the prior paragraph. Despite how smart some of them are, or how smart they think they are—they are wrong. And their assertion that their position is morally superior to mine is also wrong. They frankly do not understand that selling one's liberty for security eventually causes one to lose both security and liberty. This eternal battle about agency continues to this day, and it plays out in the political arena.

America needs to continue to be a compassionate people, but increasing government control over the people is not the best approach. Leave the people the means and the opportunity to help others. It is not best for the role of government to become that of forcing people to share their wealth and their property. Excessive control in this area undermines the free enterprise system; it undermines the role of initiative and productivity in the free enterprise (capitalism) system. That is why socialism has always failed wherever it has been practiced; socialism always dies when it runs out of the money of the rich. The only way for an entire society to rise economically is to have a system that rewards creativity, initiative and productivity. Dishing out entitlements without requiring the best efforts of recipients is called the "dole." It is a plague that harms the economic system that employs it.

In Hillary Clinton's campaign she repeatedly asserted that her position was morally superior to that of the Republicans. And based upon this she promoted a plan of unlimited entitlements, to be funded by raising taxes on the rich. But Hillary's position on this is not superior in any way; on the contrary, it is philosophically, logically and morally flawed.

III.   Who Holds the Moral High Ground?

Hillary Clinton's concession speech was dignified and appropriate, but she told her supporters that they should continue to fight for the causes that have been a part of their campaign. She and her supporters continue to believe that their political positions are morally right, and that Trump's opposing positions are morally wrong. This is disturbing to me, although it is not at all surprising—in other words, she continues to take the position of righteous superiority over Trump and his supporters. For the most part I believe that Hillary and her supporters are factually, philosophically and morally wrong. It is clear that fierce ideological battles will continue to be waged during the Trump administration. Clinton and the Democrat machine lost a battle on November 8th, but the war continues.

The narrow victory for Donald Trump would not have happened without a tremendous, concerted and effective effort of many key people, including Newt Gingrich, Rudy Giuliani, Rush Limbaugh, Sean Hannity, Mark Levin, Michael Savage, Laura Ingraham and Ann Colter. It took their massive, combined, well-reasoned efforts to secure this victory for Donald Trump. Together, these people sounded the message that in this election, the Constitution was hanging by a threat, and that the defeat of Hillary Clinton and the election of Donald Trump was needed to save it.

With the election of Donald Trump, will America continue down the path of socialism? Or will the nation right itself and re-establish the principles of a productive free enterprise system—work, initiative, creativity and sacrifice? Hopefully, America can correct it excessive socialism and embark on a period of renewal of conservatism. We shall see.

IV. President Obama's Agenda Was Way Out of Line.

President Obama was way out of line when he, in a State of the Union address (in 2010), criticized the Justices of the Supreme Court, as they sat in front of him, for their ruling in the *Citizens United* case. This act of public chastisement was rare if not unheard of, even if the President had been

right, which he was not. He was way out of line when he removed the missile defense system from eastern Europe. He was way out of line when he not only refused to enforce immigration laws, but he promulgated rules that conflicted with the law, as he sought to open America's borders to illegal aliens. He was way out of line when he worked to overthrow the Egyptian and Libyan governments—these colossal mistakes created dangerous strife and unrest in that region, and caused the unnecessary death of four Americans in Benghazi. He was way out of line when he worked to bring over a hundred thousand Syrian refugees into America—when we cannot vet them to make sure none are terrorists, and when he refused to use his influence to set up a refugee camp near Syria. He was way out of line by refusing to address the national and international problem caused by radical Islamic Extremists. He was way out of line by prematurely withdrawing all American troops from Iraq—which action led directly to the growth and spread of ISIS. He was way out of line and inept when he prepared and signed a trade agreement with Iran that effectively assured their ability to develop nuclear weapons and which gave them $400 million to boot (plus another $1.3 billion 29 days later). He was way out of line when he proclaimed that "climate change" is the greatest threat to America. He was way out of line, repeatedly, during his two administrations, when he would hastily and prematurely take sides with black criminals who proclaimed to be the subject to racism, only to have such claims repeatedly debunked when the facts came to light. President Obama's proclivity to find racism whenever a black was charged with a crime, and President Obama's own personal bias in favor of Muslims was manifest time and time again, and it served to incite more racial unrest rather than to heal and cure it. He was way

4

was way out of line when he toured the globe apologizing for America. He was way out of line in increasing free entitlements during an economic downturn. He was way out of line in thinking that he could fix the national debt by borrowing money from the Chinese and others. He was way out of line by increasing the minimum wage during a time of rising unemployment (95 million out of work)—this action only caused increased unemployment. He was way out of line by increasing the national debt from $9 Trillion to $19 Trillion in order to pay for the increasing entitlements that his programs gave to more and more people. He was way out of line by pursuing extremist, idiotic environmental policies that cost miners and other middle class Americans millions of jobs, and caused millions of jobs to go overseas—all at the expense of policies that were totally ineffective to improve the environment—The list goes on and on. America is not on board with this extremist left agenda; it has too many terrible flaws.

V. Media Bias Exposed.

As the news coverage of the 2016 presidential campaign unfolded it exposed the bias of mainstream media in favor of liberalism, and it exposed a corresponding hostility towards conservatives and towards Donald Trump.[2] The mainstream media has been caught in the very act, as it has literally campaigned for Hillary Clinton and her agenda. By the mainstream media, I mean

---

[2] While Donald Trump had a conservative platform, he is clearly not a pure conservative. He is not an ideologue (like Ted Cruz). Rather, Trump is a pragmatist. His adoption of conservatism is grounded in his economic and common sense desires to make America great again. The Conservatives all know this, and because of this we have reservations about how strong Trump's commitment will be to conservative principles. Nevertheless, for now he is carrying the conservative banner.

at least the following: *The New York Times, The Washington Post,* ABC, NBC, CBS, CNN and MSNBC. In order for Trump to win the Presidency, he had to overcome and defeat both Hillary Clinton and the mainstream media. And he did.

Most of the nation now knows of this fraudulent media bias. But will this change the mainstream media? No, I don't think so. And the reason is that they believe their biases are justified because they think they are right; the media will continue to be the lap-dog of whoever is carrying the liberal torch.

Trump will never be embraced by the mainstream media, and he should not attempt to get in their good graces.

VI. A Mandate for the Trump Agenda.

Thus, while the popular vote was close, and slightly favored Clinton, a majority of the States voted for change—voted for Trump and his agenda.

And by the way, the most important take away from the Trump election is not that the nation approves of the many flaws and mistakes for which the liberals accused Trump, but rather it was an endorsement of Trump's agenda to dismantle and correct the many flawed policies and enactments of Obama. No, Trump was not elected because of his character, but in spite of his flaws. Hillary's flaws and corruption were seen as worse than those of Trump. But Trump was unquestionably seen as a strong leader who knew how to get the economy going again.

At the time of the election, Obama continued to have an approval rating of about 56%. This rating was higher than the national approval of his agenda and policies. Obama's policies were rejected in this election. Clearly it was not Trump's character qualities that carried the day—No! It was Trump's platform. In the last three national elections, American support for conservatism has steadily grown to the point where about two-thirds of the state and local governments are conservative. Conservative Republicans took control of the House of Representatives in the 2010 election; the Republican majority in the House increased in the 2012 and 2014 elections; House Republicans remain in control in the 2016 election. The Republicans took control of the Senate in the 2014 election, and their control continues after the 2016 election. All of this constitutes a national rejection of Obama's agenda.

Thus, while the election results were close, there is nevertheless a mandate to enact his campaign promises, starting with the repeal of Obamacare and bringing back jobs to America.

VII.   A Divided Nation.

As the newly-elected President, Donald Trump will certainly attempt to build some unity in the nation.

During Barack Obama's two terms, he forged ahead with his leftist policies, disregarding or denigrating those who disagreed with him. Obama took the position that his views were morally superior to those of his opponents. The consequence of eight years of this was a rejection of Obama's agenda by the nation. President Obama did not unify the nation; he certainly did not improve racial relations in America. In fact, because he consistently and openly sided with black criminals who wrongly claimed to be victims of racism, this cause increased racial turmoil and tension in America.

Donald Trump's prospects for building increased unity are viable, but questionable. On the one hand, America is a clearly divided nation, with a large part of Hillary Clinton's supporters complaining bitterly about Trump's election. The vicious personal attacks that characterized both the

Clinton and the Trump campaigns have created a stark division as the Inauguration is set to take place.

If Donald Trump leads wisely and conducts himself with dignity and grace, he could improve national unity. But it remains to be seen if he will do this. In the 75 days following the November 8th election, Trump has continued to be combative in responding to many of the continuing attacks against him. Of course, it was Trump's combative campaign approach that helped him to victory, so perhaps he will continue to respond to and attack his accusers. (With 50 million followers on Tweeter, Trump does not need the media to get his message out.) He has certainly continued to strongly criticize the press for being dishonest and biased. It will be interesting to see if the battle between Trump and the mainstream media continues after Inauguration Day. I suspect it will. But I believe that at least half of the nation want him to continue to take on the press, and this will certainly have a negative influence on any effort to bring unity to the nation. It appears to me that Trump will not back off his criticism of the press until the press shapes up. This is a battle that may very well continue for the next four years.

Regardless of the rhetorical battles that will continue to be waged during Trump's administration, he nevertheless will be able to bring a degree of national unity if in his words, his appointments, and his actions exhibit wise leadership. Those who voted for Trump expect him to be a decisive leader, and to speak up against the leftist arguments for political correctness and for radical environmental and social causes. If Trump is loyal to his voters, we must expect an on-going battle against loud minority points of view for the next four years. Whatever unity is achieved could be a supportive majority of perhaps 60% of the public. But I fully expect the press and Obama to openly fight against Trump for the next four years.

VIII. Expected Results from the Trump Victory.

Here's what we can expect from the new administration of Donald J. Trump:

1. Obamacare will be repealed and replaced. (For most of us, whose health insurance premiums and deductibles have risen dramatically, while the benefits are being reduced—this will be a welcomed change.)[3]

2. A conservative Justice will be appointed to the Supreme Court, with other conservative Justices expected to follow in the next four years. This is a critical victory for the Constitution, as the liberal-appointed Justices have consistently voted for their ideology over traditional Constitutional principles of a restrained judiciary.

3. America will re-assert itself as a strong world leader. America will re-build its military and its arsenal and its world presence to provide protection and support for freedom around the world. America will stop apologizing to other nations, and America will again promote peace through strength.

4. America can stop President Obama's open-borders immigration policy, which has brought excessive numbers of immigrants within our borders, has caused unacceptable security risks and has cost citizens thousands and thousands of jobs.

5. America can take the lead in the better solution to the Syrian refugee problem by establishing safe-havens in the regions from which the refugees came.

6. America will build a wall across our border with Mexico to stop the unchecked entry of illegal immigrants into America. This will be one component of the nation's renewed enforcement of existing immigration laws.

7. American laws and policies that undermine a growing economy will stop, and America will put in practice sounder policies that will stimulate economic growth and create jobs. These policies include making fairer international trade policies and abandoning some of the debilitating and fanatical environmental policies that pleased the climate change extremists, but which were scientifically flawed and economically crippling.

8. America will acknowledge and combat radical Islamic extremism at home and abroad. As a part of this, I expect America to be much more effective in combating ISIS around the world.

9. America can once again re-establish itself as a wise and reliable messenger of freedom by making a sharp break away from Obama's policies of apology, disarmament, capitulation, excessive passivism, stupid war strategies, and reckless regime-change policies (i.e., Libya and Egypt).

10. America will re-establish law and order at home, as the essential foundation of liberty. The pseudo-civil rights claims of the anarchists have been exposed. The racial discord that was actually worsened under the leadership of President Obama

---

[3] In retrospect, the anticipated legislative correction of the many flaws in Obamacare will be better for America than if the Supreme Court had held the entire law unconstitutional. This is so because it maintains the position of the Court as a non-political overseer of the Constitution. Had Chief Justice Roberts voted to strike down the Individual Mandate portions of the Affordable Care Act (ACA), then liberals would have accused the Court of political partisanship. Thus, whether or not the Chief Justice voted correctly, the Supreme Court is now vindicated in that a better (legislative) remedy can now be made to correct the ACA mess.

will be replaced with true color-blind leadership that rejects the notion that rioting is justified whenever a person of color is perceived to have suffered an injustice. (To remind you, President Obama repeatedly spoke out in support of black individuals who were arrested—igniting calls of racism against law enforcement—when later those individuals were found to be fully at fault—e.g., riots in Ferguson, Missouri and Baltimore, Maryland.)

11. Some of the corruption in the federal government will be ended--including the unfair advantages and favoritism that the Obama Administration has been giving to its political supporters. The Obama Administration's multiple ethical blunders eventually added up to the point that the nation could no longer deny them or refuse to correct them. Consider the following disturbing actions by the Obama Administration: Selling arms to drug lords in Latin America; Using the IRS to target Obama's political enemies; applying a double-standard at the Department of Justice to give Hillary Clinton a pass for her violations of national security laws, while at the same time sending other people to prison for even lesser violations; and most recently, pardoning hundreds of criminals, including the convicted traitor, Chelsea Manning (formerly Bradley Manning).

The above list is actually quite extensive and significant. And these changes can all make America much better. President-elect Trump will have the opportunity to make these important improvements in America.

IX. The Future of America.

So, what will be the future of liberalism/socialism in America? The growth of socialism has been temporarily stopped. But the liberals will not stop advocating for their socialistic and fanatical environmental policies that would ruin America. The liberals will fight against Trump at every turn and on every issue. They will seek every opportunity to turn on Trump to defeat or hinder him.

The battle for freedom—the fight against those who want to sell their liberty for security—this battle will go on. In the meantime, hopefully, the American values of work, initiative, creativity, sacrifice, thrift and patriotism will have a resurgence, and will strengthen America and its economy so that we can withstand the next onslaught from the socialists.

Now the stage is set for one of the most unusual presidents the nation has ever seen.[4] Donald Trump has repeatedly violated the traditional rules of how to campaign to be president; but he has repeatedly defied the odds with his communication decisions, and this is largely responsible for his being elected to be the 45th President of the United States of America.

---

[4] Trump, a multi-billionaire, has also declined to receive a salary for his service as President. That salary would be $400,000/year.

Serious Harm to the Constitution
Averted by Trump Victory

Donald Trump's defeat of Hillary Clinton in the presidential election is a clear and important victory for the Constitution and for the principles of freedom that have made our nation great.

The election of Hillary Clinton would have been disastrous to the Constitution because she promised to appoint people to the Supreme Court who would advance her liberal agenda—this would result in two terrible problems. First, her liberal agenda would damage America. Second, her liberal, activist judges would damage the Constitution. We need Justices who do what is legally right and proper—not justices whose purpose is to advance their personal ideologies. If there is one ideology that a Justice should have it would be that he/she does not legislate from the bench; that he/she exercises judicial restraint in deciding cases based upon legal principles and precedents. There is and has been a major difference between the conservative and liberal Justices in this important area. I will explain and give examples.

It is universally understood that a judge or a Justice should not have a personal interest in any matter before him or her. When such an interest does exist, the Justice recuses himself/herself. I submit that the same type of impartiality should also exist with respect to the creation of new rights by the Court. Conservative Justices agree with this point of view. Liberal Justices do not.

A majority of liberal Justices created a woman's right to an abortion; a right to engage in private, same-sex, sexual relations outside of marriage; a right to same-sex marriage; a right of habeas corpus for enemy combatants; a right for illegal immigrants to enter and live in America; a universal right to health care; an obligation for the wealthy to pay for everybody else's health care; and the liberal Justices extinguished unborn babies' right to life. These are all acts of improper judicial activism.

The Judicial system should not act like a legislature in creating some new rights and extinguishing others. The judiciary should apply neutral principles and precedents of fairness when it resolves actual cases and controversies.

On the one hand, I do agree that it is right and proper (as provided in the Ninth Amendment) for the Supreme Court to identify and enforce rights that are not specifically enumerated, but which have long been recognized as rights throughout our country's history. But there is a big difference between this and activism—to use the Court as a tool in creating new rights that have not been recognized in our society for a long period of time.

The liberal Justices don't share these concerns—they see it as their purpose to establish whatever new rights they feel like establishing. They do not employ any restraints in recognizing new rights or in extinguishing rights that they disfavor. Thus, in *Roe v. Wade*, a woman's right to an abortion was established and the fetal right to life was killed; in *Boumediene v. Bush*, a new right to *habeas corpus* for enemy combatants was created; in *Lawrence v. Texas*, a personal liberty to engage in sexual relations with someone of the same sex was established; in *Obergefell v. Hodges*, a right to same-sex marriage was created; and in *NFIB v. Sebelius*, a right to receive health care was established, and the obligation of wealthy Americans to pay for the health care of others was created.

Liberal Justices also use their power to attempt to destroy existing rights that serve to

1

block their liberal agenda. For example, the liberal Justices voted in *Heller* to deny the existence of a personal right to bear arms; they argued in *Bush v. Gore*, that Bush should not have standing to challenge the flawed and erroneous counting of ballots in Florida; they argued in *Citizens United* that it in the 60 days prior to a general election it was good to give media corporations a right to speak and write on election issues, but that other corporations could not do so; and most recently in *U.S. v. Texas*, the liberal Justices supported President Obama's blatant defiance of immigration laws, as he sought to replace those laws with conflicting Executive orders.

For the last 40 years the Supreme Court has been pretty evenly divided in its mix of conservative and liberal Justices. Some liberal activism has been blocked by a narrow margin, and some liberal causes have been championed by a slim majority of the Court. But the next two appointments will clearly take the Court either to the left or to the right. For the sake of the Constitution and the nation, we need the next Justices to be from the conservative mold. The impact of the new Justices will have a long, and perhaps irreversible, effect on the Court and on the Constitution.

This long history of judicial activism by liberal Justices has been damaging our Constitution and the principles of liberty upon which our nation was established. If Hillary Clinton had been elected, her Supreme Court appointees would have taken control over the Court and would have caused irreparable harm.

Donald Trump has promised to appoint to the Court Justices like Antonin Scalia, a conservative and a strict constructionist. That is an important promise; that would be good for the Constitution and for America.

Of course, to those who have some expertise in judicial matters, it is clear that Donald Trump does not. His discussion of *Roe v. Wade* makes it clear that he does not fully understand that case nor the implication

of overturning *Roe v. Wade*. Nevertheless, Trump's commitment to appoint conservative Justices is much appreciated and extremely important.

With regard to *Roe v Wade*, that was a complicated case. The Court was correct in recognizing a woman's right to control her own body. That part should not be overturned. And personally (for reasons I do not have the time to explain here) at this point I do not support returning the abortion decision entirely to the states to regulate. But I wholeheartedly endorse overturning that part of *Roe v. Wade* that extinguished the fetal right to life. That was a terrible mistake in *Roe v. Wade*. The fetal right to life must be recognized and protected in a civilized society. Such a right is not an absolute—it can be subject to the mother's right to life, where the two conflict. In any event, my point is that I would support modifying *Roe v. Wade* in line with what I just mentioned. But *Roe v. Wade* does not have to be overturned to outlaw partial birth abortion. *Roe v. Wade* specifically gives the States power to protect potential human life in the third trimester. Thus outlawing partial birth abortions does not require overturning *Roe v. Wade.*

In conclusion—back to the broader point that Trump's election will help to preserve and protect the Constitution—the 2016 presidential election was very close. America is closely divided: About half of the nation supports socialism, environmental extremism and free government giveaways for all the poor. The other half of America supports limited government and a robust free enterprise economy that promotes work, creativity, initiative and a limited federal government. While the election of Donald Trump was a narrow victory for conservatism, it was nevertheless a critical victory that will preserve the wiser, conservative approach to government, and which will ultimately yield a stronger economy, greater prosperity for all, and a stronger America. These results will be best for America and for freedom lovers around the globe.

Electoral College—

Trump election highlights differences in popular vote and Electoral vote

Donald Trump's election in 2016 to be the 45th President of the United States marks the 5th time (in 58 different presidential elections) that a candidate with the most popular votes did not become President.[1] Article II, Section 1 of the Constitution and the Twelfth and Twentieth Amendments provide that each State (and the District of Columbia [23rd Amendment]) vote for Electors who elect the President and Vice President. That system, called the "Electoral College," in effect gives smaller states a little more power in presidential elections than that which they would have if each state's voting power was tied only to its population. It is because of this system that in close elections, sometimes the candidate with the most popular votes does not become President. Such was the fate of Hillary Clinton this year, receiving over 65.8 million votes (of 134 million cast)—2.9 million (2%) more than Trump's 62.9 million.

Each State can adopt its own laws for choosing its Electors. Initially it was state Legislatures who elected or appointed the Electors. But this gradually changed until today, when all States do it by popular election. The Electors are individuals other than the candidates for President. But the Electors are almost always reliable and devoted to their respective parties, such that Electors rarely vote differently from how they are expected to vote.[2]

Article II, Section 1 provides that Congress shall select the date when Electors shall meet and actually cast their votes. This date is currently in early December following the November election. The Governor of each State certifies the result of their respective elections, and sends this to the Senate, where the results are presented to both Houses of Congress at the first session of Congress for the next year, that begins on January 3rd (20th Amendment).

---

[1] In 1824, Andrew Jackson had more popular votes and more Electoral votes than any other candidate. But he did not have a majority of the Electoral votes. Therefore, the House of Representatives took the three candidates receiving the most Electoral votes, and voted for John Quincy Adams to be President. (That Congress did not like Andrew Jackson.)

In 1876, Samuel J. Tilden won the popular vote by over 250,000 votes, but he lost the Electoral College by one vote to Rutherford B. Hayes.

In 1888, Grover Cleveland won the popular vote by over 90,000 votes, but he lost the Electoral College by a large margin to Benjamin Harrison (233-168).

In 2000, Al Gore won the national vote by about 540,000 votes more than George W. Bush, but Bush won the Electoral College by a slim margin of 271-266.

Finally, in 2016, Hillary Clinton won the popular vote (48%) by receiving about 2,900,000 more votes than Donald Trump. But Trump won the Electoral College decisively (304-227).

---

[2] For a more thorough treatment of the renegade Electors, google "faithless Electors," and see the discussion in Wikipedia on Electoral College. About one half of the States have now passed laws which prohibit Electors from voting other than how their state procedures direct them to vote. In a close election, it is still conceivable that a renegade Elector or two could alter the expected result. For example, in the 2000 election, where Bush won the Electoral vote 271-266, there was one renegade Elector from the District of Columbia, who was supposed to vote for Gore, but who declined to vote as a protest that full voting rights have not been extended to residents of the District of Columbia. If she had voted for Gore, the vote would have been 271-267. Then if two of the Electors who were supposed to vote for Bush had instead voted for Gore, then the Electoral result would have been 269-269, in which case the newly elected House of Representatives would have decided the outcome when they first convened on January 3rd of the next year. (The 20th Amendment provides that January 3rd is the date for such an election to begin, if it is necessary.)

CLU 01/17

Article II, Section 1 of the Constitution gives Congress the power to determine the number of Electors, subject to the requirement that each State shall have one Elector for each of its Senators plus one Elector for each of its Representatives in Congress. Amendment Twenty-three further modifies this by giving the District of Columbia three Electors. For over one hundred years the number of members of the House of Representative were regularly increasing, as the population of the United States was growing. Thus, during the 1800s Congress regularly increased the number of Representatives following each decennial Census. But in 1929 Congress passed the Permanent Apportionment Act, which set the number of Representatives at 435. Thereafter, following each decennial Census, there is a re-apportionment of Congressional seats among the states, as dictated by the census counts. For example, after the 2010 Census, eight states gained one or more Representatives and nine states lost one or more Representatives.[3]

Article I, Section 2 of the Constitution provides that there should not be more than one Representative for every 30,000 persons. But there is no limit provided for a maximum number of persons that can be represented. Thus, today, each Representative represents about 700,000 people.

The current total number of Electors is 538. It is comprised of 100 for the number of Senators, plus 435 for the number of Representatives, plus 3 for the District of Columbia. Accordingly, 270 Electoral votes constitutes a majority of the Electoral votes. Could Congress increase the number of Representatives in Congress, which would increase the number of Electors? Yes. But there has been no inclination to do so. Having 435 members of Congress is an extremely large and unwieldy group—it is widely acknowledged to already be too big, such that increasing its size presents more problems than it would resolve.

The results of the 2016 election has given rise to some calls to discard the Electoral College in favor of a simple national, popular vote. But this would be extremely unlikely. To change this Constitutional process, it would require a two-thirds vote by both Houses of Congress to approve such an Amendment, and then it would require ratification by three-fourths of the States. There is no way this would happen at this time, where the majority of the less populous states all supported the election of Donald Trump.

Post-Election Day, Electoral College Processes

The casting of ballots on Election Day is the biggest part of electing a new President, but there are several additional, crucial steps to be taken in the electoral process before the new President can be sworn in on January 20th.

Technically, on Election Day (November 8, 2016), it is the Electors who are elected. Then, on December 19th (a day selected by Congress [pursuant to the 20th Amendment]), all of the states conduct an election where the Electors officially cast their votes. Then each State and the District of Columbia certifies its election result and sends that certification to Congress, where the new Senate will officially count and certify the Electoral votes of all the States and of the District of Columbia. (This process is prescribed in Article II of the Constitution, as modified by Amendments 12 and 20.) Normally, these steps following Election Day are taken for granted and go unnoticed by the general public. But such was not the case following the election of Donald Trump on November 8, 2016. Opponents of Trump launched three specific procedural efforts to attempt to prevent Mr. Trump from being elected by the Electoral College.

---

[3] Texas gained 4 seats and Florida gained 2 seats; Arizona, Georgia, Nevada, South Carolina, Utah and Washington each gained 1 seat. New York and Ohio each lost 2 seats, and Illinois, Iowa, Louisiana, Massachusetts, Michigan, New Jersey and Pennsylvania each lost one seat.

First, Jill Stein (a third-party candidate for President) led an effort to recount the popular vote in Michigan, Pennsylvania and Wisconsin.[4] Donald Trump's margin of victory was small in these three states, and if Hillary Rodham Clinton had won these three states then she would have become President. But all of these recount efforts failed to bring any change. In Michigan and Pennsylvania, courts blocked the recounts. In Wisconsin, the recount ended up delivering more votes to Trump than before. Consequently, none of the recount efforts yielded any change.

Second, Hillary Rodham Clinton's supporters began to campaign for some of the Electors to vote for Clinton instead of Trump. This effort was futile to begin with, and the final result did take two Electoral votes from Trump (leaving him with 304 instead of 306 votes), but it ended up taking five Electoral votes from Clinton (reducing her total from 232 to 227).[5]

Third, on January 6, 2017, after the new Congress had been sworn in, a joint session of Congress was convened to count and certify the Electoral votes that had been cast in the States on December 19th. During this process, objections were made by some of the Representatives to the election results of several of the States. Representative Sheila Jackson Lee (D-Texas), made most of these objections. However, the Constitution (Article II) gives the Senate, not the House, the authority to certify the Electoral vote, and not one Senator joined in any of the objections of Representative Lee and her colleagues of the House. Therefore, the Senate did not consider any of these objections, and the election of Donald Trump was then certified by the Senate. As this process ended, the President of the Senate, out-going Vice President Joe Biden stated, "It is over," announcing that the various

challenges to Trump's election are all now ended and unsuccessful.

The last remaining step in the process will be when the President-elect takes the oath of office at noon on January 20, 2017.

---

[4] Other candidates invoked recounts in Nevada and Florida.

[5] The votes of the seven "faithless" Electors went as follows: 3 for Colin Powell, 1 for John Kaisich, 1 for Ron Paul, 1 for Bernie Sanders, and 1 for Faith Spotted Eagle.

Fake News!—
False criticisms that Trump is a racist spark widespread demonstrations

Donald Trump's election victory was a heart-breaking loss for Hillary Clinton and her supporters. The disappointment and hurt and anger led to multiple demonstrations and protests in major cities in the days immediately following the election.

The 2016 presidential campaign featured many vicious personal attacks leveled at both Hillary Clinton and at Donald Trump. Hillary was accused of being corrupt and inept, while Trump was accused of being a racist and a bigot. But there was a strong factual basis for the criticisms leveled at Clinton, but the accusations leveled at Trump were baseless. There was a strong factual basis for the criticisms leveled at Clinton, but the accusations that Trump was a racist and a bigot were false accusations that were not supported by facts. Such accusations were a misrepresentation of Trump's words and positions. Nevertheless, these false misrepresentations were made repeatedly by Hillary Clinton and Senator Kaine and their supporters. But the making of these misrepresentations backfired on Clinton— the only people that believed them were Hillary's hard-core supporters. Most of the nation recognized that these misrepresentations were just that— misrepresentations.

Donald Trump has been a well-known public figure for decades. It is well known that he is not a racist--he has not discriminated against either blacks, Hispanics or Muslims; he has given many women high and lucrative positions; and he has not discriminated against the LGTBQs. Despite this long history, the Clinton campaign continually and vigorously accused Trump of these things--Clinton's

followers believe their own lies, and now that Trump won the election, many of them are protesting against something that does not exist. The Clintonite demonstrators are the victims of their own lies.

The misrepresentations made by Clinton on Trump were many. She called Trump a racist because he had previously challenged President Obama to produce his birth certificate. This challenge (which was also made by Hillary Clinton) is not inherently racist, but Clinton sought to characterize it that way. Trump and many others pointed out that President Obama's love of the Muslims was so excessive that he would not even utter the words "Islamic Extremist Terrorist." Clinton sought to characterize this as "racist." When Trump said that he would not allow any Muslims to enter the country unless they could be fully and properly vetted, Clinton and her supporters characterized this as "racist." Most Americans do not agree with this characterization--rather it is a logical and proper recognition that most of the terrorist threats and acts in the world are being committed by Muslims who identify themselves as "Islamist." President Obama likes to cling to a technical definition in his refusal to pronounce those three words; he would say that the people of Islam are peaceful, and therefore a terrorist cannot be Islamic. But the problem with this is that the terrorists themselves called themselves Islamic. Come on, President Obama; wake up. Trump points out that some of the illegal immigrants coming to America through the southern border are drug dealers, robbers and murderers, and therefore Trump pledges to stop this illegal immigration by building a wall. In response, Clinton and her supporters characterized this as being "racist" against

1

Hispanics. Most Americans recognize that Clinton's characterization is incorrect.

It is true that this past presidential campaign was characterized by some of the most vicious personal attacks ever made. A lot of Clinton's criticisms of Trump were these false accusations of racism. These attacks were way over the top. They were disgraceful attempts to make out Trump to be a racist. But he is not. And Clinton's attacks were despicable, because they only served to heighten racial tensions and to create unfounded fears in Clinton's ignorant followers.

Because the misrepresentations about Trump are so extensive and because many of them have been refuted, this has led conservatives to the use the phrase "fake news" as a label for many of the false news reports about Trump--at least Donald Trump and conservatives have used this term. The purveyors of "fake news" (i.e., the mainstream media) have been slow to use the new term. The misrepresentations of Trump have continued non-stop after Election Day, and so has Trump continued to repeatedly criticize and condemn the mainstream media for being dishonest and corrupt. This hostile relationship was highlighted at a President-Elect news conference on January 11, 2017, where Trump specifically refused to let CNN correspondent Jim Acosta ask any question. As Acosta continued to try to interrupt the President-Elect, Trump said to Acosta: "Your organization is terrible. I'm not going to give you a question. You are fake news."

During the presidential campaign, Trumps attacks on Clinton were also very powerful and effective--but they were not false characterizations. Trump criticized Clinton's record of ineptness in international affairs, when she was Secretary of State; the Benghazi debacle, the regime change in Egypt, the premature withdrawal of troops from Iraq, the terrible nuclear agreement with Iran, the withdrawal of missiles from

eastern Europe, the pathetic handling of the Syrian civil war (resulting in the Syrian refuge crisis), and deteriorating relations with Israel--all of these results show Clinton's ineptness in handling foreign affairs. Trump correctly pointed out Clinton's errors on economic policies, including her supporting of bad trade deals, her promoting excessive and illegal immigration into the US which caused unemployment of Americans, and her complicity with President Obama in doubling the national debt (taking it from $10 Trillion to $20 Trillion in 8 years). These economic accomplishments are facts--not misrepresentations. Trump was also correct in pointing out the corruptness in the federal government that clearly applied a double standard in law enforcement--one for Hillary Clinton, and another for all the other Americans. Hillary's email scandal brought this to light. These several criticisms of Hillary are facts, not false characterizations. Thus, Trump's criticisms of Clinton were indeed harsh, but they were true, and they were absolutely proper criticisms--unlike Hillary's false characterizations.

In summary, the 2016 presidential campaign certainly included vicious criticisms made by both sides against the other. But it was and is the criticisms made by the Clinton supporters that was out of line and improper. The recent wave of protests and accusations that Donald Trump is a racist and a hateful person are totally unjustified. They are primarily the result of ignorant Clinton supporters who are victims of their own lies about Trump. Ignorant people have the freedom of speech in America, just as much as the well-informed. But ignorant demonstrations do not legitimize false criticisms, rather they expose the ignorance and prejudice of the demonstrators.

The Evan McMullin Factor

One aspect of the 2016 election that warrants discussion is the third party candidacy of Evan McMullin, a 40-year-old conservative Mormon who had never previously held any elected office.[1] McMullin received even less votes than Libertarian candidate Gary Johnson (3%) and Green Party candidate Jill Stein (1%). The support for McMullin was so anemic that it might seem unworthy of even mentioning. But McMullin did garner 21% of the vote in Utah, finishing third behind Trump (45%) and Clinton (27%). Because this was a very close election nationally between Trump and Clinton, and because it was critical for Trump to win Utah's Electoral votes,[2] in October the Trump campaign was concerned that McMullin might take away enough votes from him to allow Clinton to win Utah.[3] Had this happened, it would have delivered the most conservative state in the union to Hillary Clinton. Ultimately, this scenario did not unfold, but because of the closeness of the election, the McMullin factor in Utah was a serious threat to Trump's national campaign.

McMullin's supporters were primarily conservative Mormons who would not vote for Trump because they felt he was "evil." They routinely referred to a reported statement of Ezra Taft Benson[4] that one should vote for a good candidate and not vote for the lesser of two evil candidates, even if the "good" candidate has no chance of winning. Here is the statement:

> If you vote for the lesser of two evils, you are still voting for evil, and you will be judged for it. You should always vote for the best possible candidate, whether they have a chance of winning or not, and then even if the worst possible candidate wins, the Lord will bless our country more because more people were willing to stand up for what's right.

During the last few months of the presidential campaign there was considerable internet discussion about this quote and the McMullin campaign. The quote was apparently reported by a man named Michael Thompson, who said that Elder Benson stated this to him privately in 1972. As far as I know this quote is not contained in any of the published writings of Ezra Taft Benson. This statement is not a part of the doctrine of The Church of Jesus Christ of Latter-day Saints. Nevertheless, even assuming the statement is true, it does not properly apply to Donald Trump in this election.

It would be a mistake to say that either Trump or Clinton was pure "evil." Such a

---

[1] McMullin is a former CIA officer, a former Mormon missionary and a former volunteer in the Mitt Romney Presidential campaign in 2012. He briefly served as a chief policy director for the House Republican Conference in the U. S. House of Representatives. As a presidential candidate in 2016 he only got on the ballot in eleven states. He said his goal was to get enough votes to prevent Trump and Clinton from getting 270 Electoral votes, so that the House of Representatives would vote to determine the President.

[2] As it turned out, the margin of victory for Trump in the Electoral vote was large enough that losing Utah to Clinton would not have mattered, but until the final votes were case, the Utah vote was a serious concern.

[3] On October 19, 2016 an Emerson College poll in Utah showed McMullin leading Trump by 4 points and Clinton by 7 points.

---

[4] Ezra Taft Benson was the President and Prophet of The Church of Jesus Christ of Latter-day Saints from 1985-1994. He was the Secretary of Agriculture from 1953-1960 during the Eisenhower Administration. Elder Benson wrote and spoke extensively on political and religious issues.

broad characterization would be superficial and overly simplistic. Both Clinton and Trump were flawed. Maybe you could say that they both had some evil flaws. But to call either of them purely "evil" is not warranted and is not accurate. If Satan and Wormwood were running, then yes—don't vote for either of them. But this was not the case. To say that Clinton and Trump are both pure "evil" is an unsupportable statement.

As one who is adamantly opposed to Clinton, I would still decline to label her as "evil." I believe she has a number of serious flaws, and I regard many of her philosophies and proposals to be terrible for America. I also believe she has some character flaws, including serious deficits in the area of honesty. But I am reluctant to call her "evil." She has some good qualities, and she wants to do some good things. But her primary flaw is that her approach to government is terrible, and her politics promote some evils that I oppose. And as for Donald Trump, although much of the media and many liberals proclaim him to be evil, he is not! He has some character flaws, but he also has some very good qualities. And for the most part his philosophy of government and his proposals are the right answer to many of America's problems.

Applying this to Elder Benson's quote, the premise is not satisfied—it is not correct that Donald Trump is "evil." Therefore, even if Elder Benson's purported advice were correct, it would not warrant the conclusion that one should not vote for Trump as the best "electable" candidate.

However, I do question the legitimacy of the quote provided by Michael Thompson. Because the standard proposed by Mr. Thompson is so easily susceptible to be misapplied without some common sense qualifiers, I don't accept is as an absolute where "evil" is interpreted too loosely. Elder Benson wrote prolifically about

politics. How is it that in all of the many books and articles and speeches by him he never gave the advice that Michael Thompson wants us to accept as something that President Benson now wants us to know. If an individual were to consistently apply this approach in voting—deciding a candidate is "evil" by using a flawed, overly broad standard—then this would consistently prevent people from supporting the best electable candidates, and it would regularly work to allow the lesser candidates to be elected. This could be terrible for the nation.

Just because a person has character flaws does not make him or her pure evil. We all sin and fall short of the ideal characters we should have. Americans have historically shown a tolerance for character short-comings. The nation was exceedingly tolerant of the marital infidelity of Democrat Presidents Roosevelt, Kennedy and Clinton. None of them were even close to approaching the evil of Hitler. And although some hateful liberals accuse Trump of being a "Hitler," such accusations are patently and grossly false.

There may be cases where not voting for the better of two flawed candidates would be the right thing to do. But where the platforms of two flawed candidates are vastly different, and where one candidate's platform would ruin the nation while the other candidate's platform would be good for the nation—then a simplistic standard of refusing to vote for a flawed candidate becomes a bad standard. There are almost always flaws in the person who is the best candidate. Sometimes the flaws are flaws in their character; other times they are flaws in their judgment and in their platforms. Many factors must be considered in making sure that we elect the best possible leaders.

Interestingly, nobody is focusing on the qualities and qualifications of Mr. McMullin—the man who admittedly never

2

had any chance whatsoever to win. I can understand why Mr. McMullin might want to vote for himself—even though he had no chance to win—his candidacy has brought him some fame. Perhaps he will run for some other office in the future. After his election loss he said that he was starting a new conservative movement. But no rational person could realistically believe that he had any chance of winning in 2016.

But back to Donald Trump, and the analysis of whether his flaws are so bad that they warrant the conclusion that he is "evil." I campaigned hard to help Senator Ted Cruz win the Republican nomination. As the Republican campaign was unfolding, I at first declined to support any one candidate, as I attentively followed the primary campaigns from Iowa, to New Hampshire, to South Carolina, and so on. At some point, I became a supporter of Ted Cruz, and I campaigned against Trump in the rest of the primaries, including doing some door-to-door campaigning for Cruz. Trump's crudeness and his name-calling and his lack of understanding of certain issues and his questionable conservative credentials all caused me to favor Senator Ted Cruz, whose views I shared on most issues, and who I believe to be a very good man. But when Donald Trump emerged from the process as the Republican Nominee, I had to subordinate my idealism to being practical and realistic. Continued support for Ted Cruz would not have led to Cruz being elected. At that point, it became clear that the next president would be either Hillary Rodham Clinton or Donald Trump—at that point the only sound way to exercise my franchise was to vote for the better of the two candidates--or the lesser bad of the two bad candidates, if you will.

And the 2016 Presidential Election was not an election where there was a viable third-party candidate--not like the Presidential election of 1992, when Ross

Perot mounted a third-party campaign and garnered enough support to allow him to participate in the televised presidential debates with George W. Bush and William J. Clinton. Perot did receive about 19% of the popular vote in 1992, but he received no Electoral votes and fell far short of winning that election in 1992.[5] His campaign did, however, cause George Bush to lose and Bill Clinton to win. But in 2016 there was no third party candidate even close to the support that Perot had. So, in 2016, it was clear that there was no way McMullin would win; all votes for McMullin were a waste-- especially when the platforms of Trump and Clinton were drastically different, and where Clinton's platform would be devastating to America. In this situation, it was important that Americans use their franchise to make sure that Trump won and to make sure that Clinton lost. Therefore, a conservative vote for McMullin would be only a futile protest vote, leaving to others to decide who will lead our nation.

Trump has used crude, sexual language. And there were women who surfaced in the fall who claimed that Trump had inappropriate contact with them. But these last-minute, desperate efforts to stop Trump seemed themselves to be trumped-up and questionable.[6] I do not trust those accusers. Trump clearly loves his wife and family, and he appears to have a good, happy family. I object to these last minute efforts at character assassination to attempt to defeat Trump. I have had false attacks made about me in my campaigns, and without credible evidence, I am reluctant to

---

[5] Perot ran again in 1996 and received only 8% of the popular vote.

[6] This calls to mind the last minute efforts by the Democrats to prevent the Senate from confirming Clarence Thomas to become a Justice of the Supreme Court in 1990. Anita Hill's allegations of sexual harassment were not credible to me, and in the ensuing years Clarence Thomas has distinguished himself as an excellent Justice.

be persuaded by accusers whom I know to be untrustworthy and biased.

Throughout 2016 many people in the press repeatedly mischaracterized Trump. They falsely exaggerated criticisms about Trump; they lied about him and wrongly criticized him repeatedly—and they have done this so much and so effectively that many people erroneously believe these misrepresentations. For example, they say that he hates Muslims, and they call him a racist; they say he loves Putin more than America; they say that he hates and mistreats women and that he mocks the disabled. But I saw and heard the incidents upon which these criticisms were based, and those criticisms are much exaggerated and mistaken. Nevertheless, the mainstream media was and continues to be relentless in making these misrepresentations and mischaracterizations.

The entire mainstream media and FOX News ridiculed Trump because he would not promise to accept the election results without any protests. And then the same press praised Hillary Clinton and her supporters for challenging the results of the election once Trump won. And then the mainstream media continues to bash Trump at every turn, including broadcasting as many people as they can find who will state that Trump is "evil" and is not a "legitimate" President-elect.

Trump is not nearly as bad as the mainstream media portrays him to be. I have been infuriated by the press during this last presidential campaign because of its unfairness and because of the many falsehoods it has promulgated. I for one do not believe all of the accusations made about Trump. And, those accusations are less egregious than the many flaws and mistakes and terrible proposals of Hillary Clinton. Trump is not "evil," and he is clearly the better choice for President than Clinton.

America will be markedly better because Trump won.

4

Presidential Powers

In 2014 and 2016 the Supreme Court made rulings on the meaning and extent of Presidential power under the Constitution in the areas of Recess Appointments and Immigration Law.

A Unanimous Supreme Court strikes down President Obama's improper recess appointments—

but the Majority's rationale actually increases the President's power and diminishes Senate power to confirm appointments.

On June 26, 2014, in *NLRB V. Canning*, 573 U. S. ___ (2014), a unanimous United States Supreme Court ruled that President Obama's recess appointment of three individuals to the National Labor Relations Board. Although the Supreme Court struck down these three particular appointments, the rationale they gave in support of their ruling served to increase the power of the President and to decrease the power of the Senate.

Justice Scalia argued for the four conservative Justices that the Constitution only allowed the President to make recess appointments (1) if the vacancy originated during a formal recess, and (2) if the appointment is exercised only during such a formal recess. The majority opinion, authored by Justice Breyer, eliminated the first condition and then expanded the definition of "recess" to include short 3-day recesses during a Congressional session. According to Justice Scalia, the result of this is to "transform" the standards for recess appointments and "is a clear conflict with our precedent and forebodes a diminution of this Court's role in controversies involving the separation of powers" (page 2 of J. Scalia's Dissent).

Immigration and Presidential Power to Legislate

United States v. Texas, 579 U.S. ___ (2016)

On June 23, 2016 an equally divided Supreme Court, in *United States v. Texas*, let stand a ruling of the Fifth Circuit Court of Appeals[1] that President Obama's overt attempt to change the nation's immigration laws to create millions of more legal immigrants was unconstitutional. This issue will continue to be one of immense importance in the 2016 Presidential Campaign for several reasons; it combines issues about our national immigration policies, economic and employment conditions, terrorism concerns, and concerns about President Obama's efforts to usurp legislative powers. All of these concerns are at the heart of current presidential debates, and the result of that election will determine how the Supreme Court will rule on these issues in the future.

For several years Congress has debated enacting changes to the nation's immigration and naturalization laws, but without success. But this is not surprising— the issues of immigration, economics and terrorism are volatile and deeply held by many people. President Obama's response to this inaction was bold and decisive, for sure, but it was also way out of line. He directed the Secretary of the Department of Homeland Security to implement drastic changes in

---

[1] *United States v. Texas*, 787 F.3d 733 (5th Cir. 2015).

national immigration policies which would have changed the status of an estimated 4.3 million immigrants from illegal to legal, and would have mandated that the states pay millions of dollars of benefits to these immigrants—all of this in direct contravention of the existing immigration laws passed by Congress. President Obama boldly declared that "it was the failure of Congress to enact such a program that prompted him . . . to change the law." *United States v. Texas*, at 65. The President's bold act of defiance
was a blatant attack on the Constitution. But even more disturbing than this is the 4-4 vote of the eight Justices. It should have been an 8-0 vote affirming the Fifth Circuit. The deeply divided nature of this situation is an indication of how compromised the Supreme Court has become. By supporting President Obama in this blatant and overt attack on the Constitution's separation of powers, those four Justices who sided with him indicate their rejection of fundamental principles of Constitutional jurisprudence for over two hundred years; this is unadulterated political partisanship on the part of the liberal Justices which shows a lack of integrity and/or repudiation of the founding principles of Constitutional law.

If another such, liberal Justice is appointed the Supreme Court, then Obama and/or the liberal who succeeds him will have accomplished a Hitler-like coup, with the complicity of a majority of ignorant citizens who follow Obama like the pied piper, oblivious of the irreparable harm that they would be supporting Obama in accomplishing. I hope this does not happen, but America is on the brink of this occurring, if Hillary Clinton is elected. That is why this case is so important.

But, for a minute, let's just review what the Fifth Circuit ruled.

In November 2014, the Department of Homeland Security (DHS) expanded the

eligibility of immigrants for state and federal benefits, making millions more persons eligible. The DHS took this action in what is called the "DAPA Memo," which disregarded Congress' five criteria of eligibility, and replaced that with only one test, and the DAPA Memo went on to require the states to provide millions of dollars of benefits to these immigrants.[2] Texas and 25 other states filed for an injunction against the implementation of DAPA. In February, 2015 the United States District Court for the Southern District of Texas granted the injunction. President Obama directed the United States to appeal the injunction to the Fifth Circuit Court of Appeals. In November, 2015, The Fifth Circuit affirmed the ruling of the District Court. President Obama again directed the United States to appeal. On June 23, 2016, a divided Supreme Court resulted in affirming the ruling of the Fifth Circuit. No opinions were filed by any of the Supreme Court Justices.

In support of the injunction granted by the District Court, the Fifth Circuit Court stated that "Congress has 'directly addressed the precise question at issue.' . . . DAPA is foreclosed by Congress's careful plan; the program in "manifestly contrary to the statute" and therefore was properly enjoined." 787 F.3d 733, __ [p. 66].

---

[2] The five criteria for an immigrant to satisfy in order to become a "lawful" immigrant are these: The immigrant must (i) have a U. S. Citizen child who is at least twenty-one years old, (ii) leave the United States, (iii) wait ten years, and then (iv) obtain one of the limited number of family-preference visas from a United States consulate. See 8 U.S.C. Sec. 1151(b)(2)(A)(i), et seq. DAPA controverted these requirements, providing that an immigrant need only show that his/her child was a U. S. citizen, and DAPA extended the time from two to three years in which to accomplish this, and also changed the burden of proof from the applicant to the government. President Obama's action could not have been more defiant, more blatant or more offensive to the Constitution.

The 2013 Same-Sex Marriage Cases
Judicial activism at the Supreme Court

On June 26, 2013, the Supreme Court announced two opinions regarding same-sex marriage that the gay community hailed as important successes for them. Indeed they were. But those cases came at a steep price. The cases show that a majority of the Justices have very lax views about judicial restraint, and that a majority of Justices are advancing their personal political agendas rather than adhering to long-established principles of Constitutional law.

1. *United States v. Windsor*, 570 U.S. (2013). In *United States v. Windsor*, the Supreme Court voted (5-4) to invalidate the Defense of Marriage Act (DOMA). The position of all the Justices in this opinion followed the predictable liberal/conservative split, with Justice Kennedy providing the swing vote and writing the majority opinion. Before the Court could get to the DOMA issue, it had to deal with the question of whether the appealing party had "standing" to appeal the case. It appears that the majority was so anxious to strike down DOMA that it hastily and erroneously ruled that the appealing parties did have standing. But, in my opinion, the Court got it wrong on the standing issue, as well on the DOMA issue. Here's what happened.

Facts and Standing. Edith Windsor and her gay partner married in Canada. They were living in New York when the partner died. Windsor received all of her partner spouse's estate. But she had to pay the federal estate tax of $363,053. The Defense of Marriage Act (enacted in 1996) prevented Windsor from having the benefit of the marital deduction. Windsor sued in federal court to have DOMA held unconstitutional and for the IRS to refund the tax she paid. Windsor won her case, which was affirmed by the Second Circuit Court of Appeals. But the IRS still didn't refund her money. Then the IRS and Windsor both appealed to the Supreme Court. Neither the United States nor Windsor had standing to appeal to the Supreme Court—they both agreed with the lower court's ruling. There was no legal issue to appeal. All that remained was for the Court to order the IRS to pay up; there was no remaining case or controversy for the Court to address. It is apparent (as Justice Scalia points out at pages 1-2 of his Dissent) that the liberal justices on the Court were so anxious to rule on the merits of the DOMA that they dispensed with the standing requirements.

Court announces a new, legal basis for creating new rights. Once the Court got to the merits of the DOMA, they proceeded to make an additional, equally bad ruling with flawed reasoning, in order to strike down the DOMA. Here's a brief summary of their substantive analysis: When Congress and the President enacted the DOMA in 1996, they did so having hatred and malice towards gays, and with the intent to punish gays. Therefore, the Court now concludes, DOMA is unconstitutional because such malicious legislative action violates a liberty protected by the Fifth Amendment's Due Process Clause. For the gays who disapprove of DOMA, they herald this ruling; but for those who understand the constitutional principles that the Court has followed for 226 years, the Majority's rationale is a total departure from the Court's acknowledged precedents and principles. I will explain.

First, the Court bases its holding on a finding that those who enacted DOMA did so with malice and hatred towards gays (Scalia, at 20-21). There is no factual basis for this. And, even if there were, such intent would not invalidate the law (Scalia, at 19, citing *United States v. O'Brien,* 391 U.S. 367, 383 (1968).) The Majority based its ruling on factual errors, and did so without articulating a legal analysis to support its conclusion. The latter point is worth highlighting—The Court's holding was not the result of sound reasoning—it was merely an erroneous edict.

Second, the Court stated that its ruling was based upon a liberty that is protected by the Due Process Clause of the Fifth Amendment. The only other case I know of that was based upon this argument was the case of *Lawrence v. Texas*, 539 U.S. 558 (2003), which ruled that a state cannot criminalize private, consensual sex acts between people of the same sex. The Fifth Amendment "liberty" argument was new in that case, and now it was invoked again ten years later in another case about gay rights. In these two cases, the Supreme Court has come up with a new, expansive theory to create whatever new right it wishes to recognize. Prior to these two cases, under the Court's interpretation of the Due Process Clause, previously unidentified substantive rights had to meet certain requirements before the Court would recognize such rights. For example, previously they would have had to prove that the newly recognized right is "deeply rooted in this Nation's history and tradition" (Scalia, at 17). In this ruling (*Windsor*), the Court dispensed with the long established principles that guard against recognizing as a constitutional right any whim of a majority of the Justices.

The Court never even got to the Full Faith and Credit Clause argument, which I had been anticipating. The Full Faith and Credit Clause

1

(Article IV of the Constitution) requires one state to give full faith and credit to the laws and judicial orders of another state unless the laws or actions of the other state are against the public policy of the state being asked to enforce them. Therefore DOMA only provided for a state to do what the Constitution already empowered the state to do by virtue of the acknowledged exception to the Full Faith and Credit Clause. With or without DOMA a state could still decline to recognize and enforce another state's same-sex marriage law by invoking the exception to the Full Faith and Credit Clause.

Windsor stands as the symbol of the Supreme Court's abandonment of judicial restraint, and its transformation into the Supreme Legislature. This ruling undermines the legislative powers of Congress and dismantles the balance of power that our Founders put in the Constitution for our protection.

2. *Hollingsworth v. Perry*, 570 U.S. ____ (2013). In *Hollingsworth v. Perry*, by a 5-4 vote, the Supreme Court dismissed (on a technicality) the case of those defending California's Proposition 8. The Court ruled that the party defending California's Proposition 8 (passed by voters in a referendum, and which provided that marriage was only between a man and a woman) did not have standing to bring its case; therefore a lower court ruling was upheld, which invalidated Proposition 8. This result is not that surprising—those who closely watch the Court expected the decision to be a close one. But the reasoning of the majority on "standing" is still wrong.

Standing. The Court never reached the substantive issue, but rather a majority of Justices ruled that Petitioner did not have standing, and therefore it never reached the substantive issue. Therefore, the ruling of the lower court which struck down Proposition 8 was left controlling. But there is a troubling aspect of the Court's ruling: In effect, it undermines the Referendum process that 27 state constitutions provide. The ruling makes it virtually impossible for the citizens who are successful in a referendum effort to enforce the law established by the referendum vote. Normally, it makes sense to only allow a State to be a party in defense of its law. But, by very nature, a law enacted by referendum will frequently be different than the law preferred by the State government. Therefore, unless those who successfully used the referendum process are also allowed to have standing to defend the law that they successfully passed through a referendum, the entire referendum process is undermined. That is exactly what happened in *Hollingsworth v. Perry*. Because the State of California was not the official party of record in this appeal, the Court ruled that the party did not have standing to bring the appeal.

Having a strict and narrow approach to standing is a vital part of the judicial restraint that the Supreme Court must exercise to prevent its being transformed into a super legislature. However, in this case, the excessively rigid interpretation of standing was unreasonable, and it effectively undermined and invalidated California's (and 26 other states') constitutional referendum or initiative law.

Had the Supreme Court found that petitioners had standing, then, if the Court also followed the legal reasoning of its prior cases, Proposition 8 would have been reinstated. On the other hand, if the Court found standing, and then proceeded to apply the rationale it introduced in *Windsor* (the DOMA case), the Court would have struck down Proposition 8.

State Referendum Procedures Undermined. The Court's ruling in *Hollingsworth* effectively invalidated the referendum process in every state that has one. This case will have profound effect. The Court could have and should have acknowledged that the existence of the important substantive, state right (the right to referendum), and then acknowledged that those states implicitly authorized the successful referring parties to have standing to defend any successfully referred law. The Court's ruling clearly undermines the referendum process in every state that has such a process.

Strange Bedfellows. One of the interesting things about this ruling is the make up of the five justices in the majority and the four justices in the minority. I don't know if we will ever see this composition again: Justices Roberts, Scalia, Ginsburg, Breyer and Kagan were the majority that found no standing; and Justices Kennedy, Thomas, Alito and Sotomayor felt there was standing. Justice Scalia has a long record of having a strict and narrow view of standing—but not so with Justices Ginsburg and Breyer. I don't expect to ever see such an alignment again.

3. Conclusion. Whether or not one is happy with the results in *Windsor* and *Hollingsworth*, it must be acknowledged that the political ideology of the liberal majority now controls the Court. This ideology is being established at the expense of precedent and judicial restraint. The brazen actions of the liberal majority are a repudiation of constitutional law—replacing it with an exhibition of pure political power. This will likely forever harm the Constitution. Never again will constitutional jurisprudence be treated as too important and too sacred to be infected with partisanship. The integrity of judicial principles has not only been compromised—it has been repudiated by the Court's liberal majority.

The Supreme Court inflicts grave damage on the Constitution in its ruling in *Obergefell v. Hodges* (2015)— Court recognizes a right to same-sex marriage

On June 26, 2015, the Supreme Court ruled in *Obergefell, et al. v. Hodges, Director, Ohio Department of Health, et al.,* 576 U. S. ___ (2015) that State laws that prohibit same-sex marriages are unconstitutional.[1] This ruling resolved the dozens of on-going legislative debates and court litigation over the assertion of gays that they have a right to marry someone of the same sex. The Court's answer to this issue is quite clear, even if it was only resolved by a 5-4 vote. However, regardless of one's personal views on the same-sex marriage question, the Court's reasoning to reach its decision has done great damage to the Constitution. Chief Justice Roberts summarized this in the final paragraph of his dissenting opinion:

> If you are among the many Americans— of whatever sexual orientation—who favor expanding same-sex marriage, by all means celebrate today's decision. Celebrate the achievement of a desired goal. Celebrate the opportunity for a new expression of commitment to a partner. Celebrate the availability of new benefits. But do not celebrate the Constitution. It had nothing to do with it. [Robert, C.J., dissenting, at p. 29.]

The damage inflicted on the Constitution by the *Obergefell* ruling consists of four serious mistakes in judgment and reasoning: First, the Court failed to restrain itself from addressing a legislative issue that belonged to the States and/or to Congress. Second, as Chief Justice Roberts observed, the Court erroneously "portrays everyone who

does not share the majority's "better informed understanding" as bigoted" (p. 29 of his Dissent). Third, the Court established a subjective, Due Process standard for identifying new rights. And fourth, the Court found a violation of the Equal Protection Clause that conflicted with all previous Court precedents. Together, these four errors have done great harm to the Constitution.

1. The Court declined to exercise proper judicial restraint. The Supreme Court has long followed the principle of "judicial self-restraint," so as not to encroach upon or usurp the rights of the people to make their own laws, in both Congress and in State Legislatures. Chief Justice Roberts points out in his dissent (pages 13-15) that the majority in *Obergefell* now "breaks sharply with decades of precedent and returns the Court to the unprincipled approach of *Lochner*." [Roberts, C.J., dissenting, p. 15.]

Chief Justice Roberts quoted from a statement by the Supreme Court just one year earlier that should have caused the majority to decline from inserting their own views over those of the States; just a year earlier the Court stated: "It is demeaning to the democratic process to presume that voters are not capable of deciding an issue of this sensitivity on decent and rational grounds." *Schuette v. BAMN*, 572 U.S. ___ (2014). Nevertheless, the majority put an end to all debates of this issue in the State legislatures. Chief Justice Roberts warned: "There will be consequences to shutting down the political process on an issue of such profound public significance. [Roberts, p. 27.]

Federal courts are blunt instruments when it comes to creating rights. They have constitutional power only to resolve concrete

---

[1] More precisely, the Court struck down statutes in Michigan and Kentucky that prohibited same-sex marriage, and the Court struck down laws in Ohio, Tennessee and Kentucky that would not recognize same-sex marriages performed in another state.

1

cases or controversies; they do not have the flexibility of legislatures to address concerns of parties not before the court or to anticipate problems that may arise from the exercise of a new right. Today's decision, for example, creates serious questions about religious liberty. Many good and decent people oppose same-sex marriage as a tenet of faith, and their freedom to exercise religion is—unlike the right imagined by the majority—actually spelled out in the Constitution. Amdt. 1. . . . [Roberts, at 27.]

2. The Majority of the Court mischaracterized and misjudged opponents of same-sex marriage. Chief Justice Roberts correctly identifies and confronts the majority with their own prejudices when he points out that many opponents of same-sex marriage take such position for sincere and legitimate religious beliefs, and that such opponents are neither bigots nor uninformed people. The Chief Justice said this:

> Hard questions arise when people of faith exercise religion in ways that may be seen to conflict with the new right to same-sex marriage—when, for example, a religious college provides married student housing only to opposite-sex married couples, or a religious adoption agency declines to place children with same-sex married couples. Indeed the Solicitor General candidly acknowledged that the tax exemptions of some religious institutions would be in question if they opposed same-sex marriage. [Roberts, at 28.]

3. A majority of the Court established an improper, subjective standard for identifying non-enumerated rights. The haste for the majority to establish a right to same-sex marriage led the Court to do so by establishing a standard that is nothing more than the personal view of a majority of the Court on an issue. This usurps the power of Congress and State legislatures. The Supreme Court should not substitute the views of legislatures and should not circumvent legislative processes unless required to do so. And the Court should not create or recognize

a heretofore unrecognized right unless they are "'so rooted in the traditions and conscience of our people as to be ranked as fundamental,' and therefore cannot be deprived without compelling justification Snyder v. Massachusetts, 291 U. S. 97, 105 (1934)." [Roberts, C.J., dissenting, pp. 10-11.] Chief Justice Roberts also wrote: "Our precedents have required that implied fundamental rights be 'objectively, deeply rooted in this Nation's history and tradition,' and 'implicit in the concept of ordered liberty, such that neither liberty nor justice would exist if they were sacrificed.'" Washington v. Glucksberg, 521 U. S. 702, 720-721 (1997). [Roberts, C. J., dissenting, pp. 13-14.] Under the existing Constitutional standards, where many Legislatures were addressing the same-sex marriage issue, and reaching contradictory results, it is not possible to conclude that such a right is "deeply rooted in this Nation's history and tradition." In Obergefell, the Court effectively overturned Snyder and Glucksberg. In its place, Chief Justice Roberts points out that the Court has re-established the flawed, subjective approach the Court took for a number of years, as articulated in the much criticized case of Lochner v. New York, 198 U. S. 45 (1905). The Court now adopts a standard that is nothing more than one of second-guessing a legislature when the Justices "believe the legislature has acted unwisely" [Roberts, C. J., dissenting, p. 13]. Thus, the Chief Justice concludes that the Obergefell ruling "breaks sharply with decades of precedent and returns the Court to the unprincipled approach of Lochner" [Roberts, C.J., dissenting, p. 15].

Chief Justice Roberts also pointed out that any reliance on the 2003 Lawrence v. Texas ruling is also misplaced because the Lawrence case (which recognized a liberty for people to engage in same-sex intimacy in private) established a particular "privacy" right, not the public requirement for a state to transform the institution of marriage.

2

4. A majority of the Court established a new and flawed interpretation of the Equal Protection Clause. The *Obergefell* ruling also overturns over a century of precedent that traditional marriage laws that prohibit same-sex marriage were rationally related to the States' interest in preserving the traditional institution of marriage. [See Roberts, C.J., dissenting, pp. 23-24.] The majority's interpretation of the Equal Protection Clause in *Obergefell* conflicts with the plain meaning of the Constitution and with the Supreme Court's own precedents. Justice Roberts wrote that the Court specifically addressed this issue in 1972:

> Shortly after this Court struck down racial restrictions on marriage in Loving,[2] a gay couple in Minnesota sought a marriage license. They argued that the Constitution required States to allow marriage between people of the same sex for the same reasons that it requires States to allow marriage between people of different races. The Minnesota Supreme Court rejected their analogy to Loving, and this Court summarily dismissed an appeal. Baker v. Nelson, 409 U.S. 810 (1972). [Roberts, C. J., dissenting, p. 8]

The *Obergefell* majority's departure from specific precedents regarding same-sex marriage was not based on proper legal analysis, but was based only upon five Justices' own opinions on same-sex marriage. As recent as 2003, when the Supreme Court recognized a privacy right for individuals to engage in same-sex intimacy, that decision did not disturb the traditional rights of the States, having a "'legitimate state interest' in 'preserving the traditional institution of marriage, and which laws were not a violation of the Equal Protection Clause of the Fourteenth Amendment. [Roberts, C.J., dissenting, p.24, referring to *Lawrence v. Texas*, 539 U.S. 558, 585 (2003).]

Regardless of one's views on same-sex marriage, the Supreme Court discarded its own precedents to establish this as a new federal right. The new standards put in place by the Court to support this result are seriously flawed. The *Obergefell* holding is an indication that a majority of the Court uses their high judicial position to establish their personal views in a way that undermines the Constitutional rights of Congress and of the State legislatures. *Obergefell* is a symbol of the Court's abandonment of disciplined judicial restraint, and replacing it with pure political favoritism for the views of their political supporters.

---

[2] *Loving v. Virginia*, 388 U.S. 1 (1967) struck down a Virginia law that prohibited inter-racial marriage.

3

Major Portion of President Obama's "Affordable Care Act" Is Struck Down by Supreme Court, But the Individual Mandate Portion Survives—

Conservative Pundits Throw Chief Justice Roberts under the Bus,
Accusing Him of Selling Out to Liberals

On Thursday, June 28, 2012, the Supreme Court announced its ruling in the controversial and politically-charged case of *National Federation of Independent Business, et al. vs. Sebelius, Secretary of Health and Human Services, et al.*, 567 U.S. _____ (2012) [hereafter *National Federation*]. The Supreme Court struck down the Medicaid expansion portion of the law, but upheld the Individual Mandate portion. The significance of invalidating the Medicaid expansion cannot be overstated, but conservative pundits have been in a frenzy speculating about why Chief Justice Roberts parted ways with the other four conservative Justices and voted to uphold the Individual Mandate portion of that law. Many conservatives have been beside themselves in anger against Chief Justice Roberts for his refusal to invalidate the Individual Mandate, and there has been considerable speculation that his vote on this issue came after he succumbed to pressure from liberal politicians and the media. I will share a few thoughts about the Chief Justice later, but first it is important to understand what the *National Federation* ruling is.

The Affordable Care Act is the signature legislative achievement of President Barack Obama, who used all of his political capital to enact the 2700-page, "Patient Protection and Affordable Care Act of 2010," which is the lynchpin of President Obama's plan to enact universal, government-provided health care for all. While the 2700-page law is extensive and complex, its two primary components are: (1) Requiring individuals to purchase a health insurance policy providing a minimum level of coverage ["Individual

mandate"]; and (2) Expanding Medicaid coverage by providing funds and requiring States to make the expanded coverage available to all citizens below a certain income level. Immediately upon passage of this law, suits were filed to challenge the constitutionality of this Act. In addition to the National Federation of Independent Business, twenty-five States joined in law suits challenging this law.

The government expansion that is called for in the Act is so extensive, and the predicted consequences of the law are so far-reaching and expensive, that the law was one of the primary issues in the 2016 presidential campaign. Sky-rocketing premiums and deductibles brought widespread and anger and dissatisfaction with the ACA. The Supreme Court's ruling in 2012 did not end the growing discontent with the ACA. Repeal of the ACA became one of the most prominent issues of the 2016 presidential campaign. The growing public dissatisfaction with the ACA over the last six years has let to a shift in political power from the Democrats to the Republicans. Donald Trump campaigned to "repeal and replace" Obamacare; and he and the new Congress are poised to do that in January 2017.

Medicaid Expansion. The Medicaid expansion aspect of the Affordable Care Act would have made an enormous change in the Medicaid program, which since its enactment in the 1960's has been to provide medical services for the poor. Currently, 20% of most States' budgets are allocated to providing Medicaid benefits. The new Act would have drastically expanded those who would be entitled to benefits—compelling States to

1

cover all individuals under 65 with incomes below 133 percent of the federal poverty line. Estimates are that his will increase Medicaid expenditures by forty percent, or $100 billion per year. Not only is the expanded coverage extensive, but the Affordable Care Act would have required all States to administer these additional funds to its citizens or else lose all funding for the existing Medicaid program for the poor. The five conservative Justices (Roberts, Scalia, Kennedy, Thomas and Alito) all agreed that this proposed expansion was vast, and was an encroachment on the sovereignty of the States. Therefore, this provision was struck down by a 5-4 vote.

Individual Mandate. The Individual Mandate provision is a little more complicated, and has spawned widespread discussion and controversy. The best way to approach this is to start with the opinion of Justice Antonin Scalia, which it appears was initially the majority opinion (to which the Chief Justice is said to have initially joined), but which ended up being the dissenting opinion on this issue.[1] I start with Justice Scalia's analysis because I find it the soundest and the most simple to follow.

Twenty-five states argued that the Individual mandate of the Affordable Care Act violated the Commerce Clause of the Constitution because it sought to compel people to engage in interstate commerce rather than to regulate existing commerce. Actually, all five of the conservative Justices agreed with this reading of the Commerce Clause. Justice Scalia wrote that this therefore should conclude the analysis—the Affordable Care Act is unconstitutional, and should be struck down in its entirety. But

here is where the Chief Justice went astray (in my opinion)—He proceeded to say that even though the Act would not survive scrutiny as interstate commerce, nevertheless he asserted that the Act was a valid exercise of Congressional authority to tax. This is a most peculiar concept because the Government insisted throughout the litigation that the Affordable Care Act was not a tax. Therefore, when Justice Roberts asserted that the Individual Mandate penalty was a tax— both conservatives and liberals were left to marvel at the consequence. The liberals marveled because although they insisted the mandate was not a tax, they saw that the Chief Justice re-designated the penalty a tax in order to sustain the mandate provision; they didn't initially agree with the reasoning, but the result was what they wanted. The conservatives marveled because Justice Roberts interpreted the mandate in a way that conflicted with its plain language in order to find the law valid. The language specifically commands that "applicable individuals shall" ensure that he and his dependents secure certain minimal health insurance coverage. (Section 5000A(a).) The Act then proceeds to impose a penalty on those who do not comply with this mandate. Nowhere does the Act describe this as a tax, but rather it consistently describes it as a penalty. This distinction between a tax and a penalty has traditionally been an important one for the Supreme Court. And the definition and context of the penalty provision in the Affordable Care Act are wholly consistent with what the Supreme Court has held to be penalties in the past. And again, it is from this point where the problem (for conservatives) and the solution (for liberals) took place.

The Chief Justice's analysis as to why the "penalty" is really a "tax" is complex at best, or convoluted and contrived, from my point of view. The result of his analysis is that Justice Roberts says that the Act doesn't mean what it says. But there was no good reason for Justice Roberts to include this analysis. And what makes Justice Roberts'

---

[1] The Scalia opinion makes no mention of the Opinion of the Chief Justice. This is a rare and strange phenomenon; typically, each opinion makes specific references to those parts of the opposing opinions with which it takes issue. Thus, the Scalia opinion reads like a majority opinion, and the absence of references to the Chief Justice's opinion leads one to believe that the Chief Justice may have parted ways with the other conservative Justices late in the process.

opinion even worse, he reasons that the Act is "not a tax" for purposes of the Anti-Injunction Act, but that the Act is a tax under the constitution. Justice Scalia said that such analysis was "verbal wizardry" (Scalia dissent, at p. 28).

But even more importantly, from my perspective, it was inappropriate for Justice Roberts to even address the taxation issue once the Act was found to violate the Commerce Clause. My reading of the Constitution is that if a tax is found to violate the commerce clause of the Constitution, then that tax should not be saved by virtue of the fact that taxes are exempt from having to comply with the Commerce Clause requirements. Especially in a case such as this, where the law does not purport to be a tax, but insists that it is only a penalty to be imposed when one does not comply with the proposed mandate to act. It appears to me that Justice Roberts had to go out of his way to find a rationale to uphold the Individual mandate. In a situation like this where the penalty is inextricably connected with a federal regulation that would violate the Commerce Clause, then whether that penalty is either a "penalty" or a "tax" should make no difference. So when Justice Roberts hangs his opinion on the "tax" versus "penalty" distinction, this is merely a technical distinction without a difference. It makes no sense to allow such a technical nomenclature issue control the substance of the legal analysis. This approach elevates form over substance. The "tax" is an enforcement mechanism—the enforcement tool should not control the validity of the exercise of federal power that is at issue.

While I disagree with Roberts' result, I can't really say that he got there by applying principles that abandoned conservative principles. Because of this, I don't think it can be said that Justice Roberts sold out to the liberal agenda. At this point it is possible that Justice Roberts believes what he wrote and is just being intellectually honest—although I find fault with his analysis. As one who has taken note of Justice Roberts

opinions in the past, I have observed that while he almost always reaches the same conservative conclusions as those reached by Justices Scalia and Thomas and Alito, the reasoning he uses to get there has frequently been different. It is likely that this is what has happened here. It is likely that his intellectual independence just took him astray in this case. He did not espouse or endorse liberal principles in support of his opinion. Only if a trend develops in his opinions would it be possible to conclude that he has gone to the other side, as some have prematurely concluded.

Of course, most of the conservative discussion I have heard about the Roberts opinion does not get into this substantive analysis—it expresses dissatisfaction with the result, not with a thorough analysis of his reasoning. But this is always an unreliable basis for judging his core philosophy. The liberal analysis of the Roberts opinion is even more disturbing—it praises the Supreme Court for rising above partisanship and restoring integrity to the Court. This is a pathetic, incorrect and insulting commentary which implies problems that are non-existent—it exposes the faulty mindset of those who espouse it; and it exposes their erroneous view that the conservative majority is driven by partisan bias, and it denies that conservative opinions are based in integrity and founded on conservative principles that are in harmony with both the Constitution and the philosophy of our framers.

At this point, the Roberts opinion, although in my view wrong, demonstrates the intellectual independence of Justice Roberts, and it confirms the integrity of the Court. And while I disagree with part of the result, I would point out that the Medicaid expansion was invalidated in this case, and I would point out that the National Federal holding does not include a majority opinion with regard to the Individual Mandate—thus leaving to the future the clear opportunity to clarify (and hopefully correct) that aspect of the case.

Affordable Care Act again upheld by the Supreme Court (2015)

On June 25, 2015, the United States Supreme Court voted 6-3 in *King v. Burwell*, 576 U.S. ___ (2015) to again uphold the Affordable Care Act (ACA). At issue in this round of litigation was whether "federal Exchanges" means "federal" or "federal and State." The significance of this issue is that if the meaning of "federal" was always limited to "federal," then the ACA would have been struck down by the Court as unconstitutional. Justice Scalia argued that the ACA must be interpreted by giving its words their plain meaning, and that therefore the ACA must be struck down. However, Chief Justice Roberts and Justice Kennedy and the four liberal Justices concluded that the language of the ACA with respect to Exchanges was "ambiguous," and that therefore they determined that Congress intended for the words "federal Exchanges" to sometimes mean "federal and State Exchanges" because that is what Congress intended.

A side issue regarding the Affordable Care Act is the question of whether Chief Justice Roberts is a true conservative. Many conservatives feel betrayed by the Chief Justice because he voted to uphold the ACA, even though it violates conservative views on the role of the federal government. For whatever its worth, I don't think the Chief Justice is a liberal. His opinion in *King v.*

Burwell (2015) is not as puzzling as his opinion in the first AFA case, *NFBI v. Sebelius* (2012). The reasons stated by the Chief Justice in *King v. Burwell* are actually conservative reasons, even though they differ from the conservative views stated by Justice Scalia.

New Frederick County Law Will Tell Us How to Pray
C. Paul Smith, County Commissioner

The Board of County Commissioners recently passed a policy to have prayer at the beginning of its BOCC meetings. In the last few days, several people have asked me why I voted against the prayer policy. I will explain.

The very thought that the government will regulate the content of our prayers is chilling. You would think that if freedom of speech means anything, it would mean that the government can't tell you what you can and cannot say. You would also think that if the Establishment Clause means anything, it would mean that the government cannot establish specific criteria for what one can and cannot say in a governmental prayer.

I do believe in prayer, and I actually would support a policy of having prayers at some of our meetings. But it is a mistake to pass a law that regulates what you can and cannot say in a prayer. A preferable policy would be to allow individuals on a rotating bases from all faiths and persuasions to say or pray something for a limited time period at the beginning of meetings. This would entail no regulation of the content of speech, and it would not establish any religion over another. Federal courts have upheld such policies in New York, Georgia, Delaware, and Indiana. But the very process of prescribing an acceptable, non-sectarian prayer is the endorsement of one religious point of view.

The new prayer policy requires (1) That the invocation must be non-sectarian with elements of the American civil religion and must not be used to proselytize or advance any one faith or belief or to disparage any other faith or belief; (2) That there be no references specific to any particular religion, denomination or sect; (3) That invocations are to be directed only at the County Commissioners; (4) That the County maintain a database of "known ordained religious leaders of monotheistic religions with established congregations in Frederick County; and (5) That prayers "should not contain references that are specific to any particular religion, denomination or sect. As examples, invocations should not include references to religious figures such as Jesus Christ, to images such as a crucifix, or to teachings from such sources as the Koran or the Book of Mormon."

Some courts have already struck down prayer policies that sought to establish a non-sectarian legislative prayer. See e.g., *Pelphrey v. Cobb County, GA*, 547 F.3d 1263 (11th Cir. 2008). Two cases from the Fourth Circuit give some support to the constitutionality of our new prayer policy. *Simpson v. Chesterfield County*, 404 F.3d 276 (4th Cir. 2005) and *Turner v. Fredericksburg*, 534 F.3d 352 (4th Cir. 2008). Both of these cases rely on *Marsh v. Chambers*, 463 U.S.783 (1983), which upholds the right of legislatures to begin their sessions with prayer. But the *Marsh* case did not address the issue of whether legislative prayers must be "non-sectarian." I do not interpret *Marsh* to hold that legislative prayers must be non-sectarian.

In my opinion, anyone who will thoughtfully consider the implication of the elements of the above prayer policy will acknowledge that this attempt to regulate prayer content is infected with problems. First of all, the very defining of a "nonsectarian" prayer creates a "sectarian" prayer. Second, the prohibition from using references to a particular denomination or sect is

1

impossible. Third, directing the prayers to be "directed only at the County Commissioners," necessarily means that the words would not be prayers, for prayers are directed at God. Fourth, maintaining a database of "known ordained religious leaders of monotheistic religion with an established congregation" necessarily excludes certain religions from the database. Fifth, prohibiting prayers that might contain references to a "particular religion, denomination or sect" creates an impossible standard to measure. Seventh, the specific prohibition from mentioning "Jesus Christ" or the "crucifix" specifically violates the standard stated in *Marsh v. Chambers*, because this prohibition disparages that particular faith. *Id.* at 794-795. Eighth, the prohibition from including "teachings from the Koran or the Book of Mormon" disparages Muslims and Mormons, and therefore also violates the *Marsh* standard, and it is also a vague standard that would be impossible to ascertain or enforce without prohibiting all prayer.

It is worthy to note that the Fourth Circuit is currently considering the constitutionality of a county's prayer policy (in North Carolina) that made a regular prayer time available to people of all religions and persuasions, and which did not dictate the content of the permissible prayers. *Joyner v. Forsyth County*, Case No. 10-1232.

What the Supreme Court said in *Lee v. Weisman*, 505 U.S. 577 (1992) is certainly applicable here:

> It is a cornerstone principle of our Establishment Clause jurisprudence that "it is no part of the business of government to compose official prayers for any group of the American People," *Engel v. Vitale*, 370 U.S. 421, 425 (1962).

If appreciating diversity in our society has any value, then we should certainly be broadminded enough to listen to and appreciate the religious beliefs and non-religious philosophies of other citizens. Personally, when I pray, I pray in the name of Jesus Christ. Should I pray differently when I pray in public? Should I change the way I pray any time my praying might offend someone? I normally begin my prayers by addressing "My Father in Heaven." Is this going to be acceptable now? Should the County generate a list of all the ways that one can legally address God in a prayer? The City of Frederick generated such a list, and no one has sued them yet. But this type of prayer law is currently being litigated around the country.

Again, my opposition to the prayer regulation is not an opposition to prayer; rather it is an opposition to government-controlled prayer that establishes one brand of prayer and prohibits all others.

C-Paul Smith
2011

Statement of Commissioner Paul Smith, Urging the BOCC
to Revise Its Prayer Policy in Light of the Supreme Court Ruling in
Town of Greece, New York vs. Galloway (2014)

July 2, 2014

Supreme Court ruling allows individual to pray in the name of Jesus Christ in governmental, legislative prayers

On May 5, 2014 the Supreme Court issued its ruling (5-4) in *Town of Greece, New York v. Galloway*, which holds that municipalities who have prayers at the beginning of legislative sessions may allow people who give such prayers to pray in the name of Jesus Christ. This ruling resolves a divisive issue that has been the subject of considerable discussion and concern around the nation for three decades. In particular, this issue has been the subject of much debate and discussion recently in both Frederick and Carroll Counties.

In Frederick County, in 2011 the Board of County Commissioners (BOCC) passed a resolution establishing a policy of praying at the beginning of its legislative meetings. However, the policy that we passed allowed only prayers that were non-denominational and non-sectarian—meaning that it was prohibited to pray in the name of Jesus Christ. Indeed, prayers in the name of Jesus were the ones that the policy was intended to prohibit. John Mathias, Frederick County's attorney advised the BOCC that this policy was in keeping with a recent ruling of the Fourth Circuit Court of Appeals (*Turner v. Fredericksburg*, 534 F.3d 352 (4th Cir. 2008) and *Simpson v. Chesterfield County*, 404 F.3d 276 (4th Cir. 2005). I argued to John and to the rest of the BOCC, that I agree that Mr. Mathias was correctly reading the recent Fourth Circuit cases, but I insisted that that interpretation was wrong because it was effectively dictating the content of protected speech—prescribing (establishing) how one could and could not pray—the very action that the Establishment Clause prohibits. I argued that the Fourth Circuit has misinterpreted the 1983 Supreme Court case of *Marsh v. Chambers*. In addition, the Fourth Circuit approach is mistakenly premised on the notion that it is possible to force people to pray in a way that would not offend anyone. This notion is also mistaken. I lost my argument before the BOCC in 2011. But the Supreme Court's ruling in *Greece v. Galloway* validates both of my arguments. Now is the time for the BOCC to revise its prayer policy to allow sectarian prayers, including prayers in the name of Jesus Christ.

In Carroll County, the import of the Greece ruling is even of greater impact. That is because just a matter of weeks before the Supreme Court ruling, a federal District Court judge in Maryland signed an Injunction ordering the Commissioners of Carroll County to cease and desist from praying in the name of Jesus at the beginning of their meetings. Then, my friend, Commissioner Robin Frazier, publicly took issue with that order, and spoke out in defiance of it, including making a statement that the Order was wrong and that she would not abide by it. Robin's defiance brought national attention to this matter, as it was covered on national

1

television. The Carroll County prayer policy was almost identical to that of the Town of Greece: Both policies allowed people of any and all persuasions to pray as they chose; and the prayers that were delivered for both governments were mostly Christian prayers, including many people mentioning the name of Jesus in their prayers.

Those who challenged the prayer policy and practice in Greece and in Carroll County complained that it is offensive and an Establishment Clause violation if any legislative prayer mentions the name of Jesus. The Supreme Court disagreed. The Court held:

> The First Amendment is not a majority rule, and government may not seek to define permissible categories of religious speech. Once it invites prayer into the public sphere, government must permit a prayer giver to address his or her own God or gods as conscience dictates, unfettered by what an administrator or judge considers to be nonsectarian. [Kennedy, at 14]

> Absent a pattern of prayers that over time denigrate, proselytize, or betray an impermissible government purpose, a challenge based solely on the content of a prayer will not likely establish a constitutional violation. *Marsh*, indeed, requires an inquiry into the prayer opportunity as a whole, rather than into the contents of a single prayer. 463 U.S., at 794-795. [Kennedy, at 17]

Consequently, it is perfectly proper for the Town of Greece, for Carroll County and for Frederick County to have a policy of allowing prayers at the beginning of its legislative meetings that permit the one praying to pray however he or she chooses to pray, without any direction from the government as to the content of those prayers, provided they do not denigrate, proselytize or otherwise establish a religion. Such prayer policies are not required to prohibit sectarian or denominational prayers. It is not a constitutional violation to allow someone to pray in the name of Jesus in his/her legislative prayer.

There has been some criticism of the *Greece* decision, including Jack Topchik's opinion piece in the May 18th *Frederick NewsPost*, which criticized the Supreme Court, saying that the Court "ignores" the nation's "changing culture." But the analysis of Topchik's piece indicates he does not understand the Court's ruling. Because the First Amendment covers several broad, completing principles, it has led to an assortment of principles that sometimes seem to be contradictory to casual readers. The area of governmental prayer speech is one of those areas. For example, in the case of prayers in public schools, the Court has said state-led prayers are not allowed in the classroom or at high school graduations or at football games. Concern about government coercion of impressionable young minds has led to this result. But government-sanctioned prayers at the beginning of legislative meetings has been allowed and practiced from the First Continental Congress in 1774 until today. As Justice Alito's concurring opinion pointed out, the group of men who convened in 1774 were from diverse religious backgrounds— so much so that they at first rejected the motion to begin their meetings with prayer. But after some reflection, they changed their minds. Although the delegates were of various different religions, they agreed that they wanted to begin their meetings with prayer, even though those prayers were sectarian and denominational. And that practice has continued until this day in Congress. Congress never intended the First Amendment to prohibit its practice of beginning legislative meetings with prayer. As the Supreme Court said in *Greece*, once the government invites a prayer, it cannot dictate the content of that prayer as long as the prayer does not exploit the opportunity to proselytize (Kennedy, at p. 12). The mere fact that a prayer or a lot of prayers are made in the name of Jesus does not run afoul the First Amendment.

In his excess zeal to criticize the Supreme Court's ruling in *Greece*, Jack Topchik included a quote that he found on the internet about a Tennessee, high school softball coach who declared that people are not going to stop his team from praying in Jesus' name before games. I acknowledge that this defiant attitude exists throughout the nation. But this is irrelevant to the legislative prayer issue.

The most disconcerting thing about the *Greece* case is that it was only a 5-4 decision. Topchik criticizes the majority for basing its decision on "political and ideological grounds." In case Mr. Topchik has not thought this through, I would point out that Justice Kagan, in her minority dissent (joined by Justices Ginsberg and Sotomayor) based their opinions on "political and ideological grounds" rather than on sound constitutional principles. They misread the *Marsh* case to require that legislative prayers must be nonsectarian and nondenominational. But the *Marsh* decision did not say that. The dissent focused on a statement in *Marsh* that indicated that there was nothing offensive about nonsectarian prayers, but the dissent misread the import of those words; such a reading is inconsistent with the history of legislative prayers in the United States. Justice Kagan's dissent is an example of sloppy analysis. You would think that if America is a tolerant society that appreciates diversity, then we should certainly be able to tolerate someone praying according to the dictates of his/her own conscience—whether it be in the name of Jesus Christ or some other god or in the name of atheism. It does appear that the litigation that spawned the *Greece* case was initiated by people who took offense at people praying in the name of Jesus. I agree with Topchik that "political and ideological grounds" rather than proper judicial analysis was manifest in some of the Justices' opinions in *Greece*, but not from the majority—it was from Justices Sotomayor, Ginsberg and Kagan.

CONCLUSION: For all of the foregoing reasons, now is the time for the BOCC to revise its prayer policy to allow sectarian prayers, including prayers in the name of Jesus Christ.

For those interested in reviewing some of the history of this debate during the term of this BOCC, please see:

"New Frederick County Law Will Tell Us How to Pray" (May 2011), and

"County's New Prayer Policy in Light of the Ruling in *Joyner v. Forsyth County*" (August 2011)

TABLE OF CASES

U. S. Courts of Appeal

U. S. District Courts

State Courts

INDEX

328

About the author—

C. Paul Smith has a general civil trial practice in Maryland, where he started a partnership with his father, the late J. Russel Smith, in 1978. Paul graduated from the J. Reuben Clark Law School at Brigham Young University in 1978. In addition to law work, Paul has been active as a leader in the Boy Scouts of America for 45 years. He was awarded the Silver Beaver Award in 2013. Paul has coached youth baseball and basketball for many years. He and his wife Terry are the parents of twelve children, with 31 grandchildren. Paul has been a leader in his church,

Paul and Terry Smith

The Church of Jesus Christ of Latter-day Saints, and he served six years as bishop of the Frederick, Maryland Ward. Paul was elected a Frederick City Alderman for four years (2006-2009) and was elected vice president of the Board of County Commissioners of Frederick County for four years (2010-2014). In 2002 Paul published the book, *The State of the Constitution*, and from 2001-2017 he published seventeen issues of *Constitutional Law Updates*, a newsletter that provided commentary and analysis on Supreme Court rulings and other major events affecting the Constitution.

www.ingramcontent.com/pod-product-compliance
Lightning Source LLC
Chambersburg PA
CBHW081717170526
45167CB00009B/3610